1998 Su

to Eightl

MODERN CRIMINAL PROCEDURE

Cases — Comments — Questions

BASIC CRIMINAL PROCEDURE

Cases — Comments — Questions

and

ADVANCED CRIMINAL PROCEDURE

Cases — Comments — Questions

By

Yale Kamisar

Clarence Darrow Distinguished University Professor of Law,
University of Michigan

Wayne R. LaFave

Professor Emeritus in the College of Law
and Center for Advanced Study,
University of Illinois

Jerold H. Israel

Alene and Allan F. Smith Professor of Law Emeritus,
University of Michigan
Ed Rood Eminent Scholar in Trial Advocacy and Procedure,
University of Florida, College of Law

AMERICAN CASEBOOK SERIES®

WEST
GROUP

ST. PAUL, MINN., 1998

TEXT IS PRINTED ON 10% POST
CONSUMER RECYCLED PAPER

Preface

This Supplement contains all significant United States Supreme Court cases decided during the 1997-98 Term. This volume also contains selected provisions of the U.S. Constitution (App. A); selected federal statutory provisions, e.g., the Bail Reform Act, the Speedy Trial Act and the Habeas Corpus provisions of Title 28 (App. B); the Federal Rules of Criminal Procedure (including recent amendments) (App. C); and proposed amendments to the Rules (App. D).

Because the controversial case of *United States* v. *Singleton* (10th Cir.) was handed down too late to be integrated into this Supplement, the case appears in a Special Appendix at the back of the volume. The *Singleton* court startled law enforcement officials when it held that 18 U.S.C. § 201 (c) (2) prohibits the federal government from promising leniency to witnesses who are defendants or potential defendants in return for their testimony against other defendants. In concluding that suppression of testimony for the prosecution is the appropriate remedy for the use of government testimony in violation of § 201 (c) (2), the Tenth Circuit relied heavily on the search and seizure exclusionary rule cases. Accordingly, *Singleton* constitutes supplementary material for both Ch. 5, § 1 and Ch. 22, § 1.

However, as this Supplement was being printed, the Tenth Circuit, acting on its own motion, vacated Judge Kelly's panel decision in *Singleton* so that it could address the issues raised by the case *en banc*. Nevertheless, the panel opinion is still an excellent teaching material.

YALE KAMISAR
WAYNE LaFAVE
JEROLD H. ISRAEL

July, 1998

*

Acknowledgments

Excerpts from the following articles appear with the kind permission of the copyright holders.

Arenella, Peter, Foreword: O.J. Lessons, 69 S.Cal.L.Rev. 501 (1996). Copyright © 1996 by the Southern California Law Review. Reprinted by permission.

Cassell, Paul G., *Miranda*'s Social Cost: An Empirical Reassessment, 90 Nw.U.L.Rev. 387 (1996). Copyright © 1996 by the Northwestern University Law Review. Reprinted by permission.

Edwards, Harry T., To Err is Human, But Not Always Harmless: When Should Legal Error Be Tolerated? 70 N.Y.U.L.Rev. 1167 (1995). Copyright © 1995 by the New York University Law Review. Reprinted by permission.

Kennedy, Randall, Race, Crime, and The Law (1997). Copyright © 1997 by Randall Kennedy. Reprinted by permission.

Livingston, Debra, Brutality in Blue: Community, Authority, and the Elusive Promise of Police Reform, 92 Mich.L.Rev. 1556 (1994). Copyright © 1994 by the Michigan Law Review. Reprinted by permission.

Pizzi, William T., Punishment and Procedure: A Different View of the American Criminal Justice System, 13 Const.Comm. 55 (1996). Copyright © 1996 by Constitutional Commentary. Reprinted by permission.

Schulhofer, Stephen J., *Miranda*'s Practical Effect: Substantial Benefits and Vanishingly Small Social Costs, 90 Nw.U.L.Rev. 500 (1996). Copyright © 1996 by the Northwestern University Law Review. Reprinted by permission.

Seidman, Louis Michael, Criminal Procedure as the Servant of Politics, 12 Const.Comm. 207 (1995). Copyright © 1995 by Constitutional Commentary. Reprinted by permission.

Thomas, George C., Plain Talk about the *Miranda* Empirical Debate: A "Steady–State" Theory of Confessions, 43 U.C.L.A.L.Rev. 933 (1966). Copyright © 1996 by the U.C.L.A.Law Review. Reprinted by permission.

*

Table of Contents

Table of Cases

The principal cases are in bold type. Cases cited or discussed in the text are roman type. References are to pages. For Commonwealth v. ___, People v. ___, State v. ___, United States v. ___, see name of other party. For Ex parte ___, In re ___, Matter of ___, see name of party. For People ex rel. ___, State ex rel. ___, United States ex rel. ___, see the name of first party. Where a case is discussed in another case, reference is made only to the first page at which it is cited. No reference is made to discussion of a principal case in the Notes and Questions that follow that case.

*

1998 Supplement

to Eighth Editions

MODERN CRIMINAL PROCEDURE

Cases — Comments — Questions

BASIC CRIMINAL PROCEDURE

Cases — Comments — Questions

and

ADVANCED CRIMINAL PROCEDURE

Cases — Comments — Questions

*

Part One

INTRODUCTION

Chapter 2

THE NATURE AND SCOPE OF FOURTEENTH AMENDMENT DUE PROCESS

SECTION 2. THE PROBLEM OF BODILY EXTRACTIONS: ANOTHER LOOK AT THE "DUE PROCESS" AND "SELECTIVE INCORPORATION" APPROACHES

8th ed., p. 46; after *Rochin* add new Note:

3. Applying the "shocks-the-conscience" test first articulated in the *Rochin* case, COUNTY OF SACRAMENTO v. LEWIS, ___ U.S. ___, ___, 118 S.Ct. 1708, ___, ___ L.Ed.2d ___ (1998) (also discussed at Supp., p. ___), held, per SOUTER, J., that a police officer did not violate substantive due process by causing death through "reckless indifference" to, or "reckless disregard" for, a person's life in a high-speed automobile chase of a speeding motorcyclist. (The chase resulted in the death of the motorcyclist's passenger when the police car skidded into the passenger after the cycle had tipped over). In such circumstances, concluded the Court, "only a purpose to cause harm unrelated to the legitimate object of arrest will satisfy the element of arbitrary conduct shocking to the conscience, necessary for a due process violation [and for police liability under 42 U.S.C. § 1983]."

The Court recalled that it had held in *Graham v. Connor*, 490 U.S. 386, 109 S.Ct. 1865, 104 L.Ed.2d 443 (1989), that "where a particular amendment provides an explicit textual source of constitutional protection against a particular sort of government behavior, that Amendment, not the more generalized notion of substantive due process, must be the guide for analyzing [claims of substantive due process violations]." But the "more-specific-provision" rule of *Graham* did not bar respondents' lawsuit because neither the high-speed chase of the motorcycle nor the accidental killing of the motorcycle passenger constituted a Fourth Amendment "seizure." The Court then addressed respondents' substantive due process claim:

"Since the time of our early explanations of due process, we have understood the core of the concept to be protection against arbitrary action * * *. Our cases dealing with abusive executive action have repeatedly emphasized that only the most egregious official conduct can be said to be 'arbitrary in the constitutional sense' * * *.

"[F]or half a century now we have spoken of the cognizable level of executive abuse of power as that which shocks the conscience. We first put the test this way in *Rochin* * * *. In the intervening years we have repeatedly adhered to *Rochin*'s benchmark. * * * Most recently, in *Collins v. Harker Heights*, 503 U.S. 115, 112 S.Ct.1061, 117 L.Ed.2d 261 (1992), we said again that the substantive component of the Due Process Clause is violated by executive action only when it 'can properly be characterized as arbitrary, or conscience shocking, in a constitutional sense.' "

The Court emphasized that much turns on the particular context in which the executive misconduct arises. Thus, in a prison custodial situation, when the state has rendered an individual unable to care for himself, and at the same time fails to provide for his basic needs, "the point of the conscience-shocking is reached" when injuries are produced by reckless or grossly negligent executive conduct. On the other hand, "deliberate indifference does not suffice for constitutional liability (albeit under the Eighth Amendment) even in prison circumstances when a prisoner's claim arises not from normal custody but from response to a violent disturbance." Continued the Court:

"Like prison officials facing a riot, the police on an occasion calling for fast action have obligations that tend to tug against each other. Their duty is to restore and maintain lawful order, while not exacerbating disorder more than necessary to do their jobs. They are supposed to act decisively and to show restraint at the same moment, and their decisions have to be made 'in haste, under pressure, and frequently without the luxury of a second chance.' [A] police officer deciding whether to give chase must balance on one hand the need to stop a suspect and show that flight from the law is no way to freedom, and, on the other, the high-speed threat to everyone within stopping range, be they suspects, their passengers, other drivers, or bystanders.

"To recognize a substantive due process violation in these circumstances when only mid-level fault has been shown [i.e., something more than simple negligence, but something less than intentional misconduct] would be to forget that liability for deliberate indifference to inmate welfare rests upon the luxury enjoyed by prison officials of having time to make unhurried judgments, upon the chance for repeated reflection, largely uncomplicated by the pulls of competing obligations. When such extended opportunities to do better are teamed with protracted failure even to care, indifference is truly shocking. But when unforeseen circumstances demand an officer's instant judgment, even precipitate recklessness fails to inch close enough to harmful purpose to spark the shock that implicates 'the large concerns of the governors and the governed.' Just as a purpose to cause harm is needed for Eighth Amendment liability in a riot case, so it ought to be needed for Due Process liability in a pursuit case. Accordingly, we hold that high-speed chases with no intent to harm suspects physically or to worsen their legal plight do not give rise to liability under the Fourteenth Amendment, redressible by an action under § 1983. * * * Regardless whether Smith's behavior offended the reasonableness held up by tort law or the balance struck in law enforcement's own codes of sound practice, it does not shock the conscience * * *."[a]

Concurring in the judgement, SCALIA, J., joined by Thomas, J. would not have decided the case by applying the "shocks-the-conscience" test but "on the ground that respondents offer no textual or historical support for their alleged due process right." The concurring Justices maintained that in *Washington v. Glucksberg*, ___ U.S. ___, 117 S.Ct. 2258, 138 L.Ed.2d 772 (1997) (upholding a criminal prohibition against physician-assisted suicide), "the Court specifically rejected the method of substantive-due-process analysis employed by Justice Souter in that case, which is the very same method employed by Justice Souter in his opinion for the Court today." Justice Scalia continued:

"Adhering to our decision in *Glucksberg*, rather than ask whether the police conduct here at issue shocks my unelected conscience, I would ask whether our Nation has traditionally protected the right respondents assert.* * * I agree with the Court's conclusion that [respondents' complaint] asserts a substantive right to be free from 'deliberate or reckless indifference to life in a high-speed automobile chase aimed at apprehending a suspected offender.' Respondents provide no textual or historical support for this alleged due process right, [and] I would 'decline to fashion a new due process right out of thin air.' Nor have respondents identified any precedential support. Indeed, precedent is to the contrary * * *.

"[To] hold, as respondents urge, that all government conduct deliberately indifferent to life, liberty, or property, violates the Due Process Clause would make 'the Fourteenth Amendment a font of tort law to be

---

a. Justice Kennedy, joined by O'Connor, J. joined the opinion of the Court, but also wrote separately: They "share[d] Justice Scalia's concerns about using the phrase 'shocks the conscience' in a manner suggesting that it is a self-defining test." The phrase, they observed, "has the unfortunate connotation of a standard laden with subjective assessments. In that respect, it must be viewed with considerable skepticism."

superimposed upon whatever systems may already be administered by
the States.' [If] the people [of] California would prefer a system that
renders police officers liable for reckless driving during high-speed
pursuits, '[t]hey may create such a system [by] changing the tort law of
the State in accordance with the regular lawmaking process.' For now,
they prefer not to [do so]. It is the prerogative of a self-governing people
to make that legislative choice. [For] judges to overrule [the] democrati-
cally adopted policy judgment [of the people of California and their
elected representatives] on the ground that it shocks their consciences is
not judicial review but judicial governance."

Chapter 3

THE RIGHT TO COUNSEL, TRANSCRIPTS AND OTHER AIDS; POVERTY, EQUALITY AND THE ADVERSARY SYSTEM

SECTION 1. THE RIGHT TO APPOINTED COUNSEL AND RELATED PROBLEMS

A. The Right to Appointed Counsel in Criminal Proceedings

8th ed., p. 75; after *Gideon* add new Notes:

4. *The unrealized dream of Gideon.* For the view, spelled out at considerable length, that more than thirty years after *Gideon* the dream of that landmark case—the dream of a country "in which every person charged with a crime will be capably defended, no matter what his economic circumstances"—remains largely unrealized, see Stephen B. Bright, *Counsel for the Poor: the Death Sentence not for the Worst Crime but for the Worst Lawyer,* 103 Yale L.J. 1835 (1994). According to Bright, id. at 1870, "a properly working adversary system will never be achieved unless defender organizations are established and properly funded to employ lawyers at wages and benefits equal to what is spent on the prosecution, to retain expert and investigative assistance, to assign lawyers to capital cases, to recruit and support local lawyers and to supervise the performance of counsel defending capital cases. Judges are not equipped to do this. Management of the defense is not a proper judicial function."

5. *"Our double standards of criminal defense."* In many jurisdictions, notes Deborah L. Rhode, *Simpson Sound Bites: What Is and Isn't News about Domestic Violence,* in Postmortem: The O.J. Simpson Case 83, 84 (Jeffrey Abramson ed. 1996), the average fee for a court-appointed defense lawyer in a felony case is under $400—a total "less than what one of [O.J.] Simpson's lawyers typically charges by the hour." As for public defenders, continues Professor Rhode, each generally handles hundreds of felony cases per year and usually lacks adequate time or resources for investigation and expert testimony. "By contrast, in the Simpson case, * * * the complete defense bill, including legal fees, many

5

have reached $10 million. That figure exceeds what some states spend on appointed counsel for thousands of indigent defendants."

Adds Rhode, id. at 85: "The current structure [of our criminal defense system] bears an awkward resemblance to the one parodied in a well-known *New Yorker* cartoon. There, a well-heeled lawyer asks his anxious client, 'So, Mr. Smith, how much justice can you afford?' * * *'" Yet virtually none of the post-Simpson reform efforts focus on reducing our double standards of criminal defense.[a]

8th ed. p. 80; end of Note 6, add:

In *Nichols v. United States,* 511 U.S. 738, 114 S.Ct. 1921, 128 L.Ed.2d 745 (1994), the Court, per Rehnquist, C.J., adhered to *Scott,* but overruled *Baldasar,* "agree[ing] with the dissent in *Baldasar* that a logical consequence of [*Scott*] is that an uncounseled [misdemeanor] conviction valid under *Scott* [because no prison term was imposed] may be relied upon to enhance the sentence for a subsequent offense, even though that sentence entails imprisonment." In 1983 Nichols had pled *nolo contendere* to a state misdemeanor, driving under the influence of alcohol (DUI) and paid a $250 fine. He was not represented by counsel. Seven years later, when Nichols pled guilty to a federal drug charge, this uncounseled misdemeanor conviction was used to enhance his prison sentence.[b]

SECTION 2. THE *GRIFFIN–DOUGLAS* "EQUALITY" PRINCIPLE

C. The Indigent Defendant's Right to Expert Services in Addition to Counsel

8th ed., p. 99; add new Note:

5. *The resource imbalance—a problem the Simpson case illustrated in reverse.* Consider Peter Arenella, *Foreword: O.J. Lessons,* 69 S.Cal. L.Rev. 1233, 1234–35 (1996):

"In [a] lawyer-dominated system, the trial's outcome may hinge on which side has the superior resources to pay for the best investigators, experts, and counsel. Money can have a greater impact on the verdict than the 'facts' because it dictates how those 'facts' are transformed into legally admissible and persuasive evidence.

"This resource factor usually favors the state because most criminal defendants are poor. The prosecutor can use law enforcement agencies, state and private forensic laboratories, and experts on the public payroll to develop, shape, and present her evidence. Crime victims and wit-

a. See also the extract from Professor Arenella's article at Supp., pp. 6–7.

b. Souter, J., concurred only in the judgment. Blackmun, J., joined by Stevens and Ginsburg, JJ., dissented, maintaining that "[i]t is more logical, and more consis-tent with the reasoning in *Scott,* to hold that a conviction that is invalid for impos-ing a sentence for the offense itself remains invalid for increasing the term of imprison-ment imposed for a subsequent conviction."

nesses usually cooperate with the prosecution. If they do not, the prosecutor can command their appearance before a grand jury and compel their testimony.

"In contrast, a skilled and experienced public defender is lucky if she gets an investigator to spend a few hours investigating the 'facts.' Crime victims and civilian witnesses frequently refuse to answer the investigator's questions. If the public defender needs expert assistance, she must petition the court for funds to pay for the expert's time. The one or two state funded experts she may obtain won't be [the caliber of O.J. Simpson's experts] and they will rarely spend hundreds of hours looking for flaws in the state's case.

"This resource imbalance is particularly egregious in death penalty prosecutions. Given the horrific nature of these crimes, the defendant's life often depends on the defense's ability and capacity to make the client's humanity apparent to the jury deciding his fate at the sentencing phase of the trial.[4] Far too often, underpaid defense lawyers in capital cases spend less time and effort on death penalty cases than the Simpson defense team expended prepping for his preliminary hearing.

"The 'trial of the century' illustrated this resource imbalance problem in reverse. One of Robert Shapiro's wisest decisions was to hire some of this country's leading medical, forensic, and legal experts before Simpson was even arrested. With the aid of [various experts], the defense's forensic attorney team * * * transformed incriminating hair, blood, DNA, and fiber data into evidence of police and criminalist incompetence and corruption. While defense counsel for the indigent can read the Simpson trial transcripts and learn new ways to attack forensic evidence, they lack the resources to buy the experts whose prestige and skills made the 'garbage in-garbage out' strategy so effective."

SECTION 3. THE RIGHT TO APPOINTED COUNSEL IN PROCEEDINGS OTHER THAN CRIMINAL PROSECUTIONS: THE CONTINUED VITALITY OF THE *BETTS v. BRADY* APPROACH

B. COLLATERAL ATTACK PROCEEDINGS

8th ed., p. 106; after discussion of *Bounds* and the duty to provide prisoners "meaningful access" to the courts, add:

Two decades after it had decided *Bounds v. Smith,* the Court shed light on that case in LEWIS v. CASEY, 518 U.S. 343, 116 S.Ct. 2174, 135

---

4. This is no easy task. Explaining how one's client became a killer will not work unless the defendant's life story includes factors that trigger the jury's compassion. Constructing such a story requires extensive investigation into the offender's past, documentation of whatever factors "victimized" the offender at an early age, evidence of how the "system" failed to address these factors, and expert testimony explaining why these factors diminished the offender's capacity to control his anti-social impulses. Accounts of the offender's early victimization may well fall on deaf ears unless the defense can also make some showing of why the offender is not beyond redemption.

L.Ed.2d 606 (1996), which arose as follows: Inmates of various prisons operated by the Arizona Department of Corrections brought a class action alleging that prison officials were furnishing them inadequate legal research facilities and thus depriving them of their right of access to the courts in violation of *Bounds*. After finding a variety of shortcomings in the Arizona prison system, the federal district court appointed a special master to investigate and report about the appropriate relief. Some months later the court adopted the special master's proposed permanent injunction, a 25–page order mandating sweeping changes designed to ensure that the prison system would "provide meaningful access to the courts for all present and future prisoners." The U.S. Court of Appeals for the Ninth Circuit affirmed both the finding of a *Bounds* violation and the injunction's major terms.

The Supreme Court, per SCALIA, J., reversed, holding that the success of the inmates' systemic challenge was dependent on their ability to show widespread "actual injury" and the district court's "failure to identify anything more than isolated instances of actual injury renders its findings of a systemic *Bounds* violation invalid." The Court emphasized that *Bounds* did *not* establish the right to a law library or to legal assistance:

"The right that *Bounds* acknowledged was the (already well-established) right of access to the courts. In the cases to which *Bounds* traced its roots, we had protected that right by prohibiting State prison officials from actively interfering with inmates' attempts to prepare legal documents or file them and by requiring state courts to waive filing fees or transcript fees for indigent inmates. *Bounds* focused on the same entitlement of access to the courts. [In] other words, prison law libraries and legal assistance programs are not ends in themselves, but only the means for ensuring 'a reasonably adequate opportunity to present claimed violations of fundamental constitutional rights to the courts' [quoting *Bounds*].

"Because *Bounds* did not create an abstract, free-standing right to a law library or legal assistance, an inmate cannot establish relevant actual injury simply by establishing that his prison's law library or legal assistance program is sub-par in some theoretical sense. That would be the precise analogue of the healthy inmate claiming constitutional violation because of the prison infirmary. Insofar as the right vindicated by *Bounds* is concerned, 'meaningful access to the courts is the touchstone' and the inmate must go one step further and demonstrate that the alleged shortcomings in the library or legal assistance program hindered his efforts to pursue a legal claim. He might show, for example, that a complaint he prepared was dismissed for failure to satisfy some technical requirement which, because of deficiencies in the prison's legal assistance facilities, he could not have known. Or that he had suffered arguably actionable harm that he wished to bring before the courts, but was so stymied by inadequacies of the law library that he was unable to file a complaint. * * *

"It must be acknowledged that several statements in *Bounds* went beyond the right of access recognized in the earlier cases on which it relied, which was a right to bring to court a grievance that the inmate wished to present. These statements appear to suggest that the State must enable the prisoner to discover grievances, and to litigate effectively once in court. These elaborations upon the right of access to the courts have no antecedent in our pre-*Bounds* cases, and we now disclaim them. To demand the conferral of such sophisticated legal capabilities upon a mostly uneducated and indeed largely illiterate prison population is effectively to demand permanent provision of counsel, which we do not believe the Constitution requires.

"Finally, we must observe that the injury requirement is not satisfied by just any type of frustrated legal claim. Nearly all of the access-to-courts cases in the *Bounds* line involved attempts by inmates to pursue direct appeals from the convictions for which they were incarcerated or habeas petitions.

" * * * *Bounds* does not guarantee inmates the wherewithal to transform themselves into litigating engines capable of filing everything from shareholder derivative actions to slip-and-fall claims. The tools it requires to be provided are those that the inmates need in order to attack their sentences, directly or collaterally, and in order to challenge the conditions of their confinement. Impairment of any other litigating capacity is simply one of the incidental (and perfectly constitutional) consequences of conviction and incarceration."

Additional reasons why the district court's injunctive order could not be sustained were the court's failure to accord adequate deference to the judgment of the prison authorities in several respects (for example, in concluding that restrictions on the access of "lockdown prisoners" to law libraries were unjustified, the court gave insufficient weight to the fact that inmates in lockdown include the most dangerous and violent prisoner in the prison system) and the fact that the injunctive order was developed through a process that failed to give adequate consideration to the views of the state prison authorities. "Having found a violation of the right of access to the courts, [the district court] conferred upon its special master [a law professor from New York], rather than upon [state prison] officials, the responsibility for devising a remedial plan. To make matters worse, it severely limited the remedies the master could choose."

Justice SOUTER, joined by Ginsburg and Breyer, JJ., concurred in the judgment and in portions of the Court's opinion, but dissented in part. "Given that adequately stocked libraries go far in satisfying the *Bounds* requirements," Justice Souter considered it "an abuse of discretion for the District Court to aggregate discrete, small-bore problems in individual prisons and to treat them as if each prevailed throughout the prison system, for the purpose of justifying a broad remedial order covering virtually every aspect of each prison library." He also thought that other elements of the injunction were unsupported by any factual finding. "It is this overreaching of the evidentiary record", he emphasized, "not the application of standing or even class action rules, that call for the judgment to be reversed." Continued Souter:

"I do not disagree with the Court that in order to meet these standards (in a case that does not involve substantial systemic deprivation of access), a prisoner suing under Bounds must assert something more than an abstract desire to have an adequate library or some other access mechanism. Nevertheless, while I believe that a prisoner must generally have some underlying claim or grievance for which he seeks judicial relief, I cannot endorse the standing requirement the Court now imposes.

"On the Court's view, a district court may be required to examine the merits of each plaintiff's underlying claim in order to determine whether he was standing to litigate a *Bounds* claim. The Court would require a determination that the claim is 'nonfrivolous' in the legal sense that it states a claim for relief that is at least arguable in law and in fact. I, in contrast, would go no further than to require that a prisoner have some concrete grievance or gripe about the conditions of his confinement, the validity of his conviction, or perhaps some other problem for which he would seek legal redress infra (even though a claim based on that grievance might well fail sooner or later in the judicial process.)

"There are three reasons supporting this as a sufficient standard. First, it is the existence of an underlying grievance, not its ultimate legal merit, that gives a prisoner a concrete interest in the litigation and will thus assure the serious and adversarial treatment of the *Bounds* claim. Second, *Bounds* recognized a right of access for those who seek adjudication, not just for sure winners or likely winners or possible winners. * * * Finally, insistence on a 'nonfrivolous claim' rather than a 'concrete grievance' as a standing requirement will do no more than guarantee a lot of preliminary litigation over nothing. There is no prison system so blessed as to lack prisoners with non-frivolous complaints. They will always turn up, or be turned up, and one way or the other the Bounds litigation will occur.

"[In] sum, I would go no further than to hold (in a case not involving substantial, systemic deprivation of access to court) that Article III requirements will normally be satisfied if a prisoner demonstrates that (1) he has a complaint or grievance, meritorious or not, about the prison system or the validity of his conviction that he would raise if his library research (or advice, or judicial review of a form complaint or other means of 'access' chosen by the State) were to indicate that he had an actionable claim; and (2) that the access scheme provided by the prison is so inadequate that he cannot research, consult about, file, or litigate the claim, as the case may be."

Finally, Justice Souter disagreed with the Court on two other points: "First, I cannot concur in the suggestion that *Bounds* should be overruled to the extent that it requires States choosing to provide law libraries for court access to make them available for a prisoner's use in the period between filing a complaint and its final disposition. [With] respect to habeas claims, for example, the need for some form of legal assistance is even more obvious now than it was [at the time of *Bounds*], because the restrictions developed since *Bounds* have created a 'substantial risk' that prisoners proceeding without legal assistance will never be able to obtain review of the merits of their claims. Nor should discouragement from the number of frivolous prison suits lead us to doubt the practical justifiability of providing assistance to a *pro se* prisoner during trial. Second, I see no reason at this point to accept the Court's view that the *Bounds* right of access is necessarily restricted to attacks on sentences or challenges to conditions of confinement. It is not clear to me that a State may force a prisoner to abandon all opportunities to vindicate rights outside those two categories no matter how significant." [a]

8th ed., p. 113; after Note 6, add new Note:

New federal legislation. For discussion of new federal legislation bearing on the right to counsel in state postconviction proceedings brought by indigent prisoners on death row, see Note 5b. at Supp., p. 180.

---

a. Justice Thomas, who joined the opinion of the Court, also wrote a separate concurring opinion in the course of which he observed that "what can be termed a right of access to the courts" is merely "a right not to be arbitrarily prevented from lodging a claimed violation of a federal right in a federal court." "Quite simply," maintained Justice Thomas, "there is no basis in constitutional text, pre-*Bounds* precedent, history, or tradition for the conclusion that the constitutional right of access imposes affirmative obligations on the States to finance and support prisoner litigation." Justice Stevens dissented from the Court's opinion. He was persuaded that the relief ordered by the district court was broader than necessary to redress the constitutional violations identified in the court's findings and therefore agreed that the case should be remanded. But he saw "no need to resolve the other constitutional issues that the Court reaches out to address."

Part Two

POLICE PRACTICES

Chapter 4

SOME GENERAL REFLECTIONS ON THE POLICE, THE COURTS AND THE CRIMINAL PROCESS

8th ed., p. 121; after extract from Robert Weisberg's article add:

For strong criticism of the American criminal justice system, see Louis Michael Seidman, *Criminal Procedure as the Servant of Politics,* 12 Const.Comm. 207 (1995). Professor Seidman maintains, inter alia, that "the Fourth Amendment is so riddled with exceptions and limitations that it rarely prevents the police from pursuing any reasonable crime control tactic" and that despite judicial insistence on "the ritualistic reading of *Miranda* warnings, judges have virtually gone out of the business of actually policing the voluntariness of confessions." He continues, id. at 209–10:

"It seems unlikely, then, that the criminal procedure [constitutional] amendments have either exacerbated our crime problem or provided an effective bulwark against police and prosecutorial overreaching. A third possibility is more plausible: constitutional protections intended to make prosecution more difficult instead serve [to] make the prosecutor's job easier.

" * * * In individual cases, criminal procedure protections make the punishment we inflict on criminal defendants seem more acceptable. Although the amendments do little to make the prosecutor's job harder, people commonly believe that they obstruct the prosecution of dangerous criminals. Some doubt and ambivalence that might otherwise accompany the use of violent and coercive sanctions is thereby dissipated. * * *

"[Although the rate of incarceration has skyrocketed in this country, this increased rate is not caused by an increase in crime, but] seems to be fed by the public *perception* that crime is out of control and that still more draconian punishments are necessary to deal with it. Popular misconceptions about criminal procedure protections feed this perception. Because people believe that 'legal technicalities' set large numbers of guilty and dangerous criminals free, they think that too many miscreants are escaping punishment. Because they believe that the problem could be brought under control if only the 'legal technicalities' were changed, they fail to focus on the bankruptcy of mass-incarceration as a crime fighting strategy."

"Professor Seidman's views are strongly challenged by William T. Pizzi, *Punishment and Procedure: A Different View of the American Criminal Justice System,* 13 Const.Comm. 55 (1996), who insists that on a comparative basis both civil law and common law countries with much lower incarceration rates "grant defendants far fewer protections than defendants receive in American courts." *Id.* at 62. Professor Pizzi continues, id. at 66–67:

"Professor Seidman seems frustrated and angry that our country would develop an elaborate system of constitutional rights that has no equivalent in other countries and, at the same time, punish defendants more severely than other countries, sometimes much more severely. But I think that it is not surprising to find extremes in procedure and punishment linked in this way because there is a synergy between procedure and punishment such that extreme in one encourage extremes in the other and vice versa. It is thus not an accident that a country with a system of criminal procedure that is the most complicated and the most expensive in the western world and, if the truth be known, a trial system that is not very reliable, would also turn out to have a system that threatens, and sometimes inflicts, punishments that are harsh compared to those in other countries. Such a system needs to put pressure on defendants by threatening them with harsh punishments if they insist on trial, so that high mandatory minimums, habitual offender statutes, tough sentencing guidelines, and the like are encouraged by such a procedural system. Essentially, the system needs to work around its own procedures, and in the United States this is done by accepting types of charge bargains and sentence bargains—even bargains from defendants who insist that they are innocent—that would not be accepted in other systems.

"Harsh punishments in turn encourage even more emphasis on procedure. Certainly, there is no better example than the death penalty, where even a single mistake in jury selection by a trial judge invalidates the death sentence no matter how heinous the crimes committed by the offender or how many such crimes he may have committed in the past. The system's reluctance to use the death penalty translates into a requirement of technical perfection in capital cases that can rarely be met. This in turn feeds anger at the system and the main outlet for that sort of anger is to pressure legislatures for ever harsher punishments for criminals."

8th ed. p. 124; after extract from Skolnick & Fyfe's *Above the Law*, add:

Does "community policing" offer a promising means of preventing the police excesses discussed in *Above the Law*? Consider Debra Livingston, *Brutality in Blue: Community, Authority, and the Elusive Promise of Police Reform* (essay review of *Above the Law*), 92 Mich.L.Rev. 1556, 1559, 1571–72 (1994):

"On its face, *Above the Law* is about constraining bad cops from misusing their authority, not about empowering good cops to address growing community concerns with the problems of neighborhood deterioration. Yet, *Above the Law* points to a connection between the twin aspirations of police reformers to control police misconduct and to improve police effectiveness in responding to problems of crime and disorder. Perhaps the book's most intriguing aspect is the authors' belief that the very turn to community policing[a]—with its attendant *deemphasis on law* as a basis for police legitimation, *decentralization of decisionmaking,* and *increase in connections* between beat cops and community residents—may itself be a means of limiting the occasions on which police ignore legal restraints. As concerns with both crime and disorder push the police back to center stage and as policymakers indulge in modest hopes that community-oriented policing might help assuage these concerns, the authors' assessment that returning cops to the community will also help keep them from acts of brutality is, indeed, good news. The most frustrating aspect of this thoughtful book, however, may be *Above the Law*'s less-than-full attention to the problems that police face in our communities today and to the possibility that developing better responses to these problems may itself be a precondition to realizing the open, humanistic style of policing that Skolnick and Fyfe believe will help minimize the tragic incidence of police brutality. * * *

"* * * Proponents of community policing understand that so-called wars on crime cannot be 'won,' if for no other reason than that crime is not an enemy that can be vanquished. Once we set the war-on-crime conception of the police mission aside, however, even ardent advocates of community policing admit that the jury is still out on a different, more modest concern: whether community policing can, in fact, augment public safety at all. Skolnick and Fyfe assert, powerfully, that officers who are placed on the front lines of unwinnable wars on crime become cynical, alienated, and even brutal (pp. 114–15). The authors spend less

---

a. Common elements of the "community" strategy, points out Professor Livingston, are "an emphasis on the community, rather than merely on police professionalism and the law, as a source of legitimation for many police tasks; the purposeful decentralization of much police decisionmaking and the reorientation of patrol in the direction of neighborhood-based policing; a redefinition of the police role to include not only response to individual criminal incidents but also matters like promoting the common welfare, solving community-nominated problems that may contribute to crime, and, for some, aggressively maintaining civil order; and, finally, the establishment of close working relationships between police and citizens, community groups, and, sometimes, relevant social service agencies."

time assessing the dangers for the beat cop of a reform philosophy that may not be fully realized or that does not, as it turns out, address current concerns about crime and disorder.

"This inattention would be less noteworthy if the philosophy of community policing did not itself raise legitimate concerns relevant to the problem of police brutality. Community policing, however, both frankly bestows discretion on the beat cop and founds the propriety of his actions in part on community norms—notwithstanding how problematic the notion of *community* really is.[48] As David Bayley has noted, implications of the theory of community policing provoke concern that this theory, in practice, may 'weaken the rule of law in the sense of equal protection and evenhanded enforcement ... lessen the protection afforded by law to unpopular persons ... [and] even encourage vigilantism' by mobilizing one part of the community against another. Community policing [as Herman Goldstein has observed] implies 'that officers are to have much greater freedom and to exercise independence' and that communities are to 'have some input into decisions made about the form of police services.' But encouraging independence in the police and input from the community, as Mastrofski and Uchida note in passing in their review of *Above the Law,* may 'place street-level officers at greater risk to be responsive to vigilante values in "defended" neighborhoods.'[51] Moreover, with the decentralized decisionmaking that community policing implies, no one may know 'precisely how patrol officers spend their time.' In first acknowledging and then promoting the beat cop's street-level discretion, community policing theorists must also be concerned that police officers not employ that discretion for their *own* ends—lest community policing in practice lead to increased slackness and time wasting on the beat and to various forms of corruption."[a]

8th ed., 127; after extract from Tracey Maclin's article, add:

Consider, too, David A. Harris, *Factors for Reasonable Suspicion: When Black and Poor Means Stopped and Frisked,* 69 Ind.L.J. 659, 679–81 (1994), maintaining that, because of the disproportionately high number of African Americans and Hispanic Americans living in high crime areas, "location plus evasion" stops and frisks (stops and frisks based on an individual's presence in a high crime location plus evasion of the police) have "widen[ed] the racial divide in the United States." (See also the extract from Professor Harris's article at Supp., p. 44) But cf. Randall Kennedy, *The State, Criminal Law, and Racial Discrimination:*

---

48. Skolnick and Fyfe recognize that if community "implies a commonality of interests, traditions, identities, values, and expectations," community may simply not exist in many areas. * * *

51. Stephen D. Mastrofski & Craig D. Uchida, *Transforming the Police,* 30 J.Res. Crime & Delinq. 330, 348 (1993).

a. See also Debra Livingston, *Police Discretion and the Quality of Life in Public*

Places: Courts, Communities, and the New Policing, 97 Colum. L. Rev. 551 (1997) (reassessing the ways in which courts have employed the facial vagueness doctrine to limit police discretion in the performance of "order maintenance" tasks and maintaining that aggressive employment of the facial vagueness doctrine could impair positive change in the direction of community and problem-oriented policing.)

A Comment, 107 Harv.L.Rev. 1255, 1259 (1994): "Although the administration of criminal justice has, at times, been used as an instrument of racial oppression, the principal problem facing African–Americans in the context of criminal justice today is not over-enforcement but *under-*enforcement of the laws. The most lethal danger facing African–Americans in their day-to-day lives is not white, racist officials of the state, but private, violent criminals (typically black) who attack those most vulnerable to them without regard to racial identity."

More recently, Professor Kennedy has observed, Randall Kennedy, *Race, Crime, and the Law* 158–60 (1997):

"When a Mexican–American motorist is selected for questioning in part on the basis of his perceived ancestry, he is undoubtedly being burdened more heavily at that moment on account of his race than his white Anglo counterpart. He is being made to pay a type of racial tax for the campaign against illegal immigration that whites, blacks, and Asians escape. Similarly, a young black man selected for questioning by police as he alights from an airplane or drives a car is being made to pay a type of racial tax for the war against drugs that whites and other groups escape. That tax is the cost of being subjected to greater scrutiny than others. But is that tax illegitimate?

"One defense of it is that, under the circumstances, people of other races are simply not in a position to pay the tax effectively. In contrast to apparent Mexican ancestry, neither apparent white nor black nor Asian ancestry appreciably raises the risk that a person near the Mexican border is illegally resident in the United States. Similarly, the argument would run that in contrast to the young black man, the young white man is not as likely to be a courier of illicit drugs. The defense could go on to say that, in this context, race is *not* being used invidiously. It is not being used as a marker to identify people to harm through enslavement, or exclusion, or segregation. Rather, race is being used merely as a signal that facilitates efficient law enforcement. In this context, apparent Mexican ancestry or blackness is being used for unobjectionable ends in the same way that whiteness is used in the affirmative action context: as a marker that has the effect, though not the purpose, of burdening a given racial group. Whereas whites are made to pay a racial tax for the purpose of opening up opportunities for people of color in education and employment, Mexican–Americans and blacks are made to pay a racial tax for the purpose of more efficient law enforcement.

"We need to pause here to consider the tremendous controversy that has surrounded affirmative action policies aimed at helping racial minorities. Many of the same arguments against race-based affirmative action are applicable as well in the context of race-based police stops. With affirmative action, many whites claim that they are victims of racial discrimination. With race-based police stops, many people of color complain that they are victims of racial discrimination. With affirmative action, many adversely affected whites claim that they are *innocent* victims of a policy that penalizes them for the misconduct of others who also happened to have been white. With race-based police stops, many adversely affected people of color maintain that they are *innocent* victims of a policy that penalizes them for the misconduct of others who also happen to be colored. Many whites claim that a major drawback of affirmative action which makes it more costly than valuable is the fact of their intense resentment against such programs. Many people of color claim that one of the drawbacks of race-based police stops that makes it more costly than valuable is their resentment against such policies.

"There exist, however, a remarkable difference in reactions to these racial policies, both of which involve race-dependent decisionmaking. While affirmative action is under tremendous pressure politically and legally, racial policing is not.* * * "

Chapter 5

ARREST, SEARCH AND SEIZURE

SECTION 1.   THE EXCLUSIONARY RULE

8th ed., p. 154; in lieu of last paragraph of Note 2, add:

In PENNSYLVANIA BOARD OF PROBATION AND PAROLE v. SCOTT, ___ U.S. ___, 118 S.Ct. 2014, ___ L.Ed.2d ___ (1998), parole officers made an illegal search of parolee Scott's residence and found weapons there, which were later admitted at his parole revocation hearing, resulting in Scott being recommitted to serve 36 months. Thereafter, the state supreme court, although following the prevailing general rule against application of the exclusionary rule at parole revocation hearings, carved out an exception for cases in which the officer who conducted the search was aware of the person's parole status. The Supreme Court, in a 5–4 decision, disagreed. THOMAS, J., for the majority, relying upon *Calandra*, supra, and *Janis* and *Lopez-Mendoza*, infra, declined "to extend the operation of the exclusionary rule beyond the criminal trial context" because "application of the exclusionary rule would both hinder the functioning of state parole systems and alter the traditionally flexible, administrative nature of parole revocation proceedings," but at the same time "would provide only minimal deterrence benefits in this context." On the matter of deterrence, the majority declared it would be "minimal" even in the special situation which concerned the state court, for if the searcher was a police officer he would be deterred by the risk of exclusion of evidence at a criminal trial and would be unaffected by what happened at the parole proceeding, which, in the words of *Janis*, "falls outside the offending officer's zone of primary interest." If the searcher was a parole officer, he will likewise be deterred by the risk of evidence exclusion at a criminal trial, and, in any event, is not "engaged in the often competitive enterprise of ferreting out crime" and thus can be sufficiently deterred by "departmental training and discipline and the threat of damages actions." The dissenters, per SOUTER, J., noted "the police very likely do know a parolee's status when they go after him," which is significant because (1) police officers with such knowledge, "especially those employed by the same sovereign that runs the parole system, * * * have every incentive not to jeopardize a recommitment by rendering evidence inadmissible," and thus could be deterred by the threat of exclusion at a parole hearing; (2) "the actual likelihood of trial is often far less than the probability of a petition for parole revocation" because, as the Court itself noted on an earlier occasion, parole revocation "is often preferred to a new prosecution because of the procedural ease of recommitting the individual on the basis of a lesser showing by the State," and this means there will be "nothing 'marginal' about the deterrence provided by an exclusionary rule operating" in the parole revocation context, and (3) "the cooperation between parole and police officers * * * casts serious doubt upon the aptness of treating police officers differently from parole officers," who themselves "are considered police officers with respect to the offenders under their jurisdiction" and who, consequently, can no more than other police be thought to be adequately deterred by the risk of departmental discipline or the threat of damages actions.

8th ed., p. 157; before Note 6, add:

5a. *Evidence obtained by virtue of conduct of nonpolice government employee, used in criminal proceedings.* The *Burdeau* rule, grounded in the proposition that the Fourth Amendment is entirely inapplicable where there is no governmental action, must be distinguished from that recognized in ARIZONA v. EVANS, 514 U.S. 1, 115 S.Ct. 1185, 131 L.Ed.2d 34 (1995): that some government searches covered by the Fourth Amendment are nonetheless inappropriate occasions for use of the exclusionary rule, considering the kind of government official who was at fault. After Evans was stopped for a traffic violation, the patrol car's computer indicated he had an outstanding arrest warrant, so Evans was arrested; incident thereto, the officer found marijuana. It was later learned that this warrant (issued because of Evans' nonappearance on several traffic violations) had been quashed upon Evans' voluntary appearance in court a few weeks earlier, but that apparently the court clerk had not thereafter followed the usual procedure of notifying the sheriff's department so that the warrant could be removed from the computer records. The state supreme court concluded this amounted to a violation of the Fourth Amendment and that consequently the evidence must be suppressed, but the Supreme Court, per REHNQUIST, C.J., considering only the latter point, disagreed:

" 'The question whether the exclusionary rule's remedy is appropriate in a particular context has long been regarded as an issue separate from the question whether the Fourth Amendment rights of the party seeking to invoke the rule were violated by police conduct.' The exclusionary rule operates as a judicially created remedy designed to safeguard against future violations of Fourth Amendment rights through the rule's general deterrent effect. As with any remedial device, the rule's application has been restricted to those instances where its remedial objectives are thought most efficaciously served. Where 'the exclusionary rule does not result in appreciable deterrence, then, clearly, its use . . . is unwarranted.' * * *

"Applying the reasoning of *Leon* [8th ed., p. 135] to the facts of this case, we conclude that the decision of the Arizona Supreme Court must be reversed. The Arizona Supreme Court determined that it could not 'support the distinction drawn ... between clerical errors committed by law enforcement personnel and similar mistakes by court employees,' and that 'even assuming ... that responsibility for the error rested with the justice court, it does not follow that the exclusionary rule should be inapplicable to these facts.'

"This holding is contrary to the reasoning of *Leon,* supra; *Massachusetts v. Sheppard* [8th ed., p. 149]; and *Krull* [8th ed., p. 151]. If court employees were responsible for the erroneous computer record, the exclusion of evidence at trial would not sufficiently deter future errors so as to warrant such a severe sanction. First, as we noted in *Leon,* the exclusionary rule was historically designed as a means of deterring police misconduct, not mistakes by court employees. Second, respondent offers no evidence that court employees are inclined to ignore or subvert the Fourth Amendment or that lawlessness among these actors requires application of the extreme sanction of exclusion. To the contrary, the Chief Clerk of the Justice Court testified at the suppression hearing that this type of error occurred once every three or four years.

"Finally, and most important, there is no basis for believing that application of the exclusionary rule in these circumstances will have a significant effect on court employees responsible for informing the police that a warrant has been quashed. Because court clerks are not adjuncts to the law enforcement team engaged in the often competitive enterprise of ferreting out crime, they have no stake in the outcome of particular criminal prosecutions. The threat of exclusion of evidence could not be expected to deter such individuals from failing to inform police officials that a warrant had been quashed.

"If it were indeed a court clerk who was responsible for the erroneous entry on the police computer, application of the exclusionary rule also could not be expected to alter the behavior of the arresting officer. As the trial court in this case stated: 'I think the police officer [was] bound to arrest. I think he would [have been] derelict in his duty if he failed to arrest.' The Chief Clerk of the Justice Court testified that this type of error occurred 'on[c]e every three or four years.' In fact, once the court clerks discovered the error, they immediately corrected it, and then proceeded to search their files to make sure that no similar mistakes had occurred. There is no indication that the arresting officer was not acting objectively reasonably when he relied upon the police computer record. Application of the *Leon* framework supports a categorical exception to the exclusionary rule for clerical errors of court employees.[5]"

5. The Solicitor General, as amicus curiae, argues that an analysis similar to that we apply here to court personnel also would apply in order to determine whether the evidence should be suppressed if police personnel were responsible for the error. As the State has not made any such argument here, we agree that "[t]he record in this

O'CONNOR, J., joined by Souter and Bryer, concurring, cautioned: "While the police were innocent of the court employee's mistake, they may or may not have acted reasonably in their reliance on the recordkeeping system itself. Surely it would not be reasonable for the police to rely, say, on a recordkeeping system, their own or some other agency's, that has no mechanism to ensure its accuracy over time and that routinely leads to false arrests, even years after the probable cause for any such arrest has ceased to exist (if it ever existed). * * *

"In recent years, we have witnessed the advent of powerful, computer-based recordkeeping systems that facilitate arrests in ways that have never before been possible. The police, of course, are entitled to enjoy the substantial advantages this technology confers. They may not, however, rely on it blindly. With the benefits of more efficient law enforcement mechanisms comes the burden of corresponding constitutional responsibilities."

STEVENS, J., dissenting, argued that the majority's reliance on *Leon* was "misplaced": "The reasoning in *Leon* assumed the existence of a warrant; it was, and remains, wholly inapplicable to warrantless searches and seizures. * * * The *Leon* Court's exemption of judges and magistrates from the deterrent ambit of the exclusionary rule rested, consistently with the emphasis on the warrant requirement, on those officials' constitutionally determined role in issuing warrants. Taken on its own terms, *Leon*'s logic does not extend to the time after the warrant has issued; nor does it extend to court clerks and functionaries, some of whom work in the same building with police officers and may have more regular and direct contact with police than with judges or magistrates."

GINSBURG, J., joined by Stevens, while mainly disagreeing with the majority's invocation of "the *Long* presumption" [see 8th ed., p. 61] to assert jurisdiction, made these comments on the merits: "In the Court's view, exclusion of evidence, even if capable of deterring police officer errors, cannot deter the carelessness of other governmental actors.[5] Whatever federal precedents may indicate—an issue on which I voice no opinion—the Court's conclusion is not the lesson inevitably to be drawn from logic or experience.

case ... does not adequately present that issue for the Court's consideration." Accordingly, we decline to address that question.

5. It has been suggested that an exclusionary rule cannot deter carelessness, but can affect only intentional or reckless misconduct. This suggestion runs counter to a premise underlying all of negligence law— that imposing liability for negligence, i.e., lack of due care, creates an incentive to act with greater care. That the mistake may have been made by a clerical worker does not alter the conclusion that application of

the exclusionary rule has deterrent value. Just as the risk of respondeat superior liability encourages employers to supervise more closely their employees' conduct, so the risk of exclusion of evidence encourages policymakers and systems managers to monitor the performance of the systems they install and the personnel employed to operate those systems. In the words of the trial court, the mistake in Evans' case was "perhaps the negligence of the Justice Court, or the negligence of the Sheriff's office. But it is still the negligence of the State."

"In this electronic age, particularly with respect to recordkeeping, court personnel and police officers are not neatly compartmentalized actors. Instead, they serve together to carry out the State's information-gathering objectives. Whether particular records are maintained by the police or the courts should not be dispositive where a single computer database can answer all calls. Not only is it artificial to distinguish between court clerk and police clerk slips; in practice, it may be difficult to pinpoint whether one official, e.g., a court employee, or another, e.g., a police officer, caused the error to exist or to persist. Applying an exclusionary rule as the Arizona court did may well supply a powerful incentive to the State to promote the prompt updating of computer records. That was the Arizona Supreme Court's hardly unreasonable expectation. The incentive to update promptly would be diminished if court-initiated records were exempt from the rule's sway."

In *New Jersey v. T.L.O.*, 8th ed., p. 341, involving search of a student by a high school administrator, the Court reaffirmed that "the Fourth Amendment [is] applicable to the activities of civil as well as criminal authorities." However, because the search was found to be reasonable, the Court avoided expressing any opinion about the question which prompted the original grant of certiorari: whether the exclusionary rule is also applicable to searches by school authorities. In light of *Evans,* what is the answer to that question?

8th ed., p. 160; before Note 3, add:

2a. *More on the scope and sufficiency of the "constitutional tort."* Could the Supreme Court do more to ensure there exists a meaningful tort remedy for Fourth Amendment violations? Consider Bandes, *Reinventing* Bivens: *The Self–Executing Constitution,* 68 So.Calif.L.Rev. 289, 292 (1995), concluding that *Bivens* "stands for the principle that enforcement of the Constitution is not dependent on the assent of the political branches or of the states," so that there could (and should) be "an expanded *Bivens* doctrine which applies to federal officials and the federal government itself, for damage remedies against state officials and state government directly under the Fourteenth Amendment, and for remedies against municipal officials and government directly under the Fourteenth Amendment when section 1983 does not provide adequate relief." In any event, should tort remedies *replace* the exclusionary rule? Consider Amar, *Fourth Amendment First Principles,* 107 Harv. L.Rev. 757, 786, 798 (1994)(yes, as they were "clearly the ones presupposed by the Framers of the Fourth Amendment" and "make much more sense, *as deterrence,*" because "the traditional civil model is not skewed to reward the guilty"). But compare Maclin, *When the Cure for the Fourth Amendment is Worse Than the Disease,* 68 So.Cal.L.Rev. 1 (1994); Steiker, *Second Thoughts About First Principles,* 107 Harv. L.Rev. 820 (1994).

SECTION 2.   PROTECTED AREAS
AND INTERESTS

8th ed., p. 176; before paragraph (b), add:

(aa) *Weapons detector*. It appears that the device imagined by Prof. Loewy back in 1983 may soon become a reality. As a result of Department of Justice funding, several organizations have undertaken to develop concealed weapons detection technology in order to produce a commercially and technologically viable device that could do an "electronic frisk" of a suspect from a distance of ten to twenty feet. Two of the detectors under development use magnetic fields, albeit in quite different ways. Ratheon's device would illuminate the subject with a low intensity electronic magnetic pulse and then measure the time decay of the radiated energy from metal objects carried by the person. The device detects only metal objects, but produces no images. Rather, by measurement of the intensity and the time decay of the secondary radiation, there are produced "signatures" which can be identified as indicating whether the detected metal object is or is not a gun. By comparison, the INEL system uses magnetic gradiometers to measure fluctuations produced when anything made of ferromagnetic material moves through the earth's magnetic field. No electronic energy is directed at the subject, as these instruments merely measure what certain objects do to the earth's magnetic field. By use of target recognition software, the readings would be compared with known "signatures" of weapons of similar mass, shape and density to determine the likelihood that the device has focused upon a weapon. The third device, the Millitech system, uses passive millimeter wave imaging technology. The amplitude of radiation at which the waves are emitted varies with the object's temperature and other properties, and thus the Millitech detector scans the waves emitted by the human body and any objects concealed on the person and produces a small image on the back of the device in which the outlines of concealed objects, usually dark, are clearly visible against the much brighter image of the body.

Would the use of any or all of these systems constitute a Fourth Amendment search? Would the answer be the same in those twenty-five jurisdictions which have enacted some variety of a concealed weapon permit statute? See David Harris, *Superman's X–Ray Vision and the Fourth Amendment: The New Gun Detection Technology*, 69 Temple L.Rev. 1 (1996).

8th ed., p. 178; after first two paragraphs, add:

(d) *Thermal imaging*.   Police sometimes use an infrared thermal detection device, which detects differences in the surface temperature of targeted objects, to acquire evidence of marijuana growing activities inside of premises.   Most appellate courts which have confronted the issue have held, often by analogy to *Greenwood*, 8th ed., p. 165, and *Place*, 8th ed., p. 174, that such use of these devices does not constitute a search. Those decisions, it was concluded in *United States v. Cusumano*, 67 F.3d 1497 (10th Cir.1995), "have reduced the Fourth Amendment inquiry to an analysis of the reasonable expectation of privacy residing in the 'waste heat' which is measured merely by 'a passive device, employed from beyond the curtilage, which emits no rays or beams and which does not intrude in any fashion upon the observed property.' " But this, the court continued, "is to ignore both the purpose of the device and the manner in which it operates," for the "imager measures not 'waste heat' but rather heat differentials" across "the exterior surface of a building" which in turn reveal "the amount of heat generated by heat sources in proximity to the interior of that wall"; in short, "the true worth of the device—the very reason that the government turned the imager on the home of the Defendants—is predicated upon the translation of these thermal records into intelligible (albeit speculative) information about the activities that generate the observed heat."

The court in *Cusumano* thus concluded the better analogy was to *Katz:* "It must be remembered that the bug at issue in *Katz* was fixed to the outside of a public phone booth. Reduced to its operational fundamentals, that bug did not monitor the interior of the phone booth at all; rather, it measured the molecular vibrations of the glass that encompassed that interior. Alternatively, it might fairly be said that the bug passively recorded the propagation of waste vibrational energy into the public sphere. Drawing upon the logic embraced by our fellow circuits, one could reason that the translation of the vibrational record into an account of that which transpired within the phone booth was simply a useful interpretation of abandoned energy—an analysis which would, we note, approve the search condemned in *Katz*. * * *

"* * * *Katz* looked not to the tools employed by the government nor to the phenomena measured by those tools but to the object of the government's efforts; we see no reason to do otherwise here. We acknowledge that the thermal imager monitors and records the heat signatures of the activities ongoing inside a structure. The pertinent inquiry is not, therefore, whether the Defendants retain an expectation of privacy in the 'waste heat' radiated from their home but, rather, whether they possess an expectation of privacy in the heat signatures of the activities, intimate or otherwise, that they pursue within their home."

This opinion was vacated on rehearing en banc, 83 F.3d 1247 (10th Cir.1996), on the ground that this issue need not be reached because evidence other than the thermal imager scan provided probable cause for the challenged search warrant.

(e) *Gas Chromatography* involves using an extremely sensitive filtering machine to break down a gas sample or a liquid mixture into its molecular subcomponents. The sample to be tested is forced through a column, which is a glass tube filled with special filtration material, and a detector attached at the outgoing end of the column records the quantity and concentration of each particular molecular compound contained in the sample. Government-funded product development in recent years has turned GC from simply "a scientific laboratory technique" to one that is also used "on the streets." A law enforcement agent can use an eight-pound sampling unit, which resembles a large flashlight and works like a vacuum, to suck in vapors and particles from the immediate vicinity of a suspected container or individual. The analytical unit, also at the scene, then takes this sample and produces a chemical sketch of it, which is then compared to the make-up of known explosives (under one version of the equipment) or drugs (under another). The assumption is that a positive GC report establishes the presence of explosives or drugs, as the case may be, upon the object person or within the object container. Is such use of a portable unit, sometimes characterized as an "electronic canine," governed by the *Place* decision, 8th ed., p.174? See Bober, *The "Chemical Signature" of the Fourth Amendment: Gas Chromatography/Mass Spectrometry and the War on Drugs*, 8 Seton Hall Const.L.J. 75 (1997).

SECTION 3. PROBABLE CAUSE

8th ed. p. 213; following *Whiteley,* add:

What is the status of *Whiteley* after *Evans,* Supp. p. 19? The defendant there relied on *Whiteley,* which the Court distinguished because it mistakenly "treated identification of a Fourth Amendment violation as synonymous with application of the exclusionary rule to evidence secured incident to that violation"?

In UNITED STATES v. RAMIREZ, ___ U.S. ___, 118 S.Ct. 992, 140 L.Ed.2d 191 (1998), the Court, per REHNQUIST, C.J., unanimously held that whether the *Richards* reasonable suspicion test has been met "depends in no way on whether police must destroy property in order to enter." The Court then concluded that no Fourth Amendment violation had occurred in the instant case, where police executing a search warrant authorizing entry to seize a wanted person broke a garage window in order to deter the occupants of the premises (who thereafter exited and surrendered) from entering the garage to obtain weapons thought to be stored there: "A reliable confidential informant had notified the police that Alan Shelby might be inside respondent's home, and an officer had confirmed this possibility. Shelby was a prison escapee with a violent past who reportedly had access to a large supply of weapons. He had vowed that he would 'not do federal time.' The police certainly had a 'reasonable suspicion' that knocking and announcing their presence might be dangerous to themselves or to others."

SECTION 4. SEARCH WARRANTS

B. Execution of the Warrant

8th ed., p. 218; Note 2 before *Gassner,* add:

In WILSON v. ARKANSAS, 514 U.S. 927, 115 S.Ct. 1914, 131 L.Ed.2d 976 (1995), a unanimous Court, per THOMAS, J., proceeded "to resolve the conflict among the lower courts" by holding that the common law doctrine which "recognized a law enforcement officer's authority to break open the doors of a dwelling, but generally indicated that he first ought to announce his presence and authority," "forms a part of the reasonableness inquiry under the Fourth Amendment." (This conclusion, the Court noted, was consistent with its prior decisions in which "we have looked to the traditional protections against unreasonable searches and seizures afforded by the common law at the time of the framing" in evaluating the scope of the Fourth Amendment's protections.) The Court cautioned that the "Fourth Amendment's flexible requirement of reasonableness should not be read to mandate a rigid rule of announcement that ignores countervailing law enforcement interests," for "the common-law principle of announcement was never stated as an inflexible rule." However, the Court did not have occasion to define just when "law enforcement interests may also establish the reasonableness of an unannounced entry," or to consider whether the requisite circumstances were present in the instant case, as these matters had not been addressed by the lower court.

In RICHARDS v. WISCONSIN, 520 U.S. 385, 117 S.Ct. 1416, 137 L.Ed.2d 615 (1997), a unanimous Court, per STEVENS, J., rejected the state supreme court's holding that police officers are *never* required to knock and announce their presence when executing a search warrant in a felony drug investigation:

"The Wisconsin court explained its blanket exception as necessitated by the special circumstances of today's drug culture, and the State asserted at oral argument that the blanket exception was reasonable in 'felony drug cases because of the convergence in a violent and dangerous form of commerce of weapons and the destruction of drugs.' But creating exceptions to the knock-and-announce rule based on the 'culture' surrounding a general category of criminal behavior presents at least two serious concerns.

"First, the exception contains considerable overgeneralization. For example, while drug investigation frequently does pose special risks to officer safety and the preservation of evidence, not every drug investigation will pose these risks to a substantial degree. For example, a search could be conducted at a time when the only individuals present in a residence have no connection with the drug activity and thus will be unlikely to threaten officers or destroy evidence. Or the police could know that the drugs being searched for were of a type or in a location that made them impossible to destroy quickly. In those situations, the asserted governmental interests in preserving evidence and maintaining safety may not outweigh the individual privacy interests intruded upon by a no-knock entry. Wisconsin's blanket rule impermissibly insulates these cases from judicial review.

"A second difficulty with permitting a criminal-category exception to the knock-and-announce requirement is that the reasons for creating an exception in one category can, relatively easily, be applied to others.

Armed bank robbers, for example, are, by definition, likely to have weapons, and the fruits of their crime may be destroyed without too much difficulty. If a per se exception were allowed for each category of criminal investigation that included a considerable—albeit hypothetical—risk of danger to officers or destruction of evidence, the knock-and-announce element of the Fourth Amendment's reasonableness requirement would be meaningless.

"Thus, the fact that felony drug investigations may frequently present circumstances warranting a no-knock entry cannot remove from the neutral scrutiny of a reviewing court the reasonableness of the police decision not to knock and announce in a particular case. Instead, in each case, it is the duty of a court confronted with the question to determine whether the facts and circumstances of the particular entry justified dispensing with the knock-and-announce requirement.

"In order to justify a 'no-knock' entry, the police must have a reasonable suspicion that knocking and announcing their presence, under the particular circumstances, would be dangerous or futile, or that it would inhibit the effective investigation of the crime by, for example, allowing the destruction of evidence. This standard—as opposed to a probable cause requirement—strikes the appropriate balance between the legitimate law enforcement concerns at issue in the execution of search warrants and the individual privacy interests affected by no-knock entries. * * * This showing is not high, but the police should be required to make it whenever the reasonableness of a no-knock entry is challenged."

The Court concluded with two additional points: (1) The trial judge had correctly concluded that the police were excused from the knock-and-announce requirement because of the facts of the particular case. The officer who knocked at the door of defendant's hotel room claimed to be a maintenance man, defendant opened the door slightly and upon seeing a uniformed officer slammed the door, at which the police kicked the door in and entered. As the Court explained, once "the officers reasonably believed that Richards knew who they were * * * it was reasonable for them to force entry immediately given the disposable nature of the drugs." (2) The refusal of the magistrate issuing the search warrant to issue a no-knock warrant did not alter this conclusion, as "a magistrate's decision not to authorize a no-knock entry should not be interpreted to remove the officers' authority to exercise independent judgment concerning the wisdom of a no-knock entry at the time the warrant is being executed."

SECTION 5.　WARRANTLESS ARRESTS

8th ed., p. 234; bottom of page, add:

If the police conduct causing death or bodily harm was not a search or seizure, then the Fourteenth Amendment due process shocks-the-conscience test, rather than the Fourth Amendment reasonableness test, applies. See *County of Sacramento v. Lewis,* Note 3, Supp. p. 1.

What is the meaning of the term "deadly force" in *Garner*? In *Vera Cruz v. City of Escondido*, 139 F.3d 659 (9th Cir.1997), an officer acting solely to terminate a person's flight released his "K–9 companion," who bit the fleeing party on the arm and held him until the officer took away the arrestee's knife, resulting in wounds requiring surgery and eight days of hospitalization. In a § 1983 action, plaintiff argued for the Model Penal Code definition, "force that the actor uses with the purpose of causing or that he knows to create a substantial risk of causing death or serious bodily injury," but the court ruled that "deadly force is that force which is reasonably likely to cause death." Which is correct?

8th ed., p. 238; before Note 11, add:

10a.   Assuming a *Gerstein* violation, what bearing should it have if the individual is later prosecuted? In *Powell v. Nevada*, 511 U.S. 79, 114 S.Ct. 1280, 128 L.Ed.2d 1 (1994), holding *McLaughlin* retroactive to that case, the Court, per Ginsburg, J., noted: "It does not necessarily follow, however, that Powell must 'be set free' or gain other relief, for several questions remain open for decision on remand," including "the appropriate remedy for a delay in determining probable cause (an issue not resolved by *McLaughlin*)." In *Powell,* an untimely probable cause determination was made four days after defendant's arrest, shortly after he gave the police an incriminating statement. In declaring that "whether a suppression remedy applies in that setting remains an unresolved question," Justice Ginsburg took note of two arguably analogous rules pointing in opposite directions: (i) that an after-the-fact judicial determination of probable cause does not make admissible evidence obtained in a search in violation of the Fourth Amendment's search warrant requirement; and (ii) that under *Harris,* 8th ed., p. 812, suppression of a statement subsequently obtained elsewhere is not required because of defendant's warrantless arrest inside premises in violation of the Fourth Amendment.

8th ed., p. 246; bottom of page, add:

Nearly a quarter of a century passed before the Supreme Court finally addressed the pretext and police regulation issues in a traffic seizure context:

WHREN v. UNITED STATES

517 U.S. 806, 116 S.Ct. 1769, 135 L.Ed.2d 89 (1996).

Justice SCALIA delivered the opinion of the Court. * * *

On the evening of June 10, 1993, plainclothes vice-squad officers of the District of Columbia Metropolitan Police Department were patrolling a "high drug area" of the city in an unmarked car. Their suspicions were aroused when they passed a dark Pathfinder truck with temporary license plates and youthful occupants waiting at a stop sign, the driver looking down into the lap of the passenger at his right. The truck remained stopped at the intersection for what seemed an unusually long time—more than 20 seconds. When the police car executed a U-turn in order to head back toward the truck, the Pathfinder turned suddenly to its right, without signalling, and sped off at an "unreasonable" speed. The policemen followed, and in a short while overtook the Pathfinder when it stopped behind other traffic at a red light. They pulled up alongside, and Officer Ephraim Soto stepped out and approached the driver's door, identifying himself as a police officer and directing the driver, petitioner Brown, to put the vehicle in park. When Soto drew up to the driver's window, he immediately observed two large plastic bags of what appeared to be crack cocaine in petitioner Whren's hands. Petitioners were arrested, and quantities of several types of illegal drugs were retrieved from the vehicle.

Petitioners were charged in a four-count indictment with violating various federal drug laws. At a pretrial suppression hearing, they challenged the legality of the stop and the resulting seizure of the drugs. They argued that the stop had not been justified by probable cause to believe, or even reasonable suspicion, that petitioners were engaged in illegal drug-dealing activity; and that Officer Soto's asserted ground for approaching the vehicle—to give the driver a warning concerning traffic violations—was pretextual. The District Court denied the suppression motion * * *.

ISSUE

Petitioners were convicted of the counts at issue here. The Court of Appeals affirmed the convictions, holding with respect to the suppression issue that, "regardless of whether a police officer subjectively believes that the occupants of an automobile may be engaging in some other illegal behavior, a traffic stop is permissible as long as a reasonable officer in the same circumstances could have stopped the car for the suspected traffic violation."

History

The Fourth Amendment guarantees "[t]he right of the people to be secure in their persons, houses, papers, and effects, against unreasonable searches and seizures." Temporary detention of individuals during the stop of an automobile by the police, even if only for a brief period and for a limited purpose, constitutes a "seizure" of "persons" within the meaning of this provision. An automobile stop is thus subject to the constitutional imperative that it not be "unreasonable" under the circumstances. As a general matter, the decision to stop an automobile is reasonable where the police have probable cause to believe that a traffic violation has occurred.

Petitioners accept that Officer Soto had probable cause to believe that various provisions of the District of Columbia traffic code [regarding inattentive driving, speeding, and turning without signalling] had been violated. They argue, however, that "in the unique context of civil traffic regulations" probable cause is not enough. Since, they contend, the use of automobiles is so heavily and minutely regulated that total compliance with traffic and safety rules is nearly impossible, a police officer will almost invariably be able to catch any given motorist in a technical violation. This creates the temptation to use traffic stops as a means of investigating other law violations, as to which no probable cause or even articulable suspicion exists. Petitioners, who are both black, further contend that police officers might decide which motorists to stop based on decidedly impermissible factors, such as the race of the car's occupants. To avoid this danger, they say, the Fourth Amendment test for traffic stops should be, not the normal one (applied by the Court of Appeals) of whether probable cause existed to justify the stop; but rather, whether a police officer, acting reasonably, would have made the stop for the reason given.

Petitioners contend that the standard they propose is consistent with our past cases' disapproval of police attempts to use valid bases of action against citizens as pretexts for pursuing other investigatory agendas. We are reminded that in *Florida v. Wells*, [8th ed., p. 305], we stated that "an inventory search must not be used as a ruse for a general rummaging in order to discover incriminating evidence"; that in *Colorado v. Bertine*, [8th ed., p. 298], in approving an inventory search, we apparently thought it significant that there had been "no showing that the police, who were following standard procedures, acted in bad faith or for the sole purpose of investigation"; and that in *New York v. Burger*, [8th ed., p. 340], we observed, in upholding the constitutionality of a warrantless administrative inspection, that the search did not appear to be "a 'pretext' for obtaining evidence of . . . violation of . . . penal laws." But only an undiscerning reader would regard these cases as endorsing the principle that ulterior motives can invalidate police conduct that is justifiable on the basis of probable cause to believe that a violation of law has occurred. In each case we were addressing the validity of a search conducted in the absence of probable cause. Our quoted statements simply explain that the exemption from the need for probable cause (and warrant), which is accorded to searches made for the purpose of inventory or administrative regulation, is not accorded to searches that are not made for those purposes.

* * * Not only have we never held, outside the context of inventory search or administrative inspection (discussed above), that an officer's motive invalidates objectively justifiable behavior under the Fourth Amendment; but we have repeatedly held and asserted the contrary. In *United States v. Villamonte–Marquez*, 462 U.S. 579, 584, n. 3, 103 S.Ct. 2573, 2577, n. 3, 77 L.Ed.2d 22 (1983), we held that an otherwise valid warrantless boarding of a vessel by customs officials was not rendered invalid "because the customs officers were accompanied by a Louisiana state policeman, and were following an informant's tip that a vessel in the ship channel was thought to be carrying marihuana." We flatly dismissed the idea that an ulterior motive might serve to strip the agents of their legal justification. In *United States v. Robinson*, [8th ed., p. 239], we held that a traffic-violation arrest (of the sort here) would not be rendered invalid by the fact that it was "a mere pretext for a narcotics search," and that a lawful postarrest search of the person would not be rendered invalid by the fact that it was not motivated by the officer-safety concern that justifies such searches. And in *Scott v.*

United States, [8th ed., p. 378], in rejecting the contention that wiretap evidence was subject to exclusion because the agents conducting the tap had failed to make any effort to comply with the statutory requirement that unauthorized acquisitions be minimized, we said that "[s]ubjective intent alone ... does not make otherwise lawful conduct illegal or unconstitutional." We described *Robinson* as having established that "the fact that the officer does not have the state of mind which is hypothecated by the reasons which provide the legal justification for the officer's action does not invalidate the action taken as long as the circumstances, viewed objectively, justify that action."

We think these cases foreclose any argument that the constitutional reasonableness of traffic stops depends on the actual motivations of the individual officers involved. We of course agree with petitioners that the Constitution prohibits selective enforcement of the law based on considerations such as race. But the constitutional basis for objecting to intentionally discriminatory application of laws is the Equal Protection Clause, not the Fourth Amendment. Subjective intentions play no role in ordinary, probable-cause Fourth Amendment analysis.

Recognizing that we have been unwilling to entertain Fourth Amendment challenges based on the actual motivations of individual officers, petitioners disavow any intention to make the individual officer's subjective good faith the touchstone of "reasonableness." They insist that the standard they have put forward—whether the officer's conduct deviated materially from usual police practices, so that a reasonable officer in the same circumstances would not have made the stop for the reasons given—is an "objective" one.

But although framed in empirical terms, this approach is plainly and indisputably driven by subjective considerations. Its whole purpose is to prevent the police from doing under the guise of enforcing the traffic code what they would like to do for different reasons. Petitioners' proposed standard may not use the word "pretext," but it is designed to combat nothing other than the perceived "danger" of the pretextual stop, albeit only indirectly and over the run of cases. Instead of asking whether the individual officer had the proper state of mind, the petitioners would have us ask, in effect, whether (based on general police practices) it is plausible to believe that the officer had the proper state of mind.

Why one would frame a test designed to combat pretext in such fashion that the court cannot take into account actual and admitted pretext is a curiosity that can only be explained by the fact that our cases have foreclosed the more sensible option. If those cases were based only upon the evidentiary difficulty of establishing subjective intent, petitioners' attempt to root out subjective vices through objective means might make sense. But they were not based only upon that, or indeed even principally upon that. Their principal basis—which applies equally to attempts to reach subjective intent through ostensibly objective means—is simply that the Fourth Amendment's concern with "reasonableness" allows certain actions to be taken in certain circumstances, whatever the subjective intent. See, e.g., *Robinson,* supra ("Since it is the fact of custodial arrest which gives rise to the authority to search, it is of no moment that [the officer] did not indicate any subjective fear of the [arrestee] or that he did not himself suspect that [the arrestee] was armed"). But even if our concern had been only an evidentiary one, petitioners' proposal would by no means assuage it. Indeed, it seems to us somewhat easier to figure out the intent of an individual officer than to plumb the collective consciousness of law enforcement in order to determine whether a "reasonable officer" would have been moved to act upon the traffic violation. While police manuals and standard procedures may sometimes provide objective assistance, ordinarily one would be reduced to speculating about the hypothetical reaction of a hypothetical constable—an exercise that might be called virtual subjectivity.

Moreover, police enforcement practices, even if they could be practicably assessed by a judge, vary from place to place and from time to time. We cannot accept that the search and seizure protections of the Fourth Amendment are so variable, and can be made to turn upon such trivialities. The difficulty is illustrated by petitioners' arguments in this case. Their claim that a reasonable officer would not have made this stop is based largely on District of Columbia police regulations which permit plainclothes officers in unmarked vehicles to enforce traffic laws "only in the case of a violation that is so grave as to pose an immediate threat to the safety of others." This basis of invalidation would not apply in jurisdictions that had a different practice. And it would not have applied even in the District of Columbia, if Officer Soto had been wearing a uniform or patrolling in a marked police cruiser.

Petitioners argue that our cases support insistence upon police adherence to standard practices as an objective means of rooting out pretext. They cite no holding to that effect, and dicta in only two cases. In *Abel v. United States,* 362 U.S. 217, 80 S.Ct. 683, 4 L.Ed.2d 668 (1960), the petitioner had been arrested by the Immigration and Naturalization Service (INS), on the basis of an administrative warrant that, he claimed, had been issued on pretextual grounds in order to enable the Federal Bureau of Investigation (FBI) to search his room after his arrest. We regarded this as an allegation of "serious misconduct," but rejected Abel's claims on the ground that "[a] finding of bad faith is ... not open to us on th[e] record" in light of the findings below, including the finding that " 'the proceedings taken by the [INS] differed in no respect from what would have been done in the case of an individual concerning whom [there was no pending FBI investigation].' " But it is a long leap from the proposition that following regular procedures is some evidence of lack of pretext to the proposition that failure to follow regular procedures proves (or is an operational substitute for) pretext. *Abel,* moreover, did not involve the assertion that pretext could invalidate a search or seizure for which there was probable cause—and even what it said about pretext in other contexts is plainly inconsistent with the views we later stated in [the cases summarized above]. In the other case claimed to contain supportive dicta, *United States v. Robinson,* in approving a search incident to an arrest for driving without a license, we noted that the arrest was "not a departure from established police department practice." That was followed, however, by the statement that "[w]e leave for another day questions which would arise on facts different from these." This is not even a dictum that purports to provide an answer, but merely one that leaves the question open.

In what would appear to be an elaboration on the "reasonable officer" test, petitioners argue that the balancing inherent in any Fourth Amendment inquiry requires us to weigh the governmental and individual interests implicated in a traffic stop such as we have here. That balancing, petitioners claim, does not support investigation of minor traffic infractions by plainclothes police in unmarked vehicles; such investigation only minimally advances the government's interest in traffic safety, and may indeed retard it by producing motorist confusion and alarm—a view said to be supported by the Metropolitan Police Department's own regulations generally prohibiting this practice. And as for the Fourth Amendment interests of the individuals concerned, petitioners point out that our cases acknowledge that even ordinary traffic stops entail "a possibly unsettling show of authority"; that they at best "interfere with freedom of movement, are inconvenient, and consume time" and at worst "may create substantial anxiety." That anxiety is likely to be even more pronounced when the stop is conducted by plainclothes officers in unmarked cars.

It is of course true that in principle every Fourth Amendment case, since it turns upon a "reasonableness" determination, involves a balancing of all relevant factors. With rare exceptions not applicable here, however, the result of that balancing is not in doubt where the search or seizure is based upon probable cause. That is why petitioners must rely upon cases like *Prouse* to provide examples of actual "balancing" analysis. There, the police action in question was a random traffic stop for the purpose of checking a motorist's license and vehicle registration, a practice that—like the practices at issue in the inventory search and administrative inspection cases upon which petitioners rely in making their "pretext" claim—involves police intrusion without the probable cause that is its traditional justification. Our opinion in *Prouse* expressly distinguished the case from a stop based on precisely what is at issue here: "probable cause to believe that a driver is violating any one of the multitude of applicable traffic and equipment regulations." It noted approvingly that "[t]he foremost method of enforcing traffic and vehicle safety regulations ... is acting upon observed violations," which afford the " 'quantum of individualized suspicion' " necessary to ensure that police discretion is sufficiently constrained. What is true of *Prouse* is also true of other cases that engaged in detailed "balancing" to decide the constitutionality of automobile stops: the detailed "balancing" analysis was necessary because they involved seizures without probable cause.

Where probable cause has existed, the only cases in which we have found it necessary actually to perform the "balancing" analysis involved searches or seizures conducted in an extraordinary manner, unusually harmful to an individual's privacy or even physical interests—such as, for example, seizure by means of deadly force, see *Tennessee v. Garner,* [8th ed., p. 233], unannounced entry into a home, see *Wilson v. Arkansas,* [Supp. p. 20], entry into a home without a warrant, see *Welsh v. Wisconsin,* [8th ed., p. 271], or physical penetration of the body, see *Winston v. Lee,* [8th ed., p. 250]. The making of a traffic stop out-of-uniform does not remotely qualify as such an extreme practice, and so is governed by the usual rule that probable cause to believe the law has been broken "outbalances" private interest in avoiding police contact.

Petitioners urge as an extraordinary factor in this case that the "multitude of applicable traffic and equipment regulations" is so large and so difficult to obey perfectly that virtually everyone is guilty of violation, permitting the police to single out almost whomever they wish for a stop. But we are aware of no principle that would allow us to decide at what point a code of law becomes so expansive and so commonly violated that infraction itself can no longer be the ordinary measure of the lawfulness of enforcement. And even if we could identify such exorbitant codes, we do not know by what standard (or what right) we would decide, as petitioners would have us do, which particular provisions are sufficiently important to merit enforcement.

For the run-of-the-mine case, which this surely is, we think there is no realistic alternative to the traditional common-law rule that probable cause justifies a search and seizure.

* * *

 Here the District Court found that the officers had probable cause to believe that petitioners had violated the traffic code. That rendered the stop reasonable under the Fourth Amendment, the evidence thereby discovered admissible, and the upholding of the convictions by the Court of Appeals for the District of Columbia Circuit correct.

Judgment affirmed.

Notes and Questions

1. As the Supreme Court was advised in the briefs of the petitioners and amici, the tactic at issue in *Whren* is one which has been commonly employed by police in recent years in their "war against drugs." Both in urban areas and on the interstates, police are on the watch for "suspicious" travellers, and once one is spotted it is only a matter of time before some technical or trivial offense produces the necessary excuse for pulling him over. Perhaps because the offenses are so often insignificant, the driver is typically told at the outset that he will merely be given a warning. But then things often turn ugly. The driver and passengers are usually closely questioned about their identities, the reason for their travels, their intended destination, and the like.

The subject of drugs comes up, and often the driver is induced to "consent" to a full search of the vehicle for and all effects therein for drugs. If such consent is not forthcoming, another police vehicle with a drug-sniffing dog may appear on the scene. See, e.g., *United States v. Mesa,* 62 F.3d 159 (6th Cir.1995); *State v. Dominguez–Martinez,* 895 P.2d 306 (Or.1995).

2. Two illustrations from the many reported cases of this genre reveal how little it takes to supply grounds for a traffic stop acceptable to the courts. In one, a Texas state trooper passing a van noticed it had four black occupants, so the officer crested a hill, pulled onto the shoulder and doused his lights. When the van approached, the driver cautiously changed lanes to distance the van from the vehicle on the shoulder, but failed to signal—hardly surprising considering that the van was the only moving vehicle on that stretch of road. Yet the stop for an illegal lane change was upheld. *United States v. Roberson,* 6 F.3d 1088 (5th Cir.1993). In the other case, the stop occurred after a Utah deputy patrolling Interstate 70 saw an automobile driven by a black man straddle the center line for about one second before proceeding to the other lane of traffic. The stop was upheld on the grounds that the officer had sufficient suspicion the operator was driving while impaired. *United States v. Lee,* 73 F.3d 1034 (10th Cir.1996).

3. In *Roberson,* the court took note of the trooper's "remarkable record" of turning traffic stops into drug arrests on 250 prior occasions! While one can only speculate as to how many innocent people were subjected to roadside indignities to produce that record, no speculation is required to figure out who—in all likelihood—many of those persons were. As *Roberson* and *Botero–Ospina* suggest, and as was documented in the *Whren* briefs, race is often a factor in the otherwise amorphous drug courier profile. See, e.g., *United States v. Harvey,* 16 F.3d 109 (6th Cir.1994); *Washington v. Vogel,* 880 F.Supp. 1534 (M.D.Fla.1995); *Lowery v. Commonwealth,* 9 Va.App. 314, 388 S.E.2d 265 (1990). As one distinguished black educator has wryly noted, "there's a moving violation that many African–Americans know as D.W.B.: Driving While Black." Henry Louis Gates, Jr., *Thirteen Ways of Looking at a Black Man,* The New Yorker 56, 59 (Oct. 23, 1995).

4. The dissent by Chief Judge Seymour in *United States v. Botero–Ospina,* 71 F.3d 783 (10th Cir.1995), a pre-*Whren* decision which squares with the *Whren* holding, provides an interesting contrast to the later Scalia opinion in *Whren.* That dissent states in part:

"In addition to producing the intrusion any individual experiences when subjected to a traffic stop, the majority's standard frees a police officer to target members of minority communities for the selective enforcement of otherwise unenforced statutes. The Supreme Court recognized in *Terry [v. Ohio,* 8th ed., p. 306] that the harassment of minority groups by certain elements of the police population does occur, and that 'the degree of community resentment aroused by particular practices is clearly relevant to an assessment of the quality of the intrusion upon reasonable expectations of personal security caused by those practices.' By refusing to examine either the arbitrariness with which a particular statute is enforced or the motivation underlying its enforcement in a particular case, the majority standard does nothing to curb the ugly reality that minority groups are sometimes targeted for selective enforcement. As a result, the majority standard adds the onus of discrimination and resentment to the already significant burden imposed by traffic stops generally. * * *

"The Supreme Court held in *Terry* that to justify a particular intrusion, a 'police officer must be able to point to specific and articulable facts which, taken together with the rational inferences from those facts, reasonably warrant that intrusion.' It is difficult to justify a stop as reasonable, even if supported by an observed violation, if the undisputed facts indicate that the violation does not ordinarily result in a stop. Moreover, the Court in *Terry* described in detail the appropriate reasonableness inquiry in language that is utterly irreconcilable with the majority standard. The Court stated that in assessing the reasonableness of a particular stop 'it is imperative that the facts be judged against an objective standard: would the facts available to the officer at the moment of the seizure or the search "warrant a man of reasonable caution in the belief" that the action taken was appropriate?' It would hardly seem necessary to point out that the Court's mandate to determine what a reasonable officer would do in the circumstances cannot be fulfilled by merely ascertaining in a vacuum what a particular officer could do under state law.

"Given the 'multitude of applicable traffic and equipment regulations' in any jurisdiction, upholding a stop on the basis of a regulation seldom enforced opens the door to the arbitrary exercise of police discretion condemned in *Terry* and its progeny. 'Anything less [than the reasonable officer standard] would invite intrusions upon constitutionally guaranteed rights based on nothing more substantial than inarticulate hunches, a result this Court has consistently refused to sanction.' *Terry*."

5. Is Chief Judge Seymour's concern about harassment of minorities met by Justice Scalia's observation that selective enforcement based on race is barred by the Equal Protection Clause? How could the petitioners in *Whren* have proved such an equal protection violation? Does/should the "rigorous standard for discovery" against the government upon a defendant's claim of race-based selective prosecution, see *United States v. Armstrong*, Supp. at p. 105, also apply in this setting? And even if the *Whren* petitioners *did* prove that the traffic stop was itself a violation of the Equal Protection Clause, would that bar prosecution on the *drug* charges? Would it require suppression of the drugs? Cf. *United v. Jennings*, 985 F.2d 562 (6th Cir.1993) (dictum by majority that if defendant had proved he had been selected for a consensual encounter solely because of his race, then the evidence obtained in a consent search during that encounter ought to be excluded, as "evidence seized in violation of the Equal Protection Clause should be suppressed";

concurring opinion notes that the case cited in support by the majority, *Elkins v. United States,* 8th ed. p. 133, "provides absolutely no support for the majority's position").

6.   Does Justice Scalia ever respond directly to the *Whren* petitioners' argument that probable cause is not enough "in the unique context of civil traffic regulations" because it is possible for a police officer to catch any given motorist in a technical violation?   Is the proper response, as Scalia says at one point, that the matter of police purpose is relevant only in situations represented by *Wells, Bertine* and *Burger,* where the search is allowed without probable cause?   Is the risk of pretext greater in those situations, where the police must show they complied with "standard procedures" or "reasonable legislative or administrative standards," than as to traffic stops?

7.   In assessing the *Mota* case, 8th ed. p. 247, consider also whether it can be squared with *Whren.*

8th ed., p. 251; end of Note 12, in lieu of last sentence, add:

In *Maryland v. Wilson,* 519 U.S. 408, 117 S.Ct. 882, 137 L.Ed.2d 41 (1997), the Court held "that an officer making a traffic stop may order passengers to get out of the car pending completion of the stop." The Court agreed that "there is not the same basis for ordering the passengers out of the car as there is for ordering the driver out," but yet deemed "the additional intrusion on the passenger" to be "minimal" and justified in light of the fact that "danger to an officer from a traffic stop is likely to be greater when there are passengers in addition to the driver in the stopped car."

SECTION 6.   WARRANTLESS SEARCHES OF PREMISES, VEHICLES AND CONTAINERS

8th ed., p. 275; replacing all after first sentence of Note 7, add:

Cf. The *Wilson* and *Richards* cases, Supp. pp. 25–26.

SECTION 7.   STOP AND FRISK

B.   POLICE ACTION SHORT OF A SEIZURE

8th ed., p. 320; before Note 3, add:

2a. After citing *Hodari D.* to support the conclusion "that a police pursuit in attempting to seize a person does not amount to a 'seizure' within the meaning of the Fourth Amendment," the Court in *County of Sacramento v. Lewis,* Note 3, Supp. p. 1, also concluded "that no Fourth Amendment seizure would take place where a 'pursuing police car sought to stop the suspect only by the show of authority represented by flashing lights and continuing pursuit,' but accidentally stopped the suspect by crashing into him." This is because for a Fourth Amendment seizure there must be "a governmental termination of freedom of movement *through means intentionally applied.*"

8th ed., p. 321; after Note 5, add:

6. What result under *Bostick* if, when an intercity bus has stopped for an equipment change, necessitating that all passengers leave the bus with their luggage, the police board the bus and announce that they have a narcotics canine outside the bus and that the dog will "alert" to anyone carrying narcotics? Does it depend upon whether "the tenor and tone of [the] announcement was informative rather than confrontational"? On whether the passengers are told to exit "in a normal fashion with your carry-on," or instead to disembark "with all their carry-on luggage in their right hand so that the luggage would pass by the dog"? Compare *United States v. Jones,* 914 F.Supp. 421 (D.Colo.1996); with *United States v. Brumfield,* 910 F.Supp. 1528 (D.Colo.1996).

C. GROUNDS FOR TEMPORARY SEIZURE FOR INVESTIGATION

8th ed., p. 327, before Note 6, add:

5a. Are there grounds for the stops made on the following facts, essentially those in *United States v. Feliciano,* 45 F.3d 1070 (7th Cir. 1995)? An officer on patrol near a train station at midnight saw F and M walking in an area of a parking lot where there were no cars and which led to the river embankment. M then approached K, who was standing near the tracks with a suitcase, spoke with him for a while, and then left, rejoined F, and departed the scene in a direction opposite of that K then headed. The officer approached K, who told the officer that M had tried to lure him to the embankment to help an injured friend, but that K had refused. K explained that he had also seen F earlier and thus knew he was not injured; K surmised that the two had been planning to mug him. The officer asked his backup officer to stop F and M. The backup officer, who recognized F as a gang member recently released from prison, where F had served time for robbery, then stopped F and M as they walked toward their homes through the apparently deserted downtown area.

8th ed., p. 327; end of Note 6, add:

Compare also David A. Harris, *Factors for Reasonable Suspicion: When Black and Poor Means Stopped and Frisked,* 69 Ind.L.J. 659, 674, 687 (1994), noting there are many lower court cases holding that "presence in a high crime location" plus "evasion" are together "enough to sustain a *Terry* stop," and proposing that instead "the law should require that something more than a location of high crime or drug activity and evasion of the police be present, something clearly indicative of criminality. For example, gestures known to be characteristic of drug activity, such as using particular hand signals to indicate the availability of contraband, in addition to location and evasion, could be enough. For a frisk, the law should require not just possible drug possession or trafficking, but an indication that the suspect is armed.

"Such a rule would not necessarily require a rethinking of *Sokolow* [8th ed., p. 325]. While all of the defendant's actions in *Sokolow* are consistent with innocence, no activity in *Sokolow* is both innocent *and* necessary, in the sense that being at one's home or place of work is necessary. Additionally, to the extent that both the 'location plus evasion' cases and *Sokolow* are about clusters of innocent activity, *Sokolow* contains more than two such activities.

"The rule proposed here would have at least two salutary effects. First, existing law that protects, separately, the rights to be in a place and to refuse to respond to police stops without reasonable suspicion would be respected and kept vital. * * * Second, it would remove from the courts a set of cases, and from the police arsenal a group of techniques, that clearly have a disproportionate impact on the poor, and on racial and ethnic minorities."

8th ed., p. 327; before Note 7, add:

6a. After reading the facts in this paragraph, decide how you would rule if it were claimed that an illegal *Terry* stop preceded the search? An officer testified that at about 5 a.m. on April 21, 1995, he and his fellow plainclothes officer in an unmarked car patrolling a part of Manhattan characterized as "a hub for the drug trade" saw a car with Michigan plates pull over and double-park, at which four males approached single file on foot. In a matter of seconds, without conversing with the vehicle's occupants, the first man lifted up the trunk lid, the second and third each placed a large black duffel bag into the trunk, and the fourth closed the trunk. The car then drove off but stopped at a light, and when the police vehicle stopped behind it the four males walked off in different directions at a rapid gait. When the light changed the vehicle proceeded, but was promptly stopped by the plainclothes officers. At the police request, the middle-aged black woman driving the car provided her license and the vehicle registration. They asked what was in the trunk; she said she didn't know; the police then asked for the keys, which she surrendered; and the police then searched the trunk. A videotape of the woman's statement to the police, deemed credible, differed from the police version of events in that she claimed the car was double parked about 10 minutes and that she was at the wheel only after the duffel bags were put in the car.

6b. The search referred to above uncovered 34 kilos of cocaine and 2 kilos of heroin, a drug cache estimated to be worth four million dollars. The woman, one Carol Bayless, was charged in federal court with involvement in a cocaine and heroin distribution conspiracy. She moved to suppress the drugs and post-arrest statements on the grounds that they were the fruits of an illegal stop. In *United States v. Bayless*, 913 F.Supp. 232 (S.D.N.Y.1996), district judge Harold Baer granted the defendant's motion. In his decision on Jan. 22, the judge discussed each of the circumstances the police had claimed contributed to a reasonable suspicion: (1) "mere presence of an individual in a neighborhood known for its drug activity, which here was characterized as from 155th Street to the end of Manhattan, fails to raise a reasonable suspicion that the person observed is there to purchase drugs"; (2) there was "nothing unusual about the time at which she was observed," as in New York City people are about "all hours of the day and night"; (3) because of the number of visitors to the city, "it is not odd to see a license plate from another state"; (4) "it is often the case that cars are double parked, even triple parked on Manhattan's busy avenues and side streets"; (5) "duffel bags are commonly and regularly used to transport things from clothing to equipment"; (6) "there is no evidence of furtive or evasive conduct by the defendant here"; and (7) "even assuming that one or more of the males ran from the corner once they were aware of the officers' presence, it is hard to characterize this as evasive conduct," for as manifested in "the public hearing and final report of the Mollen Commission, residents in this neighborhood tended to regard police officers as corrupt, abusive and violent," meaning that "had the men not run when the cops began to stare at them, it would have been unusual." Is the judge's reasoning correct? If not, in what respect was he in error?

6c. Judge Baer's decision was the subject of earnest comment in many quarters. Among the reactions appearing in print were the following: New York Daily News: "Judge Baer has become an accomplice to evil." Wall Street Journal: "We suspect the law-abiding residents of Washington Heights might take a different view about whether the bigger threat to their well-being is the police or fleeing drug runners." New York Times: "What the judge managed to do * * * through his sloppy reasoning, was to undermine respect for the legal system, encourage citizens to flee the police and deter honest cops in drug-infested neighborhoods from doing their job." New York Times columnist A.M. Rosenthal: "I understand the Judge Baers. Their arrogance is their law." New York City Police Commissioner Bratton: "He's living in a fairyland. These officers in this case definitely did it the right way." New York City Mayor Giuliani: "This decision was wrong, and it was very, very wrong." New York State Attorney General Vacco: "Judges should not be handcuffing our cops with arcane technicalities." New York Governor Pataki: "The judge's decision is despicable." Senator Moynihan (D. N.Y.): "The judge should be sentenced to live a year in Washington Heights, to see if he would run away when he saw police." House Speaker Gingrich: "A shocking and egregious example of judicial activism, the perfect reason why we are losing our civilization." Senator Dole, explaining his call for impeachment of Baer: "We don't need judges who try to find excuses for more criminal behavior." White House press secretary McCurry, explaining why the President might ask Judge Baer to resign: "The President regrets Judge Baer's decision."

At the request of the prosecution, a rehearing was held on March 15th, and on the 1st of April (!) Judge Baer reversed his earlier decision. *United States v. Bayless*, 921 F.Supp. 211 (S.D.N.Y.1996). Because the Court had now "gained a more complete and more accurate picture of the events" (only one officer's testimony and a videotape of defendant's statement to police were presented at the first hearing, while at the second hearing the second officer and the defendant took the stand and contemporaneous police reports were received), it was decided that defendant's version of the events was untrue, meaning that the "totality of the circumstances" now established reasonable suspicion. The court expressed regret that "the hyperbole (dicta) in my initial decision not only obscured the true focus of my analysis, but regretfully may have demeaned the law-abiding men and women who make Washington Heights their home and the vast majority of the dedicated men and women in blue who patrol the streets of our great City." The opinion then cautioned: "This Court and others will continue fearlessly to draw the line that separates 'investigatory stops supported by "specific, objective facts" from those stops occurring essentially at the "unfettered discretion of officers in the field." ' "[a]

What lessons are to be learned from the *Bayless* case?

6d. Assuming grounds for a *Terry* stop but not grounds for arrest, is it (sometimes)(ever) permissible for the police to enter private premises in an effort to find the person to be detained? In the O.J. Simpson case, for example, is the police conduct in scaling the wall of the compound more understandable on the ground that Simpson was *not* a suspect and the police were attempting to see if anyone within was injured (the basis on which that conduct was upheld in court), or on the ground that Simpson *was* a suspect then sought for questioning by the police?[b]

D. PERMISSIBLE EXTENT OF TEMPORARY SEIZURE

8th ed., p. 331; before section E, add:

5. Reconsider the pretext traffic stop tactic discussed in the Notes following *Whren v. United States,* Supp. p. 28. To what extent does the *Terry* requirement that the seizure be "reasonably related in scope to the circumstances which justified the interference in the first place" provide meaningful limits upon the opportunity for the police to conduct a narcotics investigation during a traffic stop? For example, on the following facts, taken from *United States v. Ramos,* 20 F.3d 348 (8th Cir.1994), on reh. 42 F.3d 1160 (8th Cir.1994), at what point, if at all, did the officer cross the line?

At 7 a.m. the trooper stopped a pickup on Interstate 80 when he saw the passenger was not wearing a seat belt. The trooper asked the

---

a. Thereafter, the court denied defendant's motion for recusal, wherein it was contended, as the court put it, "that the extensive media coverage and comment from political leaders which followed the initial decision in this matter created considerable political pressure which, in turn, prompted me to develop a personal interest and lose my impartiality," and "that media coverage and political commentary have created an appearance of partiality." However, the court then decided to avoid further delay in the case "by returning this case to the wheel * * * with a new judge to be chosen." *United States v. Bayless,* 926 F.Supp. 405 (S.D.N.Y.1996).

b. See LaFave, *Over the Wall: A New Theory Regarding Entry of the Simpson Compound,* 1994 Westlaw 562135.

passenger for identification, and the passenger produced his driver's license. The trooper then asked for the driver for his license as well, which was also produced. (The trooper later testified he needed only the passenger's identification to prepare a citation.) The trooper then asked the driver to accompany him to the patrol car, where the trooper radioed for a computer check on the two men and the truck. While awaiting a response, the trooper questioned the driver about various matters, including his precise destination, the purpose of his trip, and his employment. When a negative response was received from the computer inquiry, the trooper returned the driver's license and then asked him to stay in the patrol car while he gave the warning ticket to the passenger. The trooper gave the warning ticket, which bore the time 7:40 a.m., to the passenger and then asked him about his destination and whether there were any drugs in the truck. The trooper then went back to his patrol car and questioned the driver again about where he was from and his destination, and asked if there were drugs in the truck. The trooper then asked the driver to consent to a search of the truck, and the driver signed a consent form which also bore the time 7:40 a.m. The trooper then called for a second officer, who arrived at the scene 10 minutes later, and then the searched commenced.

6.   The cases analyzing such traffic stops usually take the view that if the officer who made the stop has checked out the driver's license and vehicle registration and has written up the traffic citation or warning, then any *extension* of the stop thereafter for the purpose of questioning about drugs or seeking consent to search for drugs is illegal. See, e.g., *United States v. Fernandez,* 18 F.3d 874 (10th Cir.1994); *People v. Banks,* 650 N.E.2d 833 (N.Y.1995). Dictum in some cases, e.g., *United States v. Cummins,* 920 F.2d 498 (8th Cir.1990), suggests that *all* of the officer's investigative activity must be limited to the offense for which the stop was made unless reasonable suspicion develops as to other criminality, e.g., drug possession. However, courts often deem questioning on unrelated matters absent such suspicion as unobjectionable *provided* it is accomplished within the permissible time span of the traffic stop. See, e.g., *United States v. Crain,* 33 F.3d 480 (5th Cir.1994).

It is thus sometimes necessary to determine whether a traffic stop was extended or instead terminated at a certain point. Even if it is apparent to the defendant that the officer has completed writing up the ·ticket or warning, that does not terminate the stop if the officer continues to hold the defendant's license, vehicle registration, or other credentials. *United States v. Fernandez,* supra. But if, on the other hand, the officer *has* returned those credentials, does this mean that the seizure has terminated even if the officer then uses the Lt. Colombo gambit ("Oh, one more thing, . . .") in order to question the defendant about drugs? See *United States v. Werking,* 915 F.2d 1404 (10th Cir.1990) (return of his papers manifested to the driver that he "was free to leave the scene," so that when he instead remained and responded to the questions he "chose to engage in a consensual encounter").

7. OHIO v. ROBINETTE, 519 U.S. 33, 117 S.Ct. 417, 136 L.Ed.2d 347 (1996), involved these facts: a sheriff's deputy on "drug interdiction patrol" stopped defendant for speeding. The deputy examined defendant's license, ran a computer check indicting no previous violations, issued a verbal warning and returned defendant's license, and then immediately asked defendant if he had drugs in the car; when defendant answered in the negative, the deputy asked to search the car and defendant consented, resulting in a search which uncovered a small amount of marijuana and a single pill which was a controlled substance. The state supreme court concluded the evidence must be suppressed, reasoning that the "right to be secure in one's person and property requires that citizens stopped for traffic offenses be clearly informed by the detaining officer when they are free to go after a valid detention, before an officer attempts to engage in a consensual interrogation." The Supreme Court, per REHNQUIST, C.J., focused on the issue stated in the certiorari petition, whether such a warning is a prerequisite to a voluntary consent, and answered in the negative. The state court's per se rule was deemed inconsistent with the approach to Fourth Amendment issues by the Supreme Court, which has "consistently eschewed bright-line rules, instead emphasizing the fact-specific nature of the reasonableness inquiry." Moreover, the Court reasoned in *Robinette*, requiring such warnings would be just as impractical as the right-to-refuse-consent warnings held unnecessary by the Court in *Schneckloth v. Bustamonte* [8th ed., p. 342].

Only Justice STEVENS, dissenting, fully considered an alternative characterization of the state court's holding, namely, that (i) the officer's failure to tell defendant he was free to leave meant that a reasonable person would continue to believe he was not free to leave, so that the seizure had not yet ended at the time the consent was obtained; (ii) the seizure by that time was illegal, as it had exceeded its lawful purpose, the giving of a warning about the traffic offense; and (iii) consequently the evidence obtained via the voluntary consent was a suppressible fruit of that poisonous tree. He concluded that the evidence in the case (including the fact that this deputy had used this tactic to make 786 consent searches in one year) supported that conclusion, so that the suppression of evidence by the state court was justified.

The *Robinette* majority was not totally silent regarding this theory. The defendant argued the Court could not reach the voluntariness issue because the state court decision set out a valid alternative ground in the following language: "When the motivation behind a police officer's continued detention of a person stopped for a traffic violation is not related to the purpose of the original, constitutional stop, and when that continued detention is not based on articulable facts giving rise to a suspicion of some separate illegal activity justifying an extension of the detention, the continued detention constitutes an illegal seizure." Relying on the *Whren* case, Supp. p. 28, the Chief Justice declared that the state court was in error because "the subjective intentions of the officer did not make the continued detention of respondent illegal under the

Fourth Amendment." Is this a proper application of *Whren*? Does it mean that in applying the *Terry* scope limitation, the fact the officer decided only to give a warning is irrelevant? Or, is Justice Stevens correct in concluding that the irrelevant subjective motivation was drug interdiction, but that the subjective purpose of warning bears on the justification for the continued detention, so that by the time the consent was obtained "the lawful traffic stop had come to an end" because the defendant "had been given his warning"?

F. PROTECTIVE SEARCH

8th ed., p. 333; before Note 2, add:

1a. Consider David A. Harris, *Frisking Every Suspect: The Withering of* Terry, 28 U.C. Davis L.Rev. 1, 5, 43–44 (1994): "Perhaps as a result of the high-visibility use of frisks as a contemporary crime control device, or because of general public antipathy to crime, lower courts have stretched the law governing frisks to the point that the Supreme Court might find it unrecognizable. Lower courts have consistently expanded the *types of offenses* always considered violent regardless of the individual circumstances. At the same time, lower courts have also found that certain *types of persons and situations* always pose a danger of armed violence to police. When confronted with these offenses, persons, or situations, police may *automatically* frisk, whether or not any individualized circumstances point to danger. Soon, *anyone* stopped by police may have to undergo a physical search at the officer's discretion, however benign the circumstances of the encounter or the conduct of the 'suspect.' * * *

" * * * African–Americans and Hispanic–Americans pay a higher personal price for contemporary stop and frisk practices than whites do. Cases from courts around the country already permit *Terry* stops of individuals based on nothing more than their presence in a high-crime or drug-involved location, and allegedly evasive behavior toward the police. Minority group members are more likely than majority race individuals to live and work in such areas. Moreover, the police often use race as a proxy for criminality in deciding whether to stop a putative suspect. Given all of this, the automatic frisk cases—especially those that allow frisks based on the character of the neighborhood—paint an ugly picture: *Minority group members can be not only stopped, but subjected to a frisk without any evidence that they are armed or dangerous, just because they are present in the neighborhoods in which they work and live.*"

SECTION 8. ADMINISTRATIVE INSPECTIONS AND REGULATORY SEARCHES: MORE ON BALANCING THE NEED AGAINST THE INVASION OF PRIVACY

8th ed., p. 342; end of Note 6, add:

The Court's latest foray into this area, while also not a criminal case, provides an excellent vehicle for considering the respective merits of the reasonable suspicion and standardized procedures approaches:

VERNONIA SCHOOL DISTRICT 47J v. ACTON

515 U.S. 646, 115 S.Ct. 2386, 132 L.Ed.2d 564 (1995).

JUSTICE SCALIA delivered the opinion of the Court.

The Student Athlete Drug Policy adopted by School District 47J in the town of Vernonia, Oregon, authorizes random urinalysis drug testing of students who participate in the District's school athletics programs. We granted certiorari to decide whether this violates the Fourth and Fourteenth Amendments to the United States Constitution.

Petitioner Vernonia School District 47J (District) operates one high school and three grade schools in the logging community of Vernonia, Oregon. As elsewhere in small-town America, school sports play a prominent role in the town's life, and student athletes are admired in their schools and in the community.

Drugs had not been a major problem in Vernonia schools. In the mid-to-late 1980's, however, teachers and administrators observed a sharp increase in drug use. Students began to speak out about their attraction to the drug culture, and to boast that there was nothing the school could do about it. Along with more drugs came more disciplinary problems. Between 1988 and 1989 the number of disciplinary referrals in Vernonia schools rose to more than twice the number reported in the early 1980's, and several students were suspended. Students became increasingly rude during class; outbursts of profane language became common.

Not only were student athletes included among the drug users but, as the District Court found, athletes were the leaders of the drug culture. This caused the District's administrators particular concern, since drug use increases the risk of sports-related injury. Expert testimony at the trial confirmed the deleterious effects of drugs on motivation, memory, judgment, reaction, coordination, and performance. The high school football and wrestling coach witnessed a severe sternum injury suffered by a wrestler, and various omissions of safety procedures and misexecutions by football players, all attributable in his belief to the effects of drug use.

Initially, the District responded to the drug problem by offering special classes, speakers, and presentations designed to deter drug use.

It even brought in a specially trained dog to detect drugs, but the drug problem persisted. According to the District Court:

"[T]he administration was at its wits end and . . . a large segment of the student body, particularly those involved in interscholastic athletics, was in a state of rebellion. Disciplinary problems had reached 'epidemic proportions.' The coincidence of an almost three-fold increase in class-room disruptions and disciplinary reports along with the staff's direct observations of students using drugs or glamorizing drug and alcohol use led the administration to the inescapable conclusion that the rebellion was being fueled by alcohol and drug abuse as well as the student's misperceptions about the drug culture."

At that point, District officials began considering a drug-testing program. They held a parent "input night" to discuss the proposed Student Athlete Drug Policy (Policy), and the parents in attendance gave their unanimous approval. The school board approved the Policy for implementation in the fall of 1989. Its expressed purpose is to prevent student athletes from using drugs, to protect their health and safety, and to provide drug users with assistance programs.

The Policy applies to all students participating in interscholastic athletics. Students wishing to play sports must sign a form consenting to the testing and must obtain the written consent of their parents. Athletes are tested at the beginning of the season for their sport. In addition, once each week of the season the names of the athletes are placed in a "pool" from which a student, with the supervision of two adults, blindly draws the names of 10% of the athletes for random testing. Those selected are notified and tested that same day, if possible.

The student to be tested completes a specimen control form which bears an assigned number. Prescription medications that the student is taking must be identified by providing a copy of the prescription or a doctor's authorization. The student then enters an empty locker room accompanied by an adult monitor of the same sex. Each boy selected produces a sample at a urinal, remaining fully clothed with his back to the monitor, who stands approximately 12 to 15 feet behind the student. Monitors may (though do not always) watch the student while he produces the sample, and they listen for normal sounds of urination. Girls produce samples in an enclosed bathroom stall, so that they can be heard but not observed. After the sample is produced, it is given to the monitor, who checks it for temperature and tampering and then transfers it to a vial.

The samples are sent to an independent laboratory, which routinely tests them for amphetamines, cocaine, and marijuana. Other drugs, such as LSD, may be screened at the request of the District, but the identity of a particular student does not determine which drugs will be tested. The laboratory's procedures are 99.94% accurate. The District follows strict procedures regarding the chain of custody and access to test results. The laboratory does not know the identity of the students whose samples it tests. It is authorized to mail written test reports only to the superintendent and to provide test results to District personnel by telephone only after the requesting official recites a code confirming his authority. Only the superintendent, principals, vice-principals, and athletic directors have access to test results, and the results are not kept for more than one year.

If a sample tests positive, a second test is administered as soon as possible to confirm the result. If the second test is negative, no further action is taken. If the second test is positive, the athlete's parents are notified, and the school principal convenes a meeting with the student and his parents, at which the student is given the option of (1) participating for six weeks in an assistance program that includes weekly urinalysis, or (2) suffering suspension from athletics for the remainder of the current season and the next athletic season. The student is then retested prior to the start of the next athletic season for which he or she is eligible. The Policy states that a second offense results in automatic imposition of option (2); a third offense in suspension for the remainder of the current season and the next two athletic seasons.

In the fall of 1991, respondent James Acton, then a seventh-grader, signed up to play football at one of the District's grade schools. He was denied participation, however, because he and his parents refused to sign the testing consent forms. The Actons filed suit, seeking declaratory and injunctive relief from enforcement of the Policy on the grounds that it violated the Fourth and Fourteenth Amendments * * *. After a bench trial, the District Court entered an order denying the claims on the merits and dismissing the action. The United States Court of Appeals for the Ninth Circuit reversed, holding that the Policy violated both the Fourth and Fourteenth Amendments * * *. We granted certiorari.

The Fourth Amendment to the United States Constitution provides that the Federal Government shall not violate "[t]he right of the people to be secure in their persons, houses, papers, and effects, against unreasonable searches and seizures...." We have held that the Fourteenth Amendment extends this constitutional guarantee to searches and seizures by state officers, including public school officials, *New Jersey v. T.L.O.*, [8th ed., p. 341]. In *Skinner v. Railway Labor Executives' Assn.*, [8th ed., p. 342], we held that state-compelled collection and testing of urine, such as that required by the Student Athlete Drug Policy, constitutes a "search" subject to the demands of the Fourth Amendment. See also *Treasury Employees v. Von Raab*, [8th ed., p. 342].

As the text of the Fourth Amendment indicates, the ultimate measure of the constitutionality of a governmental search is "reasonableness." At least in a case such as this, where there was no clear practice, either approving or disapproving the type of search at issue, at the time the constitutional provision was enacted, whether a particular search meets the reasonableness standard " 'is judged by balancing its intrusion

criminal evidence must be search by warrant

on the individual's Fourth Amendment interests against its promotion of legitimate governmental interests.'" Where a search is undertaken by law enforcement officials to discover evidence of criminal wrongdoing, this Court has said that reasonableness generally requires the obtaining of a judicial warrant. Warrants cannot be issued, of course, without the showing of probable cause required by the Warrant Clause. But a warrant is not required to establish the reasonableness of all government searches; and when a warrant is not required (and the Warrant Clause therefore not applicable), probable cause is not invariably required either. A search unsupported by probable cause can be constitutional, we have said, "when special needs, beyond the normal need for law enforcement, make the warrant and probable-cause requirement impracticable." *Griffin v. Wisconsin*, [8th ed., p. 341].

when no prob. cause needed

We have found such "special needs" to exist in the public-school context. There, the warrant requirement "would unduly interfere with the maintenance of the swift and informal disciplinary procedures [that are] needed," and "strict adherence to the requirement that searches be based upon probable cause" would undercut "the substantial need of teachers and administrators for freedom to maintain order in the schools." *T.L.O.* The school search we approved in *T.L.O.*, while not based on probable cause, was based on individualized suspicion of wrongdoing. As we explicitly acknowledged, however, " 'the Fourth Amendment imposes no irreducible requirement of such suspicion.'" We have upheld suspicionless searches and seizures to conduct drug testing of railroad personnel involved in train accidents, see *Skinner;* to conduct random drug testing of federal customs officers who carry arms or are involved in drug interdiction, see *Von Raab;* and to maintain automobile checkpoints looking for illegal immigrants and contraband and drunk drivers.

The first factor to be considered is the nature of the privacy interest upon which the search here at issue intrudes. The Fourth Amendment does not protect all subjective expectations of privacy, but only those that society recognizes as "legitimate." What expectations are legitimate varies, of course, with context, depending, for example, upon whether the individual asserting the privacy interest is at home, at work, in a car, or in a public park. In addition, the legitimacy of certain privacy expectations vis-à-vis the State may depend upon the individual's legal relationship with the State. For example, in *Griffin* we held that, although a "probationer's home, like anyone else's, is protected by the Fourth Amendmen[t]," the supervisory relationship between probationer and State justifies "a degree of impingement upon [a probationer's] privacy that would not be constitutional if applied to the public at large." Central, in our view, to the present case is the fact that the subjects of the Policy are (1) children, who (2) have been committed to the temporary custody of the State as schoolmaster.

Traditionally at common law, and still today, unemancipated minors lack some of the most fundamental rights of self-determination—including even the right of liberty in its narrow sense, i.e., the right to come and go at will. They are subject, even as to their physical freedom, to the control of their parents or guardians. When parents place minor children in private schools for their education, the teachers and administrators of those schools stand in loco parentis over the children entrusted to them. * * *

In *T.L.O.* we rejected the notion that public schools, like private schools, exercise only parental power over their students, which of course is not subject to constitutional constraints. Such a view of things, we said, "is not entirely 'consonant with compulsory education laws,'" * * *. But while denying that the State's power over schoolchildren is formally no more than the delegated power of their parents, *T.L.O.* did not deny, but indeed emphasized, that the nature of that power is custodial and tutelary, permitting a degree of supervision and control that could not be exercised over free adults. "[A] proper educational environment requires close supervision of schoolchildren, as well as the enforcement of rules against conduct that would be perfectly permissible if undertaken by an adult." * * * Thus, while children assuredly do not "shed their constitutional rights ... at the schoolhouse gate," the nature of those rights is what is appropriate for children in school. * * *

Fourth Amendment rights * * * are different in public schools than elsewhere; the "reasonableness" inquiry cannot disregard the schools' custodial and tutelary responsibility for children. For their own good and that of their classmates, public school children are routinely required to submit to various physical examinations, and to be vaccinated against various diseases. * * * Particularly with regard to medical examinations and procedures, therefore, "students within the school environment have a lesser expectation of privacy than members of the population generally."

Legitimate privacy expectations are even less with regard to student athletes. School sports are not for the bashful. They require "suiting up" before each practice or event, and showering and changing afterwards. Public school locker rooms, the usual sites for these activities, are not notable for the privacy they afford. The locker rooms in Vernonia are typical: no individual dressing rooms are provided; shower heads are lined up along a wall, unseparated by any sort of partition or curtain; not even all the toilet stalls have doors.

There is an additional respect in which school athletes have a reduced expectation of privacy. By choosing to "go out for the team," they voluntarily subject themselves to a degree of regulation even higher than that imposed on students generally. In Vernonia's public schools, they must submit to a preseason physical exam (James testified that his included the giving of a urine sample), they must acquire adequate insurance coverage or sign an insurance waiver, maintain a minimum grade point average, and comply with any "rules of conduct, dress, training hours and related matters as may be established for each sport by the head coach and athletic director with the principal's approval."

Somewhat like adults who choose to participate in a "closely regulated industry," students who voluntarily participate in school athletics have reason to expect intrusions upon normal rights and privileges, including privacy.

Having considered the scope of the legitimate expectation of privacy at issue here, we turn next to the character of the intrusion that is complained of. We recognized in *Skinner* that collecting the samples for urinalysis intrudes upon "an excretory function traditionally shielded by great privacy." We noted, however, that the degree of intrusion depends upon the manner in which production of the urine sample is monitored. Under the District's Policy, male students produce samples at a urinal along a wall. They remain fully clothed and are only observed from behind, if at all. Female students produce samples in an enclosed stall, with a female monitor standing outside listening only for sounds of tampering. These conditions are nearly identical to those typically encountered in public restrooms, which men, women, and especially school children use daily. Under such conditions, the privacy interests compromised by the process of obtaining the urine sample are in our view negligible.

The other privacy-invasive aspect of urinalysis is, of course, the information it discloses concerning the state of the subject's body, and the materials he has ingested. In this regard it is significant that the tests at issue here look only for drugs, and not for whether the student is, for example, epileptic, pregnant, or diabetic. Moreover, the drugs for which the samples are screened are standard, and do not vary according to the identity of the student. And finally, the results of the tests are disclosed only to a limited class of school personnel who have a need to know; and they are not turned over to law enforcement authorities or used for any internal disciplinary function. * * *

Finally, we turn to consider the nature and immediacy of the governmental concern at issue here, and the efficacy of this means for meeting it. In both *Skinner* and *Von Raab*, we characterized the government interest motivating the search as "compelling." *Skinner* (interest in preventing railway accidents); *Von Raab* (interest in insuring fitness of customs officials to interdict drugs and handle firearms). * * * It is a mistake, however, to think that the phrase "compelling state interest," in the Fourth Amendment context, describes a fixed, minimum quantum of governmental concern, so that one can dispose of a case by answering in isolation the question: Is there a compelling state interest here? Rather, the phrase describes an interest which appears important enough to justify the particular search at hand, in light of other factors which show the search to be relatively intrusive upon a genuine expectation of privacy. Whether that relatively high degree of government concern is necessary in this case or not, we think it is met.

That the nature of the concern is important—indeed, perhaps compelling—can hardly be doubted. Deterring drug use by our Nation's schoolchildren is at least as important as enhancing efficient enforcement of the Nation's laws against the importation of drugs, which was the governmental concern in *Von Raab,* or deterring drug use by engineers and trainmen, which was the governmental concern in *Skinner.* School years are the time when the physical, psychological, and addictive effects of drugs are most severe. * * * And of course the effects of a drug-infested school are visited not just upon the users, but upon the entire student body and faculty, as the educational process is disrupted. In the present case, moreover, the necessity for the State to act is magnified by the fact that this evil is being visited not just upon individuals at large, but upon children for whom it has undertaken a special responsibility of care and direction. Finally, it must not be lost sight of that this program is directed more narrowly to drug use by school athletes, where the risk of immediate physical harm to the drug user or those with whom he is playing his sport is particularly high. Apart from psychological effects, which include impairment of judgment, slow reaction time, and a lessening of the perception of pain, the particular drugs screened by the District's Policy have been demonstrated to pose substantial physical risks to athletes. * * *

As for the immediacy of the District's concerns: We are not inclined to question—indeed, we could not possibly find clearly erroneous—the District Court's conclusion that "a large segment of the student body, particularly those involved in interscholastic athletics, was in a state of rebellion," that "[d]isciplinary actions had reached 'epidemic proportions,'" and that "the rebellion was being fueled by alcohol and drug abuse as well as by the student's misperceptions about the drug culture." That is an immediate crisis of greater proportions than existed in *Skinner,* where we upheld the Government's drug testing program based on findings of drug use by railroad employees nationwide, without proof that a problem existed on the particular railroads whose employees were subject to the test. And of much greater proportions than existed in *Von Raab,* where there was no documented history of drug use by any customs officials.[a]

As to the efficacy of this means for addressing the problem: It seems to us self-evident that a drug problem largely fueled by the "role model" effect of athletes' drug use, and of particular danger to athletes, is effectively addressed by making sure that athletes do not use drugs. Respondents argue that a "less intrusive means to the same end" was available, namely, "drug testing on suspicion of drug use." We have

a. Compare *Chandler v. Miller*, 520 U.S. 305, 117 S.Ct. 1295, 137 L.Ed.2d 513 (1997), invalidating a Georgia statute requiring each candidate for public office to submit to drug testing, where the Court stated: "Georgia asserts no evidence of a drug problem among the State's elected officials, those officials typically do not perform high-risk, safety-sensitive tasks, and the required certification immediately aids no interdiction effort. The need revealed, in short, is symbolic, not 'special,' as that term draws meaning from our case law." As for the state's reliance on *Von Raab*, the Court noted that there the affected employees and their work product were not amenable to "day-to-day scrutiny," and then concluded: "Candidates for public office, in contrast, are subject to relentless scrutiny—by their peers, the public, and the press. Their day-to-day conduct attracts attention notable beyond the norm in ordinary work environments."

repeatedly refused to declare that only the "least intrusive" search practicable can be reasonable under the Fourth Amendment. Respondents' alternative entails substantial difficulties—if it is indeed practicable at all. It may be impracticable, for one thing, simply because the parents who are willing to accept random drug testing for athletes are not willing to accept accusatory drug testing for all students, which transforms the process into a badge of shame. Respondents' proposal brings the risk that teachers will impose testing arbitrarily upon troublesome but not drug-likely students. It generates the expense of defending lawsuits that charge such arbitrary imposition, or that simply demand greater process before accusatory drug testing is imposed. And not least of all, it adds to the ever-expanding diversionary duties of schoolteachers the new function of spotting and bringing to account drug abuse, a task for which they are ill prepared, and which is not readily compatible with their vocation. In many respects, we think, testing based on "suspicion" of drug use would not be better, but worse.

Taking into account all the factors we have considered above—the decreased expectation of privacy, the relative unobtrusiveness of the search, and the severity of the need met by the search—we conclude Vernonia's Policy is reasonable and hence constitutional.

We caution against the assumption that suspicionless drug testing will readily pass constitutional muster in other contexts. The most significant element in this case is the first we discussed: that the Policy was undertaken in furtherance of the government's responsibilities, under a public school system, as guardian and tutor of children entrusted to its care. Just as when the government conducts a search in its capacity as employer (a warrantless search of an absent employee's desk to obtain an urgently needed file, for example), the relevant question is whether that intrusion upon privacy is one that a reasonable employer might engage in, so also when the government acts as guardian and tutor the relevant question is whether the search is one that a reasonable guardian and tutor might undertake. Given the findings of need made by the District Court, we conclude that in the present case it is.

We may note that the primary guardians of Vernonia's schoolchildren appear to agree. The record shows no objection to this districtwide program by any parents other than the couple before us here—even though, as we have described, a public meeting was held to obtain parents' views. We find insufficient basis to contradict the judgment of Vernonia's parents, its school board, and the District Court, as to what was reasonably in the interest of these children under the circumstances.
* * *

JUSTICE GINSBURG, concurring. * * * I comprehend the Court's opinion as reserving the question whether the District, on no more than the showing made here, constitutionally could impose routine drug testing not only on those seeking to engage with others in team sports, but on all students required to attend school.

Justice O'Connor, with whom Justice Stevens and Justice Souter join, dissenting.

The population of our Nation's public schools, grades 7 through 12, numbers around 18 million. By the reasoning of today's decision, the millions of these students who participate in interscholastic sports, an overwhelming majority of whom have given school officials no reason whatsoever to suspect they use drugs at school, are open to an intrusive bodily search.

In justifying this result, the Court dispenses with a requirement of individualized suspicion on considered policy grounds. * * * In making these policy arguments, of course, the Court sidesteps powerful, countervailing privacy concerns. Blanket searches, because they can involve "thousands or millions" of searches, "pos[e] a greater threat to liberty" than do suspicion-based ones, which "affec[t] one person at a time." Searches based on individualized suspicion also afford potential targets considerable control over whether they will, in fact, be searched because a person can avoid such a search by not acting in an objectively suspicious way. And given that the surest way to avoid acting suspiciously is to avoid the underlying wrongdoing, the costs of such a regime, one would think, are minimal.

search should be based on individual suspicion

But whether a blanket search is "better" than a regime based on individualized suspicion is not a debate in which we should engage. In my view, it is not open to judges or government officials to decide on policy grounds which is better and which is worse. For most of our constitutional history, mass, suspicionless searches have been generally considered per se unreasonable within the meaning of the Fourth Amendment. And we have allowed exceptions in recent years only where it has been clear that a suspicion-based regime would be ineffectual. Because that is not the case here, I dissent. * * *

The *Carroll* [*v. United States*, 8th ed., p. 276] Court's view that blanket searches are "intolerable and unreasonable" is well-grounded in history. As recently confirmed in one of the most exhaustive analyses of the original meaning of the Fourth Amendment ever undertaken, what the Framers of the Fourth Amendment most strongly opposed, with limited exceptions wholly inapplicable here, were general searches—that is, searches by general warrant, by writ of assistance, by broad statute, or by any other similar authority. * * *

More important, there is no indication in the historical materials that the Framers' opposition to general searches stemmed solely from the fact that they allowed officials to single out individuals for arbitrary reasons, and thus that officials could render them reasonable simply by making sure to extend their search to every house in a given area or to every person in a given group. * * *

Perhaps most telling of all, as reflected in the text of the Warrant Clause, the particular way the Framers chose to curb the abuses of general warrants—and by implication, all general searches—was not to impose a novel "evenhandedness" requirement; it was to retain the individualized suspicion requirement contained in the typical general warrant, but to make that requirement meaningful and enforceable, for instance, by raising the required level of individualized suspicion to objective probable cause. * * *

The view that mass, suspicionless searches, however evenhanded, are generally unreasonable remains inviolate in the criminal law enforcement context. * * *

Thus, it remains the law that the police cannot, say, subject to drug testing every person entering or leaving a certain drug-ridden neighborhood in order to find evidence of crime. And this is true even though it is hard to think of a more compelling government interest than the need to fight the scourge of drugs on our streets and in our neighborhoods. Nor could it be otherwise, for if being evenhanded were enough to justify evaluating a search regime under an open-ended balancing test, the Warrant Clause, which presupposes that there is some category of searches for which individualized suspicion is non-negotiable, would be a dead letter.

Outside the criminal context, however, in response to the exigencies of modern life, our cases have upheld several evenhanded blanket searches, including some that are more than minimally intrusive, after balancing the invasion of privacy against the government's strong need. Most of these cases, of course, are distinguishable insofar as they involved searches either not of a personally intrusive nature, such as searches of closely regulated businesses, see, e.g., *New York v. Burger,* [8th ed., p. 340], or arising in unique contexts such as prisons * * *.

In any event, in many of the cases that can be distinguished on the grounds suggested above and, more important, in all of the cases that cannot, see, e.g., *Skinner* (blanket drug testing scheme); *Von Raab* (same); cf. *Camara v. Municipal Court,* [8th ed., p. 339] (area-wide searches of private residences), we upheld the suspicionless search only after first recognizing the Fourth Amendment's longstanding preference for a suspicion-based search regime, and then pointing to sound reasons why such a regime would likely be ineffectual under the unusual circumstances presented. In *Skinner,* for example, we stated outright that " 'some quantum of individualized suspicion' " is "usually required" under the Fourth Amendment, and we built the requirement into the test we announced: "In limited circumstances, where the privacy interests implicated by the search are minimal, and where an important governmental interest furthered by the intrusion would be placed in jeopardy by a requirement of individualized suspicion, a search may be reasonable despite the absence of such suspicion." The obvious negative implication of this reasoning is that, if such an individualized suspicion requirement would not place the government's objectives in jeopardy, the requirement should not be forsaken.

Accordingly, we upheld the suspicionless regime at issue in *Skinner* on the firm understanding that a requirement of individualized suspicion for testing train operators for drug or alcohol impairment following serious train accidents would be unworkable because "the scene of a serious rail accident is chaotic." (Of course, it could be plausibly argued that the fact that testing occurred only after train operators were involved in serious train accidents amounted to an individualized suspicion requirement in all but name, in light of the record evidence of a strong link between serious train accidents and drug and alcohol use.) We have performed a similar inquiry in the other cases as well. * * *

Moreover, an individualized suspicion requirement was often impractical in these cases because they involved situations in which even one undetected instance of wrongdoing could have injurious consequences for a great number of people. See, e.g., *Camara* (even one safety code violation can cause "fires and epidemics [that] ravage large urban areas"); *Skinner*, supra (even one drug- or alcohol-impaired train operator can lead to the "disastrous consequences" of a train wreck, such as "great human loss"); *Von Raab* (even one customs official caught up in drugs can, by virtue of impairment, susceptibility to bribes, or indifference, result in the noninterdiction of a "sizable drug shipmen[t]," which eventually injures the lives of thousands, or to a breach of "national security").

The instant case stands in marked contrast. One searches today's majority opinion in vain for recognition that history and precedent establish that individualized suspicion is "usually required" under the Fourth Amendment (regardless of whether a warrant and probable cause are also required) and that, in the area of intrusive personal searches, the only recognized exception is for situations in which a suspicion-based scheme would be likely ineffectual. * * *

But having misconstrued the fundamental role of the individualized suspicion requirement in Fourth Amendment analysis, the Court never seriously engages the practicality of such a requirement in the instant case. And that failure is crucial because nowhere is it less clear that an individualized suspicion requirement would be ineffectual than in the school context. In most schools, the entire pool of potential search targets—students—is under constant supervision by teachers and administrators and coaches, be it in classrooms, hallways, or locker rooms.

The record here indicates that the Vernonia schools are no exception. The great irony of this case is that most (though not all) of the evidence the District introduced to justify its suspicionless drug-testing program consisted of first- or second-hand stories of particular, identifiable students acting in ways that plainly gave rise to reasonable suspicion of in-school drug use—and thus that would have justified a drug-related search under our *T.L.O.* decision. Small groups of students, for example, were observed by a teacher "passing joints back and forth" across the street at a restaurant before school and during school hours. Another group was caught skipping school and using drugs at one of the students' houses. Several students actually admitted their drug use to school officials (some of them being caught with marijuana pipes). One student presented himself to his teacher as "clearly obviously inebriated" and had to be sent home. Still another was observed dancing and singing at the top of his voice in the back of the classroom; when the teacher asked what was going on, he replied, "Well, I'm just high on life." To take a final example, on a certain road trip, the school wrestling coach smelled marijuana smoke in a hotel room occupied by four wrestlers, an observation that (after some questioning) would probably have given him reasonable suspicion to test one or all of them.

In light of all this evidence of drug use by particular students, there is a substantial basis for concluding that a vigorous regime of suspicion-based testing (for which the District appears already to have rules in place) would have gone a long way toward solving Vernonia's school drug problem while preserving the Fourth Amendment rights of James Acton and others like him. And were there any doubt about such a conclusion, it is removed by indications in the record that suspicion-based testing could have been supplemented by an equally vigorous campaign to have Vernonia's parents encourage their children to submit to the District's voluntary drug testing program. In these circumstances, the Fourth Amendment dictates that a mass, suspicionless search regime is categorically unreasonable. * * *

The principal counterargument to all this, central to the Court's opinion, is that the Fourth Amendment is more lenient with respect to school searches. That is no doubt correct, for, as the Court explains, schools have traditionally had special guardian-like responsibilities for children that necessitate a degree of constitutional leeway. This principle explains the considerable Fourth Amendment leeway we gave school officials in *T.L.O.* In that case, we held that children at school do not enjoy two of the Fourth Amendment's traditional categorical protections against unreasonable searches and seizures: the warrant requirement and the probable cause requirement. * * *

The instant case, however, asks whether the Fourth Amendment is even more lenient than that, i.e., whether it is so lenient that students may be deprived of the Fourth Amendment's only remaining, and most basic, categorical protection: its strong preference for an individualized suspicion requirement, with its accompanying antipathy toward personally intrusive, blanket searches of mostly innocent people. [T]he answer must plainly be no.

I find unpersuasive the Court's reliance on the widespread practice of physical examinations and vaccinations, which are both blanket searches of a sort. [A] suspicion requirement for vaccinations is not merely impractical; it is nonsensical, for vaccinations are not searches for anything in particular and so there is nothing about which to be suspicious. * * * As for physical examinations, the practicability of a suspicion requirement is highly doubtful because the conditions for which these physical exams ordinarily search, such as latent heart conditions, do not manifest themselves in observable behavior the way school drug use does.

I do not believe that suspicionless drug testing is justified on these facts. But even if I agreed that some such testing were reasonable here, I see two other Fourth Amendment flaws in the District's program. First, and most serious, there is virtually no evidence in the record of a drug problem at the Washington Grade School, which includes the 7th and 8th grades, and which Acton attended when this litigation began. * * *

Second, even as to the high school, I find unreasonable the school's choice of student athletes as the class to subject to suspicionless testing—a choice that appears to have been driven more by a belief in what would pass constitutional muster, than by a belief in what was required to meet the District's principal disciplinary concern. Reading the full record in this case, it seems quite obvious that the true driving force behind the District's adoption of its drug testing program was the need to combat the rise in drug-related disorder and disruption in its classrooms and around campus. * * * And the record in this case surely demonstrates there was a drug-related discipline problem in Vernonia of " 'epidemic proportions.' " The evidence of a drug-related sports injury problem at Vernonia, by contrast, was considerably weaker.

On this record, then, it seems to me that the far more reasonable choice would have been to focus on the class of students found to have violated published school rules against severe disruption in class and around campus, disruption that had a strong nexus to drug use, as the District established at trial. Such a choice would share two of the virtues of a suspicion-based regime: testing dramatically fewer students, tens as against hundreds, and giving students control, through their behavior, over the likelihood that they would be tested. Moreover, there would be a reduced concern for the accusatory nature of the search, because the Court's feared "badge of shame," would already exist, due to the antecedent accusation and finding of severe disruption. In a lesser known aspect of *Skinner,* we upheld an analogous testing scheme with little hesitation. See *Skinner* (describing " 'Authorization to Test for Cause' " scheme, according to which train operators would be tested "in the event of certain specific rule violations, including noncompliance with a signal and excessive speeding").

It cannot be too often stated that the greatest threats to our constitutional freedoms come in times of crisis. But we must also stay mindful that not all government responses to such times are hysterical overreactions; some crises are quite real, and when they are, they serve precisely as the compelling state interest that we have said may justify a measured intrusion on constitutional rights. The only way for judges to mediate these conflicting impulses is to do what they should do anyway: stay close to the record in each case that appears before them, and make their judgments based on that alone. Having reviewed the record here, I cannot avoid the conclusion that the District's suspicionless policy of testing all student-athletes sweeps too broadly, and too imprecisely, to be reasonable under the Fourth Amendment.

SECTION 9. CONSENT SEARCHES

8th ed., p. 345; new fn. on line 14 after "warning"

b. Relying upon this language, the Court later held in *Ohio v. Robinette*, 519 U.S. 33, 117 S.Ct. 417, 136 L.Ed.2d 347 (1996), that if a person has been lawfully seized, for example, because of commission of a traffic violation, and following the point at which the detainee would be free to go he consents to a search, that consent is not involuntary because the officer failed to specifically advise the detainee that he was free to go, as a requirement of such warnings would be equally "unrealistic."

Chapter 7

POLICE "ENCOURAGEMENT" AND THE DEFENSE OF ENTRAPMENT

SECTION 3. CONTINUING CONTROVERSY OVER THE ENTRAPMENT DEFENSE

8th ed., p. 439; add new Note:

6. *More on the meaning of Jacobson.* In UNITED STATES v. GENDRON, 18 F.3d 955 (1st Cir.1994), in the course of holding that defendant was not entrapped into receiving child pornography, Chief Judge (now Supreme Court Justice) BREYER observed:

"The Supreme Court has described [the entrapment] defense as resting upon an assumption that Congress, when enacting criminal statutes, does not intend the statute to apply to violations arising out of (1) the government's *'abuse'* of its crime 'detection' and law 'enforcement' efforts by 'instigat[ing]' the criminal behavior and 'lur[ing]' to commit the crime (2) persons who are *'otherwise innocent.'* *Sorrells* (emphasis added). Consequently, the entrapment doctrine forbids punishment of an *'otherwise innocent'* person whose 'alleged offense' is 'the *product of the creative activity'* of government officials. Id. (emphasis added).

"As the Supreme Court has recently stated: 'When the Government's quest for conviction leads to the apprehension of an *otherwise law-abiding citizen* who, *if left to his own devices,* likely would never have been afoul of the law, the courts should intervene.' *Jacobson v. United States* (emphasis added). Since the Court has repeatedly expressed concern about *both* government 'abuse' of its enforcement powers (or the like) *and* the 'otherwise law-abiding citizen' (or the like), it is not surprising that the defense has two parts, one that focuses upon government 'inducement' and the other upon the defendant's 'predisposition.'

"[The Supreme Court] saw in the entrapment defense not so much a sanction used to control police conduct, but rather a protection of the ordinary law-abiding citizen against government overreaching. Consequently, it saw no need to permit a defendant to take advantage of that defense unless he himself was such a citizen. The upshot is that we must find out just who that 'innocent person' is. Who is the *otherwise* law-abiding citizen' who would not 'otherwise' have committed the crime?

"The question's difficulty lies in the word 'otherwise.' That word requires us to abstract from present circumstances. We cannot simply ask whether, without the government's present activity, the defendant would likely have committed the crime *when* he did. After all, without the government's having presented *that* opportunity, the defendant, no matter how 'predisposed,' would likely not have acted *then*. Nor can we simply ask whether the defendant would have acted similarly at some other time *had he faced similar circumstances,* since his present behavior virtually compels an affirmative answer to the question phrased in this way.

"The right way to ask the question, it seems to us, is to abstract from—to assume away—the present circumstances *insofar as they reveal government overreaching.* That is to say, we should ask how the defendant likely would have reacted to an *ordinary* opportunity to commit the crime. *See Jacobson,* n. 2. By using the word 'ordinary,' we mean an opportunity that lacked those special features of the government's conduct that made of it an 'inducement,' or an 'overreaching.' Was the defendant 'predisposed' to respond affirmatively to a *proper,* not to an *improper,* lure? * * *

"Finally, this way of phrasing the question prevents one from concluding automatically, simply from the fact that the defendant committed the crime, that he was 'predisposed' to commit it. At the same time, if the answer to the question so phrased is affirmative, the defendant would seem to be the sort of person (and his conduct in this instance is the sort of conduct) that the criminal statute intends to punish. He is, in other words, someone who would likely commit the crime under the circumstances and for the reasons normally associated with that crime, and who therefore poses the sort of threat to society that the statute seeks to control, and which the government, through the 'sting,' seeks to stop.

"We turn now to *Jacobson* * * *. In three respects [government agents] did more than provide an ordinary opportunity to buy child pornography: First, the solicitations reflected a psychologically 'graduated' set of responses to Jacobson's own noncriminal responses, beginning with innocent lures and progressing to frank offers. The government started with a 'sexual attitude questionnaire,' which elicited a general interest in 'pre-teen sex'; it followed with letters containing general, nonexplicit references implying a possibility of child pornography; it then sent Jacobson more personal correspondence; and, finally (but after Jacobson had discontinued the correspondence), it sent him child pornography catalogues. Second, the government's soliciting letters sometimes depicted their senders as 'free speech' lobbying organizations and fighters for the 'right to read what we desire'; they asked Jacobson to 'fight against censorship and the infringement of individual rights.' Third, the government's effort to provide an 'opportunity' to buy child pornography stretched out over two and a half years. Taken together, one might find in these three sets of circumstances—the graduated response, the long time period, the appeal to a proper (free speech) motive—a substantial risk of inducing an ordinary law-abiding person to commit the crime. Indeed, the government conceded in *Jacobson* that its methods amounted, for entrapment purposes, to an improper 'inducement.' Id. at n. 2.

"*Jacobson's* importance, however, concerns the 'predisposition' part of the entrapment defense. The Court held that the evidence, as a matter of law, required acquittal because a reasonable jury would have had to doubt Jacobson's predisposition. The evidence of predisposition consisted of two facts: (1) that before the government became involved Jacobson was on a private bookstore's mailing list for dubious photos; and (2) that he responded affirmatively to the government's solicitations. The first fact, the Court wrote, showed little about a predisposition to act *un*lawfully because ordering the photos was lawful at the time. The second, placing orders, could not show how Jacobson would have acted had the solicitation lacked the three elements we just mentioned, namely, the improper appeals to anti-censorship motives, the graduated response, and the lengthy time frame. The government therefore failed to show 'predisposition' (beyond a reasonable doubt). That means (as we understand it) that the government's evidence did not show how Jacobson would have acted had he been faced with an ordinary 'opportunity' to commit the crime rather than a special 'inducement.'

"[The evidence in this case,] taken together, reveals a defendant who met an initial opportunity to buy child pornography with enthusiasm, who responded to each further government initiative with a purchase order, and who, unlike Jacobson, showed no particular interest in an anti-censorship campaign. This evidence * * * permits a jury to find (beyond a reasonable doubt) that Gendron would have responded affirmatively to the most ordinary of opportunities, and, hence, was 'predisposed' to commit the crime. We therefore find the jury's entrapment decision lawful."

Compare UNITED STATES v. HOLLINGSWORTH, 27 F.3d 1196 (7th Cir.1994)(en banc). In the course of holding that the defendants, Pickard (a dentist) and Hollingsworth (a farmer), had been entrapped as a matter of law into engaging in a money laundering scheme in violation of federal law, a 6–5 majority, per POSNER, C.J., observed:

"[Until] the Supreme Court's recent decision in *Jacobson,* the courts of appeals had been drifting toward the view [that] the defense of entrapment must fail in any case in which the defendant is 'willing,' in the sense of being psychologically prepared, to commit the crime for which he is being prosecuted, even if it is plain that he would not have been engaged in criminal activity unless inveigled or assisted by the government. This drift in thinking reflected the semantic pull of the term 'predisposition,' the central element of the defense of entrapment as articulated in the modern cases. The word is suggestive of pure willingness; and it is the suggestion picked up by [various cases]. But the suggestion cannot in our view be squared with *Jacobson*. * * * Despite his lack of reluctance, emphasized by Justice O'Connor in her dissenting opinion, the Supreme Court reversed Jacobson's conviction, holding that he had been entrapped as a matter of law.

"[The] facts of *Jacobson* were unquestionably peculiar, and the government's tactics * * * bizarre and distasteful. Nevertheless, had the Court in *Jacobson* believed that the legal concept of predisposition is exhausted in the demonstrated willingness of the defendant to commit the crime without threats or promises by the government, then Jacobson was predisposed, in which event the Court's reversal of his conviction would be difficult to explain. The government did not offer Jacobson any inducements to buy pornographic magazines or threaten him with harm if he failed to buy them. It was not as if the government had had to badger Jacobson for 26 months in order to overcome his resistance to committing a crime. He *never* resisted.

" * * * [W]e are naturally reluctant to suppose that [*Jacobson*] is limited to the precise facts before the Court, or to ignore the Court's definition of entrapment, which concludes the analysis portion of the opinion and is not found in previous opinions, as 'the apprehension of an otherwise law-abiding citizen who, if left to his own devices, likely would have never run afoul of the law.' That was Jacobson. However impure his thoughts, he was law abiding. A farmer in Nebraska, his access to child pornography was limited. As far as the government was aware, over the period of more than two years in which it was playing cat and mouse with him he did not receive any other solicitations to buy pornography. So, had he been 'left to his own devices,' in all likelihood he would 'have never run afoul of the law.' If the same can be said of [the defendants in this case,] Pickard and Hollingsworth, they too are entitled to be acquitted. * * *

"Recently the First Circuit, struggling as are we to understand the scope of *Jacobson,* suggested that all it stands for is that the government may not, in trying to induce the target of a sting to commit a crime, confront him with circumstances that are different from the ordinary or typical circumstances of a private inducement. *Gendron.* The [First Circuit] thought that the government's attempt to persuade Jacobson that he had a First Amendment right to consume child pornography had departed from typicality. We are not so sure. Just as the gun industry likes to wrap itself in the mantle of the Second Amendment, so the pornography industry likes to wrap itself in the mantle of the First Amendment. But however that may be, the government made no effort in *this* case to show that a real customer for money laundering would have responded to an advertisement to sell a Grenadan bank * * *.

"We put the following hypothetical case to the government's lawyer at the reargument. Suppose the government went to someone and asked him whether he would like to make money as a counterfeiter, and the reply was, 'Sure, but I don't know anything about counterfeiting.' Suppose the government then bought him a printer, paper, and ink, showed him how to make the counterfeit money, hired a staff for him, and got everything set up so that all he had to do was press a button to print the money; and then offered him $10,000 for some quantity of counterfeit bills. The government's lawyer acknowledged that the counterfeiter would have a strong case that he had been entrapped, even though he was perfectly willing to commit the crime once the government planted the suggestion and showed him how and the government neither threatened him nor offered him an overwhelming inducement.[a]

"We do not suggest that *Jacobson* adds a new element to the entrapment defense—'readiness' or 'ability' or 'dangerousness' on top of inducement and, most important, predisposition. [Rather,] the Court clarified the meaning of predisposition. Predisposition is not a purely mental state, the state of being willing to swallow the government's bait. It has positional as well as dispositional force. The dictionary definitions of the word include 'tendency' as well as 'inclination.' The defendant must be so situated by reason of previous training or experience or occupation or acquaintances that it is likely that if the government had not induced him to commit the crime some criminal would have done so; only then does a sting or other arranged crime take a dangerous person out of circulation. A public official is in a position to take bribes; a drug addict to deal drugs; a gun dealer to engage in illegal gun sales. For these and other traditional targets of stings all that must be shown to establish predisposition and thus defeat the defense of entrapment is willingness to violate the law without extraordinary inducements; ability can be presumed. It is different when the defendant is not in a position without the government's help to become involved in illegal activity. * * *

"There is no evidence that before 'Hinch' began his campaign to inveigle them into a money-laundering scheme either Pickard or Hollingsworth had contemplated engaging in such behavior. [When] the opportunity to become *crooked* international financiers beckoned, they were willing enough, though less willing than Jacobson had been to violate the federal law against purchasing child pornography through the mails—Jacobson never evinced reluctance, even though he had received no financial inducements. Pickard and Hollingsworth had no prayer of becoming money launderers without the government's aid. Their solicitations for financial business had produced a tiny investor, but no customers. Their corporation was running out of money when they placed the ad in *USA Today* for the Grenadan banking license. No one responded to the ad, except [undercover customs agent] 'Hinch.' Suppose he hadn't responded. What would Pickard and Hollingsworth have

---

   a. Did the government's lawyer concede too much?

done next? Whatever it takes to become an international money launderer, they did not have it. Had Hinch not answered the ad, Pickard would soon have folded his financial venture.

"[The] point is not that Pickard and Hollingsworth were *incapable* of engaging in the act of money laundering. Obviously they were capable of the act. All that was involved in the act was wiring money to a bank account designated by the government agent. Anyone can wire money. But to get into the international money-laundering business you need underworld contacts, financial acumen or assets, access to foreign banks or bankers, or other assets. Pickard and Hollingsworth had none. * * * Even if they had wanted to go into money laundering before they met Hinch—and there is no evidence that they did—the likelihood that they could have done so was remote. They were objectively harmless.

"We do not wish to be understood as holding that lack of *present* means to commit a crime is alone enough to establish entrapment if the government supplies the means. Only in punishing speech is the government limited to preventing clear and present dangers. Suppose that before Hinch chanced on the scene (for *Jacobson* makes clear [that] a predisposition *created* by the government cannot be used to defeat a defense of entrapment), Pickard had decided to smuggle arms to Cuba but didn't know where to buy a suitable boat. On a hunch, a government agent sidles up to Pickard and gives him the address of a boat dealer; and Pickard is arrested after taking possession of the boat and setting sail, and is charged with attempted smuggling. That would be a case in which the defendant had the idea for the crime all worked out and lacked merely the present means to commit it, and if the government had not supplied them someone else very well might have. It would be a case in which the government had merely furnished the opportunity to commit the crime to someone already predisposed to commit it. [A] person who is likely to commit a particular type of crime without being induced to do so by government agents, although he would not have committed it when he did but for that inducement, is a menace to society and a proper target of law enforcement. The likelihood that he has committed this type of crime in the past or will do so in the future is great, and by arranging for him to commit it now, in circumstances that enable the government to apprehend and convict him, the government punishes or prevents real criminal activity. The government's inducement affects the timing of the offense; it does not create the offense by exploiting the susceptibility of a weak-minded person. The defense of entrapment reflects the view that the proper use of the criminal law in a society such as ours is to prevent harmful conduct for the protection of the law abiding, rather than to purify thoughts and perfect character.

"Our two would-be international financiers were at the end of their tether, making it highly unlikely that if Hinch had not providentially appeared someone else would have guided them into money laundering. No real criminal would do business with such tyros. Or so it appears;

perhaps the government could have shown that a Grenadan banking license has no other use but money laundering and that sooner or later Pickard and Hollingsworth would have gotten into money laundering even without the government's aid. No attempt was made to show this; and we remind that the government's acknowledged burden is to prove beyond a reasonable doubt that a defendant who raises a colorable defense of entrapment, as Pickard plainly did, has not in fact been entrapped."[b]

b. In three separate dissents, Judges Coffey, Easterbrook and Ripple voiced strong disagreement with the majority's interpretation of *Jacobson*.

Chapter 8

POLICE INTERROGATION AND CONFESSIONS

SECTION 1. SOME DIFFERENT PERSPECTIVES

8th ed., p. 452, at the end of the extract from Professor Grano's book, add new fn. b:

b. For an essay review of Professor Grano's book, a review that, inter alia, discusses the arguments for and against overruling *Miranda*, see George C. Thomas, III, *An Assault on the Temple of Miranda*, 85 J.Crim.L. & Criminology 807 (1995).

SECTION 2. HISTORICAL BACKGROUND

A. THE INTERESTS PROTECTED BY THE DUE PROCESS "VOLUNTARINESS" TEST FOR ADMITTING CONFESSIONS

8th ed., p. 455; at end of subsection, add:

According to Albert Alschuler, *Constraint and Confessions*, 74 Denv. U.L.Rev. 957 (1997), "Courts should define the term coerced confession to mean a confession caused by offensive governmental conduct, period. * * * Shifting their attention almost entirely from the minds of suspects to the conduct of government officers, courts should abandon the search for 'overborne wills' and attempts to assess the quality of individual choices."

SECTION 3. THE *MIRANDA* "REVOLUTION"

8th ed., p. 489; end of fn. 57 to *Miranda*, add:

[Ed. Note—*England curtails the right to silence.* In the fall of 1994, the British Parliament adopted various restrictions on the right to silence, effective March 1, 1995. These restrictions were similar to those Parliament had imposed on Northern Ireland in 1988. The new law permits judges and jurors to draw adverse inferences when, during interrogation, suspects do not tell the police any fact subsequently relied upon in their defense at trial if, under the circumstances, the suspects would have been "reasonably expected" to mention that fact to the police. (This section corresponds to a provision of the Northern Ireland Order which, according to the government, was designed to end terrorists' use of the "ambush defense," whereby terrorists would remain silent during interrogation and thus prevent the prosecution from preparing a rebuttal to subsequent defense claims.)

[The new law also permits judges and jurors to draw adverse inferences when suspects fail to respond to police questions about any suspicious objects, substances, or marks which are found on their persons or clothing or when suspects do not explain to the police why they were present at a place at or about the time of the crime for which they were arrested. Finally, if the defendant fails to testify at trial, the new law permits the jury to draw such adverse inferences "as appear proper"—including the "common sense" inference that there is no explanation for the evidence produced against the defendant and that the defendant is guilty. See generally, Mark Berger, *Of Policy, Politics, and Parliament: The*

Legislative Rewriting of the British Right to Silence, 22 Am.J.Crim.L. 391 (1995); Gregory W. O'Reilly, *England Limits the Right to Silence and Moves Toward an Inquisitional System of Justice,* 85 J.Crim.L. & C. 402 (1994).

[For the view that silence during police interrogation does not cause police to drop charges or prosecutors to dismiss cases or courts to acquit defendants; that using adverse inferences will not induce suspects to talk to the police or to reveal their defenses; that there is no indication that in the past a defendant's right to silence has been frequently invoked at trial; and that adverse inferences about a defendant's failure to testify at trial will not foster testimony by defendants, see O'Reilly, supra, at 431–42.]

8th ed., p. 501; after text of § 3501(c), add:

Does § 3501(c) codify a limited form of the McNabb–Mallory rule or repudiate the rule in its entirety? Does § 3501(c) apply at all to statements made by a person who is being held by local authorities solely on state charges? Consider *United States v. Alvarez–Sanchez,* 511 U.S. 350, 114 S.Ct. 1599, 128 L.Ed.2d 319 (1994), which arose as follows:

While executing a warrant to search respondent's residence for heroin, Los Angeles law enforcement officers discovered not only narcotics, but counterfeit Federal Reserve Notes. Respondent was arrested and booked on state felony narcotics charges on Friday afternoon and spent the weekend in police custody. On Monday morning Los Angeles authorities informed the U.S. Secret Service of the counterfeit currency they had found. Several hours later two Secret Service agents arrived at the Sheriff's Department and interviewed respondent. After waiving his *Miranda* rights, respondent admitted that he had known that the currency was counterfeit. Shortly thereafter, the Secret Service agents arrested respondent and took him to their field office for booking.

Respondent moved to suppress the statements he had made to the secret service agents on the ground that the delay between his arrest on state charges and his presentment on the federal charge rendered his confession inadmissible under § 3501(c). The District Court denied his motion. Respondent was subsequently convicted after a jury trial at which the statements were admitted into evidence. But the U.S. Court of Appeals overturned the conviction, reasoning that, by negative implication, § 3501(c) must in some circumstances allow suppression of a confession made more than six hours after arrest solely on the basis of pre-presentment delay, "regardless of the voluntariness of the confession." The Supreme Court, per Thomas, J., reversed.

The Ninth Circuit was of the view that § 3501(c) codified a limited form of the *McNabb–Mallory* rule and thus required the suppression of a confession made before presentment but after the expiration of the six-hour "safe harbor" period. The Government contended, on the other hand, that § 3501 repudiated the *McNabb–Mallory* rule in its entirety and that the admissibility of a confession obtained beyond the six-hour period is controlled by § 3501(a), which provides that voluntary confessions "shall be admitted in evidence." The Court saw no need to resolve this dispute because "the terms of § 3501(c) were never triggered in this case":

"[T]here can be no 'delay' in bringing a person before a federal magistrate until, at a minimum, there is some obligation to bring the person before such a judicial officer in the first place. Plainly, a duty to present a person to a federal magistrate does not arise until the person has been arrested for a *federal* offense. [Until then] there is no duty, obligation, or reason to bring [the person] before a judicial officer 'empowered to commit persons charged with offenses against the laws of the United States,' and therefore, no 'delay' under § 3501(c) can occur.

"* * * This is true even if the arresting officers (who, when the arrest is for a violation of state law, almost certainly will be agents of the State or one of its subdivisions) believe or have cause to believe that the person also may have violated federal law. Such a belief, which may not be uncommon given that many activities are criminalized under both state and federal law, does not alter the underlying basis for the arrest and subsequent custody. As long as a person is arrested and held only on state charges by state or local authorities, the provisions of § 3501(c) are not triggered."

The Court declined to discuss the effect of § 3501(c), if any, in "the situation that would arise if state or local authorities, acting in collusion with federal officers, were to arrest and detain someone in order to allow the federal agents to interrogate him in violation of his right to a prompt federal presentment." For there was "no evidence" that such collusion had taken place in this case.[a]

8th ed., p. 502; after the discussion, at pp. 501–02, of the validity of § 3501—Congress's attempt to "repeal" *Miranda*—and the reluctance of the Department of Justice to invoke this statutory provision, add:

Consider the views of Justice SCALIA, concurring in DAVIS v. UNITED STATES (1994)(discussed at Supp., p. 82):

"[Section 3501] declares that 'a confession . . . *shall be admissible in evidence if it is voluntarily given*,' and that the issue of voluntariness shall be determined on the basis of '*all* the circumstances surrounding the giving of the confession, *including* . . . whether or not [the] defendant was advised or knew that he was not required to make any statement . . . [;] . . . whether or not [the] defendant had been advised prior to questioning of his right to the assistance of counsel; [and] whether or not [the] defendant was without the assistance of counsel when questioned. . . .' §§ 3501(a), (b) (emphases added). It continues (lest the import be doubtful): "The presence or absence of any of the above-mentioned factors . . . need not be conclusive on the issue of

---

a. Ginsburg, J., joined by Blackmun, J., wrote a concurring opinion. Stevens, J., wrote a separate opinion concurring only in the judgment.

voluntariness of the confession." § 3501(b). Legal analysis of the admissibility of a confession without reference to these provisions is equivalent to legal analysis of the admissibility of hearsay without consulting the Rules of Evidence; it is an unreal exercise. Yet [that] is precisely what the United States has undertaken in this case. It did not raise § 3501(a) below and asserted that it is 'not at issue' here.*

"This is not the first case in which the United States has declined to invoke § 3501 before us—nor even the first case in which that failure has been called to its attention. In fact, with limited exceptions the provision has been studiously avoided by every Administration, not only in this Court but in the lower courts, since its enactment more than 25 years ago. * * *

"I agree with the Court that it is *proper,* given the Government's failure to raise the point, to render judgment without taking account of § 3501. But the refusal to consider arguments not raised is a sound prudential practice, rather than a statutory or constitutional mandate, and there are times when prudence dictates the contrary. [As] far as I am concerned, such a time will have arrived when a case that comes within the terms of this statute is next presented to us.

"For most of this century, voluntariness *vel non* was the touchstone of admissibility of confessions. Section 3501 of Title 18 *seems* to provide for that standard in federal criminal prosecutions today. I say 'seems' because I do not wish to prejudge any issue of law. I am entirely open to the argument that § 3501 does not mean what it appears to say; that it is inapplicable for some other reason; or even that it is unconstitutional. But I will no longer be open to the argument that this Court should continue to ignore the commands of § 3501 simply because the Executive declines to insist that we observe them.

"The Executive has the power (whether or not it has the right) effectively to nullify some provisions of law by the mere failure to prosecute—the exercise of so-called prosecutorial discretion. And it has the power (whether or not it has the right) to avoid application of § 3501 by simply declining to introduce into evidence confessions admissible under its terms. But once a prosecution has been commenced and a confession introduced, the Executive assuredly has neither the power nor the right to determine what objections to admissibility of the confession are valid in law. Section 3501 is a provision of law directed *to the courts,* reflecting the people's assessment of the proper balance to be struck between concern for persons interrogated in custody and the needs of effective law enforcement. We shirk our duty if we systematically disregard that statutory command simply because the Justice Department systematically declines to remind us of it.

"The United States' repeated refusal to invoke § 3501, combined with the courts' traditional (albeit merely prudential) refusal to consider

---

* [The] Court today bases its refusal to consider § 3501 not upon the fact that the provision is inapplicable, but upon the fact that the Government failed to argue it—and it is *that* refusal which my present statement addresses.

arguments not raised, has caused the federal judiciary to confront a host of 'Miranda' issues that might be entirely irrelevant under federal law. * * * Worse still, it may have produced—during an era of intense national concern about the problem of run-away crime—the acquittal and the nonprosecution of many dangerous felons, enabling them to continue their depredations upon our citizens. There is no excuse for this. Perhaps (though I do not immediately see why) the Justice Department has good basis for believing that allowing prosecutions to be defeated on grounds that could be avoided by invocation of § 3501 is consistent with the Executive's obligation to 'take Care that the Laws be faithfully executed,' U.S. Const., Art. II, § 3. That is not the point. The point is whether *our* continuing refusal to *consider* § 3501 is consistent with the Third Branch's obligation to decide according to the law. I think it is not."

8th ed., p. 506; add to the Note on prophylactic rules and the "legitimacy" of *Miranda*:

Consider the views of Justice Scalia, set forth at Supp., p. 68, concurring in *Davis v. United States.*

Consider the developments in UNITED STATES v. LEONG, 116 F.3d 1474 (4th Cir.1997).[a] The Fourth Circuit upheld a district court's ruling suppressing defendant's confession on the ground that the confession had been obtained in violation of *Miranda*. The Washington Legal Foundation and the Safe Streets Coalition then moved to proceed as *amici curiae*, maintaining that the confession should have been admitted, despite the *Miranda* violation, unless it did not satisfy the more lenient standard for admissibility set forth in 18 U.S.C. § 3501. These organizations also criticized the federal government for failing to assert the applicability of § 3501. In response to this motion, and to the surprise of many, the Fourth Circuit then issued an order directing the parties to consider the effect of § 3501 on the admissibility of defendant's confession.

The Department of Justice recognized that "[v]iewed in isolation" cases such as *Michigan* v. *Tucker, New York* v. *Quarles* and *Oregon* v. *Elstad* "can be argued to support the validity of § 3501, for those cases state that violations of *Miranda*'s rules do not necessarily result in statements that must be deemed 'compelled' within the meaning of the Self–Incrimination Clause." Nevertheless, continued the Department of Justice, "we do not believe that the Supreme Court's jurisprudence permits [the Fourth Circuit] or any lower court to draw the conclusion that *Miranda* may now be viewed solely as an exercise of the Court's supervisory powers. The most important indication that the Court does not regard *Miranda* as resting simply on its supervisory powers is the fact that [it] has continued to apply the *Miranda* rules to cases arising in state courts. [The Court has] consistently disclaimed [any] supervisory authority over state courts. With respect to cases tried in state courts,

a. The editors of the Supplement are indebted to Professor Paul Cassell, who served as counsel for Amici Curiae Washington Legal Foundation and Safe Streets Coalition in *Leong*, for providing much valuable material about the case.

the Court's 'authority is limited to enforcing the commands of the United States Constitution.' "

The Supreme Court, noted Justice, has recently held that "claims that a conviction rests on statements obtained in violation of *Miranda* are cognizable on federal habeas review. *Withrow* v. *Williams* (1993) [8th ed., p. 590]. Habeas corpus is available only for claims that a person 'is in custody in violation of the Constitution or the laws or treaties of the United States.' Because *Miranda* is not a 'law' or a treaty, the Court's holding in *Withrow* depends—as does its application of *Miranda* to the states—on the conclusion that the requirement of *Miranda* warning implements and protects constitutional rights."

The Burger and Rehnquist Court's description of the *Miranda* rules as "prophylactic," emphasized Justice, "does not require the conclusion that the rules are therefore extra-constitutional. The appellation may simply reflect the notion that *Miranda*, in the interest of avoiding constitutional violations, structured a regime that 'overprotects the value at stake,' and this excludes some statements that are not 'compelled' within the meaning of the Self–Incrimination Clause * * *. That a 'prophylactic' rule is not necessarily a non-constitutional rule is confirmed by the Supreme Court's description of *Edwards* v. *Arizona* (1981) [8th ed., p. 547]. [The] Court has both characterized the *Edwards* rule as 'a second layer of prophylaxis' to protect a suspect's right to counsel under *Miranda* and also unmistakably described [it] as a constitutional decision."

Finally, argued the Department of Justice, even if cases such as *Tucker, Quarles* and *Elstad* "are viewed as having eroded *Miranda*'s basic constitutional premise," it would be inappropriate for any lower court "to apply § 3501 to admit a defendant's statement in a case in which *Miranda* would require its suppression or for the Department of Justice to urge the lower courts to do so":

"[A lower court] may not disregard controlling Supreme Court precedent. *Miranda* has never expressly been overruled, and it is the Supreme Court's sole province to pass on the continuing validity of its decisions. * * * [U]ntil the Supreme Court expressly overrules *Miranda* and the more recent cases reaffirming *Miranda*'s application to the States, lower courts may not disregard its basic command. Thus, to the extent that § 3501 would require courts to admit statements obtained in violation of *Miranda*, [the Fourth Circuit] is bound by *Miranda*."

However, added Justice, if the validity or constitutional status of § 3501 were to be presented to the U.S. Supreme Court, "the same considerations would not control, since the Supreme Court (unlike the lower courts) is free to reconsider its prior decisions, and the Department of Justice is free to urge it to do so."

The Washington Legal Foundation (WLF), and Safe Streets Coalition forcefully responded to the supplemental briefs of the Department of Justice and other parties:

"The problem with [the argument by the Department of Justice] is that it only works if *Miranda* is indeed a constitutional decision in the strongest sense of the word. If *Miranda* is anything else—if it is, for example, either a decision rooted in the Court's supervisory powers or a Constitutional common law decision, in which the Court devised one form of remedy to guard against Fifth Amendment violations but acknowledged that that remedy could be replaced with an alternative so long as the alternative continued to be adequate to effectuate constitutional rights—Congress has significant authority to modify *Miranda*'s holding by legislation. And if § 3501 represents such a Congressional modification, all federal courts are not only free, but duty bound to apply the resulting statute in cases before them.

"Accordingly, this court not only may, but must decide whether *Miranda* is a constitutionally mandated holding."

The WLF amicus brief recalled that in 1986, after a comprehensive analysis of the issue, the Department of Justice's Office of Legal Policy had concluded, in a lengthy report to the Attorney General, that, because of the enactment of § 3501, "*Miranda* should no longer be regarded as controlling [in federal cases]. Since the Supreme Court now holds that *Miranda*'s rules are merely prophylactic, and that the fifth amendment is not violated by the admission of a defendant's voluntary statements despite non-compliance with *Miranda*, a decision by the Court invalidating [§ 3501] would require some extraordinary imaginative legal theorizing of an unpredictable legal nature." U.S. Department of Justice, Office of Legal Policy, *Report to the Attorney General on the Law of Pre–Trial Interrogation* 103 (1986), reprinted in 22 Mich.J.L.Ref. 437, 549 (1989).

Miranda, suggested the WLF, "may be a constitutional common law decision. In such cases, the Court is presented with an issue implicating a constitutional right for whose violation there is no legislatively specified remedy. It is conceivable that generally in such circumstances the judicial power may include the crafting of a remedy, and that the remedy may extend beyond simply redressing the constitutional violation. It is clear, however, that exercising its powers, Congress may step in and substitute an alternative remedy that sweeps more or less broadly, provided the substitute remedy is adequate to correct the violation. It is also entirely possible that the States may do so as well. This theory * * * is consistent with the suggestion made by the *Miranda* Court itself that the national and state legislatures may substitute alternative remedial schemes for the one set out in *Miranda*. Unlike this case, none of the state cases decided since *Miranda* have involved an effort by Congress on the states to modify through legislation the scope of the remedy created by *Miranda*. Thus the continued application of *Miranda* to the states in the absence of such a legislative effort may represent no more than the application of the Court's judicially-created, but not constitutionally mandated, remedial scheme in the absence of a legislatively devised alternative."

The WLF was not impressed with the Justice Department's argument that *Miranda*'s constitutional status is supported by *Withrow* v. *Williams* because habeas corpus extends to persons held in custody "in violation of the Constitution or the laws or treaties of the United States" and since *Miranda* is neither a "law" nor a "treaty" it must be a constitutional right: "The [Justice] Department must be aware [that] what is a 'law' for purposes of federal habeas review is not exclusively limited to federal statutory claims [but may include judicial decisional law]. This has led a leading commentator [Larry Yackle] to conclude that *Miranda* claims raise issues about a 'law' of the United States. * * * ('If,' [commented Professor Yackle] 'court-fashioned rules for the enforcement of constitutional rights are not themselves part and parcel of these rights, they would seem to be federal "laws" which, under the statute, may form the basis for habeas relief.')"

Although the WLF maintained that § 3501 "is a valued exercise of Congress's undoubted power to override non-constitutional procedures and establish the rules for federal courts," it added: "But an alternative, independent analysis leads to exactly the same conclusion: § 3501—read in combination with other bodies of law providing criminal, civil, and administrative remedies for coercion during interrogation along with the Fifth Amendment's exclusionary rule for coerced confessions—leaves in place a constitutionally adequate alternative to the unflexible *Miranda* exclusionary rule."

The WLF warned the Fourth Circuit:

"If the [Justice] Department's position is left unreviewed, [the] Department will have succeeded in frustrating the constitutional scheme of separated powers—by obtaining for itself not simply a role in executing the laws but effectively in writing them as well. It has long been established that the executive branch's charge to execute the law does not carry with it a power *not* to execute it. * * * As a result, the longstanding practice of the Department, reiterated over many years, is to defend the constitutionality of Acts of Congress unless no "reasonable" supporting argument could be made.

" * * * The Department's conclusion that it can make no 'reasonable' argument in defense of the law here flies in the face of the views of many apparently 'reasonable' predecessors in the Department of Justice who thought the statute constitutional, [and] is all the more astounding because there is only one clear-cut Court of Appeals ruling on the constitutionality of the statute—a ruling *upholding* it, see *United States* v. *Crocker,* 510 F.2d 1129 (10th Cir.1975), apparently at the behest of the Department. Six thoughtful members of the Senate Judiciary Committee too have carefully explained—quite "reasonably" and even persuasively, in our estimation—why the law is constitutional.[b] In taking a

b. The August, 1997 letter to Attorney General Janet Reno from Senator Orrin Hatch, Chair, U.S. Senate Committee on the Judiciary and five other members of the Committee is reprinted as an appendix to the WLF's amicus brief. The letter reminds the Attorney General that "you and other senior Department of Justice officials have

contrary position, the Department seems not to have made the kind of legal judgment that is properly the province of the Executive Branch, but rather a political judgment that (for some inscrutable and unarticulated) reason § 3501 should not have been passed by Congress—a policy judgment reserved for the Legislative Branch."

On September 19, 1997, the Fourth Circuit voiced strong disagreement with the Justice Department's view that *Miranda* "remains binding on lower federal courts notwithstanding § 3501 unless or until it is modified by the Supreme Court." However, the court declined to rehear the appeal. Since the government had not pressed § 3501 before the district court or the court of appeals as a basis for a determination that defendant's confession was admissible, review of the applicability of § 3501 had to be solely for "plain error." And the view that "a confession obtained during a custodial interrogation that was conducted without the procedural safeguards prescribed by *Miranda* is nevertheless admissible if it satisfies the requirements of § 3501 is anything but clear or obvious."

8th ed., p. 509; before Note 2, add:

1a. *The correlation between prior criminal records and invocation of Miranda rights,* Richard A. Leo, *Inside the Interrogation Room,* 86 J.Crim.L. & Criminology 263 (1996) (recent empirical study of police interrogation in three California cities) reports that "the only variable that exercised a statistically significant effect on the suspect's likelihood to waive or invoke the *Miranda* rights was whether a suspect had a prior criminal record." *Id.* at 286. Continues Professor Leo:

"[W]hile 89% of the suspects with a misdemeanor record and 92% of the suspects without any record waived their *Miranda* rights, only 70% of the suspects with a felony record waived their *Miranda* rights. Put another way, a suspect with a felony record in my sample was almost four times as likely to invoke his *Miranda* rights as a suspect with no prior record and almost three times as likely to invoke as a suspect with a misdemeanor record. This result confirms the findings of earlier studies, as well as the conventional wisdom among the detectives I studied, who complained that ex-felons frequently refuse to talk to them as a matter of course."

8th ed., p. 515; add to Note 4:

4. *"Custody" vs. "focus."*   In *Stansbury v. California,* 511 U.S. 318, 114 S.Ct. 1526, 128 L.Ed.2d 293 (1994)(per curiam), the Court held, "not for the first time, that an officer's subjective and undisclosed view concerning whether the person being interrogated is a suspect is irrelevant to the assessment whether the person is in custody."

testified before the Senate Committee on the Judiciary that the Department will urge the application of, and will defend the constitutionality of, § 3501 in what such officials consistently have identified as 'the appropriate case.' " Senator Hatch added that "clearly" *Leong* is such a case.

Stansbury, one of two suspects in the disappearance and possible murder of a young girl, agreed to answer some questions and accompanied an officer to the stationhouse. There he was questioned without being given *Miranda* warnings. Because the trial court concluded that the officer's "mind" was on the other suspect until Stansbury revealed certain information, statements Stansbury made before that time were admitted into evidence. The state supreme court affirmed, viewing "whether the investigation has focused on the subject" one of the important considerations "in deciding the custody issue." In reversing, the U.S. Supreme Court emphasized that "[s]ave as they are communicated or otherwise manifested to the person being questioned, an officer's evolving but unarticulated suspicions do not affect the objective circumstances of an interrogation or interview, and thus cannot affect the *Miranda* custody inquiry."

8th ed., p. 518, add to Note 5:

When an officer stops a motorist, must all of the officer's activity be limited to the offense for which the stop was made? Unless reasonable suspicion develops as to other criminality, is it improper for the police to question a motorist about matters unrelated to the offense for which he was stopped? See Note 6, Supp., p. 42.

8th ed., p. 541; after Notes following *Quarles*, add:

(d) *Quarles* and *Miranda.* The *Quarles* case, observes Charles Weisselberg, *Saving Miranda*, 84 Cornell L.Rev. ___ (1998) (forthcoming), "struck at the Court's original version of *Miranda* in several respects": It "reinforced the notion that the warning requirement was divorced from the Fifth Amendment"; "the majority's cost-benefit analysis represents a wholly different view of the value of the Fifth Amendment than was expressed in *Miranda*"; and "[t]hird, by creating a vague and ill-defined exception to the warning requirement, the Court reduced the efficacy of *Miranda*'s bright-line rules." However, adds Professor Weisselberg, *Quarles* "did not—as it turns out—open the door to other large exceptions to the *Miranda* rule. In the fourteen years since *Quarles* was decided, the Supreme Court has not approved any other instances of custodial interrogations in which warnings need not be given."

8th ed., p. 542; add to Note 10:

10. *Meeting the "heavy burden" of demonstrating waiver: should written records and sound recordings be required?*

Although some commentators have argued that the police should comply with *both* the *Miranda* rules *and* an electronic recording requirement, in the article extracted below Professor Cassell maintains that a recording requirement should be viewed as an *alternative* to *Miranda*.

PAUL G. CASSELL—*MIRANDA*'S SOCIAL COSTS: AN EMPIRICAL REASSESSMENT

90 Nw.U.L.Rev. 387, 486–97 (1996).

Miranda's defenders have argued that any change in the decision's requirements would "roll back the clock" to an outmoded day and age. But time has passed these Warren Court warriors by—they are, in effect, advocating a 1966 solution to the problem of preventing coerced confessions when the 1990s offer superior solutions. Consider, then, videotaping of interrogations as an alternative to *Miranda*. * * *

Videotaping interrogations would certainly be as effective as *Miranda* in preventing police coercion and probably more so. The *Miranda* regime appears to have had little effect on the police misconduct that does exist. In contrast, videotaping, when used, has often reduced claims of police coercion and probably real coercion as well. To be sure, police conceivably could alter tapes or deploy force off-camera. But if you were facing a police officer with a rubber hose, would you prefer a world in which he was required to mumble the *Miranda* warnings and have you waive your rights, all as reported by him in later testimony? Or a world in which the interrogation is videorecorded and the burden is on law enforcement to explain if it is not; where date and time are recorded on the videotape; where your physical appearance and demeanor during the interrogation are permanently recorded? Videotaping is the clear winner. Not surprisingly, those who are most concerned about police brutality have seen videotaping as a means of control.

Recording confessions also promises to be effective in preventing not only physical coercion but also in detecting, if not preventing, other fine points of coercion as well. In this regard, it is interesting that some of the most detailed assessments of voluntariness have come in cases of recorded interrogations, which permitted judges to parse implicit promises and threats made to obtain an admission. Recording also allows a review of police overbearing that might not be revealed in dry testimony. Taping is thus the only means of eliminating "swearing contests" about what went on in the interrogation room.

Videotaping also promises to offer more effective protection against the more esoteric problem of false confessions induced by non-coercive police questioning. A complete record of the proceedings promises to be the most effective means of identifying such cases. * * *

While recording maintains, and in many ways exceeds, *Miranda*'s supposed benefits of deterring coercion and preventing false confessions, it has the advantage over *Miranda* of not significantly impeding law enforcement. In 1992 the National Institute of Justice (NIJ) published a nationwide survey of representative samples of police agencies about videotaping interrogations. The survey found that about one-sixth of all police and sheriffs' departments in the United States videotaped at least some confessions. The survey found that 59.8% of the agencies believed that they obtained more incriminating information from suspects, 26.9% the same amount, while 13.2% thought they obtained less. Also, 8.6% thought suspects were more willing to talk to police, 63.1% thought there was no difference, while 28.3% reported suspects less willing to talk. Videotaping also had many other benefits, such as improving police interrogation practices, rendering confessions more convincing, facilitating their introduction into evidence, assisting prosecutors in negotiating more acceptable plea bargains and obtaining guilty pleas, and helping in securing convictions. * * *

Recent and substantial experience with a mandatory recording requirement in Britain suggests that such a requirement would not significantly harm police efforts to obtain confessions. In 1988, a Code of Practice took effect that generally required that police tape record interviews with suspects. A 1993 review of the requirement by the Royal Commission on Criminal Justice reported that "[b]y general consent, tape recording in the police station has proved to be a strikingly successful innovation providing better safeguards for the suspect and the police officer alike." No significant adverse effect on obtaining confessions has been observed in the empirical studies specifically focusing on taping, and in fact police obtain more confessions and information about other offenses when interrogations are taped. According to one survey, 91% of police officers approve of the practice with 65% reporting "very favorable" views about it. * * *

Miranda's defenders might be prepared to concede that videotaping has many advantages but argue that police should comply with both *Miranda* and videotaping requirements. But such an approach single-mindedly pursues the goal of eliminating coerced confessions without considering the countervailing costs identified in this Article. The Court has described *Miranda* as "a carefully crafted balance designed to fully protect *both* the defendants' and society's interests." [598] An approach that strikes a reasonable balance between maximizing benefits and minimizing costs would be to require taping to prevent police coercion while at the same time relaxing the features of the *Miranda* regime that extract the greatest costs in terms of lost confessions. The existing empirical literature allows us to identify the particularly harmful features of *Miranda*. These features can then be modified, without disturbing the other protections. In particular, the *Miranda* warnings can be retained without significantly lowering the confession rate, while the waiver and questioning cutoff rules should be eliminated, as they cause the bulk of *Miranda*'s harms. * * *

In light of the benefits of videotaping and the costly features of *Miranda*, what might a replacement for *Miranda* look like? Suspects could continue to be advised of their rights, as follows:

(1) You do not have to say anything.

(2) Anything you do say may be used as evidence.

598. Moran v. Burbine [8th ed., p. 572] n. 4 * * *.

(3) You have the right to be represented by a lawyer when we bring you before a judge.

(4) If you cannot afford a lawyer, the judge will appoint one for you without charge.

(5) We are required to bring you before a judge without unnecessary delay.

While adding a new, fifth warning that is not required by *Miranda,* the modified warnings would dispense with the *Miranda* offer of counsel, identified as a particularly harmful aspect of *Miranda* and, in any event, a right that has proven to be purely theoretical since police always terminate questioning rather than finding a lawyer. Also, the alternative would dispense with the requirement that police obtain an affirmative waiver of rights from suspects, another particularly harmful feature of *Miranda.* However, police could continue to ask suspects whether they understood the rights communicated to them, since nothing in the empirical literature identifies this aspect of *Miranda* as being particularly harmful. Also eliminated would be the requirement that police immediately terminate an interview whenever the suspect requests an end to the interview or an opportunity to meet with counsel. These features have been identified as harming the confession rate.[634]

While these changes would eliminate most of *Miranda*'s costs, the additional safeguard of taping confessions could be added on top of existing requirements without adversely affecting confession rates. Videotaping would be required for custodial interrogation in the stationhouse; audiotaping would be required for custodial interrogation in the field (as is currently done in Alaska). * * *

One final point should be made in favor of this proposal. Since police are still required to give modified warnings and since they will be videotaped while conducting interrogations, police will not gain the mistaken impression that any judicial supervision of the interrogation process has ended.[a]

Professor Cassell's article evoked a response from Professor Schulhofer, the article extracted below. In this article Schulhofer maintains

634. Continued persistence to convince a suspect to change his mind will, at some point, render a confession involuntary and thus inadmissible under Fifth Amendment principles. * * *

a. See also Richard A. Leo, *The Impact of Miranda Revisited,* 86 J. Crim. L. & Criminology 621, 680–82 (1996). Although he believes *Miranda* should neither be overruled nor strengthened doctrinally, Professor Leo maintains that substantive due process requires the electronic recording of custodial interrogations in all felony cases

and that such a requirement constitutes the most adequate solution to the problems *Miranda* failed to resolve, "problems that continue to bedevil the constitutional law of criminal procedure." According to Leo, these are "the problem of adjudicating the 'swearing contest' between officer and suspect in court; the problem of false allegations of police improprieties; the problem of police perjury; the problem of false confessions; and, most notably, the problem of determining the voluntariness of a confession."

that videotaping of interrogation cannot be seen as a substitute for the Miranda safeguards and that Cassell's proposed replacement for *Miranda* would expose suspects to violations of their Fifth Amendment privilege.

STEPHEN J. SCHULHOFER—*MIRANDA*'S PRACTICAL EFFECT: SUBSTANTIAL BENEFITS AND VANISHINGLY SMALL SOCIAL COSTS

90 Nw.U.L.Rev. 556–60 (1996).

Videotaping is an extremely valuable tool—for both the police and the suspect. Many police departments now use it routinely, and a number of foreign countries require it. * * *

If seen as a *supplement* to *Miranda*, videotaping would clearly help protect suspects in custody, without infringing any legitimate law enforcement interest. But a videotaping requirement would lose much of its value if it were merely a *replacement* for *Miranda*. In effect, the proposal to substitute videotaping for *Miranda* amounts to a police officer in the form, "We'll stop lying about what we do, if you allow us to do it." No doubt a videotaped record would often prevent police abuse and manipulation of the "swearing contest." But without clear substantive requirements against which to test the police behavior that the videotape will reveal, the objective record will lack any specific legal implications.

Miranda's central concern, of course, is to dispel the pressures that custodial interrogation brings to bear on the suspect. A videotaping requirement that *replaced Miranda* would do little to further this goal. Videotaping would deter most officers from beating the suspect, but it would not prevent psychological pressure, ignoring requests to consult counsel, or disregarding pleas to terminate the interview. The principal way that videotaping might help dissipate psychological coercion would be by reassuring the suspect that he won't be beaten while the camera is on. But Cassell is aware that *telling* the suspect about the videotape sometimes strengthens resistance to confessing, so he is willing to let police videotape the interrogation covertly. At that point, we lose whatever fear-dispelling effects an announced policy of videotaping might promise. And of course the tape lays down no rules of behavior and gives the police no guidance about the tactics they may use. Thus, videotaping, though an excellent idea, does not meet the constitutional concerns about compulsion to which the *Miranda* safeguards are addressed. Videotaping could provide a useful complement to the *Miranda* protections, but it cannot replace them.

The heart of the Cassell proposals is his recommendation to strip arrested suspects of their right to consult counsel during pre-arraignment interrogation, to eliminate the requirement that interrogation be preceded by an explicit waiver of rights, and to eliminate *Miranda*'s requirement that interrogation cease if a suspect makes a clear request to break off questioning or to consult with counsel. The requirements he would eliminate are not only central to the *Miranda* safeguards but have now become entrenched in the interrogation procedures of many countries around the world.[242]

Edwards v. Arizona [8th ed., p. 547] provides a suitable illustration of the difference between the *Miranda* safeguards and those Cassell would put in their place. In *Edwards* the defendant, under interrogation, invoked his *Miranda* right to counsel, and police then returned him to his cell. Later, detectives sought to question him again without counsel; when the defendant refused, a guard told him that he "had to" and led him unwillingly to the interrogation room. The Supreme Court *unanimously* held the resulting confession inadmissible. Its opinion was written by Justice White, the Court's most long-standing critic of *Miranda,* and concurring opinions were written by Chief Justice Burger and by Justice Powell, who was joined by Justice Rehnquist.

Tactics like those condemned in *Edwards* would be encouraged under the Cassell proposal and would no doubt become commonplace. Cassell estimates that 20% of arrested suspects (some 550,000 persons per year) at some point invoke their right to remain silent. Under Cassell's approach, police could require (literally *compel*) these individuals to submit to the interrogation process. We must remember that *Miranda*'s cut-off rules are triggered only by an unequivocal expression of the desire to remain silent.[245] The Cassell proposal would permit police investigators to insistently question suspects who have clearly and explicitly asked to be left alone. This is not a regime of prophylactic safeguards, but an explicit recipe for involuntary custodial interrogation, in direct violation of the Fifth Amendment.

The other elements of Cassell's package would do little to mitigate this problem. Suspects would have no right to consult with counsel prior to formal arraignment. They would be told they have a right to remain silent, but the protective effect of that warning would be immediately negated by police actions. Instead of "scrupulously honoring" a suspect's decision to remain silent, as *Miranda* requires, police would be authorized to ignore the suspect's decision and press forward with the interrogation. Will suspects treated this way really have (or think they have) the right to remain silent? All they will have (mixed messages notwithstanding) is the legally sanctioned obligation to submit to an unwanted custodial interrogation.

---

242. *See* Craig M. Bradley, *The Emerging International Consensus as to Criminal Procedure Rules,* 14 Mich.J.Int'l L. 171, 185 (1993) ("England's interrogation rules are *more stringent* than *Miranda.*") (emphasis added); id. at 197–98 (noting that in Canada, a suspect must be informed upon arrest of his right to counsel, and that police "must refrain from attempting to elicit evidence from the detainee until he has a reasonable opportunity to retain and instruct counsel") (quoting Martin's Annual Criminal Code CH–21 (1991)); id. at 214–15 (Germany requires warning of rights to silence and right "*at all times, even before his examination,* to consult with defense counsel of his choice") (emphasis added) (quoting German Code of Criminal Procedure § 136); id. at 217–18 (noting that Italian interrogation rules prohibit use of statements made in the absence of counsel).

245. Davis v. United States [Supp., p. 82].

The distinction Cassell needs to draw here, to render his proposal plausible, is the distinction between compelling the suspect *to answer,* which the Constitution clearly forbids, and compelling him to *submit to questions,* which Cassell thinks should be permissible. Involuntary *statements* would be ruled out, but not involuntary *interrogation.* In the context of custodial police interrogation, there is only a slender conceptual difference here, not a practical difference that can possibly matter. If the suspect in police custody chooses to make no statement and asks for questioning to cease, if the interrogators who hold him in their power ignore that request and continue asking him to say something, are they merely compelling him *to listen?* Or are they not, in every practical sense, compelling (or trying to compel) him *to answer?* * * *

The Cassell system would not only enhance (rather than dispel) these inherently compelling pressures, but it would fail to meet *Miranda*'s other central concerns as well. Officers interrogating an unwilling suspect would have no guidance about the tactics they could use or when they should relent, except for the rule that they should *not* stop questioning just because the suspect refuses to answer or unequivocally pleads for questioning to cease. Notoriously vague due process concepts would provide the only limits. Cassell offers nothing to fill this crucial void in his proposal, except to state that "[c]ontinued persistence to convince a suspect to change his mind will, *at some point,* render a confession involuntary...." [emphasis added].

This return to the vague due process test would compel hundreds of thousands of unwilling suspects (roughly half a million suspects per year) to submit to involuntary questioning, and it would leave police (and courts) without any predictable framework for judging how long such an involuntary interrogation could last and what kinds of tactics could be used. Worse yet, since the murky boundaries for dealing with recalcitrant suspects would sometimes be overstepped, serious instances of physical and psychological abuse would inevitably occur even among the best-intentioned officers.

All to what end? Is it the hope that law enforcement practices would eventually settle into the new regime, that truly egregious abuses would not occur too often, that society will tolerate subjecting arrested suspects to pressures the Fifth Amendment clearly forbids in every other context, and that a microscopically small increase in the net conviction rate would eventually be realized as a result? With or without a video camera to record the process, persistent custodial questioning of unwilling suspects is pragmatically undesirable and constitutionally indefensible.[a]

a. In *All Benefits, No Costs: The Grand Illusion of Miranda's Defenders,* 90 Nw. U.L.Rev. 1084, 1121–22 (1996), a rejoinder to Professor Schulhofer's response, Professor Cassell comments, inter alia:

" * * * Schulhofer appears to agree [that] videotaping would be more effective than *Miranda* in preventing police brutality and identifying fine points of coercion, but he offers no specific explanation for his conclusion that this benefit is outweighed by what he sees as the costs of modifying *Miranda.* Nor does he offer any response to my argument that videotaping would

8th ed., p. 563; add to Note 16(b):

16(b). *What constitutes an effective invocation of the right to counsel for purposes of Edwards.* See *Davis v. United States*, immediately below.

8th ed., p. 563; add to Note 17:

17. *The assumption that direct and assertive speech should be the norm.* In DAVIS v. UNITED STATES, 512 U.S. 452, 114 S.Ct. 2350, 129 L.Ed.2d 362 (1994), Justice O'CONNOR, speaking for five members of the Court, in effect rejected the position taken by Professor Ainsworth that (a) the courts should not place a premium on suspects making direct, assertive, unqualified invocations of the right to counsel and (b) all arguable references to counsel should be treated as valid invocations of the right. The *Davis* case arose as follows:

Davis, a member of the U.S. Navy, was suspected of murdering another sailor. When interviewed by agents of the Naval Investigative Service (NIS) at the NIS office, he initially waived his *Miranda* rights. About an hour and a half into the interview, he said: "Maybe I should talk to a lawyer." At this point, according to the uncontradicted testimony of one of the agents, "we made it very clear [that] we weren't going to pursue the matter unless we have it clarified is he asking for a lawyer or is he just making a comment about a lawyer" and Davis replied, "No, I'm not asking for a lawyer" and then said, "No, I don't want a lawyer."

After a short break, the agents then reminded Davis of his *Miranda* rights and the interview continued for another hour—until Davis said, "I think I want a lawyer before I say anything." At this point, questioning ceased.

A military judge admitted Davis's statements and he was convicted of murder. The U.S. Court of Appeals affirmed the conviction—as did the U.S. Supreme Court:

"The applicability of the ' "rigid" prophylactic rule' of *Edwards* requires courts to 'determine whether the accused *actually invoked* his right to counsel.' *Smith v. Illinois* (emphasis added). To avoid difficulties of proof and to provide guidance to officers conducting interrogations, this is an objective inquiry. Invocation of the *Miranda* right to counsel 'requires, at a minimum, some statement that can reasonably be

eliminate the problem of false confessions that convict the innocent. * * *

"Instead of engaging on these issues, Professor Schulhofer moves swiftly and predictably to the one part of my proposal that is designed to reduce *Miranda*'s social costs: the abolition of the prophylactic rules that require an affirmative waiver of rights and give suspects an unqualified right to avoid questioning. Here Professor Schulhofer's approach to the *Miranda* compromise is revealed to be intransigent. In essence, his stance is: 'What's mine is mine, and what's yours is negotiable.' Having conceded that '[vi]deotaping is an extremely valuable tool' for the suspect, he should be willing to admit, since *Miranda* is a 'carefully crafted balance,' that at least some part of current doctrine can be modified to reduce societal costs. Yet he puts not even a single reform on the bargaining table and, indeed, suggests only that videotaping might be piled on top of *Miranda*'s requirements."

construed to be an expression of a desire for the assistance of an attorney.' But if a suspect makes a reference to an attorney that is ambiguous or equivocal in that a reasonable officer in light of the circumstances would have understood only that the suspect *might* be invoking the right to counsel, our precedents do not require the cessation of questioning. * * *

"Rather, the suspect must unambiguously request counsel. As we have observed, 'a statement either is such an assertion of the right to counsel or it is not.' *Smith v. Illinois*. Although a suspect need not 'speak with the discrimination of an Oxford don' (Souter, J., concurring in judgment), he must articulate his desire to have counsel present sufficiently clearly that a reasonable police officer in the circumstances would understand the statement to be a request for an attorney. If the statement fails to meet the requisite level of clarity, *Edwards* does not require that the officers stop questioning the suspect. * * *

"We decline petitioner's invitation to extend *Edwards* and require law enforcement officers to cease questioning immediately upon the making of an ambiguous or equivocal reference to an attorney. See *Arizona v. Roberson,* (Kennedy, J., dissenting)('the rule of *Edwards* is our rule, not a constitutional command; and it is our obligation to justify its expansion'). The rationale underlying *Edwards* is that the police must respect a suspect's wishes regarding his right to have an attorney present during custodial interrogation. But when the officers conducting the questioning reasonably do not know whether or not the suspect wants a lawyer, a rule requiring the immediate cessation of questioning 'would transform the *Miranda* safeguards into wholly irrational obstacles to legitimate police investigative activity,' because it would needlessly prevent the police from questioning a suspect in the absence of counsel even if the suspect did not wish to have a lawyer present. Nothing in *Edwards* requires the provision of counsel to a suspect who consents to answer questions without the assistance of a lawyer. * * *

"We recognize that requiring a clear assertion of the right to counsel might disadvantage some suspects who—because of fear, intimidation, lack of linguistic skills, or a variety of other reasons—will not clearly articulate their right to counsel although they actually want to have a lawyer present. But the primary protection afforded suspects subject to custodial interrogation is the *Miranda* warnings themselves. '[F]ull comprehension of the rights to remain silent and request an attorney [is] sufficient to dispel whatever coercion is inherent in the interrogation process.' *Moran v. Burbine*. A suspect who knowingly and voluntarily waives his right to counsel after having that right explained to him has indicated his willingness to deal with the police unassisted. Although *Edwards* provides an additional protection—if a suspect subsequently requests an attorney, questioning must cease—it is one that must be affirmatively invoked by the suspect.

"In considering how a suspect must invoke the right to counsel, we must consider the other side of the *Miranda* equation: the need for effective law enforcement. Although the courts ensure compliance with the *Miranda* requirements through the exclusionary rule, it is police officers who must actually decide whether or not they can question a suspect. The *Edwards* rule—questioning must cease if the suspect asks for a lawyer—provides a bright line that can be applied by officers in the real world of investigation and interrogation without unduly hampering the gathering of information. But if we were to require questioning to cease if a suspect makes a statement that *might* be a request for an attorney, this clarity and ease of application would be lost. Police officers would be forced to make difficult judgment calls about whether the suspect in fact wants a lawyer even though he hasn't said so, with the threat of suppression if they guess wrong. We therefore hold that, after a knowing and voluntary waiver of the *Miranda* rights, law enforcement officers may continue questioning until and unless the suspect clearly requests an attorney.

"Of course, when a suspect makes an ambiguous or equivocal statement it will often be good police practice for the interviewing officers to clarify whether or not he actually wants an attorney. That was the procedure followed by the NIS agents in this case. Clarifying questions help protect the rights of the suspect by ensuring that he gets an attorney if he wants one, and will minimize the chance of a confession being suppressed due to subsequent judicial second-guessing as to the meaning of the suspect's statement regarding counsel. But we decline to adopt a rule requiring officers to ask clarifying questions. If the suspect's statement is not an unambiguous or unequivocal request for counsel, the officers have no obligation to stop questioning him.

"To recapitulate: We held in *Miranda* that a suspect is entitled to the assistance of counsel during custodial interrogation even though the Constitution does not provide for such assistance. We held in *Edwards* that if the suspect invokes the right to counsel at any time, the police must immediately cease questioning him until an attorney is present. But we are unwilling to create a third layer of prophylaxis to prevent police questioning when the suspect *might* want a lawyer. Unless the suspect actually requests an attorney, questioning may continue."[a]

Justice SOUTER, joined by Blackmun, Stevens and Ginsburg, JJ., wrote a separate opinion. Although he concurred in the judgment affirming Davis's conviction, "resting partly on evidence of statements given after agents ascertained that he did not wish to deal with them

---

a. The Court noted that "the Government has not sought to rely in this case on § 3501 [and] we therefore decline the invitation of some *amici* to consider it. Although we will consider arguments raised only in an *amicus* brief, we are reluctant to do so when the issue is one of first impression involving the interpretation of a federal statute on which the Department of Justice expressly declines to take a position." Justice Scalia wrote a concurring opinion, set forth in the Supp. at p. 68, discussing the applicability of § 3501 to *Miranda* issues and concluding that the Court's continuing refusal to consider § 3501 was inconsistent with "the Third Branch's obligation to decide according to the law."

through counsel," Justice Souter could not join the majority's "further conclusion that if the investigators here had been so inclined, they were at liberty to disregard Davis's reference to a lawyer entirely, in accordance with a general rule that interrogators have no legal obligation to discover what a custodial subject meant by an ambiguous statement that could reasonably be understood to express a desire to consult a lawyer":

"Our own precedent, the reasonable judgments of the majority of the many courts already to have addressed the issue before us, and the advocacy of a considerable body of law enforcement officials are to the contrary. All argue against the Court's approach today, which draws a sharp line between interrogated suspects who 'clearly' assert their right to counsel and those who say something that may, but may not, express a desire for counsel's presence, the former suspects being assured that questioning will not resume without counsel present, the latter being left to fend for themselves. The concerns of fairness and practicality that have long anchored our *Miranda* case law point to a different response: when law enforcement officials 'reasonably do not know whether or not the suspect wants a lawyer,' they should stop their interrogation and ask him to make his choice clear.

"While the question we address today is an open one, its answer requires coherence with nearly three decades of case law addressing the relationship between police and criminal suspects in custodial interrogation. Throughout that period, two precepts have commanded broad assent: that the *Miranda* safeguards exist 'to assure that *the individual's right to choose* between speech and silence remains unfettered throughout the interrogation process,' and that the justification for *Miranda* rules, intended to operate in the real world, 'must be consistent [with] practical realities.' *Arizona v. Roberson* (Kennedy, J., dissenting). A rule barring government agents from further interrogation until they determine whether a suspect's ambiguous statement was meant as a request for counsel fulfills both ambitions. It assures that a suspect's choice whether or not to deal with police through counsel will be 'scrupulously honored' and it faces both the real-world reasons why misunderstandings arise between suspect and interrogator and the real-world limitations on the capacity of police and trial courts to apply fine distinctions and intricate rules.

"Tested against the same two principles, the approach the Court adopts does not fare so well. First, as the majority expressly acknowledges, criminal suspects who may (in *Miranda*'s words) be 'thrust into an unfamiliar atmosphere and run through menacing police interrogation procedures,' would seem an odd group to single out for the Court's demand of heightened linguistic care. A substantial percentage of them lack anything like a confident command of the English language, many are 'woefully ignorant,' and many more will be sufficiently intimidated by the interrogation process or overwhelmed by the uncertainty of their predicament that the ability to speak assertively will abandon them.[4]

---

4. Social science confirms what common sense would suggest, that individuals who feel intimidated or powerless are more likely to speak in equivocal or nonstandard

Indeed, the awareness of just these realities has, in the past, dissuaded the Court from placing any burden of clarity upon individuals in custody, but has led it instead to require that requests for counsel be 'give[n] a broad, rather than a narrow, interpretation' and that courts 'indulge every reasonable presumption,' *Johnson v. Zerbst,* that a suspect has not waived his right to counsel under *Miranda.*

"[Nor] may the standard governing waivers as expressed in these statements be deflected away by drawing a distinction between initial waivers of *Miranda* rights and subsequent decisions to reinvoke them, on the theory that so long as the burden to demonstrate waiver rests on the government, it is only fair to make the suspect shoulder a burden of showing a clear subsequent assertion. *Miranda* itself discredited the legitimacy of any such distinction. The opinion described the object of the warning as being to assure 'a continuous opportunity to exercise [the right of silence].' '[C]ontinuous opportunity' suggests an unvarying one, governed by a common standard of effectiveness.

"[The] Court defends as tolerable the certainty that some poorly expressed requests for counsel will be disregarded on the ground that *Miranda* warnings suffice to alleviate the inherent coercion of the custodial interrogation. But, 'a once-stated warning, delivered by those who will conduct the interrogation cannot itself suffice' to 'assure that [the] right to choose between silence and speech remains unfettered throughout the interrogation process.' Nor does the Court's defense reflect a sound reading of the case it relies on, *Moran v. Burbine.* * * * While *Moran* held that a subject's knowing and voluntary waiver of the right to counsel is not undermined by the fact that police prevented an unsummoned lawyer from making contact with him, it contains no suggestion that *Miranda* affords as ready a tolerance for police conduct frustrating the suspect's subjectively held (if ambiguously expressed) desire for counsel. * * *

"Indeed, it is easy, amidst the discussion of layers of protection, to lose sight of a real risk in the majority's approach, going close to the core of what the Court has held that the Fifth Amendment provides. The experience of the timid or verbally inept suspect (whose existence the Court acknowledges) may not always closely follow that of the defendant in *Edwards* (whose purported waiver of his right to counsel, made after having invoked the right, was held ineffective, lest police be tempted to 'badge[r]' others like him.) Indeed, it may be more like that of the defendant in *Escobedo,* whose sense of dilemma was heightened by his interrogators' denial of his requests to talk to a lawyer. When a suspect understands his (expressed) wishes to have been ignored (and by hypothesis, he has said something that an objective listener could 'reasonably,' although not necessarily, take to be a request), in contravention of the

terms when no ambiguity or equivocation is meant. Suspects in police interrogation are strong candidates for these effects. Even while resort by the police to the 'third de-gree' has abated since *Miranda,* the basic forms of psychological pressure applied by police appear to have changed less. * * *

'rights' just read to him by his interrogator, he may well see further objection as futile and confession (true or not) as the only way to end his interrogation.

"Nor is it enough to say [as the majority does] that a 'statement either is [an] assertion of the right to counsel or it is not' [quoting *Smith v. Illinois*]. In *Smith*, we neither denied the possibility that a reference to counsel could be ambiguous nor suggested that particular statements should be considered in isolation. While it might be fair to say that every statement is meant either to express a desire to deal with police through counsel or not, this fact does not dictate the rule that interrogators who hear a statement consistent with either possibility may presume the latter and forge ahead; on the contrary, clarification is the intuitively sensible course.

"The other justifications offered for the 'requisite level of clarity' rule are that, whatever its costs, it will further society's strong interest in 'effective law enforcement', and maintain the 'ease of application' that has long been a concern of our *Miranda* jurisprudence. With respect to the first point, the margin of difference between the clarification approach advocated here and the one the Court adopts is defined by the class of cases in which a suspect, if asked, would make it plain that he meant to request counsel (at which point questioning would cease). While these lost confessions do extract a real price from society, it is one that *Miranda* itself determined should be borne.

"[As] for practical application, while every approach, including the majority's, will involve some 'difficult judgment calls,'[7] the rule argued for here would relieve the officer of any responsibility for guessing 'whether the suspect in fact wants a lawyer even though he hasn't said so.' To the contrary, it would assure that the 'judgment call' will be made by the party most competent to resolve the ambiguity, who our case law has always assumed should make it: the individual suspect.

"Although I am convinced that the Court has taken the wrong path, I am not persuaded by [Davis's] contention, that even ambiguous statements require an end to all police questioning. [While] it is plainly wrong, for example, to continue interrogation when the suspect wants it to stop (and so indicates), the strong bias in favor of individual choice may also be disserved by stopping questioning when a suspect wants it to continue (but where his statement might be understood otherwise).

---

7. In the abstract, nothing may seem more clear than a "clear statement" rule, but in police stations and trial courts the question, "how clear is clear?" is not so readily answered. When a suspect says, "uh, yeah, I'd like to do that" after being told he has a right to a lawyer, has he "clearly asserted" his right? Compare *Smith v. Illinois (per curiam)* (statement was " 'neither indecisive nor ambiguous' ") with [Justice Rehnquist's dissent in that case]. * * * (questioning clarity). * * *

As a practical matter, of course, the primary arbiters of "clarity" will be the interrogators themselves, who tend as well to be courts' preferred source in determining the precise words a suspect used. And when an inculpatory statement has been obtained as a result of an unrecorded, incommunicado interrogation, these officers rarely lose "swearing matches" against criminal defendants at suppression hearings.

[The] costs to society of losing confessions would, moreover, be especially hard to bear where the suspect, if asked for his choice, would have chosen to continue. One need not sign the majority's opinion here to agree that resort to the rule [Davis] argues for should be had only if experience shows that less drastic means of safeguarding suspects' constitutional rights are not up to the job * * *.

"Our cases are best respected by a rule that when a suspect under custodial interrogation makes an ambiguous statement that might reasonably be understood as expressing a wish that a lawyer be summoned (and questioning cease), interrogators' questions should be confined to verifying whether the individual meant to ask for a lawyer. While there is reason to expect that trial courts will apply today's ruling sensibly (without requiring criminal suspects to speak with the discrimination of an Oxford don) and that interrogators will continue to follow what the Court rightly calls 'good police practice' (compelled up to now by a substantial body of state and Circuit law), I believe that the case law under *Miranda* does not allow them to do otherwise."

THE IMPACT OF *MIRANDA* IN PRACTICE

8th ed., p. 600; after discussion of *Miranda*'s effects, add:

Almost all the early *Miranda* studies (cited in fn. c to p. 599 of the 8th ed.) indicate that the landmark case had only a negligible adverse impact on the effectiveness of police investigation. However, maintains Richard A. Leo, *The Impact of Miranda Revisited*, 86 J. Crim. L. & Criminology 621, 646–47 (1996), these studies are "outdated" and thus "largely irrelevant for assessing the current and ongoing impact of *Miranda* in America today." Moreover, adds Professor Leo, who has both a Ph.D. in sociology and a law degree, "with one or two exceptions, these studies—virtually all of which were conducted by lawyers or law professors not trained in the research methods of social science—are replete with methodological weaknesses." However, Professor Leo's own recent empirical study "does not support the assertion that *Miranda* has exercised an adverse impact on law enforcement." Id. at 677.

According to Leo, *id.* at 675, "the historical impact of *Miranda* on law enforcement has been largely to reframe how police talk and think about the process of custodial questioning and in so doing to professionalize interrogation practices and contribute to the declining use of coercion." Leo further concludes that "although the requirement of warnings undoubtedly causes some suspects to avoid cooperating with their interrogators, police have successfully adapted their practices to the legal requirements of *Miranda* by using conditioning, de-emphasizing, and persuasive strategies to orchestrate consent to custodial questioning in most cases." Id.

In *Miranda's Social Costs: An Empirical Reassessment*, 90 Nw. U.L.Rev. 387, 390 (1996), Professor Paul G. Cassell contends that despite the "conventional academic wisdom" to the contrary, "*Miranda* has significantly harmed law enforcement efforts in this country." *Mi-*

randa's effects, maintains Professor Cassell, "should be measured not by looking at suppression motions filed after police have obtained a confession, but rather by examining how many confessions police never obtain because of *Miranda*." Id. at 391.

According to Cassell, "the existing empirical data supports the tentative estimate that *Miranda* has led to lost cases against almost four percent [3.8%] of all criminal suspects in this country who are questioned."[a] Id. at 438. "While defenders of *Miranda* may argue that a 3.8% 'cost' is acceptable given *Miranda*'s benefits, critics will respond that the apparently small percentage figure multiplied across the run of criminal cases constitutes a large number of criminals."

Continues Cassell, id. at 440: For 1993 (the most recent year for which statistics are available) the Uniform Crime Reports (UCR) Crime Index reports 754,110 arrests for violent crimes and 2,094,300 arrests for property crimes. Multiplying the *Miranda* cost figure (3.8%) by the UCR index arrest figures suggests that in 1993 *Miranda* produced roughly 28,000 lost cases against suspects for index violent crimes and 79,000 lost cases against suspects for index property crimes." According to Cassell, the available data suggests that *Miranda* results in plea bargains to reduced charges in almost the same number of cases.[b]

Responding to Professor Cassell's article, Stephen J. Schulhofer, *Miranda's Practical Effect: Substantial Benefits and Vanishingly Small Social Costs,* 90 Nw.U.L.Rev. 500, 502 (1996), maintains that if one reexamines the old studies with all necessary qualifications in mind, "the properly adjusted attrition rate is not 3.8% but *at most* only 0.78%." Moreover, adds Professor Schulhofer, id. at 546–47, even this adjusted figure "still substantially overstates *Miranda*'s current effect. One major source of overestimation is organizational failure and general chaos in the criminal justice system. The resulting attrition dwarfs the 0.78% (or 3.8%) figure. To be sure, weak evidence often causes such attrition, and more confessions would thereby help reduce it. But much of the attrition is *unrelated* to the strength of the evidence. Cassell's own empirical research [referring to the 1994 Cassell–Hayman study of Salt Lake County discussed infra] indicates, for example, that 'questioning [was] successful' in 20% of the cases that prosecutors *chose to drop*. To focus on a 0.78% estimate as a concrete, quantifiable gain—in the porous, rough-and-tumble world of criminal justice—is simply unreal."

a. Professor Cassell recognizes that "in the empirical debate over the costs of the search and seizure exclusionary rule, defenders of the rule have made the plausible argument that the concept of a 'cost' is simply inappropriate" because "a case that is lost, either because the police did not unreasonably search or because the results of such a search were later suppressed, is simply the logical consequence of the Fourth Amendment." Id. at 471. However, continues Cassell: "Whatever force such an argument might have in the exclusionary rule context disappears in the *Miranda* context. * * * *Miranda*'s costs are generated regulations on police not required by the Constitution and to which reasonable alternatives clearly exist." Id. at 472.

b. Professor Cassell goes on to say that alternatives such as videotaping of police interrogations can "more effectively prevent coercion while reducing harms to society." See the extracts from his article at Supp., p. 76.

Most important, argues Schulhofer, "the great weight of the evidence confirms that police have now adjusted to the *Miranda* requirements and overcome the limited difficulties experienced in the immediate post-*Miranda* period. Altogether, a realistic working estimate of *Miranda*'s impact on current law enforcement must be placed for lower than the 0.78% figure. For practical purposes, *Miranda*'s demonstrable impact on conviction rates today is virtually nil."

In his rejoinder, *All Benefits, No Costs: The Grand Illusion of Miranda's Defenders,* 90 Nw.U.L.Rev. 1084, 1091–92 (1996), Professor Cassell maintains that both clearance rate data and confession rate data demonstrate that "over the long haul, law enforcement never recovered from the blow inflicted by *Miranda.*" Cassell relies, inter alia, on his own 1994 study of police interrogation in Salt Lake County, Paul G. Cassell & Bret Hayman, *Police Interrogation in the 1990s: An Empirical Study of the Effects of Miranda,* 43 UCLA L.Rev. 839 (1996), which found that suspects confessed or gave incriminating statements in only about a third "of all cases presented by police for prosecution"— according to Cassell, a confession rate well below the average rate before *Miranda.*[a]

The Salt Lake County study's low confession rate, charges Schulhofer, supra at 509 n. 28, "results from a good deal of unjustified juggling of the numbers": Cassell and Hayman include cases in which suspects were never questioned at all, they include non-custodial interrogations (although the best reading of the pre-*Miranda* studies is that they involved only custodial interrogation)[b] and they *exclude* cases in which the suspect gave "denials with explanation" although a substantial number of such "denials" probably should have been classified as incriminating statements.[c]

---

a. Professor Cassell recognizes that a 1994 study of interrogation by detectives in three California cities found an incriminating rate of about 64%. See Richard A. Leo, *Inside the Interrogation Room,* 86 J.Crim.L. & Criminology 266, 280 (1996); Richard A. Leo, Police Interrogation in America: A Study of Violence, Civility, and Social Change (1994) (unpublished Ph.D. dissertation, University of California (Berkley)). But Cassell argues that Leo's sample "needs to be adjusted to reflect suspects who are never questioned, suspects questioned in less productive noncustodial settings, and suspects questioned not only by detectives but also by less effective patrol officers. Such adjustments produce a confession rate of somewhere below 38.7%, quite close to what we found." Cassell rejoinder at 1091–92.

However, George C. Thomas III, *Plain Talk about the Miranda Empirical Debate: A "Steady–State" Theory of Confessions,* 43 UCLA L.Rev. 933, 953–54 (1996) maintains that Leo's methodology "is consistent with

the pre-*Miranda* studies," and that the attempt by Cassell to whittle down Leo's confession rate on methodological grounds "must be rejected." Id. at 954. According to Professor Thomas, it is not the Leo confession rate, but the Cassell–Hayman rate that should be adjusted—upward. See id. at 946–55.

b. Of the total Cassell–Hayman interrogations, 30.1% were in non-custodial settings, where one would naturally expect the police to be less successful. The Salt Lake County data confirm that non-custodial settings produce fewer successful interrogations (30.0%) than the custodial interrogations (56.9%)." Thomas, fn. a supra, at 946–47.

c. As pointed out in Thomas, fn. a supra, at 948, because not all suspects' responses to the police are incriminating, "researchers are forced to draw a distinction between incriminating and non-incriminating statements. Different researchers will classify borderline statements differently;

As already indicated, Professor Thomas, fn. a supra, criticizes the Cassell–Hayman Salt Lake County study on grounds similar to Schulhofer's (in fact Schulhofer relied in part on Thomas's article). Thomas concludes that if the adjustments to the Cassell–Hayman study he would make were accepted, "the Salt Lake County data looks remarkably like the pre-*Miranda* studies" and support the hypothesis that *Miranda* has had no effect on confession rates. *Id.* at 953. Adds Professor Thomas, id. at 956–57:

"Cassell and Hayman conclude that 12.1% of felony suspects 'who were questioned invoked their rights before police were successful in interrogation.' Two observations can be made about this figure. First, if the *Miranda*-dissenters and the police in 1966 had been told that the effect of *Miranda* would be limited to 12.1% of felony suspects, they would have cheered in relief. Thus, while significant, 12.1% is hardly crippling to the law enforcement enterprise.

"But another observation must be made: There is no way to credit *Miranda* with all of that 12.1%. Some suspects refused to cooperate with police prior to *Miranda*. The 12.1% who invoke their rights includes that category of suspects, now given an easier way to refuse to cooperate. On this point, though, Cassell and Hayman can find support among *Miranda*'s defenders. If *Miranda* is to have any of the effects envisioned by its supporters (reduce pressure in the interrogation room, level the playing field, increase equality among suspects), it simply must cause more invocations. Otherwise, *Miranda* is (as some cynics have charged) merely about symbolism and appearances. Thus, *Miranda* supporters should cheer an increase in invocations. Though the paucity of the pre-*Miranda* data makes hazardous any guess as to the magnitude of the difference, the Cassell–Hayman data, together with Leo's data, suggest that the effect may be rather substantial.[93]

"The available data thus seems to demonstrate that more suspects invoke their right to remain silent, and the rate of confessions is roughly the same. This divergence supports my steady-state theory: *Miranda* encourages some suspects not to talk and encourages others to talk too much. It is possible that, in the pre-*Miranda* era, fewer suspects refused to talk but more suspects gave terse answers. Perhaps more suspects refuse to talk today, but those who do talk have a *Miranda*-created incentive to tell a fuller story. The *Miranda* warnings might make suspects believe they can avoid being prosecuted only if they tell a story close enough to the truth that the police will be fooled into letting them

this is a problem with all *Miranda* studies." Adds Professor Thomas, id. at 949:

"The Cassell–Hayman study methodology here is more problematic than most. They use a category of unsuccessful outcomes called 'denial with explanation.' The test they use to decide whether a statement is 'incriminating' (and thus more than merely an 'explanation') is whether the statement had a 'primary import' to 'assist police in proving their case.' I think that is the wrong test. It is not the test used by at least one of the pre-*Miranda* studies and it is narrower than the *Miranda* Court's use of 'self-incrimination.' "

93. Leo's study finds an even greater rate of invocation: 21.7%. [See Richard A. Leo, *Inside the Interrogation Room,* 86 J.Crim.L. & Criminology 266, 275–76, 286 (1996).]

go. In the NIJ study, for example, more robbery suspects admitted being at the scene of the crime than gave an outright confession." [d]

In 1997, the Cassell–Schulhofer debate continued in the pages of another law journal. As evidence of Miranda's harmful effects, Professor Cassell notes that in 1965 the clearance rate for violent crime had been stable for several years and stood at nearly 60 percent—only to plunge more than twelve percentage points in the next three years. See Paul G. Cassell, *Miranda's "Negligible" Effect on Law Enforcement: Some Skeptical Observations*, 20 Harv. J. L. Pub. Pol'y 327, 333–35 (1997). Professor Schulhofer responds that clearance capacity (the number of officers and dollars available to investigate each reported crime) collapsed in the late 1960s as crime rose sharply and that the dramatic reduction in clearance *capacity* provides "the most likely explanation" for the significant decline in the clearance *rates* that occurred at the same time. Schulhofer points out that after *Miranda* the *number* of crimes cleared continued to rise. See Stephen J. Schulhofer, *Bashing Miranda is Unjustified—and Harmful*, 20 Harv. J.L. Pub. Pol'y 347, 357–62 (1997). Cassell concedes that rising crime rates, which stretched police resources thinner, may have had some effect on declining clearance rates, but insists that *Miranda* is partly to blame. See Cassell, supra, at 333–35.

At this point, another law professor joined the debate, Peter Arenella, *Miranda Stories*, 20 Harv. J.L. Pub. Pol'y 375 (1997), observing, id. at 375–76:

"Neither the 'conservative' nor the 'liberal' tale provides a fully plausible account of *Miranda*'s impact on our criminal justice system because both stories commit the same fundamental error: exaggerating either *Miranda*'s costs (Cassell) or benefits (Schulhofer). Moreover, each story generates an obvious question that neither author answers persuasively. If Cassell's account is accurate, why have the police and a conservative Supreme Court shown no interest in eliminating the *Miranda* regime? Conversely, if Schulhofer is right (and I believe he is) that the *Miranda* regime has not impaired law enforcement's ability to secure incriminating admissions, how exactly does *Miranda*'s negligible impact demonstrate its success in eliminating the 'inherent coerciveness' of police interrogation?"

As this supplement went to press, the controversy, revivified by Professor Cassell, over *Miiranda*'s costs and benefits had spilled into the pages of the *Stanford Law Review*. See Paul Cassell & Richard Fowles, *Handcuffing the Cops? A Thirty-Yeae Perspective on Miranda's Harmful Effects on Law Enforcement*, 50 Stan.L.Rev. 1055 1998); John J. Dono-

---

d. See also George C. Thomas III, *Is Miranda A Real-World Failure? A Plea for More (and Better) Empirical Evidence,* 43 UCLA L.Rev. 821, 823–24 (1996): "I believe the *Miranda* warnings have simultaneous, and roughly off-setting, effects. The warnings discourage suspects from making outright acknowledgments of guilt, but they encourage suspects to talk to police and thus often incriminate themselves indirectly. Second, I believe the most important predictor of success in interrogation is how much the police think they need a confession. Because what the police need is extraneous to the suspect's mental calculus about the advisability of confessing, warnings are irrelevant."

hue, III, *Did Miranda Diminish Police Effectiveness?*, Stan.L.Rev. 1147 (1998); Paul Cassell & Richard Fowles, *Falling Clearance Rates after Miranda: Coincidence or Consequence?*, 50 Stan.L.rev. 1181 (1998).

ANOTHER LOOK AT *MIRANDA:* " 'TWAS A FAMOUS VICTORY"

8th ed., p. 607, end of fn. e to David Simon's *Homicide*, add:

But consider Richard A. Leo, *The Impact of Miranda Revisited*, 86 J. Crim. L. & Criminology 621, 680–81 (1996): [To adopt Professor Ogletree's proposal to provide all custodial suspects with a nonwaivable right to counsel before being questioned by the police] would not merely affirmatively discourage admissions and confessions to police, but would altogether eliminate them as a source of evidence in the criminal process. That is simply too high a price to pay in as violent and crime-ridden a society as America: neither the Constitution nor common sense would warrant such a legal requirement. The Fifth Amendment prohibits only compelled testimony; it should not be invoked as legal authority with which to discourage or render impossible non-compelled testimony to police." See also Donald Dripps, *Against Police Interrogation—and the Privilege Against Self-Incrimination,* 78 J. Crim. L & C. 699, 723 (1988).

8th ed., p. 608, end of fn. g to David Simon's *Homicide*, add:

Does *Davis v. United States,* Supp., p. 82, vindicate the detective's view of the *Miranda–Edwards* rule?

8th ed., p. 609; after the extract from David Simon's *Homicide*, add:

Pointing to police training materials uncovered in the course of litigation seeking to stop officers in two California police departments from questioning custodial suspects after they have asserted their *Miranda* rights, Professor Charles Weisselberg maintains, *Saving Miranda*, 84 Cornell L.Rev. ___ (1998) (forthcoming), that "[in] California and, to a certain extent in other states, police have developed the tactics of questioning 'outside *Miranda*,' meaning questioning over the direct and unambiguous assertion of Fifth Amendment rights." Set forth below are extracts from the remarks of Devallis Rutledge in a California police training videotape. Mr. Rutledge is an Orange County Deputy District Attorney and a member of the California Commission on Peace Officer Standards and Training. The full transcript of the videotape is reprinted in the Appendix to Professor Weisselberg's forthcoming article.

CALIFORNIA POLICE TRAINING VIDEOTAPE— QUESTIONING " OUTSIDE *MIRANDA*" (1990)

This has to do with questioning "outside *Miranda*." * * *

What if you've got a guy [in custody] that you've only got one shot at? This is it, it's now or never because you're gonna lose him—he's gonna bail out or a lawyer's on the way down there, or you're gonna have to take him over to some other officials—you're never gonna have another chance at this guy, this is it. And you Mirandize him and he invokes. What you can do—legally do—in that instance is go "outside *Miranda*" and continue to talk to him because you've got other legitimate purposes in talking to him other than obtaining an admission of guilt that can be used in his trial. And that's what *Miranda* protects him against—you compelling him to make a statement that is later used in trial to convict him of the charge. But you may want to go "outside *Miranda*" and get information to help you clear cases. * * * Or, maybe it will help you recover a dead body or missing person. * * * You may be able to recover stolen property. He tells you where the property is ditched, his statement will not be admissible against him in trial if you go "outside *Miranda*," but you'll get the property back and the owner will get the property back. That's a legitimate function. Maybe his statement "outside *Miranda*" will reveal methods—his methods of operation. How he was able to obtain these credit cards and how he was able to pull off this scam or whatever. * * *

Or his statements might reveal the existence and the location of physical evidence. You've got him, but you'd kinda like to have the gun that he used or the knife that he used or whatever else it was. But he ditched it somewhere and you can't find it. And so you've arrested him, he's invoked *Miranda* and you say, "Well I'd still like to find the evidence in the case." So you go "outside *Miranda*," and if he talks "outside *Miranda*"—if the only thing that was shutting him up was the chance of it being used against him in court—and then you go "outside *Miranda*" and take a statement and then he tells you where the stuff is, we can go and get all that evidence.[1]

And it forces the defendant to commit to a statement that will prevent him from pulling out some defense and using it at trial—that he's cooked up with some defense lawyer—that wasn't true. So if you get a statement "outside *Miranda*" and he tells you that he did it and how he did it or if he gives you a denial of some sort, he's tied to that, he is married to that, because the U.S. Supreme Court [and] the California Supreme Court [have] told us that we can use statements "outside *Miranda*" to impeach or to rebut.[2] We can't use them for our case in chief. The D.A. can't trot them out to the jury before he says, "I rest," but if the defendant then gets up there and gets on the stand and lies and says something different, we can use his "outside *Miranda*" statements to impeach him. We can use it to rebut his case.

* * * The *Miranda* exclusionary rule is limited to the defendant's own statement out of his mouth. That is all that is excluded under *Miranda*. It doesn't have a fruits of the poisonous tree theory attached to it the way constitutional violations do. When you violate *Miranda*, you're not violating the Constitution. *Miranda* is not in the Constitution. It's a court-created decision that affects the admissibility of testimonial evidence and that's all it is. [There's] no law says you can't question people "outside *Miranda*." You don't violate the Constitution. The Constitution

---

1. Consider *Oregon v. Elstad*, 8th ed., p. 824, and the Notes & Questions that follow.

2. See *Harris v. New York*, 8th ed., p. 833, and *Oregon v. Hass*, 8th ed., p. 834.

doesn't say you have to do that. It's a court decision. So all you're violating is a court decision controlling admissibility of evidence. So you're not doing anything unlawful, you're not doing anything illegal, you're not violating anybody's civil rights, you're doing nothing improper. [When we question someone who has invoked his *Miranda* rights] [a]ll we lose is the statement taken in violation of *Miranda*. We do not lose physical evidence that resulted from that. We do not lose the testimony of other witnesses that we learned about only by violating his *Miranda* invocation.[3]

SECTION 4. THE "DUE PROCESS"— "VOLUNTARINESS" TEST REVISITED

A. *MILLER V. FENTON:* WHAT KINDS OF TRICKERY OR DECEPTION, IF ANY, MAY THE POLICE EMPLOY *AFTER* A SUSPECT HAS WAIVED HIS RIGHTS?

8th ed., p. 609; after first ¶ of subsection, add:

A recent empirical study of police interrogation in three California cities, Richard A. Leo, *Inside the Interrogation Room,* 86 J.Crim.L. & Criminology 263 (1996), indicates that a number of the police interrogation techniques the *Miranda* Court lamented "—undermining a suspect's confidence in his denial of guilt, offering moral justification for the behavior, and confronting suspects with fabricated evidence of their guilt, to name but a few—appear to be exceedingly common in contemporary American police interrogations." Id. at 302. Certain interrogation tactics were highly likely to elicit incriminating information. Appealing to the suspect's conscience was successful in 97% of the interrogations in which it was used; the tactics of identifying contradictions in the suspect's denial of involvement, of offering the suspect a moral justification or psychological excuse for his behavior, and using praise or flattery was successful in 90% or more of the interrogations in which they were used. See id. at 293.

8th ed., p. 610; after 2nd full ¶, add:

Recently, there has been much thoughtful writing about police lying and other deception in interrogations and/or the extent to which such police tactics produce false confessions. See Albert Alschuler, *Constraint and Confession,* 74 Denv.U.L.Rev. 957 (1997); Paul Cassell, *Balanced Approaches to the False Confession Problem: A Brief Comment on Ofshe, Leo and Alschuler,* 74 Denv.U.L.Rev. 1123 (1997); Richard Ofshe & Richard Leo, *The Decision to Confess Falsely: Rational Choices and Irrational Action,* 74 Denv.U.L.Rev. 979 (1997); Christopher Slobogin, *Deceit, Pretext, and Trickery: Investigative Lies By the Police,* 76 Or. L.Rev. 101 (1997) (forthcoming); Welsh White, *False Confessions and the Constitution: Safeguards Against Untrustworthy Confessions,* 32 Harv.

---

3. See *Michigan v. Tucker,* 8th ed., pp. 502, 825.

C.R.-C.L. L.Rev. 105 (1997); Deborah Young, *Unnecessary Evil: Police Lying in Interrogations,* 28 Conn.L.Rev. 425 (1996).

B. *COLORADO V. CONNELLY*: DID THE COURT DECLINE TO EXPAND THE "VOLUNTARINESS" TEST OR DID IT REVISE THE TEST SIGNIFICANTLY?

8th ed., p. 626; add to Note 3:

Albert Alschuler, *Constraint and Confession,* 74 Denv.U.L.Rev. 957, 959 (1997), maintains that "pre-*Connelly* efforts to assess whether confessions were the product of free will were always misguided—incoherent in concept, unadministerable in practice, and incompatible with our general understanding of the Bill of Rights as a body of restraints on improper governmental conduct." Professor Alschuler continues: "One can, if one likes, find sufficient governmental action to satisfy the governmental-action requirements of the Fifth and Fourteenth Amendments simply in the admission at trial of a mentally disturbed person's confession—but I do not know why one would want to. Especially in a constitutional system incorporating the principle that 'the trial of all Crimes * * * shall be by Jury' permitting a jury rather than a judge to assess the evidentiary value of a confession obtained without governmental misconduct seems fully compatible with due process."

8th ed., p. 627; add to Note 4:

But consider Alschuler, supra Note 3, at 959–60: "Just as the Constitution does not mandate the exclusion of unreliable eyewitness testimony, it does not mandate the exclusion of unreliable confessions. An almost blind witness may tell a jury she saw the defendant commit a crime despite the fact she previously gave four inconsistent statements and has been convicted of perjury five times. The Constitution requires the exclusion of unreliable eyewitness testimony only when improper governmental conduct—for example, an impermissibly suggestive police line-up—has produced it.

"The rule should be no different for unreliable confessions. Unless improper governmental conduct has generated a confession, the Constitution should give the defendant only a right to present evidence of the confession's unreliability to the jury. With few exceptions, the Constitution makes juries the appropriate judges of the probative value of evidence in criminal cases."

SECTION 5. *MASSIAH* REVISITED; *MASSIAH* AND *MIRANDA* COMPARED AND CONTRASTED

A. THE REVIVIFICATION OF *MASSIAH*

8th ed., p. 642; add to Note on the "no-contact" rule:

A rule promulgated by Attorney General Janet Reno (codified at 28 C.F.R. pt. 77 and set forth in its entirety in 53 Crim.L.Rep. 2269 (Aug.

10, 1994)) purporting to exempt federal government lawyers from state ethical rules prohibiting ex parte communications with parties represented by counsel was struck down in part in *United States ex rel. O'Keefe v. McDonnell Douglas Corp.*, 132 F.3d 1252 (8th Cir.1998). The particular regulation at issue, 28 C.F.R. § 77.10(a), dealt with employees of organizations represented by counsel, but the Eighth Circuit opinion seems to apply to the entire set of regulations of which § 77.10(a) is a part.

Because Missouri Supreme Court rules based on Model Rule 4.2 (and adopted by the U.S. District Court for the Eastern district of Missouri) barred such ex parte contacts, the federal district court issued a protective order preventing federal government attorneys from engaging in ex parte communications with employees of defendant corporation without the consent of the corporation's counsel. The government argued that the protective order was unwarranted because its lawyers' conduct was authorized by 28 C.F.R. § 77.10(a).

The Eighth Circuit, per Hansen, J., disagreed. It concluded that neither the "Housekeeping Statute," 5 U.S.C. § 301 (which provides that the head of an executive agency may prescribe regulations for the governance of his or her department and the conduct of department employees) nor various provisions of Title 28 relating to the powers and duties of the Attorney General and the role of U.S. Attorneys provide a basis for the regulation promulgated by the Attorney General.

––––––

The Department of Justice has voiced support for a proposal being discussed by the Chief Justices of the State Supreme Courts which would allow the ex parte contacts permitted by the Justice Department regulation. For the text of this proposal see 62 Crim.L.Rep. 2043 (Jan. 14, 1998). See also 63 Crim.L.Rep. 337 (June 17, 1998).

Chapter 10

GRAND JURY INVESTIGATIONS

SECTION 4. APPLICATION OF THE PRIVILEGE AGAINST SELF–INCRIMINATION

8th ed., p. 729; replacing Note 3:

3. *Incrimination under the laws of another sovereign.* For many years, American courts took the position that the privilege protected only against incrimination under the laws of the sovereign which was attempting to compel the incriminating testimony. Then, in *Murphy v. Waterfront Comm.*, 378 U.S. 52, 84 S.Ct. 1594, 12 L.Ed.2d 678 (1964), the Supreme Court rejected this "separate sovereign" limitation as applied to state and federal inquiries. The Court concluded that the "policies and purposes" of the Fifth Amendment required that the privilege protect "a state witness against incrimination under federal as well as state law and a federal witness against incrimination under state as well as federal law." In UNITED STATES v. BALSYS, ___ U.S. ___, 118 S.Ct. 2218, ___ L.Ed.2d ___ (1998), the Court majority (7–2) held that the separate sovereign doctrine continued to apply as to incrimination under the laws of a foreign country. Thus, respondent Balsys, a resident alien subpoenaed to testify about his possible participation in Nazi persecution during World War II, could not utilize the privilege to refuse to provide answers which could subject him to a "real and substantial danger of prosecution of Lithuania and Israel." (The only consequence of his testimony in this country was deportation, long established as having a "civil character").

The Court majority [per SOUTER, J.] initially rejected respondent's contention that the phrase "any criminal case" in the self-incrimination clause literally encompasses all prosecutions, no matter where they might occur. That phrase, the Court noted, must be read in the context of a Fifth Amendment which encompasses various other guarantees (grand jury indictment, double jeopardy, due process, and just compensation), which are only implicated "by action of the government that it binds." The phrase "any criminal case" sensibly should be read as aimed simply at making clear that the self-incrimination clause, as distinguished from the grand jury clause, was not limited to capital or otherwise infamous crimes. In the absence of "legislative history" or "common law practice at the time of the Framing" which suggested otherwise, the Court would "read the Clause contextually as apparently providing a witness with the right against compelled self-incrimination when reasonably fearing prosecution by the government whose power the Clause limits, but not otherwise."

Further support for excluding foreign prosecution was found in a series of pre-*Murphy* rulings (e.g., *United States v. Murdock*) that had recognized the separate sovereign limitation in the context of federal/state prosecutions, relying in part on the English recognition of that limitation in the context of prosecutions by other nations. The Court majority acknowledged that *Murphy,* in overturning that earlier precedent as to federal/state prosecutions, included reasoning that supported a complete rejection of the separate sovereign limitation. Thus, the two dissenting justices (Ginsberg, J. and Breyer, J.), relied in part on *Murphy*'s reading of the legal history of the privilege (including the English common law), and on *Murphy*'s analysis of the purposes of the privilege, as inconsistent with a separate sovereign limitation. As to legal history, the *Balsys* majority rejected *Murphy*'s conclusion that the earlier cases recognizing a separate sovereign limitation had misread the English common law precedent. As to policy, the Court noted that, while *Murphy* catalogued multiple "aspirations" of the self-incrimination clause [see 8th ed., p. 750], some of which might support its extension to the fear of foreign prosecution, *Murphy* had failed "to weigh the host of competing policy concerns that would be raised in a legitimate reconsideration of the Clause's scope."[a] Those costs included the loss of evidence in domestic courts, resulting in arguably "serious consequences" for domestic law enforcement, due to the government's inability to grant immunity that would extend to foreign prosecution.

The *Balsys* majority concluded that *Murphy* is better read as resting on an "alternative rationale," which tied its rejection of the separate sovereign limitation to the applicability of the self-incrimination privilege to both the federal and state governments. The Court explained:

"*[M]urphy* was undoubtedly correct, given the decision rendered that very day in *Malloy v. Hogan* [8th ed., p. 36, fn.a], which applied the doctrine of Fourteenth Amendment due process incorporation to the Self–Incrimination Clause, so as to bind the States as well as the National Government to recognize the privilege. * * * As the Court immediately thereafter said in *Murphy, Malloy* 'necessitate[d] a reconsideration' of the unqualified *Murdock* rule that a witness subject to testimonial compulsion in one jurisdiction, state or federal, could not plead fear of prosecution in the other. After *Malloy,* the Fifth Amend-

---

a. Justices Scalia and Thomas did not join Part IV of the opinion for the Court, which considered relevant (and discussed) *Murphy*'s discussion of self-incrimination policies and competing policy concerns not considered in *Murphy.*

ment limitation could no longer be seen as framed for one jurisdiction alone, each jurisdiction having instead become subject to the same claim of privilege flowing from the one limitation. Since fear of prosecution in the one jurisdiction bound by the Clause now implicated the very privilege binding upon the other, the *Murphy* opinion sensibly recognized that if a witness could not assert the privilege in such circumstances, the witness could be 'whipsawed into incriminating himself under both state and federal law even though the constitutional privilege against self-incrimination is applicable to each.' 378 U.S., at 55. The whipsawing was possible owing to a feature unique to the guarantee against self-incrimination among the several Fifth Amendment privileges. In the absence of waiver, the other such guarantees are purely and simply binding on the government. But under the Self–Incrimination Clause, the government has an option to exchange the stated privilege for an immunity to prosecutorial use of any compelled inculpatory testimony. *Kastigar v. United States* [8th ed., p. 744]. The only condition on the government when it decides to offer immunity in place of the privilege to stay silent is the requirement to provide an immunity as broad as the privilege itself. After *Malloy* had held the privilege binding on the state jurisdictions as well as the National Government, it would therefore have been intolerable to allow a prosecutor in one or the other jurisdiction to eliminate the privilege by offering immunity less complete than the privilege's dual jurisdictional reach. *Murphy* accordingly held that a federal court could not receive testimony compelled by a State in the absence of a statute effectively providing for federal immunity, and it did this by imposing an exclusionary rule prohibiting the National Government 'from making any such use of compelled testimony and its fruits.'

"This view of *Murphy* as necessitated by *Malloy* was adopted in the subsequent case of *Kastigar v. United States,* supra. Read this way, *Murphy* rests upon the same understanding of the Self–Incrimination Clause that *Murdock* recognized and to which the earlier cases had pointed. Although the Clause serves a variety of interests in one degree or another, at its heart lies the principle that the courts of a government from which a witness may reasonably fear prosecution may not in fairness compel the witness to furnish testimonial evidence that may be used to prove his guilt. After *Murphy,* the immunity option open to the Executive Branch could only be exercised on the understanding that the state and federal jurisdictions were as one, with a federally mandated exclusionary rule filling the space between the limits of state immunity statutes and the scope of the privilege. As so understood, *Murphy* stands at odds with Balsys's claim."

8th ed., p. 758; add to Note 5:

In *United States v. Balsys,* discussed above, the majority questioned *Murphy*'s suggestion that self-incrimination privilege reflects " 'the inviolability of the human personality and * * * the right of each individual to a private enclave where he may lead a private life' " (quoting

Murphy). The *Balsys* Court noted: "If in fact these values were reliable guides to the actual scope of protection under the Clause, they would be seen to demand a very high degree of protection indeed: 'inviolability' is, after all, an uncompromising term, and we know as well from Fourth Amendment law as from a layman's common sense that breaches of privacy are complete at the moment of illicit intrusion, whatever use may or may not later be made of their fruits. * * * The Fifth Amendment tradition, however, offers no such degree of protection. If the Government is ready to provide the requisite use and derivative use immunity, the protection goes no further: no violation of personality is recognized and no claim of privilege will avail. One might reply that the choice of the word 'inviolability' was just unfortunate; while testimonial integrity may not be inviolable, it is sufficiently served by requiring the Government to pay a price in the form of use (and derivative use) immunity before a refusal to testify will be overruled. But that answer overlooks the fact that when a witness's response will raise no fear of criminal penalty, there is no protection for testimonial privacy at all. Thus, what we find in practice is not the protection of personal testimonial inviolability, but a conditional protection of testimonial privacy subject to basic limits recognized before the framing and refined through immunity doctrine in the intervening years."

Chapter 11

THE SCOPE OF THE EXCLUSIONARY RULES

SECTION 2. THE "FRUIT OF THE POISONOUS TREE"

B. The "Inevitable Discovery" Doctrine: The Sequel to *Brewer v. Williams*

8th ed., p. 823; add new Note:

5. *The issue not reached in Wilson v. Arkansas.* In *Wilson v. Arkansas*, Supp., p. 25, the Court declined to reach an argument put forward as an alternative ground for affirming denial of defendant's suppression motion: "that exclusion is not a constitutionally compelled remedy where the unreasonableness of a search stems from the failure of announcement. Analogizing to the 'independent source' doctrine applied in *Segura* [8th ed., p. 814], and the 'inevitable discovery' rule adopted in *Nix v. Williams*, respondent and its amici argue that any evidence seized after an unreasonable, unannounced entry is causally disconnected from the constitutional violation and that exclusion goes beyond the goal of precluding any benefit to the government flowing from the constitutional violation."

Assuming that the Court had reached this issue, what (would) (should) the result be?

C. Is a Confession Obtained in Violation of *Miranda* a "Poisonous Tree"?

8th ed., p. 832; add new Note:

6. *The physical fruits of coerced confessions.* Should courts admit physical evidence derived from coerced confessions? Is this a logical extension of the sharp distinction the Court drew in *Schmerber v. California* (8th ed., p. 45) between words and physical evidence? Did Justice O'Connor point the way in *Quarles* (8th ed., p. 823)? Could the

same result also be reached by simply expanding the inevitable discovery doctrine adopted in *Nix v. Williams* (8th ed., p. 818), i.e., by simply presuming that the fruits of a coerced confession could or would always have come to light anyway? Compare Akhil Reed Amar and Renée B. Lettow, *Fifth Amendment First Principles: The Self–Incrimination Clause*, 93 Mich.L.Rev. 857 (1995) (yes) *with* Yale Kamisar, *On the Fruits of Miranda Violations, Coerced Confessions and Compelled Testimony*, 93 Mich.L.Rev. 929 (1995) (no).

SECTION 3. USE OF ILLEGALLY OBTAINED EVIDENCE FOR IMPEACHMENT PURPOSES

A. THE EXPANSION OF A ONCE-NARROW EXCEPTION

8th ed., p. 834; after Note 4, add:

4a. *Does the Harris–Hass exception apply even when a police officer deliberately fails to honor a suspect's request for counsel with the objective of obtaining evidence for impeachment purposes? Even when an officer fails to honor a suspect's request for counsel pursuant to a police department policy to violate Miranda in order to obtain evidence for impeachment purposes?* In PEOPLE v. PEEVY, 73 Cal.Rptr.2d 865 (1998), the California Supreme Court, per GEORGE, J., answered the first question in the affirmative. However, it did not reach the second question because the issue had not been timely raised below. As for the first question, the court rejected the defendant's argument that the *Harris-Hass* rule was based upon the assumption that a *purposeful* or *deliberate* violation of *Miranda* and *Edwards* would not occur:

"Language in *Hass* and subsequent cases [demonstrates the U.S. Supreme Court's belief] that the *Harris* rule sufficiently deters individual police misconduct, *whether the misconduct occurred as the result of negligence or design.* In *Hass*, there is some indication that the violation of the suspect's rights was deliberate. * * * In *Michigan v. Harvey* [8th ed., p. 843], it is even more apparent that the interrogating police officer's failure to honor the defendant's Sixth Amendment right to counsel was deliberate.

"[Moreover,] it would be anomalous to hold that the applicability of the *Harris* rule depends upon the subjective intent of the interrogating police officer, when other applications of the *Miranda* rule generally do not turn upon the individual officer's state of mind, but rather upon the accused's perception of his or her circumstances. * * * [To] the extent we wish to serve *Edwards's* goal of protecting the suspect from the coercive pressure to waive the privilege against self-incrimination that is inherent in custodial interrogation and to recognize only waivers of constitutional rights that are knowing and voluntary, the suspect's perception of the coerciveness of his or her circumstances is not altered when the officer possesses an *unspoken* intent to violate *Edwards* for the purpose of securing impeachment evidence. * * * [E]vidence of deliberation on the part of the police and—as apparent in this case—of a purpose to violate the suspect's rights in order to secure evidence * * * may call into question the accuracy of the high court's conclusion in *Harris* that police misconduct will be deterred adequately by excluding improperly obtained evidence from the prosecution's case-in-chief, but such evidence does not render the *Harris* rule inapplicable."

Although concurring Justice MOSK concurred in the result, he made clear his belief that if a statement secured in violation of a suspect's right to counsel had been obtained by a member of a law enforcement agency pursuant to that agency's policy to violate *Miranda* the statement could not be used for impeachment purposes:

"Any policy of a law enforcement agency to obtain statements from criminal suspects in violation of *Miranda* would strike through the suspect's 'prophylactic' rights towards his substantive Fifth Amendment privilege against self-incrimination itself. * * * Moreover, any policy of a law enforcement agency to obtain statements from criminal suspects in violation of *Miranda* would necessarily constitute proof that 'sufficient deterrence' of [police misconduct] does not, in fact, 'flow from exclusion of such statements from the prosecution's case-in-chief' [quoting from *Harris*]. At the same time, it would necessarily constitute proof that a more than sufficient incentive to such conduct is given by their admissibility under the impeachment exception * * *. For, in a situation of this sort, 'proscribed * * * conduct' would not figure merely as a 'speculative possibility' [quoting from *Harris*]. It would rather present itself as an actual fact.

"[It] may indeed be true, as stated in *Michigan v. Tucker,* that '[where] official action [is] pursued in complete good faith [the] deterrence rationale loses much of its force.' But if so, it must also be true that, where official action is pursued in utter bad faith, as in accordance with the type of policy in question, the deterrence rationale retains its force without any diminution whatsoever."

Part Three

THE COMMENCEMENT OF FORMAL PROCEEDINGS

Chapter 13

THE DECISION WHETHER TO PROSECUTE

SECTION 3. CHALLENGING THE PROSECUTOR'S DISCRETION

II. THE DECISION TO PROSECUTE
8th ed., p. 917; replacing *Wayte*

UNITED STATES v. ARMSTRONG

517 U.S. 456, 116 S.Ct. 1480, 134 L.Ed.2d 687 (1996).

Chief Justice REHNQUIST delivered the opinion of the Court. * * *

In April 1992, respondents were indicted in the United States District Court for the Central District of California on charges of conspiring to possess with intent to distribute more than 50 grams of cocaine base (crack) and conspiring to distribute the same, in violation of 21 U.S.C. §§ 841 and 846, and federal firearms offenses. For three months prior to the indictment, agents of the Federal Bureau of Alcohol, Tobacco, and Firearms and the Narcotics Division of the Inglewood, California, Police Department had infiltrated a suspected crack distribution ring by using three confidential informants. On seven separate occasions during this period, the informants had bought a total of 124.3 grams of crack from respondents and witnessed respondents carrying firearms during the sales. The agents searched the hotel room in which

105

the sales were transacted, arrested respondents Armstrong and Hampton in the room, and found more crack and a loaded gun. The agents later arrested the other respondents as part of the ring.

In response to the indictment, respondents filed a motion for discovery or for dismissal of the indictment, alleging that they were selected for federal prosecution because they are black. In support of their motion, they offered only an affidavit by a "Paralegal Specialist," employed by the Office of the Federal Public Defender representing one of the respondents. The only allegation in the affidavit was that, in every one of the 24 §§ 841 or 846 cases closed by the office during 1991, the defendant was black. Accompanying the affidavit was a "study" listing the 24 defendants, their race, whether they were prosecuted for dealing cocaine as well as crack, and the status of each case.

The Government opposed the discovery motion, arguing, among other things, that there was no evidence or allegation "that the Government has acted unfairly or has prosecuted non-black defendants or failed to prosecute them." The District Court granted the motion. It ordered the Government (1) to provide a list of all cases from the last three years in which the Government charged both cocaine and firearms offenses, (2) to identify the race of the defendants in those cases, (3) to identify what levels of law enforcement were involved in the investigations of those cases, and (4) to explain its criteria for deciding to prosecute those defendants for federal cocaine offenses.

The Government moved for reconsideration of the District Court's discovery order. With this motion it submitted affidavits and other evidence to explain why it had chosen to prosecute respondents and why respondents' study did not support the inference that the Government was singling out blacks for cocaine prosecution. The federal and local agents participating in the case alleged in affidavits that race played no role in their investigation. An Assistant United States Attorney explained in an affidavit that the decision to prosecute met the general criteria for prosecution, because "there was over 100 grams of cocaine base involved, over twice the threshold necessary for a ten year mandatory minimum sentence; there were multiple sales involving multiple defendants, thereby indicating a fairly substantial crack cocaine ring; . . . there were multiple federal firearms violations intertwined with the narcotics trafficking; the overall evidence in the case was extremely strong, including audio and videotapes of defendants; . . . and several of the defendants had criminal histories including narcotics and firearms violations." The Government also submitted sections of a published 1989 Drug Enforcement Administration report which concluded that "[l]arge-scale, interstate trafficking networks controlled by Jamaicans, Haitians and Black street gangs dominate the manufacture and distribution of crack."

In response, one of respondents' attorneys submitted an affidavit alleging that an intake coordinator at a drug treatment center had told her that there are "an equal number of caucasian users and dealers to minority users and dealers." Respondents also submitted an affidavit from a criminal defense attorney alleging that in his experience many nonblacks are prosecuted in state court for crack offenses, and a newspaper article reporting that Federal "crack criminals . . . are being punished far more severely than if they had been caught with powder cocaine, and almost every single one of them is black."

The District Court denied the motion for reconsideration. When the Government indicated it would not comply with the court's discovery order, the court dismissed the case.[2]

A divided three-judge panel of the Court of Appeals for the Ninth Circuit reversed, holding that, because of the proof requirements for a selective-prosecution claim, defendants must "provide a colorable basis for believing that 'others similarly situated have not been prosecuted'" to obtain discovery. The Court of Appeals voted to rehear the case en banc, and the en banc panel affirmed the District Court's order of dismissal, holding that "a defendant is not required to demonstrate that the government has failed to prosecute others who are similarly situated." We granted certiorari to determine the appropriate standard for discovery for a selective-prosecution claim.

Neither the District Court nor the Court of Appeals mentioned Federal Rule of Criminal Procedure 16, which by its terms governs discovery in criminal cases. Both parties now discuss the Rule in their briefs, and respondents contend that it supports the result reached by the Court of Appeals. Rule 16 provides, in pertinent part: "Upon request of the defendant the government shall permit the defendant to inspect and copy or photograph books, papers, documents, photographs, tangible objects, buildings or places, or copies or portions thereof, which are within the possession, custody or control of the government, and which are material to the preparation of the defendant's defense or are intended for use by the government as evidence in chief at the trial, or were obtained from or belong to the defendant." Fed.R.Crim.P. 16(a)(1)(C). Respondents argue that documents "within the possession . . . of the government" that discuss the government's prosecution strategy for cocaine cases are "material" to respondents' selective-prosecution claim. Respondents argue that the Rule applies because any claim that "results in nonconviction" if successful is a "defense" for the Rule's purposes, and a successful selective-prosecution claim has that effect.

We reject this argument, because we conclude that in the context of Rule 16 "the defendant's defense" means the defendant's response to the Government's case-in-chief. While it might be argued that as a general matter, the concept of a "defense" includes any claim that is a "sword," challenging the prosecution's conduct of the case, the term

---

2. We have never determined whether dismissal of the indictment, or some other sanction, is the proper remedy if a court determines that a defendant has been the victim of prosecution on the basis of his race. Here, "it was the government itself that suggested dismissal of the indictments to the district court so that an appeal might lie."

may encompass only the narrower class of "shield" claims, which refute the Government's arguments that the defendant committed the crime charged. Rule 16(a)(1)(C) tends to support the "shield-only" reading. If "defense" means an argument in response to the prosecution's case-in-chief, there is a perceptible symmetry between documents "material to the preparation of the defendant's defense," and, in the very next phrase, documents "intended for use by the government as evidence in chief at the trial."

If this symmetry were not persuasive enough, paragraph (a)(2) of Rule 16 establishes beyond peradventure that "defense" in section (a)(1)(C) can refer only to defenses in response to the Government's case-in-chief. Rule 16(a)(2), as relevant here, exempts from defense inspection "reports, memoranda, or other internal government documents made by the attorney for the government or other government agents in connection with the investigation or prosecution of the case."

Under Rule 16(a)(1)(C), a defendant may examine documents material to his defense, but, under Rule 16(a)(2), he may not examine Government work product in connection with his case. If a selective-prosecution claim is a "defense," Rule 16(a)(1)(C) gives the defendant the right to examine Government work product in every prosecution except his own. Because respondents' construction of "defense" creates the anomaly of a defendant's being able to examine all Government work product except the most pertinent, we find their construction implausible. We hold that Rule 16(a)(1)(C) authorizes defendants to examine Government documents material to the preparation of their defense against the Government's case-in-chief, but not to the preparation of selective-prosecution claims. * * *

A selective-prosecution claim is not a defense on the merits to the criminal charge itself, but an independent assertion that the prosecutor has brought the charge for reasons forbidden by the Constitution. Our cases delineating the necessary elements to prove a claim of selective prosecution have taken great pains to explain that the standard is a demanding one. These cases afford a "background presumption" that the showing necessary to obtain discovery should itself be a significant barrier to the litigation of insubstantial claims.

A selective-prosecution claim asks a court to exercise judicial power over a "special province" of the Executive. The Attorney General and United States Attorneys retain " 'broad discretion' " to enforce the Nation's criminal laws. They have this latitude because they are designated by statute as the President's delegates to help him discharge his constitutional responsibility to "take Care that the Laws be faithfully executed." U.S. Const., Art. II, § 3. As a result, "[t]he presumption of regularity supports" their prosecutorial decisions and "in the absence of clear evidence to the contrary, courts presume that they have properly discharged their official duties." In the ordinary case, "so long as the prosecutor has probable cause to believe that the accused committed an offense defined by statute, the decision whether or not to prosecute, and what charge to file or bring before a grand jury, generally rests entirely in his discretion."

Of course, a prosecutor's discretion is "subject to constitutional constraints." One of these constraints, imposed by the equal protection component of the Due Process Clause of the Fifth Amendment, is that the decision whether to prosecute may not be based on "an unjustifiable standard such as race, religion, or other arbitrary classification," *Oyler v. Boles*, 368 U.S. 448, 82 S.Ct. 501, 7 L.Ed.2d 446 (1962). A defendant may demonstrate that the administration of a criminal law is "directed so exclusively against a particular class of persons ... with a mind so unequal and oppressive" that the system of prosecution amounts to "a practical denial" of equal protection of the law. *Yick Wo v. Hopkins*, 118 U.S. 356, 6 S.Ct. 1064, 30 L.Ed. 220 (1886).

In order to dispel the presumption that a prosecutor has not violated equal protection, a criminal defendant must present "clear evidence to the contrary." We explained in *Wayte* [*v. United States*, 470 U.S. 598, 105 S.Ct. 1524, 84 L.Ed.2d 547 (1985)], why courts are "properly hesitant to examine the decision whether to prosecute." Judicial deference to the decisions of these executive officers rests in part on an assessment of the relative competence of prosecutors and courts. "Such factors as the strength of the case, the prosecution's general deterrence value, the Government's enforcement priorities, and the case's relationship to the Government's overall enforcement plan are not readily susceptible to the kind of analysis the courts are competent to undertake." It also stems from a concern not to unnecessarily impair the performance of a core executive constitutional function. "Examining the basis of a prosecution delays the criminal proceeding, threatens to chill law enforcement by subjecting the prosecutor's motives and decisionmaking to outside inquiry, and may undermine prosecutorial effectiveness by revealing the Government's enforcement policy."

The requirements for a selective-prosecution claim draw on "ordinary equal protection standards." The claimant must demonstrate that the federal prosecutorial policy "had a discriminatory effect and that it was motivated by a discriminatory purpose." To establish a discriminatory effect in a race case, the claimant must show that similarly situated individuals of a different race were not prosecuted. This requirement has been established in our case law since *Ah Sin v. Wittman*, 198 U.S. 500, 25 S.Ct. 756, 49 L.Ed. 1142 (1905). Ah Sin, a subject of China, petitioned a California state court for a writ of habeas corpus, seeking discharge from imprisonment under a San Francisco county ordinance prohibiting persons from setting up gambling tables in rooms barricaded to stop police from entering. He alleged in his habeas petition "that the ordinance is enforced 'solely and exclusively against persons of the Chinese race and not otherwise.' " We rejected his contention that this averment made out a claim under the Equal Protection Clause, because it did not allege "that the conditions and practices to which the ordinance was directed did not exist exclusively among the Chinese, or that there were other offenders against the ordinance than the Chinese as to whom it was not enforced."

The similarly situated requirement does not make a selective-prosecution claim impossible to prove. Twenty years before *Ah Sin*, we invalidated an ordinance, also adopted by San Francisco, that prohibited the operation of laundries in wooden buildings. *Yick Wo*, supra. The plaintiff in error successfully demonstrated that the ordinance was applied against Chinese nationals but not against other laundry-shop operators. The authorities had denied the applications of 200 Chinese subjects for permits to operate shops in wooden buildings, but granted the applications of 80 individuals who were not Chinese subjects to operate laundries in wooden buildings "under similar conditions." We explained in *Ah Sin* why the similarly situated requirement is necessary: "No latitude of intention should be indulged in a case like this. There should be certainty to every intent. Plaintiff in error seeks to set aside a criminal law of the State, not on the ground that it is unconstitutional on its face, not that it is discriminatory in tendency and ultimate actual operation as the ordinance was which was passed on in the *Yick Wo* case, but that it was made so by the manner of its administration. This is a matter of proof, and no fact should be omitted to make it out completely, when the power of a Federal court is invoked to interfere with the course of criminal justice of a State." Although *Ah Sin* involved federal review of a state conviction, we think a similar rule applies where the power of a federal court is invoked to challenge an exercise of one of the core powers of the Executive Branch of the Federal Government, the power to prosecute.[a] * * *

Having reviewed the requirements to prove a selective-prosecution claim, we turn to the showing necessary to obtain discovery in support of such a claim. If discovery is ordered, the Government must assemble from its own files documents which might corroborate or refute the defendant's claim. Discovery thus imposes many of the costs present when the Government must respond to a prima facie case of selective prosecution. It will divert prosecutors' resources and may disclose the Government's prosecutorial strategy. The justifications for a rigorous standard for the elements of a selective-prosecution claim thus require a correspondingly rigorous standard for discovery in aid of such a claim.

The parties, and the Courts of Appeals which have considered the requisite showing to establish entitlement to discovery, describe this

---

a. At this juncture, respondents urged that *Batson*, 8th ed., p. 1420, "cut against any absolute requirement that there be a showing of failure to prosecute similarly situated individuals," but the Court responded that *Batson* was different: "During jury selection, the entire res gestae take place in front of the trial judge. Because the judge has before him the entire venire, he is well situated to detect whether a challenge to the seating of one juror is part of a 'pattern' of singling out members of a sin-gle race for peremptory challenges. He is in a position to discern whether a challenge to a black juror has evidentiary significance; the significance may differ if the venire consists mostly of blacks or of whites. Similarly, if the defendant makes out a prima facie case, the prosecutor is called upon to justify only decisions made in the very case then before the court. The trial judge need not review prosecutorial conduct in relation to other venires in other cases."

showing with a variety of phrases, like "colorable basis," "substantial threshold showing," "substantial and concrete basis," or "reasonable likelihood." However, the many labels for this showing conceal the degree of consensus about the evidence necessary to meet it. The Courts of Appeals "require some evidence tending to show the existence of the essential elements of the defense," discriminatory effect and discriminatory intent.

In this case we consider what evidence constitutes "some evidence tending to show the existence" of the discriminatory effect element. The Court of Appeals held that a defendant may establish a colorable basis for discriminatory effect without evidence that the Government has failed to prosecute others who are similarly situated to the defendant. We think it was mistaken in this view. The vast majority of the Courts of Appeals require the defendant to produce some evidence that similarly situated defendants of other races could have been prosecuted, but were not, and this requirement is consistent with our equal protection case law. * * *[3]

The Court of Appeals reached its decision in part because it started "with the presumption that people of all races commit all types of crimes—not with the premise that any type of crime is the exclusive province of any particular racial or ethnic group." It cited no authority for this proposition, which seems contradicted by the most recent statistics of the United States Sentencing Commission. Those statistics show that: More than 90% of the persons sentenced in 1994 for crack cocaine trafficking were black; 93.4% of convicted LSD dealers were white; and 91% of those convicted for pornography or prostitution were white. Presumptions at war with presumably reliable statistics have no proper place in the analysis of this issue.

The Court of Appeals also expressed concern about the "evidentiary obstacles defendants face." But all of its sister Circuits that have confronted the issue have required that defendants produce some evidence of differential treatment of similarly situated members of other races or protected classes. In the present case, if the claim of selective prosecution were well founded, it should not have been an insuperable task to prove that persons of other races were being treated differently than respondents. For instance, respondents could have investigated whether similarly situated persons of other races were prosecuted by the State of California, were known to federal law enforcement officers, but were not prosecuted in federal court. We think the required threshold— a credible showing of different treatment of similarly situated persons— adequately balances the Government's interest in vigorous prosecution and the defendant's interest in avoiding selective prosecution.

In the case before us, respondents' "study" did not constitute "some evidence tending to show the existence of the essential elements of" a

3. We reserve the question whether a defendant must satisfy the similarly situated requirement in a case "involving direct admissions by [prosecutors] of discriminatory purpose."

selective-prosecution claim. The study failed to identify individuals who were not black, could have been prosecuted for the offenses for which respondents were charged, but were not so prosecuted. This omission was not remedied by respondents' evidence in opposition to the Government's motion for reconsideration. The newspaper article, which discussed the discriminatory effect of federal drug sentencing laws, was not relevant to an allegation of discrimination in decisions to prosecute. Respondents' affidavits, which recounted one attorney's conversation with a drug treatment center employee and the experience of another attorney defending drug prosecutions in state court, recounted hearsay and reported personal conclusions based on anecdotal evidence. The judgment of the Court of Appeals is therefore reversed, and the case is remanded for proceedings consistent with this opinion.

It is so ordered.[b]

Justice STEVENS, dissenting. * * *

The Court correctly concludes that in this case the facts presented to the District Court in support of respondents' claim that they had been singled out for prosecution because of their race were not sufficient to prove that defense. Moreover, I agree with the Court that their showing was not strong enough to give them a right to discovery, either under Rule 16 or under the District Court's inherent power to order discovery in appropriate circumstances. Like Chief Judge Wallace of the Court of Appeals, however, I am persuaded that the District Judge did not abuse her discretion when she concluded that the factual showing was sufficiently disturbing to require some response from the United States Attorney's Office. Perhaps the discovery order was broader than necessary, but I cannot agree with the Court's apparent conclusion that no inquiry was permissible.

The District Judge's order should be evaluated in light of three circumstances that underscore the need for judicial vigilance over certain types of drug prosecutions. First, the Anti–Drug Abuse Act of 1986 and subsequent legislation established a regime of extremely high penalties for the possession and distribution of so-called "crack" cocaine. Those provisions treat one gram of crack as the equivalent of 100 grams of powder cocaine. The distribution of 50 grams of crack is thus punishable by the same mandatory minimum sentence of 10 years in prison that applies to the distribution of 5,000 grams of powder cocaine. The Sentencing Guidelines extend this ratio to penalty levels above the

---

b. Justice Souter, concurring, joined the Court's discussion of Rule 16 "only to the extent of its application to the issue in this case." Justice Ginsburg, concurring, emphasized that the "Court was not called upon to decide here whether Rule 16(a)(1)(C) applies in any other context, for example, to affirmative defenses unrelated to the merits." Justice Breyer, concurring in part and concurring in the judgment, though concluding that "neither the alleged 'symmetry' in the structure of Rule 16(a)(1)(C), nor the work product exception of Rule 16(a)(2), supports the majority's limitation of discovery under Rule 16(a)(1)(C) to documents related to the government's 'case-in-chief,'" concluded that the defendants' discovery request failed to satisfy the Rule's requirement that the discovery be "material to the preparation of the defendant's defense."

mandatory minimums: for any given quantity of crack, the guideline range is the same as if the offense had involved 100 times that amount in powder cocaine. These penalties result in sentences for crack offenders that average three to eight times longer than sentences for comparable powder offenders.

Second, the disparity between the treatment of crack cocaine and powder cocaine is matched by the disparity between the severity of the punishment imposed by federal law and that imposed by state law for the same conduct. For a variety of reasons, often including the absence of mandatory minimums, the existence of parole, and lower baseline penalties, terms of imprisonment for drug offenses tend to be substantially lower in state systems than in the federal system. The difference is especially marked in the case of crack offenses. The majority of States draw no distinction between types of cocaine in their penalty schemes; of those that do, none has established as stark a differential as the Federal Government. For example, if respondent Hampton is found guilty, his federal sentence might be as long as a mandatory life term. Had he been tried in state court, his sentence could have been as short as 12 years, less worktime credits of half that amount.

Finally, it is undisputed that the brunt of the elevated federal penalties falls heavily on blacks. While 65% of the persons who have used crack are white, in 1993 they represented only 4% of the federal offenders convicted of trafficking in crack. Eighty-eight percent of such defendants were black. During the first 18 months of full guideline implementation, the sentencing disparity between black and white defendants grew from preguideline levels: blacks on average received sentences over 40% longer than whites. Those figures represent a major threat to the integrity of federal sentencing reform, whose main purpose was the elimination of disparity (especially racial) in sentencing. The Sentencing Commission acknowledges that the heightened crack penalties are a "primary cause of the growing disparity between sentences for Black and White federal defendants."

The extraordinary severity of the imposed penalties and the troubling racial patterns of enforcement give rise to a special concern about the fairness of charging practices for crack offenses. Evidence tending to prove that black defendants charged with distribution of crack in the Central District of California are prosecuted in federal court, whereas members of other races charged with similar offenses are prosecuted in state court, warrants close scrutiny by the federal judges in that District. In my view, the District Judge, who has sat on both the federal and the state benches in Los Angeles, acted well within her discretion to call for the development of facts that would demonstrate what standards, if any, governed the choice of forum where similarly situated offenders are prosecuted.

Respondents submitted a study showing that of all cases involving crack offenses that were closed by the Federal Public Defender's Office in 1991, 24 out of 24 involved black defendants. To supplement this evidence, they submitted affidavits from two of the attorneys in the defense team. The first reported a statement from an intake coordinator at a local drug treatment center that, in his experience, an equal number of crack users and dealers were caucasian as belonged to minorities. The second was from David R. Reed, counsel for respondent Armstrong. Reed was both an active court-appointed attorney in the Central District of California and one of the directors of the leading association of criminal defense lawyers who practice before the Los Angeles County courts. Reed stated that he did not recall "ever handling a [crack] cocaine case involving non-black defendants" in federal court, nor had he even heard of one. He further stated that "[t]here are many crack cocaine sales cases prosecuted in state court that do involve racial groups other than blacks."

The majority discounts the probative value of the affidavits, claiming that they recounted "hearsay" and reported "personal conclusions based on anecdotal evidence." But the Reed affidavit plainly contained more than mere hearsay; Reed offered information based on his own extensive experience in both federal and state courts. Given the breadth of his background, he was well qualified to compare the practices of federal and state prosecutors. In any event, the Government never objected to the admission of either affidavit on hearsay or any other grounds. It was certainly within the District Court's discretion to credit the affidavits of two members of the bar of that Court, at least one of whom had presumably acquired a reputation by his frequent appearances there, and both of whose statements were made on pains of perjury.

The criticism that the affidavits were based on "anecdotal evidence" is also unpersuasive. I thought it was agreed that defendants do not need to prepare sophisticated statistical studies in order to receive mere discovery in cases like this one. Certainly evidence based on a drug counselor's personal observations or on an attorney's practice in two sets of courts, state and federal, can "ten[d] to show the existence" of a selective prosecution.

Even if respondents failed to carry their burden of showing that there were individuals who were not black but who could have been prosecuted in federal court for the same offenses, it does not follow that the District Court abused its discretion in ordering discovery. There can be no doubt that such individuals exist, and indeed the Government has never denied the same. In those circumstances, I fail to see why the District Court was unable to take judicial notice of this obvious fact and demand information from the Government's files to support or refute respondents' evidence. The presumption that some whites are prosecuted in state court is not "contradicted" by the statistics the majority cites, which show only that high percentages of blacks are convicted of certain federal crimes, while high percentages of whites are convicted of other federal crimes. Those figures are entirely consistent with the allegation of selective prosecution. The relevant comparison, rather, would be with the percentages of blacks and whites who commit those crimes. But, as discussed above, in the case of crack far greater numbers of whites are believed guilty of using the substance. The District Court, therefore, was entitled to find the evidence before her significant and to require some explanation from the Government.[6]

In sum, I agree with the Sentencing Commission that "[w]hile the exercise of discretion by prosecutors and investigators has an impact on sentences in almost all cases to some extent, because of the 100–to–1 quantity ratio and federal mandatory minimum penalties, discretionary decisions in cocaine cases often have dramatic effects."[7] The severity of the penalty heightens both the danger of arbitrary enforcement and the need for careful scrutiny of any colorable claim of discriminatory enforcement. In this case, the evidence was sufficiently disturbing to persuade the District Judge to order discovery that might help explain the conspicuous racial pattern of cases before her Court. I cannot accept the majority's conclusion that the District Judge either exceeded her power or abused her discretion when she did so. I therefore respectfully dissent.

8th ed., p. 927; Note 5, delete paragraphs (b), (c) and (d)

6. Also telling was the Government's response to respondents' evidentiary showing. It submitted a list of more than 3,500 defendants who had been charged with federal narcotics violations over the previous 3 years. It also offered the names of 11 non-black defendants whom it had prosecuted for crack offenses. All 11, however, were members of other racial or ethnic minorities. The District Court was authorized to draw adverse inferences from the Government's inability to produce a single example of a white defendant, especially when the very purpose of its exercise was to allay the Court's concerns about the evidence of racially selective prosecutions. As another court has said: "Statistics are not, of course, the whole answer, but nothing is as emphatic as zero...."

7. For this and other reasons, the Sentencing Commission in its Special Report to Congress "strongly recommend[ed] against a 100–to–1 quantity ratio." The Commission shortly thereafter, by a 4–to–3 vote, amended the guidelines so as to equalize the treatment of crack and other forms of cocaine, and proposed modification of the statutory mandatory minimum penalties for crack offenses. In October 1995, Congress overrode the Sentencing Commission's guideline amendments. Nevertheless, Congress at the same time directed the Commission to submit recommendations regarding changes to the statutory and guideline penalties for cocaine distribution, including specifically "revision of the drug quantity ratio of crack cocaine to powder cocaine."

Chapter 14

THE PRELIMINARY HEARING

SECTION 2. THE DEFENDANT'S RIGHT
TO A PRELIMINARY HEARING

8th ed., p. 960; end of Note 1 add:

In *Albright v. Oliver,* 510 U.S. 266, 114 S.Ct. 807, 127 L.Ed.2d 114 (1994), the Court addressed the question of whether substantive due process affords protection against initiation of prosecution without probable cause. The Court majority (7–2) sustained the dismissal of a federal civil rights action (filed under 42 U.S.C. § 1983), concluding that the complaint did not set forth an actionable claim under the single constitutional theory advanced there. The complaint alleged that a police detective, relying solely upon information supplied by a clearly unreliable informant, had filed charges against the plaintiff, alleging that he sold a substance that simulated an illegal drug, and had then obtained an arrest warrant based on those charges. Upon learning of the issuance of the warrant, the plaintiff surrendered to the detective and was subsequently released after posting bond. At a preliminary hearing, the detective testified as to the alleged sale and the plaintiff was bound over for trial. The charge was later dismissed at a pretrial hearing on the ground that it did not state an offense under state law.

Chief Justice Rehnquist, in a plurality opinion joined by Justices O'Connor, Scalia, and Ginsburg, stressed that petitioner had framed his claim solely as a substantive due process claim, and had not relied on either procedural due process or the Fourth Amendment. Dismissal was therefore required under previous precedent holding that where a particular Amendment "provides an explicit textual source of constitutional protection," then "that Amendment, not the more generalized notion of 'substantive due process' must be the guide for analyzing [that claim]." The Fourth Amendment, the Chief Justice noted, specifically addresses pretrial deprivations of liberty, and they "go hand in hand with criminal prosecutions, see *Gerstein v. Pugh.*" Also the Court had noted in *Gerstein* and *Lem Woon* that "the accused is not entitled to judicial oversight or review of the decision to prosecute." Accordingly, any claim here would have to be based on the Fourth Amendment rather than "substantive due process, with its 'scarce and open-ended guideposts.'"[a]

Justice Kennedy joined by Justice Thomas, concurred in the judgment. Justice Kennedy concluded that the plaintiff's due process claim focused not on his arrest, but on his malicious prosecution on baseless charges, which presented a separate issue. Nonetheless, dismissal was still required since due process does not "include a standard for the initiation of prosecution." This was evidenced by the common law, which while it provided for "grand jury indictment and speedy trial, * * * did not provide a specific evidentiary standard applicable to a pretrial hearing on the merits of the charges or subject to later review by the courts. See *United States v. Williams* [8th ed., p. 1013]; *Costello v. United States* [8th ed., p. 1004]." Moreover, insofar as the common law of torts might reflect some notion of due process protection against malicious prosecution, prior precedent established that a state actor's "random and unauthorized" deprivation of such an interest could not be challenged under 42 U.S.C. § 1983 so long as the state provides "an adequate post-deprivation remedy" (here found in the state's tort remedy). Also concurring in the judgment, Justice Souter concluded that none of the injuries cited by plaintiff as flowing from his prosecution without probable cause went to a substantial liberty interest that stood apart from the custodial deprivations establishing a potential Fourth Amendment claim. He left open the possibility that due process could come into play in an "exceptional case * * * where some quantum of harm occurs in the interim after groundless criminal charges are filed but before any Fourth Amendment seizure."

In dissent, Justice Stevens, joined by Justice Blackmun, argued that freedom from prosecution except upon probable cause is a deeply-rooted substantive liberty interest protected by Fourteenth Amendment due process. At stake are a range of consequences, producing "'a wrenching disruption of everyday life,' regardless of whether the initiation of criminal prosecution prompts an arrest." While *Hurtado* held that due process does not require states to proceed by grand jury indictment, it had allowed the states to do so "only if the substance of the probable cause requirement remains adequately protected." Here, the state had established procedures to ensure that probable cause was present, but, as evidenced by cases such as *Mooney v. Holohan*, involving the prosecution's knowing use of perjured testimony (see 8th ed., Note 1, p. 1297), a "state compliance with facially valid procedures" should not invariably

a. Although joining the plurality opinion, Justices Scalia and Ginsburg each wrote separate concurring opinions. Justice Scalia noted that he thought it "unlikely that the procedures constitutionally 'due' with regard to an arrest consist of anything more than what the Fourth Amendment specifies, but petitioner has in any case not invoked 'procedural' due process." Justice Ginsburg cited various elements of the case—the issuance of an arrest warrant, the petitioner's voluntary submission based on the warrant, his subsequent release subject to bail restrictions, and preliminary hearing testimony by the detective which "served to maintain and reinforce" any "Fourth Amendment violation"—that supported "viewing this case through a Fourth Amendment lens."

"meet the demands of due process, without regard to the substance of the resulting probable cause determination."

8th ed., p. 963, at the end of Note 6, add:

Consider the defense tactics adopted in response to a prosecutorial attempt to bypass a preliminary hearing in the O.J. Simpson case, as described by two of the Simpson defense lawyers. California is an information state which allows for mooting by indictment an otherwise required preliminary hearing (as a result of an amendment to the state constitution adopted in 1990, see Note 7, infra). When defendant Simpson was arrested, the magistrate set his preliminary hearing for June 30th, the last day within the ten-day deadline established by state law. On the same day, the prosecution began presenting its evidence before the grand jury, and the defense assumed that task would be completed and an indictment issued before June 30th. Indeed, the defense believed that one of the factors that led the prosecutor to have the case placed before the court in downtown Los Angeles rather than in Santa Monica was that "the only grand jury in Los Angeles county sits downtown." The defense was concerned about the impending loss of a preliminary hearing, although defense counsel recognized that a preliminary hearing would have some disadvantages. The preliminary hearing would be televised and the viewers would be seeing "a parade of prosecution witnesses, with no defense witnesses to counteract them." This was especially important because "the jurors [would] come from the same public that would be watching the preliminary hearing on television." On the other hand, the defense's forensic experts were convinced "that the prosecution was not yet prepared to present a well-organized case." Many of its forensic tests were not complete, and "several important witness interviews had not been conducted." If a preliminary hearing were held on the 30th, that "could force the prosecution to put its witnesses on the stand without the kind of preparation that avoids contradictions and other mistakes," presenting "the prospect of a long-term advantage for the defense at the trial itself."

On June 22nd, the defense saw the opportunity to force a preliminary hearing. The police department, in response to a media request under the California Public Records Act, released tapes of 911 emergency telephone calls relating to earlier incidents of domestic violence. The defense decided to "bite the bullet and go for the preliminary hearing by filing * * * [a] motion to dismiss the grand." It filed an "Emergency Motion for Voir Dire of Grand Jurors and Determination of Prejudice from Improper Pretrial Publicity." Shortly thereafter, the chief presiding judge, without directly referring to the motion, announced that he had determined, based on a "personal inquiry," that "some jurors have become aware of potentially prejudicial matter not officially presented to them by the District Attorney" and therefore, in order to "protect the due process rights of Mr. Simpson and the integrity of the grand jury process," he was removing the case from the grand jury.[a] The case

a. As to the uniqueness of this ruling, see Note 5, 8th ed., p. 997.

would now "proceed to the preliminary hearing already scheduled for the 30th."

In retrospect, the defense counsel considered this an important victory. While its "initial effect * * * was to allow the prosecution to put its case on in public" without the rebuttal of defense witnesses, and the "vast majority of those who watched [the hearing] concluded that Simpson was guilty," the defense was able to lay the groundwork for the plan of attack it later advanced at trial through a "strategy that locked the prosecution into its initial mistakes at * * * [the] preliminary hearing." See Alan Dershowitz, *Reasonable Doubts* 27–33, 100–101 (1996); Gerald F. Uelmen, *Lessons From the Trial* 18–23 (1996).

Chapter 15

GRAND JURY REVIEW

SECTION 2. CHALLENGES TO GRAND JURY COMPOSITION

8th ed., p. 997; new footnote, after reference to Powers v. Ohio, 7 lines from bottom of Note 4:

Campbell v. Louisiana, ___ U.S. ___, 118 S.Ct. 1419, 140 L.Ed.2d 551 (1998), held that the standing rule of *Powers v. Ohio* [8th ed., p. 1430] applies to grand jury selection as well as petit jury selection and therefore a "white criminal defendant has standing to object to discrimination against black persons in the selection of the grand jurors." The state had argued that *Powers* was distinguishable because the discrimination there occurred in the exercise of peremptory challenges, "in open court and in front of the entire jury pool," leading the *Powers* Court to "express concern that this tactic might encourage the jury to be lawless in its own actions." Here, the discrimination occurred in the judge's selection of the grand jury foreperson (see Note 4 below) and was "invisible to the grand jurors on the panel," only becoming "apparent when a pattern [of discrimination] emerges over the years." Rejecting this distinction, the Court reasoned: "This argument, however, underestimates the seriousness of the allegations. In *Powers,* even if the prosecutor had been motivated by racial prejudice, those responsible for the defendant's fate, the judge and the jury, had shown no actual bias. If, by contrast, the allegations here are true, the impartiality and discretion of the judge himself would be called into question."

8th ed., p. 997; end of Note 4, add:

In *Campbell v. Louisiana,* ___ U.S. ___, 118 S.Ct. 1419, 140 L.Ed.2d 551 (1998), the Louisiana Supreme Court relied on *Hobby* in holding that the defendant lacked standing to challenge racial discrimination in the selection of the grand jury foreperson. It noted that the foreperson in Louisiana, like the foreperson in *Hobby,* had only ministerial duties. Rejecting this analysis, the Supreme Court noted that in Louisiana, the supervising judge "selects the foreperson from the grand jury venire before the remaining members of the grand jury have been chosen by lot." Thus, the defendant here was objecting to discrimination in the composition of the grand jury (the foreperson having the full voting powers of a panel member), not simply the exercise of the foreperson's duties, and *Hobby* was inapplicable. The "significance of this distinction," the Court noted, "was acknowledged by *Hobby*'s discussion of * * * *Rose v. Mitchell.*"

The *Campbell* Court also recognized defendant's standing to claim that the alleged discrimination there violated defendant's right to due process under the rationale of *Peters v. Kiff*. The Court added that it was unnecessary at this point "to discuss the nature and full extent of due process protection in the context of grand jury selection." Since the defendant had standing, "that issue, to the extent it is still open based on our earlier precedents, should be determined on the merits" by the state court.

Chapter 18

THE SCOPE OF THE PROSECUTION: JOINDER AND SEVERANCE OF OFFENSES AND DEFENDANTS

SECTION 2. FAILURE TO JOIN RELATED OFFENSES

8th ed., p. 1098; in the Notes and Questions, before Note 1, add:

0. When only the greater offense has been charged, as in *Harris v. Oklahoma*, joinder sometimes occurs as a consequence of the well-established rule of procedure under which a defendant is entitled to a jury instruction on the uncharged lesser included offense whenever such an alternative disposition is rationally justified by the evidence in the case. As noted in *Beck v. Alabama*, 447 U.S. 625, 100 S.Ct. 2382, 65 L.Ed.2d 392 (1980): "In the federal courts, it has long been 'beyond dispute that the defendant is entitled to an instruction on a lesser included offense if the evidence would permit a jury rationally to find him guilty of the lesser offense and acquit him of the greater.' Similarly, the state courts that have addressed the issue have unanimously held that a defendant is entitled to a lesser included offense instruction where the evidence warrants it. * * * Although the States vary in their descriptions of the quantum of proof necessary to give rise to a right to a lesser included offense instruction, they agree that it must be given when supported by the evidence." This procedure, the Court noted in *Beck*, "originally developed as an aid to the prosecution in cases in which the proof failed to establish some element of the crime charged. But it has long been recognized that it can also be beneficial to the defendant because it affords the jury a less drastic alternative than the choice between conviction of the offense charged and acquittal."

In *Beck*, the Court concluded that "the nearly universal acceptance of the rule in both state and federal courts establishes the value to the defendant of this procedural safeguard," which is "especially important * * * when the evidence unquestionably establishes that the defendant is guilty of a serious, violent offense—but leaves some doubt with respect to an element that would justify conviction of a capital offense." Thus the Court held as a matter of due process that when "the unavailability of a lesser included offense instruction enhances the risk of an unwarranted conviction," that option may not be withdrawn from the jury in a capital case. The *Beck* rule does not require a state court to instruct the jury on offenses that, under state law, are not considered lesser included offenses of the crime charged. *Hopkins v. Reeves,* ___ U.S. ___, 118 S.Ct. 1895, ___ L.Ed.2d ___ (1998) (second-degree murder, which requires intent, is not lesser included offense of felony-murder, which does not).

8th ed., p. 1099; new fn. c, 8 lines from bottom after "848":

    c. The Court later so held. *Rutledge v.*
United States, 517 U.S. 292, 116 S.Ct. 1241,
134 L.Ed.2d 419 (1996).

8th ed., p. 1101; after Note 3, add:

    4. While it has long been settled that the Double Jeopardy Clause has to do only with multiple *criminal* punishment, the Supreme Court has encountered difficulty over the years in determining how to go about making the civil-criminal distinction in this context. The method used in *United States v. Halper,* 490 U.S. 435, 109 S.Ct. 1892, 104 L.Ed.2d 487 (1989), under which the outcome depended primarily on whether the sanction imposed served the traditional "goals of punishment," namely "retribution and deterrence," was abandoned in HUDSON v. UNITED STATES, ___ U.S. ___, 118 S.Ct. 488, 139 L.Ed.2d 488 (1997). There, bank officers indicted for misapplication of bank funds claimed the prosecution was barred because monetary penalties and occupational debarment had previously been imposed upon them by the Office of Comptroller of Currency. The Court, per REHNQUIST, C.J., rejected that contention:

    "Whether a particular punishment is criminal or civil is, at least initially, a matter of statutory construction. A court must first ask whether the legislature, 'in establishing the penalizing mechanism, indicated either expressly or impliedly a preference for one label or the other.' Even in those cases where the legislature 'has indicated an intention to establish a civil penalty, we have inquired further whether the statutory scheme was so punitive either in purpose or effect,' as to 'transfor[m] what was clearly intended as a civil remedy into a criminal penalty.'

    "In making this latter determination, the factors listed in *Kennedy v. Mendoza–Martinez,* 372 U.S. 144, 83 S.Ct. 554, 9 L.Ed.2d 644 (1963), provide useful guideposts, including: (1) '[w]hether the sanction involves an affirmative disability or restraint'; (2) 'whether it has historically been regarded as a punishment'; (3) 'whether it comes into play only on a finding of scienter'; (4) 'whether its operation will promote the traditional aims of punishment-retribution and deterrence'; (5) 'whether the behavior to which it applies is already a crime'; (6) 'whether an alternative purpose to which it may rationally be connected is assignable for it'; and (7) 'whether it appears excessive in relation to the alternative purpose assigned.' It is important to note, however, that 'these factors must be considered in relation to the statute on its face,' and 'only the clearest proof' will suffice to override legislative intent and transform what has been denominated a civil remedy into a criminal penalty."

As for the instant case, the Court concluded "that Congress intended the OCC money penalties and debarment sanctions * * * to be civil in nature," and found "little evidence" that the sanctions were so punitive as to make them criminal, considering that "neither money penalties nor debarment have historically been viewed as punishment," and that the sanctions imposed "do not involve an 'affirmative disability or restraint' " or come "into play 'only' on a finding of scienter," Moreover, though "the conduct for which OCC sanctions are imposed may also be criminal" and though the sanctions will serve to deter others, "a traditional goal of criminal punishment," neither of those factors "renders such sanctions 'criminal' for double jeopardy purposes."[a]

8th ed., pp. 1105–06; end of fn. e, add:

But in *Schiro v. Farley*, 510 U.S. 222, 114 S.Ct. 783, 127 L.Ed.2d 47 (1994), the Court held that the "failure to return a verdict does not have collateral estoppel effect * * * unless the record establishes that the issue was actually and necessarily decided in the defendant's favor." In that case, defendant's trial for a single killing resulted in the jury being given ten possible verdicts, including three murder counts ("knowingly" killing, rape felony-murder, deviate conduct felony-murder), voluntary and involuntary manslaughter, guilty but mentally ill, not guilty by reason of insanity, and not guilty. Because the jury returned a guilty verdict as to rape felony murder and left the other verdict sheets blank, defendant claimed the state was collaterally estopped from now showing intentional killing as an aggravated factor supporting a death sentence. The Court disagreed, concluding that because the jury (i) was not instructed to return more than one verdict but (ii) was instructed that intent was required for each variety of murder, defendant had "not met his 'burden ... to demonstrate that the issue whose relitigation he seeks to foreclose was actually decided' in his favor."

8th ed., p. 1109; following Note 6, add:

7. *Sentencing guidelines and multiple prosecutions for related offenses.* In *Witte v. United States*, 515 U.S. 389, 115 S.Ct. 2199, 132 L.Ed.2d 351 (1995), the Supreme Court considered the bearing of federal guideline sentencing upon separate prosecutions for offenses that are distinct offenses under *Blockburger* but involve the same criminal enterprise. Defendant there entered into a conspiracy in June 1990 to participate in the transportation of large amounts of marijuana and cocaine from Central America. One of the participants in the planned operation was an undercover agent, who later arranged for the arrest of several of the participants in Mexico as they were about to ship cocaine to the United States. In January 1991, the defendant agreed with the undercover agent to purchase and distribute a shipment of marijuana, using equipment purchased for distributing the 1990 shipment that never arrived. Defendant was arrested after receiving that marijuana. He subsequently was charged with attempted possession with intent to

a. *Hudson* produced four concurring opinions by six Justices. All but one of them agreed that a departure from pre-*Hudson* doctrine was necessary, but three expressed reservations about the extent of the departure in the Rehnquist opinion.

distribute, based solely upon the planned distribution of the 1991 shipment, and he entered a guilty plea to that charge. The statutorily authorized penalty for that offense was 5–40 years in prison.

Under the federal sentencing guidelines, the sentencing court is directed to take account of all "relevant conduct" in which the defendant was engaged. As applied to narcotics offenses, the relevant conduct provision holds the defendant "accountable for all quantities of contraband with which he was directly involved, and in the case of jointly undertaken criminal activity, all reasonably foreseeable quantities of contraband that were within the scope of criminal activity that he jointly undertook." In defendant's case, this meant consideration of the marijuana and cocaine that was to have been received under the failed 1990 plan, as well as the amount to be received in January 1991, as those shipments were part of "the same continuing conspiracy." The quantities involved in the anticipated Central America shipments added considerably to the offense-level score of 40, which produced (with adjustments for defendant's cooperation) the defendant's ultimate sentence of 144 months. Defendant was subsequently prosecuted for conspiring to import cocaine based upon the arrangements entered into in 1990. He moved to dismiss that charge on the ground that punishing him for that offense would violate the double jeopardy prohibition against multiple punishments as he had already been punished for the anticipated cocaine shipment in the calculation of his 144 month sentence.

Rejecting defendant's double jeopardy contention, the Supreme Court majority (per O'Connor, J.) held that consideration of the 1990 relevant conduct in setting the sentence for the 1991 offense did not constitute punishment for the criminal activity involved in that earlier conduct. Sentencing courts, in setting the sentence for the offense of conviction, traditionally have been allowed to consider a broad range of behavior, "including past criminal behavior, even if no conviction resulted from that behavior. *Nichols v. United States* [Supp. p. 2]." Such behavior guides the court in assessing defendant's range of culpability and thereby determining precisely where his sentence should fall within the range legislatively authorized for the offense of conviction. The sentence imposed consequently constitutes punishment only for the offense of conviction. Indeed, on the same principle, the Court had repeatedly upheld recidivist statutes, reasoning that the enhanced punishment "imposed for the later offenses is not to be viewed as either a new jeopardy or additional penalty for the earlier crimes."

The Court majority rejected the contention of Justice Stevens in dissent that the Guidelines altered the above analysis because they treated relevant conduct not as reflecting upon the character of the offender, but as a measure of the character of the offense. It noted that while relevant conduct "may relate to the severity of the particular crime, the commission of multiple offenses in the same course of conduct also necessarily provides important evidence that the character of the offender requires special punishment." The "offender is still punished only for the fact that the present offense was carried out in a manner that warrants increased punishment, not for a different offense." Concurring in the judgment, Justice Scalia, joined by Justice Thomas, suggested that the majority's analysis rested upon "perceiv[ed] lines that do not really exist," and the proper approach was to recognize, contrary to recent precedent (e.g., *Department of Revenue v. Kurth Ranch*, Supp. p. 101 n. a), that the double jeopardy clause simply does not prohibit multiple punishment for the same offense.

The Court majority in *Witte* also spoke to the appropriate interpretation of the Guidelines. This portion of the opinion was not joined by two members of the six justice majority (the Chief Justice and Justice Kennedy), but was joined by Justice Stevens. It noted that the Guidelines include significant safeguards that would protect Witte against having the length of his second sentence multiplied by duplicative consideration of the same criminal conduct already considered as "relevant conduct" for the marijuana sentence. These included a provision for concurrent sentencing where a charged offense was fully considered in a prior sentence. Moreover, even if the Sentencing Commission had not formalized such protective standards for multiple convictions, district courts retain enough flexibility under the Guideline provisions on variances to take into account the fact that conduct underlying the offense at issue has previously been treated as relevant conduct in the sentencing for another offense.

Consider also, Elizabeth Lear, *Contemplating the Successive Prosecution Phenomenon in the Federal System,* 85 J.Crim.L. & Criminology 625 (1995) (concluding that "while the Guidelines may eliminate some incentives for [a second] prosecution in the Federal system, substantial pressures favoring piecemeal litigation remain").

SECTION 3. JOINDER AND SEVERANCE OF DEFENDANTS

8th ed., p. 1113; in lieu of *Richardson* case and Notes 4–7 following, add:

GRAY v. MARYLAND

___ U.S. ___, 118 S.Ct. 1151, 140 L.Ed.2d 294 (1998).

Justice BREYER delivered the opinion of the Court.

The issue in this case concerns the application of *Bruton v. United States*, 391 U.S. 123, 88 S.Ct. 1620, 20 L.Ed.2d 476 (1968). *Bruton* involved two defendants accused of participating in the same crime and tried jointly before the same jury. One of the defendants had confessed. His confession named and incriminated the other defendant. The trial judge issued a limiting instruction, telling the jury that it should consider the confession as evidence only against the codefendant who had confessed and not against the defendant named in the confession. *Bruton* held that, despite the limiting instruction, the Constitution forbids the use of such a confession in the joint trial.[a]

The case before us differs from *Bruton* in that the prosecution here redacted the codefendant's confession by substituting for the defendant's name in the confession a blank space or the word "deleted." We must decide whether these substitutions make a significant legal difference. We hold that they do not and that *Bruton*'s protective rule applies.

[Bell confessed to Baltimore police that he, Gray, and Vanlandingham had participated in the beating that resulted in Stacey Williams' death. Bell and Gray were indicted for murder. The trial judge, after denying Gray's motion for a separate trial, permitted the State to introduce a redacted version of Bell's confession. Other witnesses said that six persons (including Bell, Gray, and Vanlandingham) participated in the beating. Gray testified and denied his participation; Bell did not testify. The jury was instructed not to use the confession as evidence against Gray. Bell and Gray were convicted.]

In deciding whether *Bruton*'s protective rule applies to the redacted confession before us, we must consider both *Bruton*, and a later case, *Richardson v. Marsh*, 481 U.S. 200, 107 S.Ct. 1702, 95 L.Ed.2d 176 (1987), which limited *Bruton*'s scope. We shall briefly summarize each of these two cases.

Bruton, as we have said, involved two defendants—Evans and Bruton—tried jointly for robbery. Evans did not testify, but the Government introduced into evidence Evans' confession, which stated that both he (Evans) and Bruton together had committed the robbery. The trial judge told the jury it could consider the confession as evidence only against Evans, not against Bruton.

This Court held that, despite the limiting instruction, the introduction of Evans' out-of-court confession at Bruton's trial had violated Bruton's right, protected by the Sixth Amendment, to cross-examine witnesses. The Court recognized that in many circumstances a limiting instruction will adequately protect one defendant from the prejudicial effects of the introduction at a joint trial of evidence intended for use only against a different defendant. But it said that

> there are some contexts in which the risk that the jury will not, or cannot, follow instructions is so great, and the consequences of failure so vital to the defendant, that the practical and human limitations of the jury system cannot be ignored. Such a context is presented here, where the powerfully incriminating extrajudicial statements of a codefendant, who stands accused side-by-side with the defendant, are deliberately spread before the jury in a joint trial. Not only are the incriminations devastating to the defendant but their credibility is inevitably suspect.... The unreliability of such evidence is intolerably compounded when the alleged accomplice, as here, does not testify and cannot be tested by cross-examination.

---

a.　See footnote a, 8th ed., p. 1113.

The Court found that Evans' confession constituted just such a "power-fully incriminating extrajudicial statemen[t]," and that its introduction into evidence, insulated from cross-examination, violated Bruton's Sixth Amendment rights.

In *Richardson v. Marsh*, the Court considered a redacted confession. The case involved a joint murder trial of Marsh and Williams. The State had redacted the confession of one defendant, Williams, so as to "omit all reference" to his codefendant, Marsh—"indeed, to omit all indication that *anyone* other than ... Williams" and a third person had "partici-pated in the crime." (emphasis in original). The trial court also instruct-ed the jury not to consider the confession against Marsh. As redacted, the confession indicated that Williams and the third person had dis-cussed the murder in the front seat of a car while they traveled to the victim's house. The redacted confession contained no indication that Marsh—or any other person—was in the car. Later in the trial, however, Marsh testified that she was in the back seat of the car. For that reason, in context, the confession still could have helped convince the jury that Marsh knew about the murder in advance and therefore had participated knowingly in the crime.

The Court held that this redacted confession fell outside *Bruton*'s scope and was admissible (with appropriate limiting instructions) at the joint trial. The Court distinguished Evans' confession in *Bruton* as a confession that was "incriminating on its face" and which had "express-ly implicat[ed]" Bruton. By contrast, Williams' confession amounted to "evidence requiring linkage" in that it "became" incriminating in re-spect to Marsh "only when linked with evidence introduced later at trial." The Court held

> that the Confrontation Clause is not violated by the admission of a nontestifying codefendant's confession with a proper limiting in-struction when, as here, the confession is redacted to eliminate not only the defendant's name, but any reference to his or her existence.

The Court added: "We express no opinion on the admissibility of a confession in which the defendant's name has been replaced with a symbol or neutral pronoun."

Originally, the codefendant's confession in the case before us, like that in *Bruton*, referred to, and directly implicated another defendant. The State, however, redacted that confession by removing the noncon-fessing defendant's name. Nonetheless, unlike *Richardson*'s redacted confession, this confession refers directly to the "existence" of the nonconfessing defendant. The State has simply replaced the nonconfess-ing defendant's name with a kind of symbol, namely the word "deleted" or a blank space set off by commas. The redacted confession, for example, responded to the question "Who was in the group that beat Stacey," with the phrase, "Me,   , and a few other guys." And when the police witness read the confession in court, he said the word "deleted" or "deletion" where the blank spaces appear. We therefore must decide a question that *Richardson* left open, namely whether redaction that replaces a defendant's name with an obvious indication of deletion, such as a blank space, the word "deleted," or a similar symbol, still falls within *Bruton*'s protective rule. We hold that it does.

Bruton, as interpreted by *Richardson*, holds that certain "powerfully incriminating extrajudicial statements of a codefendant"—those naming another defendant—considered as a class, are so prejudicial that limiting instructions cannot work. Unless the prosecutor wishes to hold separate trials or to use separate juries or to abandon use of the confession, he must redact the confession to reduce significantly or to eliminate the special prejudice that the *Bruton* Court found. Redactions that simply replace a name with an obvious blank space or a word such as "deleted" or a symbol or other similarly obvious indications of alteration, however, leave statements that, considered as a class, so closely resemble Bruton's unredacted statements that, in our view, the law must require the same result.

For one thing, a jury will often react similarly to an unredacted confession and a confession redacted in this way, for the jury will often realize that the confession refers specifically to the defendant. This is true even when the State does not blatantly link the defendant to the deleted name, as it did in this case by asking whether Gray was arrested on the basis of information in Bell's confession as soon as the officer had finished reading the redacted statement. Consider a simplified but typical example, a confession that reads "I, Bob Smith, along with Sam Jones, robbed the bank." To replace the words "Sam Jones" with an obvious blank will not likely fool anyone. A juror somewhat familiar with criminal law would know immediately that the blank, in the phrase "I, Bob Smith, along with   , robbed the bank," refers to defendant Jones. A juror who does not know the law and who therefore wonders to whom the blank might refer need only lift his eyes to Jones, sitting at counsel table, to find what will seem the obvious answer, at least if the juror hears the judge's instruction not to consider the confession as evidence against Jones, for that instruction will provide an obvious reason for the blank. A more sophisticated juror, wondering if the blank refers to someone else, might also wonder how, if it did, the prosecutor could argue the confession is reliable, for the prosecutor, after all, has been arguing that Jones, not someone else, helped Smith commit the crime.

For another thing, the obvious deletion may well call the jurors' attention specially to the removed name. By encouraging the jury to speculate about the reference, the redaction may overemphasize the importance of the confession's accusation—once the jurors work out the reference. That is why Judge Learned Hand, many years ago, wrote in a similar instance that blacking out the name of a codefendant not only "would have been futile.... [T]here could not have been the slightest doubt as to whose names had been blacked out" but "even if there had been, that blacking out itself would have not only laid the doubt, but underscored the answer."

Finally, *Bruton*'s protected statements and statements redacted to leave a blank or some other similarly obvious alteration, function the same way grammatically. They are directly accusatory. Evans' statement in *Bruton* used a proper name to point explicitly to an accused defendant. And *Bruton* held that the "powerfully incriminating" effect of what Justice Stewart called "an out-of-court accusation," creates a special, and vital, need for cross-examination—a need that would be immediately obvious had the codefendant pointed directly to the defendant in the courtroom itself. The blank space in an obviously redacted confession also points directly to the defendant, and it accuses the defendant in a manner similar to Evans' use of Bruton's name or to a testifying codefendant's accusatory finger. By way of contrast, the factual statement at issue in *Richardson*—a statement about what others said in the front seat of a car—differs from directly accusatory evidence in this respect, for it does not point directly to a defendant at all.

We concede certain differences between *Bruton* and this case. A confession that uses a blank or the word "delete" (or, for that matter, a first name or a nickname) less obviously refers to the defendant than a confession that uses the defendant's full and proper name. Moreover, in some instances the person to whom the blank refers may not be clear: Although the follow-up question asked by the State in this case eliminated all doubt, the reference might not be transparent in other cases in which a confession, like the present confession, uses two (or more) blanks, even though only one other defendant appears at trial, and in which the trial indicates that there are more participants than the confession has named. Nonetheless, as we have said, we believe that, considered as a class, redactions that replace a proper name with an obvious blank, the word "delete," a symbol, or similarly notify the jury that a name has been deleted are similar enough to *Bruton*'s unredacted confessions as to warrant the same legal results.

The State, in arguing for a contrary conclusion, relies heavily upon *Richardson*. But we do not believe *Richardson* controls the result here. We concede that *Richardson* placed outside the scope of *Bruton*'s rule those statements that incriminate inferentially. We also concede that the jury must use inference to connect the statement in this redacted confession with the defendant. But inference pure and simple cannot make the critical difference, for if it did, then *Richardson* would also place outside *Bruton*'s scope confessions that use shortened first names, nicknames, descriptions as unique as the "red-haired, bearded, one-eyed man-with-a-limp," and perhaps even full names of defendants who are always known by a nickname. This Court has assumed, however, that nicknames and specific descriptions fall inside, not outside, *Bruton*'s protection. * * *

That being so, *Richardson* must depend in significant part upon the kind of, not the simple fact of, inference. *Richardson*'s inferences involved statements that did not refer directly to the defendant himself and which became incriminating "only when linked with evidence introduced later at trial." The inferences at issue here involve statements that, despite redaction, obviously refer directly to someone, often obviously the defendant, and which involve inferences that a jury ordinarily could make immediately, even were the confession the very first item introduced at trial. Moreover, the redacted confession with the blank prominent on its face, in *Richardson*'s words, "*facially* incriminat[es]" the codefendant. (emphasis added). Like the confession in *Bruton* itself, the accusation that the redacted confession makes "is more vivid than inferential incrimination, and hence more difficult to thrust out of mind."

Nor are the policy reasons that *Richardson* provided in support of its conclusion applicable here. *Richardson* expressed concern lest application of *Bruton*'s rule apply where "redaction" of confessions, particularly "confessions incriminating by connection," would often "not [be] possible," thereby forcing prosecutors too often to abandon use either of the confession or of a joint trial. Additional redaction of a confession that uses a blank space, the word "delete," or a symbol, however, normally is possible. Consider as an example a portion of the confession before us: The witness who read the confession told the jury that the confession (among other things) said,

Question: Who was in the group that beat Stacey?

Answer: Me, deleted, deleted, and a few other guys.

App. 11.

Why could the witness not, instead, have said:

Question: Who was in the group that beat Stacey?

Answer: Me and a few other guys.

Richardson itself provides a similar example of this kind of redaction. The confession there at issue had been "redacted to omit all reference to respondent—indeed, to omit all indication that anyone other than Martin and Williams participated in the crime," and it did not indicate that it had been redacted. * * *

The *Richardson* Court also feared that the inclusion, within *Bruton*'s protective rule, of confessions that incriminated "by connection" too often would provoke mistrials, or would unnecessarily lead prosecutors to abandon the confession or joint trial, because neither the prosecutors nor the judge could easily predict, until after the introduction of all the evidence, whether or not *Bruton* had barred use of the confession. To include the use of blanks, the word "delete," symbols, or other indications of redaction, within *Bruton*'s protections, however, runs no such risk. Their use is easily identified prior to trial and does not depend, in any special way, upon the other evidence introduced in the case. We also note that several Circuits have interpreted *Bruton* similarly for many years, yet no one has told us of any significant practical difficulties arising out of their administration of that rule.

For these reasons, we hold that the confession here at issue, which substituted blanks and the word "delete" for the respondent's proper name, falls within the class of statements to which *Bruton*'s protections apply. * * *

Justice SCALIA, with whom THE CHIEF JUSTICE, Justice KEN-NEDY, and Justice THOMAS join, dissenting. * * *

The almost invariable assumption of the law is that jurors follow their instructions. This rule "is a pragmatic one, rooted less in the absolute certitude that the presumption is true than in the belief that it represents a reasonable practical accommodation of the interests of the state and the defendant in the criminal justice process." We have held, for example, that the state may introduce evidence of a defendant's prior convictions for the purpose of sentencing enhancement, or statements elicited from a defendant in violation of *Miranda v. Arizona*, [8th ed., p. 477], for the purpose of impeachment, so long as the jury is instructed that such evidence may not be considered for the purpose of determining guilt. *Spencer v. Texas*, 385 U.S. 554, 87 S.Ct. 648, 17 L.Ed.2d 606 (1967); *Harris v. New York*, [8th ed., p. 812]. The same applies to codefendant confessions: "a witness whose testimony is introduced at a joint trial is not considered to be a witness 'against' a defendant if the jury is instructed to consider that testimony only against a codefendant." *Richardson*, supra. In *Bruton*, we recognized a "narrow exception" to this rule: "We held that a defendant is deprived of his Sixth Amendment right of confrontation when the facially incriminating confession of a nontestifying codefendant is introduced at their joint trial, even if the jury is instructed to consider the confession only against the codefendant."

We declined in *Richardson*, however, to extend *Bruton* to confessions that incriminate only by inference from other evidence. When incrimination is inferential, "it is a less valid generalization that the jury will not likely obey the instruction to disregard the evidence." Today the Court struggles to decide whether a confession redacted to omit the defendant's name is incriminating on its face or by inference. On the one hand, the Court "concede[s] that the jury must use inference to connect the statement in this redacted confession with the defendant," but later asserts, on the other hand, that "the redacted confession with the blank prominent on its face ... 'facially incriminat[es]' " him. The Court should have stopped with its concession: the statement "Me, deleted, deleted, and a few other guys" does not facially incriminate anyone but the speaker. The Court's analogizing of "deleted" to a physical description that clearly identifies the defendant (which we have assumed *Bruton* covers, see *Harrington v. California*, [8th ed., p. 1610]) does not survive scrutiny. By "facially incriminating," we have meant incriminating independent of other evidence introduced at trial. *Richardson*, supra,. Since the defendant's appearance at counsel table is not evidence, the description "red-haired, bearded, one-eyed man-with-a-limp," would be facially incriminating—unless, of course, the defendant had dyed his hair black and shaved his beard before trial, and the prosecution introduced evidence concerning his former appearance. Similarly, the statement "Me, Kevin Gray, and a few other guys" would be facially incriminating, unless the defendant's name set forth in the indictment was not Kevin Gray, and evidence was introduced to the effect that he sometimes used "Kevin Gray" as an alias. By contrast, the person to whom "deleted" refers in "Me, deleted, deleted, and a few other guys" is not apparent from anything the jury knows independent of the evidence at trial. Though the jury may speculate, the statement expressly implicates no one but the speaker.

Of course the Court is correct that confessions redacted to omit the defendant's name are more likely to incriminate than confessions redacted to omit any reference to his existence. But it is also true—and more relevant here—that confessions redacted to omit the defendant's name are less likely to incriminate than confessions that expressly state it. The latter are "powerfully incriminating" as a class, *Bruton,* supra; the former are not so. Here, for instance, there were two names deleted, five or more participants in the crime, and only one other defendant on trial. The jury no doubt may "speculate about the reference," as it speculates when evidence connects a defendant to a confession that does not refer to his existence. The issue, however, is not whether the confession incriminated petitioner, but whether the incrimination is so "powerful" that we must depart from the normal presumption that the jury follows its instructions. *Richardson,* supra. I think it is not—and I am certain that drawing the line for departing from the ordinary rule at the facial identification of the defendant makes more sense than drawing it anywhere else.

The Court's extension of *Bruton* to name-redacted confessions "as a class" will seriously compromise "society's compelling interest in finding, convicting, and punishing those who violate the law." We explained in *Richardson* that forgoing use of codefendant confessions or joint trials was "too high" a price to insure that juries never disregard their instructions. The Court minimizes the damage that it does by suggesting that "[a]dditional redaction of a confession that uses a blank space, the word 'delete,' or a symbol . . . normally is possible." In the present case, it asks, why could the police officer not have testified that Bell's answer was "Me and a few other guys"? The answer, it seems obvious to me, is because that is not what Bell said. Bell's answer was "Me, Tank, Kevin and a few other guys." Introducing the statement with full disclosure of deletions is one thing; introducing as the complete statement what was in fact only a part is something else. And of course even concealed deletions from the text will often not do the job that the Court demands. For inchoate offenses—conspiracy in particular—redaction to delete all reference to a confederate would often render the confession nonsensical. If the question was "Who agreed to beat Stacey?", and the answer was "Me and Kevin," we might redact the answer to "Me and [deleted]," or perhaps to "Me and somebody else," but surely not to just "Me"—for that would no longer be a confession to the conspiracy charge, but rather the foundation for an insanity defense. To my knowledge we have never before endorsed—and to my strong belief we ought not endorse—the redaction of a statement by some means other than the deletion of certain words, with the fact of the deletion shown. The risk to the integrity of our system (not to mention the increase in its complexity) posed by the approval of such free-lance editing seems to me infinitely greater than the risk posed by the entirely honest reproduction that the Court disapproves.

The United States Constitution guarantees, not a perfect system of criminal justice (as to which there can be considerable disagreement), but a minimum standard of fairness. Lest we lose sight of the forest for the trees, it should be borne in mind that federal and state rules of criminal procedure—which can afford to seek perfection because they can be more readily changed—exclude non-testifying-codefendant confessions even where the Sixth Amendment does not. Under the Federal Rules of Criminal Procedure (and Maryland's), a trial court may order separate trials if joinder will prejudice a defendant. See Fed. Rule Crim. Proc. 14; Md.Crim. Rule 4–253(c) (1998). Maryland courts have described the term "prejudice" as a "term of art," which "refers only to prejudice resulting to the defendant from the reception of evidence that would have been inadmissible against that defendant had there been no joinder." The federal rule expressly contemplates that in ruling on a severance motion the court will inspect "in camera any statements or confessions made by the defendants which the government intends to introduce in evidence at the trial." Fed. Rule Crim. Proc. 14. Federal and most state trial courts (including Maryland's) also have the discretion to exclude unfairly prejudicial (albeit probative) evidence. Here, petitioner moved for a severance on the ground that the admission of Bell's confession would be unfairly prejudicial. The trial court denied the motion, explaining that where a confession names two others, and the evidence is that five or six others participated, redaction of petitioner's name would not leave the jury with the "unavoidable inference" that Bell implicated Gray.

I do not understand the Court to disagree that the redaction itself left unclear to whom the blank referred.[2] That being so, the rule set forth in *Richardson* applies, and the statement could constitutionally be admitted with limiting instruction. This remains, insofar as the Sixth Amendment is concerned, the most "reasonable practical accommodation of the interests of the state and the defendant in the criminal justice process." * * *

---

2. The Court does believe, however, that the answer to a "follow-up question"—"All right, now, officer, after he gave you that information, you subsequently were able to arrest Mr. Kevin Gray; is that correct?" ("That's correct")—"eliminated all doubt" as to the subject of the redaction. That is probably not so, and is certainly far from clear. Testimony that preceded the introduction of Bell's confession had already established that Gray had become a suspect in the case, and that a warrant had been issued for his arrest, before Bell confessed. Respondent contends that, given this trial background, and in its context, the prosecutor's question did not imply any connection between Bell's confession and Gray's arrest, and was simply a means of making the transition from Bell's statement to the next piece of evidence, Gray's statement. That is at least arguable, and an appellate court is in a poor position to resolve such a contextual question de novo. * * * But if the question did bring the redaction home to the defendant, surely that shows the impropriety of the question rather than of the redaction—and the question was not objected to. The failure to object deprives petitioner of the right to complain of some incremental identifiability added to the redacted statement by the question and answer. Of course the Court's reliance upon this testimony belies its contention that name-redacted confessions are powerfully incriminating "as a class."

Chapter 19

THE RIGHT TO A "SPEEDY TRIAL"—AND TO "SPEEDY DISPOSITION" AT OTHER STEPS IN THE CRIMINAL PROCESS

SECTION 1. SPEEDY TRIAL

8th ed., p. 1130; before Note 2, add:

1a. *Barker "rebalanced"?* Was the *Barker* test "revised" in *Reed v. Farley,* 512 U.S. 339, 114 S.Ct. 2291, 129 L.Ed.2d 277 (1994)(also discussed at Supp., p. 148)? The Court there held that a state court's failure to observe the 120–day time-for-trial rule of the Interstate Agreement on Detainers was not cognizable on federal habeas corpus when, as there, the defendant registered no objection to the trial date when it was set and suffered no prejudice from the delay. In responding to Reed's argument the result should be otherwise because the IAD's speedy trial provision "effectuates" the Sixth Amendment speedy trial guarantee, the Court asserted, citing *Barker:* "A showing of prejudice is required to establish a violation of the Sixth Amendment Speedy Trial Clause, and that necessary ingredient is entirely missing here."

Part Four

THE ADVERSARY SYSTEM AND THE DETERMINATION OF GUILT OR INNOCENCE

Chapter 20

THE ASSISTANCE OF COUNSEL

SECTION 3. THE RIGHT TO "EFFECTIVE" ASSISTANCE OF COUNSEL

8th ed., p. 1188; before Note 3, add:

2a. *Did Strickland bring the standard of effective representation "down to the level of ineffective practice"?* Yes, answers Stephen B. Bright, *Counsel for the Poor: The Death Sentence Not for the Worst Crime but for the Worst Lawyer,* 103 Yale L.J. 1835, 1857–58 (1994). Observes Bright, id. at 1858: "Much less than mediocre assistance passes muster under the *Strickland* standard. Errors in judgment and other mistakes may readily be characterized as 'strategy' or 'tactics' and thus are beyond review. Indeed, courts employ a lesser standard for judging the competence of lawyers in a capital case than the standard for malpractice for doctors, accountants, and architects."

8th ed., p. 1189; add to Note 5:

In applying *Strickland,* maintains Stephen Bright, Note 2a supra, at 1862–63, "courts indulge in presumptions and assumptions that have no relation to the reality of legal representation for the poor, particularly in capital cases. One scholar [Bruce A. Green, *Lethal Fiction: The Meaning of "Counsel" in the Sixth Amendment,* 78 Iowa L.Rev. 433, 454 (1993)] has aptly called the idea that bar membership automatically qualifies one to defend a capital case [a] 'lethal fiction.' The reality is

136

that most attorneys are not qualified to represent criminal defendants and certainly not those accused of a capital crimes." Adds Bright, id. at 1864:

"The [*Strickland*] prejudice standard is particularly inappropriate for application to deficient representation at the penalty phase of a capital case. [The Supreme Court has repeatedly said that the sentencer must consider any aspect of a capital defendant's life or background that the defense offers as a basis for a sentence less than death, but it] is impossible for reviewing courts to assess the difference that investigation into mitigating circumstances and the effective presentation of mitigating circumstances might make on a jury's sentencing decision." [a]

8th ed., p. 1191; add to Note on *Kimmelman v. Morrison*:

In *Holman v. Page,* 95 F.3d 481 (7th Cir.1996), petitioner argued that he was denied the rights to the effective assistance of appellate counsel when his attorney failed to appeal the denial of his motion to suppress post-arrest statements allegedly obtained in violation of the Fourth Amendment. "Follow[ing] the reasoning of Justice Powell and the two justices who joined his concurrence in *Morrison,*" the court, per Manion, J., rejected petitioner's claim:

"The harm suffered by a defendant whose counsel was ineffective in attempting to have reliable evidence suppressed 'is not the denial of a fair and reliable adjudication of his guilt, but rather the absence of a windfall' (Powell, J., concurring in *Morrison*). * * * Fairness to the accused has nothing to do with the purpose of the exclusionary rule, which is why Fourth Amendment claims cannot be raised on habeas review. Thus, although counsel may be ineffective in dealing with a defendant's Fourth Amendment claims, the defendant suffers no prejudice as a result,"

The Seventh Circuit denied rehearing *en banc,* 102 F.3d 872, but Wood, J., joined by Ripple and Rovner, JJ., dissented from the denial of rehearing, maintaining that the three-judge panel's decision "squarely conflicts" with the Supreme Court's holding in *Morrison* that "defendants may properly base ineffective assistance of counsel claims in a habeas corpus action on the assertion that their attorney failed properly to litigate a Fourth Amendment claim." The dissenting judges emphasized that Justice Powell's opinion "did *not* speak for the Court."

SECTION 4. MULTIPLE REPRESENTATION AND CONFLICTS OF INTEREST

8th ed., p. 1223; at end of section add new Note:

10. *Which standard applies to attorney breaches of loyalty outside the multiple representation context—Cuyler or Strickland?* Consider BEETS v. SCOTT, 65 F.3d 1258 (5th Cir.1995) (*en banc*). After defendant's conviction for capital murder of her husband, she sought federal

---

a. See also the extract from Professor Arenella's article at Supp., pp. 6–7.

habeas relief, claiming ineffective assistance of counsel based on (1) a transfer, shortly after the trial commenced, of all of her literary and media rights in the case to her lawyer's son; (2) a failure of defendant's lawyer to withdraw as counsel and to testify as a material witness. Does *Strickland* apply in such situations or *Cuyler*, which sets a lower threshold for overturning a conviction than does *Strickland*? In *Beets*, a 13–5 majority of the Seventh Circuit, per EDITH JONES, J., held that *Strickland* offers a "superior framework" for addressing "attorney self-interest conflicts":

"Although the federal circuit courts have unblinkingly applied *Cuyler*'s 'actual conflict' and 'adverse effect' standards to all kinds of alleged attorney ethical conflicts, a careful reading of the Supreme Court cases belies this expansiveness. Neither *Cuyler* nor its progeny strayed beyond the ethical problems of multiple representation. * * *

"If *Cuyler*'s more rigid rule applies to attorney breaches of loyalty outside the multiple representation context, *Strickland*'s desirable and necessary uniform standard of constitutional ineffectiveness will be challenged. Recharacterization of ineffectiveness claims to duty of loyalty claims will be tempting because of *Cuyler*'s lesser standard of prejudice. A blurring of the *Strickland* standard is highly undesirable. As a result of the uncertain boundary between *Cuyler* and *Strickland*, the focus of Sixth Amendment claims would tend to shift mischievously from the overall fairness of the criminal proceedings—the goal of 'prejudice' analysis—to slurs on counsel's integrity—the 'conflict' analysis. Confining *Cuyler* to multiple representation claims poses no similar threat to *Strickland*."[a]

Dissenting Judge KING, joined by four other judges, disagreed with what he called "the majority's unprecedented decision to limit the rule of *Cuyler* to cases involving multiple or serial representation":

"[The majority] thereby excludes from the ambit of *Cuyler* an exceptional conflict between an attorney's self-interest and his client's interest stemming from a highly particularized and powerfully focused source, a media rights contract. If we reserve *Cuyler* for extraordinary attorney-client conflicts of that sort, not normally encountered in law practice, and we apply *Strickland* to alleged deficiencies in an attorney's performance having their sources in the more common incidents of the attorney-client relationship, we avoid having the *Cuyler* exception swallow the *Strickland* rule. At the same time we preserve the benefit of the

a. Applying *Strickland,* the Court concluded that petitioner was not prejudiced by either one of her lawyer's alleged two ethical breaches: "While the media rights contract posed a serious potential conflict of interest, [petitioner] failed to show how it hindered [her lawyer's] presentation of her defense or prejudiced her by rendering the result of her criminal prosecution fundamentally unreliable." As for her lawyer's other alleged ethical breach, his "potential testimony for [petitioner] was cumulative, he was not a necessary witness for her defense and did not face substantial advocate/witness conflict. His failure to withdraw and testify was not professionally unreasonable under *Strickland*."

Cuyler inquiry for those exceptional cases that lie at the heart of the principles animating it.''[b]

b. Although the majority concluded that even if attorney conflicts of interest, apart from the multiple representation context, were governed by the *Cuyler* standard, petitioner's claim would fail, the dissenters saw the matter differently:

"Under *Cuyler*, relief is proper * * * when a defendant 'demonstrates that an actual conflict of interest adversely affected his lawyer's performance.' In the instant case, [the defense lawyer] was faced with an actual conflict because, while [petitioner's] interest lay in having [her lawyer] with-draw and testify, [his] interest lay in re-maining as her counsel, because only then would he be entitled to the potentially lucrative media rights. Additionally, because [her lawyer] did not withdraw and testify, [petitioner's] representation was adversely affected. A Sixth Amendment violation will be shown if the district court concludes that the conflict was the cause of [the lawyer's] failure to withdraw and testify. I would vacate the district court's judgment and remand with instructions to resolve that issue."

Chapter 21

DISCOVERY AND DISCLOSURE

SECTION 2. DISCOVERY BY THE DEFENSE

8th ed., p. 1248: add to Note 3:

Consider also the discussions of Rule 16 "materiality" in the several opinions in *United States v. Armstrong,* Supp. p. 105.

8th ed., p. 1252; add to Note 4:

The third edition of the A.B.A. Standards defines a "written statement" as including: "the substance of a statement of any kind made by that person that is embodied or summarized in any writing or recording, whether or not specifically signed or adopted by that person. The term is intended to include statements contained in police or investigative reports, but does not include attorney work product." A.B.A. Standards for Criminal Justice: Discovery (3rd ed., 1994).

SECTION 5. THE PROSECUTION'S CONSTITUTIONAL DUTY TO DISCLOSE

8th ed., p. 1298; following Note 1, add:

1(a). *Materiality.* In KYLES v. WHITLEY, 514 U.S. 419, 115 S.Ct. 1555, 131 L.Ed.2d 490 (1995), a closely divided Court (5–4) found a *Brady* violation in a state capital murder conviction challenged in the federal courts on habeas review. The prosecution's evidence at trial consisted largely of eyewitness identification by four persons who had been at the scene of the killing in a grocery store parking lot (three of those witnesses having previously picked out defendant from a photo lineup) and physical evidence that linked the defendant to the crime (in particular, the victim's purse, found in the rubbish behind the defendant's house, and the murder weapon, found behind the defendant's kitchen stove). The defense contended (as it had in an earlier trial resulting in a hung jury) that the eyewitnesses were mistaken and that the physical evidence had been planted by an acquaintance ("Beanie") who had instigated the police investigation of defendant and had urged the police to search his apartment and trash. Before trial, defense counsel had filed what was described as "a lengthy motion for disclosure by the state of any exculpatory or impeachment evidence" but the prosecution had "responded that there was 'no exculpatory evidence of any nature.' " Following defendant's conviction and sentence to death, it was discovered that the prosecution had failed to disclose various evidentiary items known to the police. The non-disclosed items included: (1) the initial eyewitness statements taken by police, which offered conflicting descriptions of the murderer, some inconsistent with the defendant's height, age, and hair style (and arguably closer to fitting Beanie); (2) police records establishing Beanie's initial call to the police, his inconsistent statements to the police, and his suggestion that the police search the rubbish; (3) evidence linking Beanie to other crimes committed at the same grocery store and to an unrelated murder; and (4) a computer print-out of the license numbers of the cars police found in the parking lot on the night of the murder (which did not include defendant's car, although it was the police theory that the killer had left his car in the lot after driving off with the victim's car and the jury had been shown a "grainy enlargement" of a crime scene photograph that supposedly had defendant's car in the background).

The Supreme Court majority (per SOUTER, J.) initially discussed "four aspects of materiality under *Bagley*" that guided its assessment of materiality in this case. Following that discussion, which is quoted below, the majority analyzed the nondisclosed evidence as it related to the proof at trial and concluded that the potential cumulative effect of the nondisclosed evidence established a *Brady* violation. The dissent (per SCALIA, J.) initially questioned whether certiorari should have been granted in the case, arguing that there was no dispute as to governing legal principles, but only as to the application of those principles to the facts of this particular case. Turning to those facts, the dissent concluded that there had been no *Brady* violation, as the state had presented a "massive core of evidence" establishing defendant's guilt and "the effect that *Brady* materials would have had in chipping away at the edges of the State's case can only be called immaterial."

While the *Kyles* ruling rested in the end on a fact-intensive analysis that has limited precedential value (especially in light of Court's close division as to that analysis), the opinion for the Court is noteworthy for its initial discussion of general character of "materiality" under *Bagley*. The majority stated in this regard:

"Four aspects of materiality under *Bagley* bear emphasis. Although the constitutional duty is triggered by the potential impact of favorable but undisclosed evidence, a showing of materiality does not require demonstration by a preponderance that disclosure of the suppressed evidence would have resulted ultimately in the defendant's acquittal (whether based on the presence of reasonable doubt or acceptance of an explanation for the crime that does not inculpate the defendant). * * * *Bagley*'s touchstone of materiality is a 'reasonable probability' of a different result, and the adjective is important. The question is not whether the defendant would more likely than not have received a different verdict with the evidence, but whether in its absence he received a fair trial, understood as a trial resulting in a verdict worthy of confidence. A 'reasonable probability' of a different result is accordingly shown when the Government's evidentiary suppression 'undermines confidence in the outcome of the trial.' *Bagley*.

"The second aspect of *Bagley* materiality bearing emphasis here is that it is not a sufficiency of evidence test. A defendant need not demonstrate that after discounting the inculpatory evidence in light of the undisclosed evidence, there would not have been enough left to convict. The possibility of an acquittal on a criminal charge does not imply an insufficient evidentiary basis to convict. One does not show a *Brady* violation by demonstrating that some of the inculpatory evidence should have been excluded, but by showing that the favorable evidence could reasonably be taken to put the whole case in such a different light as to undermine confidence in the verdict.

"Third, we note that, contrary to the assumption made by the Court of Appeals, once a reviewing court applying *Bagley* has found constitutional error there is no need for further harmless-error review. Assuming *arguendo* that a harmless error enquiry were to apply, a *Bagley* error could not be treated as harmless, since 'a reasonable probability that, had the evidence been disclosed to the defense, the result of the proceeding would have been different,' *Bagley,* necessarily entails the conclusion that the suppression must have had ' "substantial and injurious effect or influence in determining the jury's verdict," ' *Brecht v. Abrahamson* [8th ed., p. 1684] * * *.

"The fourth and final aspect of *Bagley* materiality to be stressed here is its definition in terms of suppressed evidence considered collectively, not item-by-item. As Justice Blackmun emphasized in the portion of his opinion written for the Court, the Constitution is not violated every time the government fails or chooses not to disclose evidence that might prove helpful to the defense. We have never held that the Constitution demands an open file policy (however such a policy might work out in practice), and the rule in *Bagley* (and, hence, in *Brady*) requires less of the prosecution than the ABA Standards for Criminal Justice, which call generally for prosecutorial disclosures of any evidence tending to exculpate or mitigate. * * *

"While the definition of *Bagley* materiality in terms of the cumulative effect of suppression must accordingly be seen as leaving the government with a degree of discretion, it must also be understood as imposing a corresponding burden. On the one side, showing that the prosecution knew of an item of favorable evidence unknown to the defense does not amount to a *Brady* violation, without more. But the prosecution, which alone can know what is undisclosed, must be assigned the consequent responsibility to gauge the likely net effect of all such evidence and make disclosure when the point of 'reasonable probability' is reached. This in turn means that the individual prosecutor has a duty to learn of any favorable evidence known to the others acting on the government's behalf in the case, including the police. But whether the prosecutor succeeds or fails in meeting this obligation (whether, that is, a failure to disclose is in good faith or bad faith, see *Brady*), the prosecution's responsibility for failing to disclose known, favorable evidence rising to a material level of importance is inescapable.

"The State of Louisiana would prefer an even more lenient rule. It pleads that some of the favorable evidence in issue here was not disclosed even to the prosecutor until after trial, and it suggested below that it should not be held accountable under *Bagley* and *Brady* for evidence known only to police investigators and not to the prosecutor. To accommodate the State in this manner would, however, amount to a serious change of course from the *Brady* line of cases. In the State's favor it may be said that no one doubts that police investigators sometimes fail to inform a prosecutor of all they know. But neither is there any serious doubt that 'procedures and regulations can be established to carry [the prosecutor's] burden and to insure communication of all relevant information on each case to every lawyer who deals with it.' *Giglio v. United States* [8th ed., p. 1289, fn. b]. Since, then, the prosecutor has the means to discharge the government's *Brady* responsibility if he will, any argument for excusing a prosecutor from disclosing what he does not happen to know about boils down to a plea to substitute the police for the prosecutor, and even for the courts themselves, as the final arbiters of the government's obligation to ensure fair trials.

"Short of doing that, we were asked at oral argument to raise the threshold of materiality because the *Bagley* standard 'makes it difficult . . . to know' from the 'perspective [of the prosecutor at] trial . . . exactly what might become important later on.' The State asks for 'a certain amount of leeway in making a judgment call' as to the disclosure of any given piece of evidence. * * * Uncertainty about the degree of further 'leeway' that might satisfy the State's request for a 'certain amount' of it is the least of the reasons to deny the request. At bottom, what the State fails to recognize is that, with or without more leeway, the prosecution cannot be subject to any disclosure obligation without at some point having the responsibility to determine when it must act. Indeed, even if due process were thought to be violated by every failure to disclose an item of exculpatory or impeachment evidence (leaving harmless error as the government's only fallback), the prosecutor would still be forced to make judgment calls about what would count as favorable evidence, owing to the very fact that the character of a piece of evidence as favorable will often turn on the context of the existing or potential evidentiary record. Since the prosecutor would have to exercise some judgment even if the State were subject to this most stringent disclosure obligation, it is hard to find merit in the State's complaint over the responsibility for judgment under the existing system, which does not tax the prosecutor with error for any failure to disclose, absent a further showing of materiality. Unless, indeed, the adversary system of prosecution is to descend to a gladiatorial level unmitigated by any prosecutorial obligation for the sake of truth, the government simply cannot avoid responsibility for knowing when the suppression of evidence has come to portend such an effect on a trial's outcome as to destroy confidence in its result.

"This means, naturally, that a prosecutor anxious about tacking too close to the wind will disclose a favorable piece of evidence. * * * This is as it should be. Such disclosure will serve to justify trust in the prosecutor as 'the representative . . . of a sovereignty . . . whose interest . . . in a criminal prosecution is not that it shall win a case, but that justice shall be done.' *Berger v. United States.* And it will tend to preserve the criminal trial, as distinct from the prosecutor's private deliberations, as the chosen forum for ascertaining the truth about criminal accusations. * * * The prudence of the careful prosecutor should not therefore be discouraged."

8th ed., p. 1298; add to Note 2:

In *Wood v. Bartholomew*, 516 U.S. 1, 116 S.Ct. 7, 133 L.Ed.2d 1 (1996), the Ninth Circuit found a *Brady* violation in the prosecution's failure to disclose to defense the results of polygraph tests it had administered to two of its witnesses. Those results were inadmissible under state law, even for impeachment purposes, but as the Supreme Court later noted, "[t]o get around this problem, the Ninth Circuit reasoned that the information, had it been disclosed to the defense, might have led [defense] counsel to conduct additional discovery that might have led to some additional evidence that could have been utilized." In a per curiam summary reversal, the Supreme Court majority characterized this conclusion as based on "mere speculation" and therefore failing to meet the *Bagley* standard. Indeed, defense counsel, at the habeas hearing," had acknowledged that "disclosure would not have affected the scope of his cross examination in light of the character of the key witness testimony and the relationship to the false responses on the polygraph test to that testimony.

Chapter 22

COERCED, INDUCED AND NEGOTIATED GUILTY PLEAS; PROFESSIONAL RESPONSIBILITY

SECTION 2. REJECTED, KEPT AND BROKEN BARGAINS; UNREALIZED EXPECTATIONS

8th ed., p. 1325; before Note 7, add:

Is the problem in *Marsh* one of prosecutorial "overcharging" to gain unfair leverage in plea bargaining? If so, is there some other solution to this problem? Consider Tracey L. Meares, *Rewards for Good Behavior: Influencing Prosecutorial Discretion and Conduct with Financial Incentives,* 64 Fordham L.Rev. 851, 873 (1995): "I propose a model that financially rewards prosecutors for obtaining convictions either by trial or by plea under the condition that the defendant is convicted on the same charge or charges that the prosecutor pursues at the outset of the case."

8th ed., p. 1325; following first paragraph of Note 8, add:

In UNITED STATES v. MEZZANATTO, 513 U.S. 196, 115 S.Ct. 797, 130 L.Ed.2d 697 (1995), when defendant and his attorney met with the prosecutor for plea discussions, the prosecutor conditioned the discussions on defendant agreeing that any statements he made could be used to impeach any contradictory testimony defendant might give if the case went to trial. Defendant, after consulting his lawyer, agreed to those terms. The case later did go to trial and such impeachment occurred, but defendant's conviction was overturned on appeal on the ground that the agreement was unenforceable. The Supreme Court, per THOMAS, J., disagreed, reasoning that defendant had not shown "that the plea-statement Rules [a] depart from the presumption of waivability" which exists as to "legal rights generally, and evidentiary provisions

---

a. The reference is to Fed.R.Crim.P. 11(e)(6) and virtually identical Fed.R.Evid. 410.

specifically": (1) defendant's claim that the Rules "guarantee fair procedure" and thus cannot be waived is in error, for the "admission of plea statements for impeachment purposes *enhances* the truth-seeking function of trials and will result in more accurate verdicts"; (2) defendant's claim that waiver is inconsistent with the Rules' goal of encouraging voluntary settlement is in error, as "it simply makes no sense to conclude that mutual settlement will be encouraged by precluding negotiation over an issue that may be particularly important to one of the parties to the transaction"; and (3) defendant's claim that waivers should be forbidden because they invite prosecutorial overreaching is in error, as "the appropriate response to [such] predictions of abuse is to permit case-by-case inquiries into whether waiver agreements are the product of fraud or coercion." [b]

8th ed., p. 1334; before Note 8, add:

7a. One very common variety of plea bargain includes as an ingredient a promise by the defendant to assist in the investigation or prosecution of others, which if broken will likewise serve as a basis for the prosecution to withhold the concessions it promised.[c] It once was the view that "the question whether defendant did in fact fail to perform the condition precedent is an issue not to be finally determined unilaterally by the government, but only on the basis of adequate evidence by the Court." *United States v. Simmons,* 537 F.2d 1260 (4th Cir.1976). However, cases of this genre now arising under the federal sentencing guidelines, which per § 5K1.1 recognize that the prosecution may make a downward departure motion because of the defendant's substantial assistance to the government, typically receive different treatment. This is attributable to *Wade v. United States,* 504 U.S. 181, 112 S.Ct. 1840, 118 L.Ed.2d 524 (1992), where it was held (i) that a sentencing court may not grant defendant a downward departure under § 5K1.1 in the absence of a government motion for same,[d] and (ii) that whether to make such a motion is discretionary with the government, so that even a defendant who provides substantial assistance is not entitled to a remedy unless an unconstitutional motive underlies the government's refusal to

b. Three concurring Justices speculated "that a waiver to use such statements in the case-in-chief would more severely undermine a defendant's incentive to negotiate, and thereby inhibit plea bargaining." Two dissenters concluded the record showed Congress found that "conditions of unrestrained candor are the most effective means of encouraging plea discussions" and thus meant to bar waiver.

c. It does not necessarily follow that the prosecutor may at the same time hold defendant to his plea. See, e.g., *United States v. Fernandez,* 960 F.2d 771 (9th Cir.1992) (where defendant failed to cooperate as promised in a type (C) plea agreement for 6–year sentence, prosecutor could not both hold defendant to his plea and obtain sentence over 6 years, as defendant "could only

have reasonably understood" the agreement "to mean that if he failed to live up to his end of the bargain, the entire plea agreement would be null and void").

d. Likewise, a sentencing court may not grant a defendant a downward departure below the statutory minimum sentence absent a government motion for same made pursuant to 18 U.S.C. § 3553(e). In *Melendez v. United States,* 518 U.S. 120, 116 S.Ct. 2057, 135 L.Ed.2d 427 (1996), the Court held that a government motion made pursuant to § 5K1.1 of the sentencing guidelines that does not request a sentence below the minimum level established by statute does not qualify as the government motion required by § 3553(e).

so move. Although the Court added that the government could sacrifice its discretion and obligate itself to move for downward departure in exchange for a plea, since *Wade* it has become common procedure for federal prosecutors drafting such plea agreements to reserve the "sole discretion" as to whether or not to file a downward departure motion. When that is the case, the courts conclude there is simply "no enforceable obligation" absent the unconstitutional motive mentioned in *Wade*. See, e.g., *United States v. Underwood,* 61 F.3d 306 (5th Cir.1995).

In *United States v. Jones,* 58 F.3d 688 (D.C.Cir.1995), the prosecution did not dispute defendant's claim of complete cooperation but nonetheless claimed the plea agreement was not violated, though the prosecutor's Departure Committee did not find defendant's assistance substantial, because the plea agreement expressly stated the prosecutor's office "retains its discretion" whether to file a downward departure motion. The court found two aspects of the case troubling: (1) "that prosecutors might dangle the suggestion of a [substantial assistance] motion in front of defendants to lure them into plea agreements, all the while knowing that the defendant's cooperation could not possibly constitute assistance valuable enough for the Departure Committee to find it 'substantial,'"; and (2) "the Government's contention at oral argument that, under the terms of its agreement with Jones, its decision not to file a departure motion can only be reviewed for constitutional infirmities proves too much," as even without any contractual arrangements those constitutional limitations exist, but here the plea agreement "provides additional protection" for defendant. "Like all contracts, it includes an implied obligation of good faith and fair dealing," meaning the defendant "was entitled to an honest and fully informed evaluation by the Committee." To ensure that commitment is kept, the court suggested, in cases such as this the prosecution should summarize for the court what information it gave the Departure Committee and any explanation given by that group for finding defendant's assistance insubstantial.

SECTION 3. PROFESSIONAL RESPONSIBILITY: THE ROLE OF PROSECUTOR AND DEFENSE COUNSEL

8th ed., p. 1349; end of footnote, add:

With regard to this "no-contact" rule, reconsider Note 5, 8th ed., p. 641.

SECTION 4. RECEIVING THE PLEA; PLEA WITHDRAWAL

C. Determining Guilty Plea Is Understandingly Made

8th ed., p. 1371; end of Note 4, add:

Fed.R.Crim.P. 11(c) lists the rights waived by a guilty plea about which a federal defendant must be advised, including the "right to be tried by a jury." In *Libretti v. United States*, 516 U.S. 29, 116 S.Ct. 356, 133 L.Ed.2d 271 (1995), the Court held this was only a codification of *Boykin*'s requirement re waiver of constitutional rights, so that the defendant was not entitled to be advised of the right to jury trial re property forfeiture conferred by Fed.R.Crim. 31(e).

D. Determining Factual Basis of Guilty Plea

8th ed., p. 1371; end of Note 1, add:

Libretti v. United States, 516 U.S. 29, 116 S.Ct. 356, 133 L.Ed.2d 271 (1995), held that Rule 11(f) does not require a factual basis showing for a stipulated asset forfeiture embodied in a plea agreement: "Forfeiture is an element of the sentence imposed *following* conviction or, as here, a plea of guilty, and thus falls outside the scope of rule 11(f)." The Court cautioned it did "not mean to suggest that a district court must simply accept a defendant's agreement to forfeit property, particularly when that agreement is not accompanied by a stipulation of facts supporting forfeiture," but added that in the instant case it "need not determine the precise scope of a district court's independent obligation, if any, to inquire into the propriety of a stipulated asset forfeiture embodied in a plea agreement," for here the judge acted upon "ample evidence that * * * the statutory requisites for criminal forfeiture * * * were satisfied."

E. Plea Withdrawal Generally

8th ed., p. 1375; before Note 4, add:

3a. In *United States v. Hyde*, ___ U.S. ___, 117 S.Ct. 1630, 137 L.Ed.2d 935 (1997), the defendant and the government entered into a plea agreement whereby if the defendant pleaded guilty to four of the counts in the indictment the government would dismiss the other four. The agreement was submitted to the district court, which accepted defendant's guilty plea but stated it was deferring decision on acceptance of the plea agreement pending completion of the presentence report. A month later, before sentencing and before the court's decision on the plea agreement, defendant sought to withdraw his plea, but his motion was denied because he had not provided a "fair and just reason." The court of appeals reversed, reasoning that defendant had an absolute right to withdraw his guilty plea before the court accepted the plea agreement because the plea and the agreement are "inextricably bound up together," so that the district court's deferral of acceptance of the plea agreement also constituted a deferral of the decision whether to accept the guilty plea. A unanimous Supreme Court, per Chief Justice Rehnquist, disagreed, noting that the court of appeals' conclusion was contradicted by Fed.R.Crim.P. 11(e)(4), which states the defendant may withdraw his plea as a matter of right only if "the court rejects the plea agreement" (which did not happen in the instant case). Moreover, the Court emphasized, the court of appeals' holding "debases the judicial

proceeding at which a defendant pleads and the court accepts his plea"
and "would degrade the otherwise serious act of pleading guilty into
something akin to a move in a game of chess."

F. SIGNIFICANCE OF NONCOMPLIANCE WITH REQUIREMENTS
FOR RECEIVING GUILTY PLEA

8th ed., p. 1378; new fn. end of second sentence of Note 6:

a. As for the possibility of permitting *no* challenge of prior guilty pleas during sentencing following a later conviction, consider *Custis v. United States,* 511 U.S. 485, 114 S.Ct. 1732, 128 L.Ed.2d 517 (1994). The Court there held that it is constitutionally permissible to bar, as in the Armed Career Criminal Act, 18 U.S.C. § 924(e), virtually all collateral attacks upon prior state convictions being used for sentence enhancement in a federal trial. While a defendant may raise the "unique constitutional defect" of "failure to appoint counsel for an indigent defendant," challenge of other constitutional defects, such as an invalid guilty plea, may constitutionally be barred entirely in this setting. "Ease of administration" and the "interest in promoting the finality of judgments" (said to "bear extra weight in cases in which the prior convictions, such as the ones challenged by Custis, are based on guilty pleas") were the considerations relied upon by the *Custis* Court in support of that conclusion.

SECTION 5. THE EFFECT OF A GUILTY PLEA: MORE ON THE EFFECTIVE ASSISTANCE OF COUNSEL AND THE WAIVER (OR FORFEITURE) OF RIGHTS

8th ed., p. 1387; before Note 6, add:

5a. In BOUSLEY v. UNITED STATES, ___ U.S. ___, 118 S.Ct.
1604, 828 L.Ed.2d 140 (1998), Bousley pleaded guilty to drug possession
with intent to distribute and also to "using" a firearm "during and in
relation to a drug trafficking crime" in violation of 18 U.S.C. § 924(c)(1).
On appeal, he did not challenge the plea's validity, but later sought
habeas relief on the ground that his plea lacked a factual basis; the
district court dismissed his petition. While his appeal was pending, the
Supreme Court held in *Bailey v. United States,* 516 U.S. 137, 116 S.Ct.
501, 133 L.Ed.2d 472 (1995), that a conviction for using a firearm under
§ 924(c)(1) requires proof of "active employment of the firearm." The
court of appeals held Bousley could not obtain relief based on *Bailey,* but
the Supreme Court concluded this was not necessarily so. The Court
concluded there was no nonretroactivity problem because *Bailey* had
decided what the statute had always meant, and that Bousley could
prevail on habeas regarding an issue not previously raised if on remand
he showed he was "actually innocent" [see Supp. p. 211].

Regarding the merits of Bousley's claim, "that his guilty plea was
unintelligent" because he was misinformed as to the elements of a § 924
(c)(1) offense, and, indeed, "that the record reveals that neither he, nor
his counsel, nor the court correctly understood the essential elements of
the crime with which he was charged," the Court, per REHNQUIST,
C.J., agreed that if this contention were proven it would make his guilty
plea "constitutionally invalid." As for *Brady, McMann* and *Parker,* they

"are not to the contrary. Each of those cases involve a criminal defendant who pleaded guilty after being correctly informed as to the essential nature of the charge against him. Those defendants later attempted to challenge their guilty pleas when it became evident that they had misjudged the strength of the Government's case or the penalties to which they were subject. * * * In this case, by contrast, petitioner asserts that he was misinformed as to the true nature of the charge against him."

Chapter 23

TRIAL BY JURY

SECTION 1. RIGHT TO JURY TRIAL; WAIVER

8th ed., p. 1390; end of second line of last paragraph, add fn. aa:

aa. The distinction between a criminal contempt and a civil contempt, as to which there is no right to jury trial, is often difficult to draw. In *International Union, UMW v. Bagwell*, 512 U.S. 821, 114 S.Ct. 2552, 129 L.Ed.2d 642 (1994), a state court enjoined the union from conducting unlawful strike-related activities against certain mining companies, later fined the union for its disobedience and announced the union would be fined for any future breaches according to a specified fine schedule, and still later levied fines against the union totalling over $64,000,000. The state supreme court held these fines were civil and thus could be imposed without jury trial, but a unanimous Supreme Court reversed. The Court, per Blackmun, J., stressed these points: (1) While a contempt fine is civil if it merely compensates the complainant for losses sustained, such was not the case here, as the complainants neither requested compensation nor presented evidence regarding their injuries. (2) While traditionally a contempt fine has been considered civil if it forced a defendant into compliance with a court order, this does *not* mean (a) that the fines here were civil because there was a prospective fine schedule, for the "union's ability to avoid the contempt fines was indistinguishable from the ability of any ordinary citizen to avoid a criminal sanction by conforming his behavior to the law"; or (b) that the fines are criminal where they prohibit conduct but not when they mandate affirmative action, as often "injunctive provisions containing essentially the same command can be phrased either in mandatory or prohibitory terms." (3) While direct contempts in the presence of the court are subject to immediate summary adjudication without jury trial, the union's conduct did not occur in the court's presence. (4) Civil contempt without jury trial is appropriate for certain indirect contempts, "such as failure to comply with document discovery, [which] impedes the court's ability to adjudicate the proceedings before it," but the union's conduct was also not of that variety. (5) Because the state court "levied contempt fines for widespread, ongoing, out-of-court violations of a complex injunction," and thereby "effectively policed petitioner's compliance with an entire code of conduct that the court itself had imposed," resulting in fines which "unquestionably" were not at the petty offense level, the contempt must be deemed criminal, as in "such circumstances disinterested factfinding and even-handed adjudication were essential," and thus "petitioners were entitled to a criminal jury trial."

8th ed., p. 1391; before Note 2, add:

In LEWIS v. UNITED STATES, 518 U.S. 322, 116 S.Ct. 2163, 135 L.Ed.2d 590 (1996), petitioner argued "that, where a defendant is charged with multiple petty offenses in a single prosecution, the Sixth Amendment requires that the aggregate potential penalty be the basis for determining whether a jury trial is required." The Court, per O'CONNOR, J., disagreed, noting that per *Blanton* "we determine

151

whether an offense is serious by looking to the judgment of the legislature, primarily as expressed in the maximum authorized term of imprisonment. Here, by setting the maximum authorized prison term at six months, the legislature categorized the offense of obstructing the mail as petty. The fact that the petitioner was charged with two counts of a petty offense does not revise the legislative judgment as to the gravity of that particular offense, nor does it transform the petty offense into a serious one, to which the jury-trial right would apply." As for petitioner's reliance on *Codispoti v. Pennsylvania,* 418 U.S. 506, 94 S.Ct. 2687, 41 L.Ed.2d 912 (1974), where the defendant was deemed entitled to jury trial because the aggregate penalties actually imposed exceeded six months, the Court distinguished that case on two grounds: (1) there "the legislature had not set a specific penalty for criminal contempt," in which case "courts use the severity of the penalty actually imposed as the measure of the character of the particular offense," and (2) the "benefit of a jury trial, ' "as a protection against the arbitrary exercise of official power," ' " was deemed particularly important in [the criminal contempt] context."

KENNEDY, J., joined by Breyer, J., concurring, concluded that the "right to jury trial extends as well to a defendant who is sentenced in one proceeding to more than six months' imprisonment." The majority's efforts to distinguish *Codispoti* were deemed "not convincing," as (1) the "absence of a statutory maximum sentence * * * has nothing whatever to do with whether a court must aggregate the penalties that are in fact imposed for each crime," and (2) that case concerned post-trial contempt proceedings, said there to be governed by the "ordinary rudiments of due process." Moreover, *Codispoti* "must not be confused with the line of cases entitling a defendant to a jury trial if he is charged with a crime punishable by more than six months' imprisonment, regardless of the sentence he in fact receives. The two lines of cases are consistent. Crimes punishable by sentences of more than six months are deemed by the community's social and ethical judgments to be serious. Opprobrium attaches to conviction of those crimes regardless of the length of the actual sentence imposed, and the stigma itself is enough to entitle the defendant to a jury. This rationale does not entitle a defendant to trial by jury if he is charged only with petty offenses; even if they could result in a long sentence when taken together, convictions for petty offenses do not carry the same stigma as convictions for serious crimes.

"The imposition of stigma, however, is not the only or even the primary consequence a jury trial serves to constrain. As *Codispoti* recognizes, and as ought to be evident, the Sixth Amendment also serves the different and more practical purpose of preventing a court from effecting a most serious deprivation of liberty—ordering a defendant to prison for a substantial period of time—without the Government's persuading a jury he belongs there. A deprivation of liberty so significant may be exacted if a defendant faces punishment for a series of crimes, each of which can be punished by no more than six months' imprisonment. The stakes for a defendant may then amount in the aggregate to many years in prison, in which case he must be entitled to interpose a jury between himself and the Government. If[, as in the instant case,] the trial court rules at the outset that no more than six months' imprisonment will be imposed for the combined petty offenses, however, the liberty the jury serves to protect will not be endangered, and there is no corresponding right to jury trial."

STEVENS, J., joined by Ginsburg, J., agreed with Justice Kennedy "to the extent he would hold that a prosecution which exposes the accused to a sentence of imprisonment longer than six months, whether for a single offense or for a series of offenses, is sufficiently serious to confer on the defendant the right to demand a jury," but not otherwise:

"All agree that a judge may not strip a defendant of the right to a jury trial for a serious crime by promising a sentence of six months or less. This is so because '[o]pprobrium attaches to conviction of those crimes regardless of the length of the actual sentence imposed' (Kennedy, J., concurring in judgment). In my view, the same rule must apply to prosecutions involving multiple offenses which are serious by virtue of their aggregate possible sentence. I see no basis for assuming that the dishonor associated with multiple convictions for petty offenses is less than the dishonor associated with conviction of a single serious crime. Because the right attaches at the moment of prosecution, a judge may not deprive a defendant of a jury trial by making a pretrial determination that the crimes charged will not warrant a sentence exceeding six months."

8th ed., p. 1397; before Note 6, add:

In *United States v. Thomas*, 116 F.3d 606 (2d Cir.1997), the court answered in the affirmative the question of "whether a juror's intent to convict or acquit regardless of the evidence constitutes a basis for the juror's removal during the course of deliberations under Rule 23(b)": "Nullification is, by definition, a violation of a juror's oath to apply the law as instructed by the court in the words of the standard oath administered to jurors in the federal courts, to render a true verdict according to the law and the evidence. * * * We categorically reject the idea that, in a society committed to the rule of law, jury nullification is desirable or that courts may permit it to occur when it is within their authority to prevent it. Accordingly, we conclude that a juror who intends to nullify the applicable law is no less subject to dismissal than is a juror who disregards the court's instructions due to an event or relationship that renders him biased or otherwise unable to render a fair and impartial verdict." But the court then went on to explain why the instances in which such removal could occur would be rare: "Where, however, as here, a presiding judge receives reports that a deliberating juror is intent on defying the court's instructions on the law, the judge may well have no means of investigating the allegation without unduly breaching the secrecy of deliberations. [T]o determine whether a juror is bent on defiant disregard of the applicable law, the court would generally need to intrude into the juror's thought processes. * * * A presiding judge faced with anything but unambiguous evidence that a juror refuses to apply the law as instructed need go no further in his investigation of the alleged nullification; in such circumstances, the juror is not subject to dismissal on the basis of his alleged refusal to follow the court's instructions. * * * Where the duty and authority to prevent defiant disregard of the law or evidence comes into conflict with the principle of secret jury deliberations, we are compelled to select the lesser of two evils. Achieving a more perfect system for monitoring the conduct of jurors in the intense environment of a jury deliberation room entails an unacceptable breach of the secrecy that is essential to the work of juries in the American system of justice."

Paul Butler, *Racially Based Jury Nullification: Black Power in the Criminal Justice System*, 105 Yale L.J. 677, 679, 705 (1995), "examines the question of what role race should play in black jurors' decisions to acquit defendants in criminal cases. Specifically, I consider trials that include both African–American defendants and African–American jurors. I argue that the race of a black defendant is sometimes a legally and morally appropriate factor for jurors to consider in reaching a verdict of not guilty or for an individual juror to consider in refusing to vote for conviction.

"My thesis is that, for pragmatic and political reasons, the black community is better off when some nonviolent lawbreakers remain in the community rather than go to prison. The decision as to what kind of conduct by African–Americans ought to be punished is better made by African–Americans themselves, based on the costs and benefits to their community, than by the traditional criminal justice process, which is controlled by white lawmakers and white law enforcers. Legally, the doctrine of jury nullification gives the power to make this decision to African–American jurors who sit in judgment of African–American defendants. Considering the costs of law enforcement to the black community and the failure of white lawmakers to devise significant nonincarcerative responses to black antisocial conduct, it is the moral responsibility of black jurors to emancipate some guilty black outlaws."

"* * * I distinguish racially based nullification by African–Americans from recent right-wing proposals for jury nullification on the ground that the former is sometimes morally right and the latter is not." For strong criticism of Professor Butler's views, see Randall Kennedy, *Race, Crime and the Law* 295–310 (1997); Andrew Leipold, *The Dangers of Race–Based Jury Nullification: A Response to Prof. Butler*, 44 U.C.L.A. L.Rev. 109 (1996).

Andrew Leipold, *Rethinking Jury Nullification*, 82 Va.L.Rev. 253, 258–59 (1996), asserts that the nullification doctrine "as currently recognized should be abolished and replaced with a two-part scheme": (1) "legislatures [would] create an affirmative 'nullification defense' that would allow a jury to return a not-guilty verdict against the evidence, but only when certain statutory criteria are satisfied"; and (2) "the use of error-correcting procedures in criminal cases, including appeals from acquittals," would be allowed, as once "the jury's nullification power is *limited* to [the statutory] defense, the justification for barring these procedures would end."

8th ed., p. 1397; replace Note 6:

6. *Fact or Law.* In United States v. Gaudin, 515 U.S. 506, 115 S.Ct. 2310, 132 L.Ed.2d 444 (1995), the defendant was charged under 18 U.S.C. § 1001 with having made false statements on federal loan documents. Although "materiality" is an element of the offense, at the close of the evidence the trial judge instructed the jury: "The issue of materiality . . . is not submitted to you for your decision but rather is a matter for the decision of the court. You are instructed that the statements charged in the indictment are material statements." A unanimous Court, per Scalia, J., in affirming the court of appeals' reversal of defendant's conviction, relied on the Fifth Amendment due process clause and the Sixth Amendment right to jury trial, which "require criminal convictions to rest upon a jury determination that the defendant is guilty of every element of the crime with which he is charged." Although the government argued that this principle "actually applies to *only the factual components* of the essential elements," the Court disagreed. Specifically, the Court reasoned that though it is for the judge to "instruct the jury on the law and to insist that the jury follow his instructions," "the jury's constitutional responsibility is not merely to determine the facts, but to apply the law to those facts and draw the ultimate conclusion of guilt or innocence."

SECTION 2. JURY SELECTION

8th ed., p. 1405; before Note 5, add:

Do we need an affirmative action program for minority jurors? Consider Albert W. Alschuler, *Racial Quotas and the Jury*, 44 Duke L.J. 704, 716–17, 723 (1995), concluding that proposals to ensure proportionate minority representation on all jury panels would be constitutional, as "affirmative action in the context of jury selection presents a different issue from any that the Supreme Court has considered. * * * These quotas would not deprive individuals of significant tangible benefits; they would not brand any group as inferior or evaluate any individual on the basis of racial stereotypes; and * * * would be likely to enhance the * * * jury's achievement of its objectives."

8th ed., p. 1408; before Note 2, add:

Should anonymous juries be the exception or the rule? Consider Nancy J. King, *Nameless Justice: The Case for the Routine Use of American Juries in Criminal Trials*, 49 Vand.L.Rev. 123, 125 (1996), proposing "the routine use of anonymous juries in criminal cases, at least in urban areas where anonymity is feasible. By alleviating jury fear, anonymity can enhance the participation of citizens in jury service, the reliability of the voir dire process, the quality of jury deliberations, and the fairness of criminal verdicts."

8th ed., p. 1408; following Note 3, add:

3a.   Many courts now utilize detailed questionnaires to obtain information about the backgrounds and attitudes of prospective jurors.

Questions From the Jury Pool on Privacy, N.Y. Times, May 13, 1994, p. B9, col. 1, reports that a prospective juror was sentenced to a three-day jail term for contempt of court for answering "not applicable" to 12 questions in a 100–question questionnaire posed to prospective jurors in a murder case.   She gave that answer "to queries about her income, her religion, her political affiliation and books and TV shows she enjoys, among other questions."   What should the result be on her appeal of the contempt citation?   This article notes: "But prosecutors and criminal defense lawyers alike contend that a prospective juror's right to privacy must yield to the imperatives of a fair trial, particularly in a murder case.   Questions that appear entirely irrelevant to a member of a jury pool, they say, may nonetheless help lawyers develop a well-rounded profile."

The O.J. Simpson trial, where prospective jurors in advance of voir dire were required to answer 294 questions running over 75 pages, has focused further attention upon the practice of using juror questionnaires. See Craig M. Bradley & Joseph L. Hoffman, *Public Perception, Justice, and the "Search for Truth" in Criminal Cases,* 69 S.Cal.L.Rev. 1267, 1284 (1996) (suggesting courts should prohibit the use of questionnaires); Peter Arenella, *Foreword: O.J. Lessons,* 69 S.Cal.L.Rev. 1240, 1233 (1996) (suggesting ban on juror questionnaires "in all cases except those where the defendant's right to a fair trial has been threatened by extremely prejudicial pretrial publicity").

8th ed., p. 1412; new fn. end of Note 5:

b.   *Witt* also held that a trial judge's conclusion a prospective juror is disqualified for bias is to be accorded a presumption of correctness, but this was because the case arose on federal habeas corpus, and thus a state appellate court may but need not adopt that standard of review. *Greene v. Georgia,* 519 U.S. 145, 117 S.Ct. 578, 136 L.Ed.2d 507 (1996).

8th ed., p. 1431; following Note 7, add:

J.E.B. v. ALABAMA EX REL. T.B.
511 U.S. 127, 114 S.Ct. 1419, 128 L.Ed.2d 89 (1994).

Justice BLACKMUN delivered the opinion of the Court.   * * *

On behalf of relator T.B., the mother of a minor child, respondent State of Alabama filed a complaint for paternity and child support against petitioner J.E.B. in the District Court of Jackson County, Alabama.   On October 21, 1991, the matter was called for trial and jury selection began.   The trial court assembled a panel of 36 potential jurors, 12 males and 24 females.   After the court excused three jurors for cause, only 10 of the remaining 33 jurors were male. The State then used 9 of its 10 peremptory strikes to remove male jurors; petitioner used all but one of his strikes to remove female jurors. As a result, all the selected jurors were female.

Before the jury was empaneled, petitioner objected to the State's peremptory challenges on the ground that they were exercised against male jurors solely on the basis of gender, in violation of the Equal Protection Clause of the Fourteenth Amendment. * * * The court rejected petitioner's claim and empaneled the all-female jury. The jury found petitioner to be the father of the child and the court entered an order directing him to pay child support. On post-judgment motion, the court reaffirmed its ruling that *Batson* does not extend to gender-based peremptory challenges.

We granted certiorari to resolve a question that has created a conflict of authority—whether the Equal Protection Clause forbids peremptory challenges on the basis of gender as well as on the basis of race. Today we reaffirm what, by now, should be axiomatic: Intentional discrimination on the basis of gender by state actors violates the Equal Protection Clause, particularly where, as here, the discrimination serves to ratify and perpetuate invidious, archaic, and overbroad stereotypes about the relative abilities of men and women.

Discrimination on the basis of gender in the exercise of peremptory challenges is a relatively recent phenomenon. Gender-based peremptory strikes were hardly practicable for most of our country's existence, since, until the 19th century, women were completely excluded from jury service. So well-entrenched was this exclusion of women that in 1880 this Court, while finding that the exclusion of African–American men from juries violated the Fourteenth Amendment, expressed no doubt that a State "may confine the selection [of jurors] to males." *Strauder v. West Virginia,* 100 U.S. 303, 310, 25 L.Ed. 664.

Many States continued to exclude women from jury service well into the present century, despite the fact that women attained suffrage upon ratification of the Nineteenth Amendment in 1920. States that did permit women to serve on juries often erected other barriers, such as registration requirements and automatic exemptions, designed to deter women from exercising their right to jury service.

The prohibition of women on juries was derived from the English common law which, according to Blackstone, rightfully excluded women from juries under "the doctrine of *propter defectum sexus,* literally, the 'defect of sex.'" In this country, supporters of the exclusion of women from juries tended to couch their objections in terms of the ostensible need to protect women from the ugliness and depravity of trials. Women were thought to be too fragile and virginal to withstand the polluted courtroom atmosphere. * * *

Taylor [*v. Louisiana,* 8th ed., p. 1400] relied on Sixth Amendment principles, but the opinion's approach is consistent with the heightened equal protection scrutiny afforded gender-based classifications. Since

Reed v. Reed, 404 U.S. 71, 92 S.Ct. 251, 30 L.Ed.2d 225 (1971), this Court consistently has subjected gender-based classifications to heightened scrutiny in recognition of the real danger that government policies that professedly are based on reasonable considerations in fact may be reflective of "archaic and overbroad" generalizations about gender, or based on "outdated misconceptions concerning the role of females in the home rather than in the 'marketplace and world of ideas.'"

Despite the heightened scrutiny afforded distinctions based on gender, respondent argues that gender discrimination in the selection of the petit jury should be permitted, though discrimination on the basis of race is not. Respondent suggests that "gender discrimination in this country ... has never reached the level of discrimination" against African–Americans, and therefore gender discrimination, unlike racial discrimination, is tolerable in the courtroom. While the prejudicial attitudes toward women in this country have not been identical to those held toward racial minorities, the similarities between the experiences of racial minorities and women, in some contexts, "overpower those differences." As a plurality of this Court observed in *Frontiero v. Richardson,* 411 U.S. 677, 93 S.Ct. 1764, 36 L.Ed.2d 583 (1973):

> "[T]hroughout much of the 19th century the position of women in our society was, in many respects, comparable to that of blacks under the pre-Civil War slave codes. Neither slaves nor women could hold office, serve on juries, or bring suit in their own names, and married women traditionally were denied the legal capacity to hold or convey property or to serve as legal guardians of their own children.... And although blacks were guaranteed the right to vote in 1870, women were denied even that right—which is itself 'preservative of other basic civil and political rights'—until adoption of the Nineteenth Amendment half a century later."

Certainly, with respect to jury service, African–Americans and women share a history of total exclusion, a history which came to an end for women many years after the embarrassing chapter in our history came to an end for African–Americans.

We need not determine, however, whether women or racial minorities have suffered more at the hands of discriminatory state actors during the decades of our Nation's history. It is necessary only to acknowledge that "our Nation has had a long and unfortunate history of sex discrimination," a history which warrants the heightened scrutiny we afford all gender-based classifications today. Under our equal protection jurisprudence, gender-based classifications require "an exceedingly persuasive justification" in order to survive constitutional scrutiny. Thus, the only question is whether discrimination on the basis of gender in jury selection substantially furthers the State's legitimate interest in achieving a fair and impartial trial. In making this assessment, we do not weigh the value of peremptory challenges as an institution against our asserted commitment to eradicate invidious discrimination from the courtroom. Instead, we consider whether peremptory challenges based on gender stereotypes provide substantial aid to a litigant's effort to secure a fair and impartial jury.

Far from proffering an exceptionally persuasive justification for its gender-based peremptory challenges, respondent maintains that its decision to strike virtually all the males from the jury in this case "may reasonably have been based upon the perception, supported by history, that men otherwise totally qualified to serve upon a jury might be more sympathetic and receptive to the arguments of a man alleged in a paternity action to be the father of an out-of-wedlock child, while women equally qualified to serve upon a jury might be more sympathetic and receptive to the arguments of the complaining witness who bore the child." [9]

We shall not accept as a defense to gender-based peremptory challenges "the very stereotype the law condemns." Respondent's rationale, not unlike those regularly expressed for gender-based strikes, is reminiscent of the arguments advanced to justify the total exclusion of women from juries. Respondent offers virtually no support for the conclusion that gender alone is an accurate predictor of juror's attitudes; yet it urges this Court to condone the same stereotypes that justified the wholesale exclusion of women from juries and the ballot box.[11] Respondent seems to assume that gross generalizations that would be deemed impermissible if made on the basis of race are somehow permissible when made on the basis of gender.

Discrimination in jury selection, whether based on race or on gender, causes harm to the litigants, the community, and the individual jurors who are wrongfully excluded from participation in the judicial process. The litigants are harmed by the risk that the prejudice which motivated the discriminatory selection of the jury will infect the entire proceedings. The community is harmed by the State's participation in the perpetuation of invidious group stereotypes and the inevitable loss of

---

9. Respondent cites one study in support of its quasi-empirical claim that women and men may have different attitudes about certain issues justifying the use of gender as a proxy for bias. See R. Hastie, S. Penrod & N. Pennington, Inside the Jury 140 (1983). The authors conclude: "Neither student nor citizen judgments for typical criminal case material have revealed differences between male and female verdict preferences. * * * The picture differs [only] for rape cases, where female jurors appear to be somewhat more conviction-prone than male jurors". The majority of studies suggest that gender plays no identifiable role in jurors' attitudes. See, e.g., V. Hans & N. Vidmar, Judging the Jury 76 (1986) ("[I]n the majority of studies there are no significant differences in the way men and women perceive and react to trials; yet a few studies find women more defense-oriented, while still others show women more favorable to the prosecutor").

Even in 1956, before women had a constitutional right to serve on juries, some commentators warned against using gender as a proxy for bias. See 1 F. Busch, Law and Tactics in Jury Trials § 143, p. 207 (1949)("In this age of general and specialized education, availed of generally by both men and women, it would appear unsound to base a peremptory challenge in any case upon the sole ground of sex...."").

11. Even if a measure of truth can be found in some of the gender stereotypes used to justify gender-based peremptory challenges, that fact alone cannot support discrimination on the basis of gender in jury selection. We have made abundantly clear in past cases that gender classifications that rest on impermissible stereotypes violate the Equal Protection Clause, even when some statistical support can be conjured up for the generalization. * * *

confidence in our judicial system that state-sanctioned discrimination in the courtroom engenders. When state actors exercise peremptory challenges in reliance on gender stereotypes, they ratify and reinforce prejudicial views of the relative abilities of men and women. Because these stereotypes have wreaked injustice in so many other spheres of our country's public life, active discrimination by litigants on the basis of gender during jury selection "invites cynicism respecting the jury's neutrality and its obligation to adhere to the law." The potential for cynicism is particularly acute in cases where gender-related issues are prominent, such as cases involving rape, sexual harassment, or paternity. Discriminatory use of peremptory challenges may create the impression that the judicial system has acquiesced in suppressing full participation by one gender or that the "deck has been stacked" in favor of one side.

In recent cases we have emphasized that individual jurors themselves have a right to nondiscriminatory jury selection procedures. Contrary to respondent's suggestion, this right extends to both men and women. All persons, when granted the opportunity to serve on a jury, have the right not to be excluded summarily because of discriminatory and stereotypical presumptions that reflect and reinforce patterns of historical discrimination.[13] Striking individual jurors on the assumption that they hold particular views simply because of their gender is "practically a brand upon them, affixed by law, an assertion of their inferiority." It denigrates the dignity of the excluded juror, and, for a woman, reinvokes a history of exclusion from political participation.[14] The message it sends to all those in the courtroom, and all those who may later learn of the discriminatory act, is that certain individuals, for no reason other than gender, are presumed unqualified by state actors to decide important questions upon which reasonable persons could disagree.

Our conclusion that litigants may not strike potential jurors solely on the basis of gender does not imply the elimination of all peremptory challenges. Neither does it conflict with a State's legitimate interest in using such challenges in its effort to secure a fair and impartial jury. Parties still may remove jurors whom they feel might be less acceptable than others on the panel; gender simply may not serve as a proxy for

13. It is irrelevant that women, unlike African–Americans, are not a numerical minority and therefore are likely to remain on the jury if each side uses its peremptory challenges in an equally discriminatory fashion. Because the right to nondiscriminatory jury selection procedures belongs to the potential jurors, as well as to the litigants, the possibility that members of both genders will get on the jury despite the intentional discrimination is beside the point. The exclusion of even one juror for impermissible reasons harms that juror and undermines public confidence in the fairness of the system.

14. The popular refrain is that all peremptory challenges are based on stereotypes of some kind, expressing various intuitive and frequently erroneous biases. But where peremptory challenges are made on the basis of group characteristics other than race or gender (like occupation, for example), they do not reinforce the same stereotypes about the group's competence or predispositions that have been used to prevent them from voting, participating on juries, pursuing their chosen professions, or otherwise contributing to civic life.

bias. Parties may also exercise their peremptory challenges to remove from the venire any group or class of individuals normally subject to "rational basis" review. Even strikes based on characteristics that are disproportionately associated with one gender could be appropriate, absent a showing of pretext.[16] * * *

Failing to provide jurors the same protection against gender discrimination as race discrimination could frustrate the purpose of *Batson* itself. Because gender and race are overlapping categories, gender can be used as a pretext for racial discrimination. Allowing parties to remove racial minorities from the jury not because of their race, but because of their gender, contravenes well-established equal protection principles and could insulate effectively racial discrimination from judicial scrutiny.

Justice O'CONNOR, concurring.

I agree with the Court that the Equal Protection Clause prohibits the government from excluding a person from jury service on account of that person's gender. * * *. I therefore join the Court's opinion in this case. But today's important blow against gender discrimination is not costless. I write separately to discuss some of these costs, and to express my belief that today's holding should be limited to the government's use of gender-based peremptory strikes.

Batson v. Kentucky itself was a significant intrusion into the jury selection process. *Batson* mini-hearings are now routine in state and federal trial courts, and *Batson* appeals have proliferated as well. Demographics indicate that today's holding may have an even greater impact than did *Batson* itself. In further constitutionalizing jury selection procedures, the Court increases the number of cases in which jury selection—once a sideshow—will become part of the main event.

For this same reason, today's decision further erodes the role of the peremptory challenge. * * *

* * * Our belief that experienced lawyers will often correctly intuit which jurors are likely to be the least sympathetic, and our understanding that the lawyer will often be unable to explain the intuition, are the very reason we cherish the peremptory challenge. But, as we add, layer by layer, additional constitutional restraints on the use of the peremptory, we force lawyers to articulate what we know is often inarticulable.

In so doing we make the peremptory challenge less discretionary and more like a challenge for cause. We also increase the possibility that biased jurors will be allowed onto the jury, because sometimes a lawyer will be unable to provide an acceptable gender-neutral explanation even though the lawyer is in fact correct that the juror is unsympathetic. Similarly, in jurisdictions where lawyers exercise their strikes in open

---

16. For example, challenging all persons who have had military experience would disproportionately affect men at this time, while challenging all persons employed as nurses would disproportionately affect women. Without a showing of pretext, however, these challenges may well not be unconstitutional, since they are not gender- or race-based.

court, lawyers may be deterred from using their peremptories, out of the fear that if they are unable to justify the strike the court will seat a juror who knows that the striking party thought him unfit. Because I believe the peremptory remains an important litigator's tool and a fundamental part of the process of selecting impartial juries, our increasing limitation of it gives me pause.

Nor is the value of the peremptory challenge to the litigant diminished when the peremptory is exercised in a gender-based manner. We know that like race, gender matters. A plethora of studies make clear that in rape cases, for example, female jurors are somewhat more likely to vote to convict than male jurors. Moreover, though there have been no similarly definitive studies regarding, for example, sexual harassment, child custody, or spousal or child abuse, one need not be a sexist to share the intuition that in certain cases a person's gender and resulting life experience will be relevant to his or her view of the case.

Today's decision severely limits a litigant's ability to act on this intuition, for the import of our holding is that any correlation between a juror's gender and attitudes is irrelevant as a matter of constitutional law. But to say that gender makes no difference as a matter of law is not to say that gender makes no difference as a matter of fact. * * * In extending *Batson* to gender we have added an additional burden to the state and federal trial process, taken a step closer to eliminating the peremptory challenge, and diminished the ability of litigants to act on sometimes accurate gender-based assumptions about juror attitudes. * * *

Accordingly, I adhere to my position that the Equal Protection Clause does not limit the exercise of peremptory challenges by private civil litigants and criminal defendants. This case itself presents no state action dilemma, for here the State of Alabama itself filed the paternity suit on behalf of petitioner. But what of the next case? Will we, in the name of fighting gender discrimination, hold that the battered wife—on trial for wounding her abusive husband—is a state actor? Will we preclude her from using her peremptory challenges to ensure that the jury of her peers contains as many women members as possible? I assume we will, but I hope we will not.

Chief Justice REHNQUIST, dissenting.

* * * Unlike the Court, I think the State has shown that jury strikes on the basis of gender "substantially further" the State's legitimate interest in achieving a fair and impartial trial through the venerable practice of peremptory challenges. The two sexes differ, both biologically and, to a diminishing extent, in experience. It is not merely "stereotyping" to say that these differences may produce a difference in outlook which is brought to the jury room. Accordingly, use of peremptory challenges on the basis of sex is generally not the sort of derogatory and invidious act which peremptory challenges directed at black jurors may be. * * *

Justice SCALIA, with whom the CHIEF JUSTICE and Justice THOMAS join, dissenting. * * *

The core of the Court's reasoning is that peremptory challenges on the basis of any group characteristic subject to heightened scrutiny are inconsistent with the guarantee of the Equal Protection Clause. That conclusion can be reached only by focusing unrealistically upon individual exercises of the peremptory challenge, and ignoring the totality of the practice. Since all groups are subject to the peremptory challenge (and will be made the object of it, depending upon the nature of the particular case) it is hard to see how any group is denied equal protection. That explains why peremptory challenges coexisted with the Equal Protection Clause for 120 years. This case is a perfect example of how the system as a whole is even-handed. While the only claim before the Court is petitioner's complaint that the prosecutor struck male jurors, for every man struck by the government petitioner's own lawyer struck a woman. To say that men were singled out for discriminatory treatment in this process is preposterous. The situation would be different if both sides systematically struck individuals of one group, so that the strikes evinced group-based animus and served as a proxy for segregated venire lists. The pattern here, however, displays not a systemic sex-based animus but each side's desire to get a jury favorably disposed to its case. That is why the Court's characterization of respondent's argument as "reminiscent of the arguments advanced to justify the total exclusion of women from juries" is patently false. Women were categorically excluded from juries because of doubt that they were competent; women are stricken from juries by peremptory challenge because of doubt that they are well disposed to the striking party's case. * * *

Even if the line of our later cases guaranteed by today's decision limits the theoretically boundless *Batson* principle to race, sex, and perhaps other classifications subject to heightened scrutiny (which presumably would include religious belief[a]), much damage has been done. It has been done, first and foremost, to the peremptory challenge system, which loses its whole character when (in order to defend against "imper-

---

a. In *State v. Davis,* 504 N.W.2d 767 (Minn.1993), defendant objected to the prosecutor's use of a peremptory challenge against a black venireman, but the prosecutor explained she had struck the venireman because he was a Jehovah's Witness and explained that "[i]n my experience Jahovah Witness [sic] are reluctant to exercise authority over their fellow human beings in this Court House." Reading *Batson* as being limited to race-based peremptory challenges, the state supreme court affirmed.

The Supreme Court denied certiorari. *Davis v. Minnesota,* 115 U.S. 511, 114 S.Ct. 2120, 128 L.Ed.2d 679 (1994). Thomas, J., joined by Scalia, J., dissenting, objected that "no principled reason immediately appears for declining to apply *Batson* to any strike based on a classification that is accorded heightened scrutiny under the Equal Protection Clause," and thus concluded "that the Court's decision to deny certiorari stems from an unwillingness to confront forthrightly the ramifications of the decision in *J.E.B.*" Justice Ginsburg, concurring in denial of certiorari, responded that "the dissent's portrayal of the opinion of the Minnesota Supreme Court is incomplete. That court made two key observations: (1) '[R]eligious affiliation (or lack thereof) is not as self-evident as race or gender'; (2) 'Ordinarily ..., inquiry on voir dire into a juror's religious affiliation and beliefs is irrelevant and prejudicial, and to ask such questions is improper.' "

missible stereotyping" claims) "reasons" for strikes must be given.
* * * And make no mistake about it: there really is no substitute for the
peremptory.   Voir dire (though it can be expected to expand as a
consequence of today's decision) cannot fill the gap. The biases that go
along with group characteristics tend to be biases that the juror himself
does not perceive, so that it is no use asking about them. It is fruitless
to inquire of a male juror whether he harbors any subliminal prejudice
in favor of unwed fathers. * * *

8th ed., p. 1433; end of Note 10, add:

11. At Elem's trial, he objected to the prosecutor's use of peremptory challenges to strike two black men from the jury panel, but when
the prosecutor explained his strikes the trial court overruled Elem's
objection. Elem's conviction was affirmed on appeal, but on habeas
corpus the federal court of appeals directed the district court to grant the
writ. The court of appeals reasoned that under *Batson* the prosecutor
was obligated to "articulate some plausible race-neutral reason," which
the prosecutor had not done here in saying that the two prosecutive
jurors' "mustaches and ... beards look suspicious to me." But the
Supreme Court reversed per curiam in PURKETT v. ELEM, 514 U.S.
765, 115 S.Ct. 1769, 131 L.Ed.2d 834 (1995).

The Court explained that under *Batson,* "once the opponent of a
peremptory challenge has made out a prima facie case of racial discrimination (step 1), the burden of production shifts to the proponent of the
strike to come forward with a race-neutral explanation (step 2). If a
race-neutral explanation is tendered, the trial court must then decide
(step 3) whether the opponent of the strike has proved purposeful racial
discrimination. * * *

"The Court of Appeals erred by combining *Batson* 's second and
third steps into one, requiring that the justification tendered at the
second step be not just neutral but also at least minimally persuasive
* * *. It is not until the *third* step that the persuasiveness of the
justification becomes relevant—the step in which the trial court determines whether the opponent of the strike has carried his burden of
proving purposeful discrimination. At that stage, implausible or fantas-
tic justifications may (and probably will) be found to be pretexts for
purposeful discrimination. But to say that a trial judge *may choose to
disbelieve* a silly or superstitious reason at step 3 is quite different from
saying that a trial judge *must terminate* the inquiry at step 2 when the
race-neutral reason is silly or superstitious. The latter violates the
principle that the ultimate burden of persuasion regarding racial motivation rests with, and never shifts from, the opponent of the strike."

STEVENS and Breyer, JJ., dissenting, objected that "it is unwise
for the Court to announce a law-changing decision without first ordering
full briefing and argument on the merits of the case," and then concluded: "It is not too much to ask that a prosecutor's explanation for his
strikes be race neutral, reasonably specific, *and* trial related. * * *
Indeed, in *Hernandez* the Court explained that a trial judge could find

pretext based on nothing more than a consistent policy of excluding all Spanish-speaking jurors if that characteristic was entirely unrelated to the case to be tried. Parallel reasoning would justify a finding of pretext based on a policy of excusing jurors with beards if beards have nothing to do with the pending case.''

8th ed., p. 1433; end of Note 3, add:

In *Liteky v. United States,* 510 U.S. 540, 114 S.Ct. 1147, 127 L.Ed.2d 474 (1994), the Court held that *both* the federal challenge-for-cause statute, 28 U.S.C. § 144, and the federal recusal statute, 28 U.S.C. § 455, are subject to an "extrajudicial source" limitation, meaning: "First, judicial rulings alone almost never constitute valid basis for a bias or partiality motion. In and of themselves (i.e., apart from surrounding comments or accompanying opinion), they cannot possibly show reliance upon an extrajudicial source; and can only in the rarest circumstances evidence the degree of favoritism or antagonism required (as discussed below) when no extrajudicial source is involved. Almost invariably, they are proper grounds for appeal, not for recusal. Second, opinions formed by the judge on the basis of facts introduced or events occurring in the course of the current proceedings, or of prior proceedings, do not constitute a basis for a bias or partiality motion unless they display a deep-seated favoritism or antagonism that would make fair judgment impossible. Thus, judicial remarks during the course of a trial that are critical or disapproving of, or even hostile to, counsel, the parties, or their cases, ordinarily do not support a bias or partiality challenge. They *may* do so if they reveal an opinion that derives from an extrajudicial source; and they *will* do so if they reveal such a high degree of favoritism or antagonism as to make fair judgment impossible.''

Chapter 24

"TRIAL BY NEWSPAPER"— AND TELEVISION

SECTION 3. CONDUCT OF THE TRIAL

B. Broadcasting, Photographing and Televising Courtroom Proceedings

8th ed., p. 1448; following discussion of *Chandler*, add:

One of the questions raised by the O.J. Simpson case is whether high profile trials should be televised or, to put it another way, whether the benefits of increased public education about our legal system outweigh the costs generated by televising a high profile trial. Professor Arenella addresses this issue in the article extracted below.

PETER ARENELLA—FOREWORD: O.J. LESSONS

69 S.Cal.L.Rev. 1233, 1253–58 (1996).

[L]et us put questions of constitutional access aside and grant [the premise of Sager and Frederiksen[a]] that there should be a presumption in favor of televising most criminal cases. The harder question the Simpson trial raises is whether there are sound reasons for not televising those few high profile cases that create the greatest media frenzy.

I can hear Steve Brill of Court TV gnashing his teeth in agony and responding to those who want to pull the plug on televising high profile cases. "You can't lump televising the trial proceedings with all the other media coverage of the trial outside the courtroom. Televising the trial is the only accurate way of showing the public the difference between tabloid coverage of the case and what is actually going on inside the courtroom—so don't blame the courtroom cameras for media excesses outside the courtroom which our cameras can correct! If you don't televise such trials, you will only increase the public's dependence on the irresponsible tabloid coverage that always comes in high profile cases."

a. See Kelli L. Sager & Karen N. Frederiksen, *Televising the Judicial Branch:* *In Furtherance of the Public's First Amendment Rights*, 69 S.Cal.L.Rev. 1519 (1996).

While there is considerable merit to such a defense, there are several flaws in the argument. First, it ignores how much televising a high profile trial feeds the media frenzy outside the courtroom. There is a chicken and egg problem here. Courtroom cameras are not responsible for the irresponsible media coverage that takes place outside the courtroom, but their absence from the courtroom tends to diminish the national media's interest in the case. For better or worse, most Americans rely on television for their news and without video, there is far less incentive for the network news shows to cover high profile cases extensively. The dilution of national TV news coverage of a case tends to lower public interest in it, thereby weakening its commercial value for tabloid TV and the press.

Menendez II, which was not televised, graphically illustrates the point. While there is always less interest in a retrial because some of the drama and mystery is lost the second time around, Menendez II generated little sustained interest from national and local media. Has the public suffered? Have we missed an opportunity for public education about our legal system?

The answer to this question depends in part on how well the media educates the public in high profile cases. Apart from Court TV, the networks and local TV did an abominable job in Menendez I by latching on to the "abuse excuse" theme, creating the false impression that the brothers were seeking an acquittal when what was at stake was a determination of whether they were guilty of murder or voluntary manslaughter. Moreover, even if the media were to act more responsibly, the public education justification for televising high profile cases runs into a second problem: The factors that make a case "high profile" tend to decrease its educational value as a window into how our criminal justice system usually functions. One of the wonderful things about Court TV is that it shows the American public *ordinary* criminal and civil trials that do educate citizens about how our system usually works, warts and all. Simpson was not such a case.

Many of the preceding arguments against televising high profile cases reflect a mistrust about how the media *outside* the courtroom handles its responsibilities. But there are also problems with televising *some* high profile trials that would occur even if the media outside the courtroom were acting as responsibly and professionally as Court TV does its job inside the courtroom. Sager and Frederiksen cite empirical studies showing that the "impact of electronic media coverage of courtroom proceedings—whether civil or criminal—is virtually nil." But these studies focused on two essential issues: Did the cameras distract witnesses, attorneys, and jurors by making them so self-conscious that they performed their roles less competently and did the presence of the camera make witnesses and jurors less willing to participate in the process. Left unasked was a critical question: Does televising some high profile cases provide incentives for all of the trial participants to view their own roles somewhat differently with consequent changes in their behavior and decision-making? The Simpson case provides a telling example of how televising a high profile case alters the behavior and experiences of all the trial's participants.

Both sides in Simpson realized from the outset that there was a very good chance that the trial might end in a hung jury necessitating a retrial. The courtroom camera gave them an opportunity to address the court of public opinion when arguing legal motions outside the presence of the jury. Of course, Judge Ito could and should have exerted greater control over the attorneys when they made such appeals but the camera's eye probably affected his judicial behavior. Cutting off the lawyers' arguments when they strayed from the legal point in question might have created the appearance that he was favoring one side or the other.

What about the witnesses? Some research suggests that everyone in the courtroom soon forgets the camera's presence in the *ordinary* case. But, in a high profile case being watched by millions, it is impossible to forget that talk show guests, legal pundits, and ordinary citizens glued to their sets will scrutinize what you say. This notoriety will provide an incentive for some witnesses to get involved in the case and discourage others, who don't want their fifteen minutes of fame, from coming forward.

The jurors in high profile cases pay the greatest price. The chances of sequestration [57] increase to protect jurors from contamination by the nightly analysis of legal pundits. More significantly, televising a high profile case increases the risk that the public will not defer to the jury's resolution of the case. The viewing public becomes the thirteenth juror but is privy to information that the jury has not considered and is not bound by the legal instructions that the jury tries to follow in good faith.

Consider the public hostility expressed when one juror acknowledged that she and other jurors did not attribute great weight to the prosecution's domestic violence evidence. With condescension, many commentators suggested that the jury just "didn't get it." Perhaps the commentators didn't get it. They were exposed to far more information about domestic abuse than the jury, including evidence of stalking behavior which the prosecution promised to present but never did.
* * *

Televising ordinary criminal and civil cases that are not attracting an extraordinary amount of media attention can educate the public without generating significant costs to the system of justice. Televising high profile cases educates a far greater audience but at a far higher price.[59] There are some high profile cases (Rodney King) whose social

57. The law needs to reconsider both the necessity as well as the manner of sequestering juries in high profile cases. Jurors should not be treated like prisoners of the state. If sequestration is necessary, thought should be given to a proposal that would permit jurors and alternates to return home after each day's proceedings with a deputy who could ensure that jurors did not have access to the media. Eliminating "pillow talk" is impossible regardless of whether jurors have conjugal visits in hotel rooms or spend evenings home with their loved ones.

59. An additional price of televising high profile cases is the extent to which the

and political significance justifies the risks involved. Simpson was not such a case unless the media had used it to educate the public about how race and racism affect the criminal justice system. Instead, the media mistakenly lumped the two issues together under its pejorative "race card" label, a move that both reflected and enhanced a simplistic and misleading public discourse about race and the criminal justice system.[b]

Consider, too, Peter Arenella, *Televising High Profile Trials: Are We Better Off Pulling the Plug*, 37 Santa Clara L. Rev. 701, ___ (1997) (forthcoming):

"If the courtroom camera provides the public with *more undistorted* information, how can one quibble about the camera's educational value without sounding like an arrogant elitist? And, isn't a process that makes the viewing public *less* dependent on media interpretative filters to be applauded? [T]he answers to these questions are far from obvious once we realize that the courtroom camera is a media filter and that the 'viewing public' is not a monolith but two very different public audiences—the 'hard core' daily trial viewers and the far larger public audience that primarily catches video snippets from the trial on evening programming. Once this two audience distinction is made, it becomes easier to see why many of the benefits of the courtroom camera are realized primarily by daily trial watchers while serious costs result from the second audience's complete and unwitting dependence on television's judgments about which video snippets should be shown. My tentative answers to these questions will therefore paint a picture of modest benefits and significant costs.

" * * *Without the courtroom camera, [those in the second viewing audience] would remain totally dependent on the media's interpretive judgments but they would not see any video snippets form the trial. I shall argue [that] the electronic media's interpretive power is actually enhanced when its reporters can select video snippets to persuade viewers that their account of what is significant is 'objectively' true because the viewers can 'see it for themselves.' "

8th ed., p. 1449; at end of section, add:

C. OTHER REFORMS

Is there a need for special rules to ensure "fairness to the victim" in highly publicized cases, especially those that arise in a context presenting socially divisive, larger issues? A series of acquittals (or convictions

mainstream media fosters an implicit story line about what should be the "just" result of the trial. The media and the public then evaluate the trial's progress and outcome by how well it correlates to this presupposed just result. In the Simpson case, there was little doubt that most of the mainstream media, reflecting the attitudes of their consumers, believed Simpson was guilty of the two murders. This type of "subtext bias" is inevitable because the media, like the rest of us, comes to conclusions about the defendant's guilt or innocence long before the case goes to the jury. * * *

b. See also Jeffrey Abramson, *The Pros and Cons of Televising Trials,* in Postmortem: The O.J. Simpson Case 195 (Jeffrey Abramson ed. 1996).

of lesser-included offenses) in high profile cases arguably fit that description—the O.J. Simpson case, the original prosecution of Los Angeles police officers for the beating of Rodney King, the prosecution for the murder of Yankel Rosenbaum during the Crown Heights riots in Brooklyn, and the acquittal of William Kennedy Smith for rape. Cases such as these have generated a reexamination of the trial process and the potential it offers the defense to take advantage of external pressures that favor acquittals or "compromise verdicts."

A number of commentators have argued that there is a need for reforms such as: (1) restricting changes of venue; (2) shortening the jury selection process; (3) reducing or eliminating peremptory challenges in order to obtain more diverse juries; (4) prohibiting the use of, or at least reducing the length of, jury questionnaires, thereby diluting the role of jury consultants; (5) permitting, indeed encouraging, jurors to ask questions of the judges; (6) allowing the victim or next of kin to ask questions, either directly or through attorneys; (7) eliminating potential celebrity status for jurors by protecting their anonymity and prohibiting them from "cashing in" on book deals and interviews; (8) abolishing the requirement of jury unanimity or reducing the size of juries. For a discussion of these and other proposals, see Peter Arenella, *Foreword: O.J. Lessons,* 69 S.Cal.L.Rev. 1233 (1996); Craig M. Bradley & Joseph L. Hoffman, *Public Perception, Justice, and the "Search for Truth" in Criminal Cases,* 69 S.Cal.L.Rev. 1267 (1996); George P. Fletcher, *With Justice for Some: Victims' Rights in Criminal Trials* (1995); Robert P. Mosteller, *Popular Justice,* 109 Harv.L.Rev. 487 (1995); Stephen J. Schulhofer, *The Trouble with Trials: The Trouble with Us,* 105 Yale L.J. 825 (1995) and the collection of short articles by Albert W. Alschuler, Barbara Allen Babcock, Andrew Hacker, Kenneth Jost, Nancy J. King, and Michael Lind in Part IV of *Postmortem: The O.J. Simpson Case* (Jeffrey Abramson ed. 1996).

SECTION 4.   PREVENTING PREJUDICIAL PUBLICITY

A.   RESTRICTING PUBLIC STATEMENTS

8th ed., p. 1458; after Notes following *Gentile* add new Note:

(f) *The impact of Gentile on Model Rule 3.6.* In the wake of *Gentile* the ABA House of Delegates significantly amended Model Rule 3.6 in August 1994. Companion amendments to Rule 3.8 were approved at the same time. The amended rules delete qualifying terms that the *Gentile* Court found unconstitutionally vague, but continue to prohibit statements that a lawyer "reasonably should know * * * will have a substantial likelihood of materially prejudicing an adjudicative proceeding." The amended rules also establish a new "safe harbor" provision allowing a lawyer to protect his client against publicity initiated by someone else and make clear that all lawyers "associated in a firm or government agency" are covered. The amended rule is set forth below:

RULE 3.6   TRIAL PUBLICITY

(a) A lawyer who is participating or has participate in the investigation or litigation of a matter shall not make an extrajudicial statement that a reasonable person would expect to be disseminated by means of public communication if the lawyer knows or reasonably should know that it will have a substantial likelihood of materially prejudicing an adjudicative proceeding in the matter.

(b) Notwithstanding paragraph (a), a lawyer may state:

(1) the claim, offense or defense involved and, except when prohibited by law, the identity of the persons involved;

(2) information contained in a public record;

(3) that an investigation of a matter is in progress;

(4) the scheduling or result of any step in litigation;

(5) a request for assistance in obtaining evidence and information necessary thereto;

(6) a warning of danger concerning the behavior of a person involved, when there is reason to believe that there exists the likelihood of substantial harm to an individual or to the public interest; and

(7) in a criminal case, in addition to subparagraphs (1) through (6):

(i) the identity, residence, occupation and family status of the accused;

(ii) if the accused has not been apprehended, information necessary to aid in apprehension of that person;

(iii) the fact, time and place of arrest; and

(iv) the identity of investigating and arresting officers or agencies and the length of the investigation.

(c) Notwithstanding paragraph (a), a lawyer may make a statement that a reasonable lawyer would believe is required to protect a client from the substantial undue prejudicial effect of recent publicity not initiated by the lawyer or the lawyer's client. A statement made pursuant to this paragraph shall be limited to such information as is necessary to mitigate the recent adverse publicity.

(d) No lawyer associated in a firm or government agency with a lawyer subject to paragraph (a) shall make a statement prohibited by paragraph (a).

Chapter 25

THE CRIMINAL TRIAL

SECTION 3.   THE DEFENDANT'S RIGHT TO REMAIN SILENT AND TO TESTIFY

8th ed., p. 1490; end of fn. 3, add:

[Ed. Note—Compare the English position
described in the supplement addition p. 489
at Supp. p. 66.]

8th ed., p. 1493; before Note 5, add:

4a.   Craig M. Bradley & Joseph L. Hoffman, *Public Perception, Justice, and the "Search for Truth" in Criminal Cases,* 69 S.Cal.L.Rev. 1267, 1285–86 (1996), suggest that *Griffin* should be overruled once states (1) bar impeachment by prior conviction (or conversely permit priors to be used in the government's case in chief), and (2) allow trial courts not to give the adverse inference instruction in those exceptional cases where the defendant can justify his trial silence by some special circumstances, such as his mental condition.   But Peter Arenella, *Foreword: O.J. Lessons,* 69 S.Cal.L.Rev. 1233, 1246 (1996), fears that if *Griffin* were abolished prosecutors would "make different charging decisions in weak cases that do not have much physical evidence linking the defendant to the crime but which pass the directed verdict screening standard because of the presence of a shaky eyewitness identification."

SECTION 5.   SUBMITTING THE CASE TO THE JURY

8th ed., p. 1511; end of Note 1, add:

Can *Heald* be squared with *United States v. Gaudin,* Supp. p. 155?

Chapter 26

REPROSECUTION AND THE BAN AGAINST DOUBLE JEOPARDY

SECTION 1. REPROSECUTION AFTER A MISTRIAL

8th ed., p. 1517, add to fn. a:

As to the combination of criminal prosecutions and civil proceedings, see Note 4, Supp. p. 123. As to the impact of the double jeopardy prohibition on various aspects of state law governing the treatment of lesser included offenses, see James Shel-lenberger and James Strazzella, *The Lesser Included Offense Doctrine and the Constitution: The Development of Due Process and Double Jeopardy Remedies,* 79 Marq.L.Rev. 1 (1995).

SECTION 2. REPROSECUTION FOLLOWING AN ACQUITTAL

8th ed., p. 1550, after Note 5, add:

5a. *The fraudulently obtained acquittal.* Should an acquittal bar reprosecution when the prosecution has established that the defendant bribed the judge or tampered with the jury? Consider David Rudstein, *Double Jeopardy and the Fraudulently Obtained Acquittal,* 60 Mo.L.Rev. 607 (1995), and Anne Bowen Poulin, *Double Jeopardy and Judicial Accountability: When is an Acquittal Not an Acquittal,* 27 Ariz.St.L.J. 953 (1995), both taking note of an Illinois trial court ruling allowing a reprosecution where the judge had been bribed, the court concluding that the defendant had never truly been in jeopardy of conviction, *People v. Aleman,* 1994 WL 684499 (Ill.Cir.1994).

SECTION 3. REPROSECUTION FOLLOWING A CONVICTION

8th ed., p. 1563; add to Note 9:

In *Monge v. California,* ___ U.S. ___, 118 S.Ct. 2246, ___ L.Ed.2d ___ (1998), the Supreme Court majority held that *Bullington* did not extend beyond the capital sentencing context and therefore double jeopardy did not bar a retrial on the issue of whether a prior conviction met the prerequisites for recidivist sentencing in a noncapital sentencing proceeding. All but Justice Stevens agreed with this conclusion, but three dissenters concluded that the recidivism enhancement in this case was an element of the petitioner's offense and therefore had placed the defendant in jeopardy for an "offence" (in contrast to a sentencing determination). See also *Witte v. United States,* discussed at Supp. p. 124.

SECTION 4. REPROSECUTION BY A DIFFERENT SOVEREIGN

8th ed., p. 1571; add to footnote d:

The federal prosecutions in the "King beating case" also have sparked a reexamination of the *Bartkus* ruling in the scholarly literature, producing a variety of views as to when (if ever) a federal prosecution should be allowed following a state prosecution based on the same events. See Akhil Amar and Jonathan Marcus, *Double Jeopardy Law After Rodney King,* 95 Colum.L.Rev. 1 (1995); Paul Cassell, *The Rodney King Trials and the Double Jeopardy Clause: Some Observations on Original Meaning and the ACLU's Schizophrenic Views of the Dual Sovereign Doctrine,* 41 UCLA L.Rev. 693 (1994); Robert Gorman, *The Second Rodney King Trial: Justice in Jeopardy,* 27 Akron L.Rev. 57 (1993); Susan Herman, *Double Jeopardy All Over Again: Dual Sovereignty, Rodney King, and the ACLU,* 41 UCLA L.Rev. 609 (1994); Susan Herman, *Reconstructing The Bill of Rights: A Reply to Amar and Marcus's Triple Play on Double Jeopardy,* 93 Colum.L.Rev. 1090 (1995); Paul Hoffman, *Double Jeopardy Wars: The Case for a Civil Rights "Exception,"* 41 UCLA L.Rev. 649 (1994); Laurie Levenson, *The Future of State and Federal Civil Rights Prosecutions: the Lessons of the Rodney King Trial,* 41 UCLA L.Rev. 509 (1994).

Consider also Sandra Guerra, *The Myth of Dual Sovereignty, Multijurisdictional Drug Law Enforcement and Double Jeopardy,* 73 N.C.L.Rev. 1159 (1995).

Part Five

APPEALS, POST–CONVICTION REVIEW

Chapter 27

APPEALS

SECTION 5. THE HARMLESS ERROR RULE

8th ed., p. 1613, after Note 4, add:

5. Consider also the analysis of Chief Judge Harry Edwards of the D.C. Circuit in *To Err is Human, But Not Always Harmless: When Should Legal Error Be Tolerated?,* 70 N.Y.U.L.Rev. 1167 (1995). Judge Edwards views *Harrington* and its progeny as having advanced "a guilt-based theory of harmless error focusing on the reliability of the trial outcome," but finds in the Supreme Court rulings of the 1990s a rejection of that approach and a return to a true "effect on the verdict" analysis. Judge Edwards notes that this movement began with *Arizona v. Fulminante,* 8th ed., p. 1618, a case known more for its refusal to treat admission of a coerced confession as *per se* reversible error, but one in which the majority also held that the admission of the coerced confession in the case before it could not be deemed harmless under *Chapman.* So too, *Sullivan v. Louisiana,* 8th ed., p. 1621, another case dealing with the boundaries of the "automatic reversal" category, reached the conclusion that a constitutionally deficient reasonable-doubt instruction was a *per se* reversible error on the basis of reasoning that "cast doubt upon the continuing vitality of the *Harrington* Court's approach." For the *Sullivan* Court noted that "harmless error review looks * * * to the basis on which the jury *actually rested* its verdict" (see 8th ed., p. 1621), and rejected the concept that a deficient reasonable-doubt instruction could be held harmless if the evidence of guilt was so overwhelming that

a hypothetical reasonable jury obviously would have convicted even with a proper instruction. Finally, *O'Neal v. McAninch,* Supp. p. 217, although concerned with the extent to which a court must be convinced that an error is harmless (and applying *Kotteakos* rather than *Chapman*), included reasoning that made it the "crown jewel in the decisions moving away from guilt-based applications of the harmless-error doctrine." *O'Neal,* in its description of the "grave doubt" standard, made it clear that "the proper measure of harmlessness is whether the error 'had substantial and injurious effect or influence in determining the jury verdict,' *not* whether the record evidence is sufficient absent the minor error to warrant a verdict of guilt."

To illustrate where application of the "*Sullivan/O'Neal* standard of harmless error" should "make a difference," Judge Edwards offered the following hypothetical: "Joe Didit, who is six-feet five-inches tall, about two-hundred-and-seventy pounds, Caucasian, and bald-headed, was recently tried for the murder of a convenience-store proprietor. The indictment charged that, sometime near midnight on the evening in question, Didit entered the convenience store, with a loaded gun, intending to rob the proprietor. It was further charged that, when he faced resistance from his victim, Didit purposefully shot the proprietor in the head and face six times, and then fled the store. Two customers, who were in the store at the time of the murder, called the police and identified Didit, a well-known neighborhood thug, as the murderer. Following this lead, the police located Didit at his girlfriend's apartment, arrested him, and took him to police headquarters for interrogation. After being given his Miranda warning, Didit refused to say anything. His refusal agitated one of the police officers, who then proceeded to slap and punch Didit repeatedly. The officers then left Didit in an isolated room, telling him, 'you'll stay here unless you talk to us.' Two hours later, Didit summoned the officers and asked for a sandwich and coffee, which he was given. After eating, he told the officers that he wanted to talk. Then, without giving any further Miranda warning, the officers took a confession from Didit.

"At trial, one of the customers testified that he was about thirty feet from the place of the murder, but could 'clearly' see Didit shoot the proprietor. The other customer testified that she did not have a clear view of Didit, but she was 'sure' that she recognized the defendant's voice when he threatened to kill the store owner. A third witness testified that he had seen Didit at about midnight on the night in question, running down a street about a block away from the convenience store. A fourth witness testified that he had seen Didit with what he thought was a .45–caliber pistol two days before the shooting. No gun was ever found, but police experts testified that bullets that killed the murder victim came from a .45–caliber. All four witnesses claimed that they personally knew Didit from the neighborhood. The prosecutor also introduced a videotape recording of the murder, showing a view of the murderer from the rear; the recorded view of the murderer strongly resembled the defendant. Finally, over strong objection, the trial judge allowed Didit's confession to be introduced in evidence, along with evidence indicating that the defendant had been beaten several hours before he confessed.　For the defense, Didit's girlfriend testified that he had been with her all evening;　on cross-examination, however, she admitted that she was 'unsure' whether he may have left the apartment once during the evening to buy some cigarettes.　The jury returned a verdict of guilty within two hours after commencing deliberations.　The case is now on appeal, and the defendant seeks reversal on a claim that the trial judge committed error in admitting what amounted to a coerced confession.　Government counsel responds that any error committed by the trial judge was harmless."

Judge Edwards argues that a "judge who follows *Sullivan/O'Neal* will reverse [in this hypothetical case] because, at the very least, a judge should have 'grave doubts' as to the harmlessness of the error.　If a judge believes what Justice Kennedy said in *Fulminante,* that almost nothing is more damaging to defendant's plea of innocence than a confession, then he or she could not reasonably find that the erroneous admission of the confession could not have contaminated the judgment." Judge Edwards notes, however, that this conclusion is at odds with the majority of the responses he received in a survey which asked participants for their "first reaction" to the hypothetical.　Reversal was favored over a harmless-error affirmance by only 2 of the 11 responding judges from the D.C. Circuit, by only 7 of the 25 responding appellate attorneys from the U.S. Attorney's office, but by all 6 of the responding appellate attorneys from the Federal Defender's office, and 10 of 11 of the responding attorneys from the D.C. Public Defender Service.　The survey response, Judge Edwards notes, lends support to his concern that, "since there is no way for a judge to consider the possible effect of an error on the verdict without also considering the entire record of evidence" and since it is "hard for a judge to discount a strong feeling that the defendant is guilty" where the record so indicates (especially with appellate judges hesitant to add to the trial court's increasingly heavy caseload an additional trial that seems almost certain only to repeat the original result), the focus reflected in *Harrington* and its progeny will be "difficult to reverse."

Chapter 28

HABEAS CORPUS AND RELATED COLLATERAL REMEDIES

SECTION 1. THE BASIC STRUCTURE OF FEDERAL HABEAS FOR STATE PRISONERS

8th ed., p. 1628; end of Note 2, add:

Congress enacted a substantial revision of federal habeas corpus law in Title I of the Antiterrorism and Effective Death Penalty Act of 1996. The primary components of that revision are a series of deletions and additions in §§ 2244, 2253, 2254, and 2255 and the addition of chapter 154 (§§ 2261–66) establishing special requirements for habeas challenges in capital cases coming from states which adopt an appropriate mechanism for the appointment of competent counsel in state postconviction proceedings. These revisions have been incorporated in the selected habeas corpus provisions reproduced in Appendix B of this Supplement. The 1996 legislation added the following provisions set forth in Appendix B: subsections (b) and (d) of § 2244; the whole of § 2253; subsections (b), (d), (e), (h), and (i) of § 2254; the last three paragraphs of § 2255 (dealing with a one-year period of limitation, appointment of counsel, and successive motions); and the whole of §§ 2261–2266.

Section 107(c) of the Act provides that "Chapter 154 * * * shall apply to cases pending on or after the date of the enactment of this Act." In *Lindh v. Murphy*, ___ U.S. ___, 117 S.Ct. 2059, 138 L.Ed.2d 481 (1997), the Supreme Court read this provision "as indicating implicitly that the amendments to chapter 153 [i.e., the amendments to §§ 2244, 2253, 2254, and 2255] were assumed and meant to apply to the general run of habeas cases only when those cases had been filed after the date of the Act." As to chapter 154, which applies to qualified capital cases (see Note 5b, Supp. p. 180), the Court noted that it would consider when the issue arose the bearing of § 107(c) on the retroactive application of the various provisions of that chapter (dealing with substance as well as procedure).

178

8th ed., p. 1630; end of Note 4, add:

The Antiterrorism and Effective Death Penalty Act of 1996 modified the § 2254 provision on exhaustion in its revision of subsection (b) of § 2254. The primary changes are contained in subsections (b)(2), and (b)(3). Subsection (b)(2) allows a federal habeas court to deny a habeas petition on the lack of merit in the claim notwithstanding a lack of exhaustion. There is no need for the court to send the petitioner back to the state courts where the claim presented clearly is without merit. Subsection (b)(3) provides that a state cannot be estopped from advancing the exhaustion requirement, or be presumed to have waived its right to insist upon exhaustion, unless it has expressly waived that requirement. Thus, the state's failure to raise the lack of exhaustion at the outset does not preclude it from subsequently raising that point.

8th ed., p. 1630; after Note 5, add:

5a. *Time limitations.* Prior to the enactment in 1996 of the Antiterrorism and Effective Death Penalty Act, the only time limitation imposed on the filing of a federal habeas petition was that flowing from the application of Habeas Rule 9(a). That Rule allows for dismissal if the state "has been prejudiced in its ability to respond to the petition" by the petitioner's unexcused delay in filing the petition. The Supreme Court has concluded that dismissal under this Rule requires a specific showing as to how the government will be prejudiced in responding to the petitioner's constitutional claim, see *Vasquez v. Hillery* (8th ed., p. 1001), and that the habeas court lacks any additional authority to dismiss a petition on equitable grounds relating to delay. See *Lonchar v. Thomas,* 517 U.S. 314, 116 S.Ct. 1293, 134 L.Ed.2d 440 (1996) (a district court could not rely on general equitable principles—independent of those embodied in Rule 9(a)—to dismiss a death row inmate's first habeas petition on the ground that the inmate waited until the last moment before filing it).

The 1996 legislation, in contrast, adopted a general time limitation for the filing of habeas and § 2255 petitions and a special time limit for qualified capital cases. Initially, the newly adopted subsection (d) of § 2244 imposes a one-year time limitation on the filing of a habeas petition (with the same limitation also included in the revised § 2255). The one-year time period ordinarily runs from the date on which the judgment being challenged became final on direct review, while excluding any period during which a properly filed collateral attack was pending before the state courts. A later starting point is provided where: (1) state action in violation of the Constitution or other federal law impeded the timely filing of the habeas petition (see Note 5a, Supp. p. 190); (2) the petition relies on a constitutional right that was initially recognized by the Supreme Court after the date of finality and that was held to be retroactive in application (see Note 2a, Supp. p. 188); or (3) the petition relies on a constitutional claim as to which the factual predicate could not have been discovered at the date of finality by the exercise of due diligence (see Note 5b, Supp. p. 190).

For states that qualify for chapter 154's special habeas procedures for capital cases (see Note 5b below), § 2263 imposes a shorter, 180–day time limitation. The time limitation here runs from the "final state court affirmance of the conviction and sentence on direct review or the expiration of the time for seeking [such] review," but then is tolled during the pendency of a petition for certiorari filed with the Supreme Court and the pendency of an initial state collateral challenge.[a] In addition, subsection (3) provides for a 30–day extension under special circumstances. The appropriateness (and even the constitutionality) of such a short time limitation has been questioned. See ABA Criminal Justice Section, Task Force on Death Penalty Habeas Corpus, *Toward a More Just and Effective System of Review in State Death Penalty Cases: Recommendations and Report of the ABA Task Force on Death Penalty Habeas Corpus* 280–91, 330–39 (1989); Vivian Burger, *Justice Delayed or Justice Denied?—A Comment on Recent Proposals to Reform Death Penalty Habeas Corpus,* 90 Colum.L.Rev. 1665, 1695–98 (1990); Michael Mello and Donna Duffy, *Suspending Justice: The Unconstitutionality of the Proposed Six–Month Time Limit on the Filing of Habeas Corpus Petitions by State Death Row Inmates,* 18 N.Y.U.Rev.L. & Soc.Change 451 (1990–91).

5b. *Capital cases.* Chapter 154 of 28 U.S.C.A., containing §§ 2261–2266, is titled "Special Habeas Corpus Procedures in Capital Cases." Added by the Antiterrorism and Effective Death Penalty Act of 1996, this chapter tracks in large part a proposal, advanced in 1989 by a Committee of the United States Judicial Conference (chaired by retired Supreme Court Justice Lewis F. Powell, Jr. and commonly referred to as the "Powell Committee"). See Ad Hoc Committee on Federal Habeas Corpus in Capital Cases, *Report on Habeas Corpus in Capital Cases,* 45 Crim.L.Rep. 3239 (Sept. 27, 1989). The Powell Committee endorsed the adoption of a series of procedural requirements designed to promote a promptly adjudicated "one-shot" federal habeas challenge in state capital cases. Application of these requirements was to be conditioned, however, on a state voluntarily establishing a program under which it made available to indigent convicted capital defendants the assistance of adequate counsel in presenting their challenges in the state's postconviction procedure (the Supreme Court having held that the state had no constitutional obligation to provide appointed counsel at this stage, see *Murray v. Giarratano,* 8th ed., p. 107). Once a state established that it had such a program, federal habeas petitions by its death row inmates would be subject to a streamlined procedure that had three primary components. First, the petitions would be subject to a time limitation (basically 180 days from the end of the state proceedings), but the prisoners would receive an automatic stay of execution, allowing them

a. Sections 2244(d) and 2263 describes differently their respective starting points, and only the latter provision refers to the period during which a certiorari petition is pending before the Supreme Court. This distinction raises the question of whether the direct review referred to in § 2244(d)(1)(A) does not become "final" until after the Supreme Court has disposed of a certiorari petition or the time for filing a certiorari petition has expired. Consider fn. a, 8th ed., p. 1673.

the full period to prepare their petition. Second, the habeas court would be limited to consideration of constitutional claims properly presented in the state proceedings, with an exception created only for those claims that had not been presented in those proceedings as a result of (1) state action that violated the Constitution, (2) the Supreme Court's subsequent recognition of a new right given retroactive application, or (3) a factual predicate that could not have been timely discovered through the exercise of due diligence. Third, once a denial of relief on the first federal habeas application completed the appellate process with the capital sentence left undisturbed, the stay of execution would terminate and the federal courts would lack authority to grant a further stay, or to award relief on any subsequent petition, unless (1) the prisoner presented a constitutional claim not previously raised, (2) the failure to raise that claim previously was the product of one of the same three factors that would extend the time limitation, and (3) "the facts underlying the [new] claim would be sufficient, if proven, to undermine the court's confidence in the jury's determination of guilt on the offense or offenses for which the death penalty was imposed," 45 Crim.L.Rptr. 3243. The Powell Committee reasoned that with competent counsel having assisted the prisoner in the state postconviction proceeding, ordinarily all possible constitutional contentions should have been presented in the state proceedings, and with counsel also provided in capital cases in federal habeas proceedings (see fn. 7, 8th ed., p. 110), the prisoner should be able to present all of his claims in a single habeas petition and do so in a fairly prompt fashion.

Section 2261, following the recommendation of the Powell Committee, conditions the application of the remainder of chapter 154 on the state's adoption of a "mechanism for the appointment, compensation, and payment of reasonable litigation expenses of competent counsel in State postconviction proceedings brought by indigent prisoners whose capital sentences have been upheld on direct review." Recognizing that some states utilize a unitary appeal procedure in capital cases, which allows the defendant in a single proceeding to both appeal trial court rulings and raise issues that otherwise would be considered only in collateral attack, § 2265 also makes the chapter applicable to states that provide counsel that meet the standards of § 2261 in such a proceeding. Section 2261 insists that the state prescribe "standards of competency for the appointment of counsel," but itself imposes only one specific requirement—that the counsel appointed not have been the trial or appellate counsel (or simply not the trial counsel in a state with a unitary review procedure), unless "the prisoner and counsel expressly request continued representation." The focus of § 2261 is on the general standards utilized in appointing counsel and in providing "reasonable litigation expenses." Should the counsel provided under a satisfactory appointment mechanism turn out to be ineffective in the assistance rendered in the state postconviction proceeding or in subsequent federal habeas proceedings, the state does not bear the responsibility for that incompetence. Section 2261(e) provides that "the ineffectiveness or the incompetence" of counsel at either stage "shall not be grounds for relief" under § 2254. Cf. *Pennsylvania v. Finley,* 8th ed., p. 107 (no constitutional right to effective assistance at this stage and therefore no constitutional claim of ineffective assistance); *Coleman v. Thompson,* 8th ed., p. 1664 (since attorney error at this stage cannot be constitutionally ineffective, it does not constitute cases under the *Wainwright v. Sykes* "cause and prejudice standard").

Once a state enters an order establishing its compliance with the requirements of § 2261, the provisions in the remainder of chapter 154 take effect. Initially, § 2262 requires an automatic stay of execution upon request of the state prisoner, thereby insuring that the prisoner will be able to utilize the postconviction procedures anticipated under chapter 154. The stay continues in effect until either (1) the prisoner waives in open court his right to seek federal habeas relief, (2) the period allowed for filing under § 2263 expires without a filing, (3) the prisoner files a petition but fails to make a substantial showing of a denial of federal claim, or (4) the prisoner files and relief is denied "in the district court or at any subsequent stage of review."

The time limitation for filing, specified in § 2263, adopts the basic time period urged by the Powell Committee (180 days), although it shortens the length of the extension allowed for extraordinary circumstances to 30 days. As discussed in Note 5a, supra, § 2263 utilizes a starting point for the time limitation roughly parallel to that utilized for the general, one-year limitation imposed under § 2244(d), but § 2263 describes somewhat differently the period that is excluded due to pending proceedings. Section 2266 supplements the time limitation for filing by imposing a time limitation for judicial disposition once the petition is filed. The district court ordinarily must render a final ruling on the petition within 180 days of the filing, although here too, a 30-day extension is possible under special circumstances. If an appeal is taken to the court of appeals, that court must issue its ruling within 120 days after the final brief is filed.

Section 2264 limits the scope of the issues to be considered by the habeas court, here again following the recommendation of the Powell Committee. As a general matter, the federal habeas court may consider only "claims that have been raised and decided on the merits" in the state courts. The Powell Committee recognized three exceptions to this principle, and § 2264 also includes those exceptions—instances in which the failure to raise the claim in the state courts was the result of (1) state action itself violating the Constitution or laws of the United States, (2) a factual predicate that could not have been discovered through due diligence in time to present the claim in the state proceedings, and (3) the Supreme Court's subsequent recognition of a new federal right that is made "retroactively applicable." The Powell Committee recommended that a combination of one of these three circumstances and a factual showing that undermined confidence in the accuracy of the guilty verdict should also create an exception to its general rule limiting the prisoner to one habeas challenge. Such a limitation is not included in chapter 154 because a new 2244(b) was adopted, and that provision imposes even more stringent limits on successive petitions that are applicable to *all* petitions by state prisoners. See Note 6a, Supp. p. 185.

5c. *Appeals.* The Antiterrorism and Effective Death Penalty Act provides in 28 U.S.C.A. § 2253(c) that federal and state prisoners must obtain a certificate of appealability from "a circuit justice or judge" as a prerequisite for appealing the denial of a § 2255 or a habeas petition. Certificates of appealability may issue "only if the applicant has made a substantial showing of the denial of a constitutional right." In *Hohn v. United States,* ___ U.S. ___, 118 S.Ct. 1969, ___ L.Ed.2d ___ (1998), the Supreme Court held that it had jurisdiction, on petition for a writ of certiorari, to review the denial of an application for a certificate of appealability by a circuit judge or a circuit court panel.

SECTION 2. ISSUES COGNIZABLE

8th ed., p. 1644; following Withrow add:

7. In *Reed v. Farley,* 512 U.S. 339, 114 S.Ct. 2291, 129 L.Ed.2d 277 (1994), also discussed at Supp. p. 135, a state prisoner sought habeas relief on the ground that he was being held in custody in violation of a federal statute, the Interstate Agreement on Detainers, 18 U.S.C. App. § 2, which imposes a 120 day speedy trial requirement as to prisoners transferred under its provisions. The Court of Appeals, relying on *Stone v. Powell,* held that such a claim was not cognizable on habeas review. Three justices (per Ginsburg, J.) rejected reliance on *Stone,* held petitioner's claim to be cognizable, but concluded that petitioner would only be entitled to relief upon a showing that met the "complete miscarriage of justice" standard traditionally applied on § 2255 proceedings to claims by federal prisoners based on violations of federal statutory law. See fn. b, 8th ed. p. 1626. That standard was not met here where the petitioner did not object to the initial setting of the trial date beyond the 120 day period and suffered no prejudice due to the delayed commencement of his trial. Justice Scalia, joined by Justice Thomas, agreed that the traditional § 2255 standard was also applicable to state prisoner claims under federal law, but concluded that a claimed violation of the 120 day time limit therefore was not a cognizable claim. The 120 day requirement, applicable only to prisoners involved in interstate transfer, simply was too "technical" to fall within that small class of statutory rights whose denial could produce a complete miscarriage of justice. Speaking for four dissenters, Justice Blackmun concluded that the claim not only was cognizable, but that the Court majority erred in assuming without full discussion that the standard applicable to state prisoners presenting claims under federal law was the same as that applied under § 2255 to federal-law claims of federal prisoners, rather than the standard traditionally applied under § 2254 to constitutional claims presented by state prisoners.

SECTION 3. CLAIMS FORECLOSED
BY PROCEDURAL DEFAULTS

8th ed., p. 1660; after Note 5, add:

5a. *The 1996 amendments.* Section 2264 is the only provision of the Antiterrorism and Effective Death Penalty Act speaking specifically to the authority of a habeas court to consider a claim that was not raised and decided on the merits in the state courts. In those capital cases that are covered by chapter 154 (i.e., where the state has met the counsel-appointment prerequisites of § 2261), the habeas court cannot consider such a claim unless the failure to gain a state court ruling on the merits of the claim was due to one of three factors—state action that itself violated the Constitution, an intervening Supreme Court ruling recognizing a new constitutional rule that is given retroactive effect on collateral attack, or a factual predicate not capable of timely discovery with due diligence. See Note 5b, Supp. p. 180. The extent to which these factors alter the character of the "cause and prejudice standard" is discussed infra, in Notes 2a, 3a, 5a, 5b, and 6a, Supp. pp. 188–92.

Although the 1996 amendments to the general provisions governing habeas petitions (i.e., §§ 2244–2254) do not speak directly to procedural defaults in the state courts, those amendments in several contexts alter the bearing of the *Wainwright v. Sykes* standards upon considering claims procedurally defaulted in state proceedings. Where the defaulted claim is filed more than one year after the prisoner's conviction became final on direct review (adding on any time taken up by state collateral review), the petitioner must first establish that he is entitled to a later starting point for the time limitation due to one of three factors also recognized in § 2244(d). See Note 5a, Supp. p. 179. So too, if the procedurally defaulted claim has a factual basis that is not established by the record in the state court proceedings, § 2254(e)(2) may be applicable, and it precludes an evidentiary hearing unless the habeas petitioner meets two prerequisites—first, that the claim either (i) relies on a "new rule of constitutional law, made retroactive to cases on collateral review by the Supreme Court, that was previously unavailable," or (ii) is based on a "factual predicate that could not have been previously discovered through the exercise of due diligence," and, second, that the facts underlying the claim are sufficient "to establish by clear and convincing evidence that but the constitutional error, no reasonable factfinder would have found the applicant guilty of the underlying offense." See Note 7a, Supp. p. 219. Finally, if a claim procedurally defaulted in the state proceedings is raised for the first time in a second or successive petition, the habeas petition must satisfy either of two prerequisites set forth in § 2244(b)(2), which are similar to the prerequisites of § 2254(e)(2) described above. See Note 6a below. As suggested below, if the habeas petitioner can first meet the requirements of these provisions, the petitioner is most likely also to have established at least "cause" and often "actual prejudice" as well.

8th ed., p. 1661; after Note 6, add:

6a. *The new successive-petitions provision.*[a] The 1996 Antiterrorism and Effective Death Penalty Act replaced the § 2244(b) provision interpreted in *McCleskey* with a quite different provision. The former provision stated that the federal habeas court "need not entertain" a successive petition "unless the application alleges and is predicted on a factual or other ground not adjudicated on the hearing of the earlier application * * * and unless the court * * * is satisfied that the applicant has not on the earlier application deliberately withheld the newly asserted ground or otherwise abused the writ." The new subsection (b)(2) directs that a second or successive application presenting "a claim" not advanced in a prior application "shall be dismissed" unless one of two specified exceptions is found applicable.

The first exception, contained in § 2244(b)(2)(A), is that the claim relies on a new rule of constitutional law, previously unavailable, that the Supreme Court has made retroactively applicable on collateral review. This standard takes its content from *Teague v. Lane* (8th ed., p. 1670). The Court there held that new rules of constitutional law ordinarily would not be applied retroactively on collateral review, but there would be two exceptions, where new rules would be carried over to habeas cases even though the convictions being challenged became final before the new rules were announced. The first exception—a new rule holding unconstitutional the criminalization of particular conduct— would allow a prisoner to take advantage via a second petition of an intervening new rule rendering unconstitutional the state's punishment of the behavior for which the prisoner was charged and convicted. See Note 4, 8th ed., p. 1682. The second *Teague* exception—a "new watershed rule of criminal procedure" held to be "essential to providing fundamental fairness"—is even rarer, as the Court itself recognized in *Teague*. See 8th ed., p. 1676 and Note 5, p. 1682. The relationship of this exception to the cause and prejudice standard applied in *McCleskey* is considered in Note 2a, Supp. p. 188.

a. In Calderon v. Thompson, ___ U.S. ___, 118 S.Ct. 1489, 140 L.Ed.2d 728 (1998), the Court held that the successive petition provision would apply to a habeas petitioner's motion to have the habeas court recall a mandate denying habeas relief in order for petitioner to gain reconsideration of the merits of a previously raised claim [governed by § 2244(b)(1)—see Note 6(a), Supp. p. 217] or initial consideration of a claim not previously raised [governed by § 2244(b)(2)]. The Court added that the successive petition provision could also apply where the habeas court recalled its mandate *sua sponte*, but not where, as in the case before it, the Ninth Circuit did so not to consider "new claims or evidence," but because it wished to review the first petition en banc and its internal processes had malfunctioned, resulting in an order denying a rehearing. In Stewart v. Martinez–Villareal, ___ U.S. ___, 118 S.Ct. 1618, 140 L.Ed.2d 849 (1998), the Court held that where the habeas petitioner's original petition was dismissed as premature (state remedies not having been exhausted), his post-exhaustion petition raising the same claim was not a successive petition. In dissent Justice Scalia, joined by Justice Thomas, contended that the court "flouts the unmistakable language of the statute" to avoid a result which "contradicts pre-existing judge made-law, which it was precisely the purpose of the statute to change."

The second exception, recognized in § 2244(b)(2)(B), has two prongs. First, the factual predicate for the new claim recognized in the successive petition must be one that "could not have been discovered previously through due diligence." Second, the "facts underlying the claim, if proven and viewed in light of the evidence as a whole" must be "sufficient to establish by clear and convincing evidence that but for the constitutional error, no reasonable factfinder would have found the applicant guilty of the underlying offense." The relationship of these two prongs to the "cause," "actual prejudice" and "miscarriage of justice" components of the *McCleskey* standard is considered below in Note 5b, Supp. p. 190; Note 6a, Supp. p. 191; and Note 2, Supp. p. 210.

One consequence of the new § 2244(b)(2) is to treat successive petitions under a standard different than that applied to a first petition as to claims procedurally defaulted in state courts (in contrast to *McCleskey,* which imposed the same standard for both situations). Section 2264, governing consideration of procedurally defaulted claims on a first petition in a qualified capital case, includes in its subsection (a)(1) the "intervening-new-rule" exception also found in § 2244(b)(2)(A), but it includes only the first prong of the § 2244(b)(2)(B) exception, and it adds another exception (state action violating the constitution that resulted in failure to properly raise the claim) that is not recognized in § 2244(b)(2). See Note 5b, Supp. p. 180. As for first petitions in cases other than qualified death penalty cases, the 1996 amendments offered no new provision directed specifically at claims procedurally defaulted in the state courts, so *Wainwright v. Sykes* presumably would still apply. See Note 5a supra. However, where the procedurally defaulted claim advanced in a first petition requires an evidentiary hearing to "develop [its] factual basis," then § 2254(e)(2) could possibly govern, and it applies standards parallel to (though differently worded than) the two exceptions of § 2244(b)(2). See Note 7a, Supp. p. 219.

Another innovation of new § 2244(b) is to make the court of appeals the "gatekeeper" in applying the standards described above for second or successive applications. The applicant must seek from the court of appeals of the particular circuit an order authorizing the district court to consider the application. A three judge panel of that circuit must rule on the application within thirty days, and its granting or denying of the application is "not appealable" and "shall not be the subject of a petition for rehearing or for a writ of certiorari." § 2244(b)(3)(E). In FELKER v. TURPIN, 518 U.S. 651, 116 S.Ct. 2333, 135 L.Ed.2d 827 (1996), the Supreme Court granted certiorari to determine whether this latter provision was an unconstitutional restriction of its jurisdiction or operated in this case as a suspension of the writ in violation of Article 1, § 9, cl. 2 of the Constitution (see Note 1, 8th ed., p. 1626). A unanimous Court, per Rehnquist, C.J., concluded that § 2244(b)(3)(E) did not deprive the Court of its authority to entertain original habeas petitions, as provided in § 2241, and therefore did not properly present the question of whether Congress has authority under Article III, § 2 to deprive the Court of all appellate jurisdiction in habeas cases. It also concluded that the restrictions imposed on successive petitions did not violate the Suspension Clause. In separate concurring opinions, Justice Stevens (joined by Justices Souter and Breyer) and Justice Souter (joined by Justices Stevens and Breyer) noted that the continuing jurisdiction of the Court was not limited to its authority to entertain original writs of habeas corpus under § 2241, but also included avenues other than the writ of certiorari for reviewing the gatekeeping function of the court of appeals, such as the extraordinary writs that may issue under the All Writs Act.

In the course of discussing the original habeas jurisdiction retained by the Supreme Court under § 2241, Chief Justice Rehnquist noted that: (1) as provided in § 2254 itself, the Court's authority to grant habeas relief to state prisoners is limited by the conditions specified in § 2254; (2) the restrictions on successive petitions imposed in subsection (b)(1) and (b)(2) of § 2244 "apply without qualification to any 'second or successive' habeas corpus application under section 2254," and "whether or not we are bound by these restrictions, they certainly inform our consideration of original habeas petitions"; and (3) the Court's own Rule 20.4(a) governing exercise of its § 2241 original habeas authority mandates that the petitioner "show exceptional circumstances warranting the exercise of the Court's discretionary powers" (which was not shown by the petitioner in this case) and, as a result, " 'these writs are rarely granted.' "

Speaking to the habeas petitioner's contention under the Suspension Clause, Chief Justice Rehnquist initially noted that "the writ of habeas corpus known to the Framers was quite different from that which exists today," as the writ at that time was available "only to prisoners confined under the authority of the United States, not under state authority" and "[t]he class of judicial actions reviewable by the writ was more restricted." Nonetheless, the Court would "assume for purposes of decision here, that the Suspension Clause of the Constitution refers to the writ as it exists today, rather than as it existed in 1989." Turning to the newly adopted provisions on successive petitions, and their relationship to the modern writ, Chief Justice Rehnquist noted that while these provisions were not simply "codifications of preexisting limits on successive petitions," but "further restric[t] the availability of relief to habeas petitioners," the Court had "long recognized" that "judgments about the proper scope of the writ are 'normally for Congress to make.' " The "new restrictions * * * constitute a modified res judicata rule," building upon "a doctrine of abuse of the writ" that the Court in *McCleskey v. Zant* had characterized as reflecting "a complex and evolving body of equitable principles informed and controlled by historical usage, statutory developments, and judicial decisions". The "added restrictions" of § 2244(b), the Chief Justice concluded, "are well within the compass of this evolutionary process, and we hold that they do not amount to a 'suspension' of the writ contrary to Article I, § 9."

8th ed., p. 1662; after Note 2, add:

2a. The 1996 amendments to the federal habeas provisions in several places recognize as a justification for the failure to have timely asserted a claim that a subsequent Supreme Court ruling furnished the basis for that claim by establishing a new rule of constitutional law applicable retroactively on collateral review. Under § 2244(d)(1)(C), such a ruling extends the one-year period of limitation (with a similar extension also recognized for § 2255 motions by federal prisoners). Under § 2254(e)(2)(A)(i), such a ruling justifies holding an evidentiary hearing where the factual basis of a claim was not developed adequately in state proceedings. Under § 2244(b)(2)(A), such a ruling justifies allowing a claim to be raised initially in a second or successive petition (with an identical provision applicable to second or successive § 2255 motions). Under § 2264(a)(2), in qualified capital cases, such a ruling justifies consideration of a claim that was not raised and decided on the merits in the state courts.[a] As to the character of "new rules" that will be given retroactive effect, see Notes 4 and 5, 8th ed., p. 1682 and Note 6a, Supp. p. 185. To what extent do these provisions codify the concept of cause first recognized in *Reed v. Ross,* taking account of the *Teague v. Lane* limits on retroactivity (see fn. c, 8th ed., p. 1662)?

8th ed., p. 1664; after Note 3, add:

3a. None of the provisions of the Antiterrorism and Effective Death Penalty Act recognizing justifications for the failure to have timely presented a constitutional claim refer to counsel error as such a factor. Indeed, one of the repeatedly included justifications—that the factual predicate for the claim could not have been discovered earlier with due diligence (see Note 5b, Supp. p. 190)—by implication appears to reject as a justification (or excuse) counsel's failure to exercise due diligence.

Where a claim was not properly presented by trial counsel in the state courts and that failure precludes consideration of the claim under the provisions of the Antiterrorism and Effective Death Penalty Act (as under § 2254(e)(2) where the factual basis of the claim was not developed in the state proceedings, or under § 2264 where the claim in a capital case was not "raised and decided on the merits in the state courts"), the habeas petitioner apparently cannot look to trial counsel's

---

a. The description of the requisite ruling is somewhat different in the various provisions. For example, § 2264(a)(2) refers to "the Supreme Court's recognition of a new federal right that is made retroactively applicable," while § 2244(b)(2)(A) refers to "a new rule of constitutional law, made retroactive to cases on collateral review by the Supreme Court," and § 2244(d)(1)(C) refers to a "constitutional" right that is "newly recognized by the Supreme Court and made retroactively applicable to cases in collateral review." Section 2254(e)(2) requires for holding the eviden-

tiary hearing both a claim based on a "previously unavailable" new rule of constitutional law "made retroactive to cases in collateral review by the Supreme Court" *and* "facts underlying the claim" that are "sufficient to establish by clear and convincing evidence that but for constitutional error, no reasonable factfinder could have found the applicant guilty of the underlying offense." Of course, if the new rule held retroactive falls within *Teague*'s "beyond-the-power-exception," see Note 4, 8th ed., p. 1682, it would mean that the case should not even have been sent to the factfinder.

error to justify consideration of that claim, even if the error rendered counsel's performance constitutionally ineffective under the *Strickland* standard. Should that limitation have any practical consequence, however, since ineffective assistance can be presented as an independent constitutional claim (provided, of course, that it was timely presented in the state appellate or postconvictions proceedings and in the federal habeas proceeding)?

8th ed., p. 1665; end of Note 4, add:

Consider the comments on *Coleman* of former Attorney General Nicholas deB. Katzenbach, presenting to the Senate Judiciary Committee a statement on behalf of the Emergency Committee to Save Federal Habeas Corpus:

> In the *Coleman v. Thompson* case in 1991, a death row inmate with strong new evidence of actual innocence—evidence so powerful and disturbing that Time magazine featured it as a cover story—was denied an opportunity to even have his new evidence heard in federal court, because his lawyer had unwittingly missed a filing deadline by three days. The Court ruled that the mistake of the otherwise competent lawyer, who was with the respected Washington firm of Arnold & Porter, barred any habeas review of the evidence.[b] Mr. Coleman was executed. Such rulings devalue the protections of the Bill of Rights. No person should pay with his life for the neglect or ignorance of his lawyer. 1995 WL 143182 (F.D.C.H.) (March 28, 1995).

The Emergency Committee also urged the Congress to include in any revision of the habeas statutes that followed the lead of the Powell Committee Report a requirement that the state provide competent counsel *at trial* as well as on state postconviction proceedings.[c] However, Congress limited the appointment prerequisite for the applicability of chapter 154 to postconviction counsel, and further provided that the "ineffectiveness of counsel during State or Federal postconviction proceedings shall not be a ground for relief in a proceeding arising under section 2254." See § 2261(e). Consider also § 2254(i).[d]

b. In *Coleman v. Thompson*, 798 F.Supp. 1209 (W.D.Va.1992), aff'd, 966 F.2d 1441 (4th Cir.1992), the district court held that "Coleman has not made a colorable showing of 'actual innocence' that would entitle him to an evidentiary hearing or habeas corpus relief." The court noted that "all of Coleman's evidence which he claims is new and shows his 'actual innocence' does nothing more than attack the credibility of witnesses and evidence at the original trial," and if all such evidence had been introduced at trial, "it would have raised nothing more than credibility questions which the jury still could have re-solved against Coleman when considering all of the probative evidence."

c. This reform was also urged by various other groups, pointing in particular to studies arguing that there had been widespread ineffective assistance in such cases. See Stephen Bright, *Counsel for the Poor: The Death Sentence Not for the Worst Crime, But for the Worst Lawyer*, 103 Yale L.J. 1835 (1994).

d. As for the appointment of counsel in federal habeas proceedings, see § 2254(h) and fn. 7, 8th ed., p. 110.

8th ed., p. 1666; after Note 5, add:

5a. Three provisions adopted in the Antiterrorism and Effective Death Penalty Act treat state interference as a justification for failing to timely present constitutional claims.[e] Under § 2244(d)(1)(B) and a corresponding provision in § 2255, the one-year period of limitation receives a later starting date where "state action in violation of the Constitution or laws of the United States" constituted an "impediment" preventing the earlier filing of the postconviction petition. Under § 2264(a)(1), in a qualified capital case, the restriction limiting review to claims "raised and decided on the merits" in the state courts is lifted where the "failure to raise the claim properly * * * [was] the result of state action in violation of the Constitution or laws of the United States."[f] Do these provisions utilize a narrower concept of "cause" than that envisioned in *Amadeo v. Zant* and *Brown v. Allen* by requiring that the state action constitutes a violation of the Constitution or federal law?

5b. *Non-discoverable factual predicates.* Where the habeas provisions adopted in 1996 excuse what would otherwise be a procedural default, they treat as one of those excuses the inability to present the claim in a timely fashion because it was based on a factual predicate that could not have been earlier discovered through the exercise of due diligence.[g] Would such a non-discoverable factual predicate also constitute "cause" under the cause and prejudice standard of *Sykes?* As for the due diligence component of this standard, consider the Federal Rule 33 standard on new evidence, described at fn. d, 8th ed., p. 1291, and Note 4, 8th ed., p. 1516. Note in this regard that the 1996 amendment

e. Unlike the other two justifications recognized in these three provisions (i.e., the new rule applied retroactively and the non-discoverable factual predicate), interference by state action is not included also as a justification under § 2244(b) for the filing of a second or successive petition or as a justification under § 2254(e) for having failed to develop the factual basis of a claim in state court proceedings. Where state action at the trial level precludes the development of the factual basis for a claim, and that action itself violates the Constitution, it presumably would constitute a ground for habeas relief in and of itself where appropriately raised in the state courts on direct or collateral review. As for second and successive petitions, the Powell Committee had suggested treating state interference in the first petition as a justification for considering a second petition, though restricting that justification to cases in which the claim was one that would undermine the court's confidence in the jury's determination of guilt. See 45 Crim.L.Rptr. 3243. Congress, however, did not follow this recommendation in § 2244(b).

f. Is this provision limited to state action that prevented presentation of the issue in accordance with state procedural requirements? Might it also apply to a state court ruling procedurally defaulting a claim (i.e., refusing to consider it on the merits) in such an arbitrary or discriminatory fashion as to constitute "a violation of the Constitution or laws of the United States?" If so, to what extent does that standard differ from the *Wainwright v. Sykes* requirement that a procedural default must be based on an adequate state ground? See Note 1, 8th ed., p. 1656. Does § 2264(a)(1) replace that requirement as to procedural defaults in qualified capital cases?

g. See § 2244(d)(1)(C) (later starting point for one-year time limitation), § 2255 (same); § 2264(a) (consideration in capital case of a claim not raised and decided on the merits in the state proceeding); § 2254(b)(2)(B) (successive petition, where combined with showing of innocence); § 2254(e)(2) (holding of evidentiary hearing on factual basis not developed in state proceeding, where combined with showing of innocence).

of § 2255 regarding successive petitions refers simply to "newly discovered evidence" that presents a clear and convincing showing as to actual innocence.

The due diligence standard raises numerous questions of interpretation. One of the most significant is its applicability to claims of incompetent representation by trial counsel where that claim was not raised on appeal or promptly presented in a state postconviction proceeding, but the defendant was represented on appeal by trial counsel and had no counsel (or no different counsel) for the state postconviction proceedings. Cf. *Kimmelman v. Morrison*, 8th ed., p. 1190 ("A layman will ordinarily be unable to recognize counsel's errors and to evaluate counsel's professional performance; * * * consequently a criminal defendant will rarely know that he has not been represented competently until after trial or appeal, usually when he consults another lawyer about his case. Indeed, an accused will often not realize that he has a meritorious ineffectiveness claim until he begins collateral review proceedings, particularly if he retained trial counsel on direct appeal"). Consider also *Coleman v. Thompson*, 8th ed., p. 1664 (leaving open the issue of whether an indigent prisoner might have a constitutional right to the assistance of appointed counsel at a state postconviction proceeding, for the purpose of raising a claim of ineffective assistance of trial counsel, where the jurisdiction prohibits the presentation of such a claim on direct appeal, insisting that it be raised only via collateral attack).

8th ed., p. 1666; after Note 6, add:

6a. Actual prejudice is not always a component of the Antiterrorism and Effective Death Penalty Act provisions that excuse what would otherwise be procedural defaults. In particular, § 2264(a), applicable to qualified capital cases, directs the habeas court to consider claims not raised and decided on the merits in the state proceeding upon a showing of any one of three specified justifications for that procedural default— with no reference to prejudice. See Note 5b, Supp. p. 180. Arguably, the second justification—the Supreme Court's recognition of a new federal right made retroactively applicable—implicitly provides an element of actual prejudice by virtue of the character of the new rules that will fall in that category. See Notes 4 and 5, 8th ed., pp. 1682–83. However, actual prejudice certainly is not inherent in a constitutional claim recognized because its factual predicate was not previously discoverable or because state action prevented the raising of that claim in state proceedings. Here, § 2264 would appear to eliminate a prejudice showing as to the death penalty cases that come within its scope.

On the other hand, as to successive petitions and as to evidentiary hearings where the factual basis was not developed in the state courts, the provisions adopted in 1996 require a showing that goes beyond the "actual prejudice" standard of *Wainwright v. Sykes*. These provisions include as a necessary component for excusing a prior default a showing of an "actual innocence" that would fit within the "miscarriage of justice" exception that *Sykes* and its progeny treated as an alternative to cause the prejudice. See Notes 2 and 3, Supp. p. 210. Under § 2244(b), such a showing is required where the petitioner seeks to justify raising a new claim in a second or successive petition on the ground that the factual predicate was not previously discoverable with due diligence. See Note 6a, Supp. p. 185. Under § 2254(e)(2), governing evidentiary hearings where the factual basis for the claim was not developed in the state proceedings, such a showing is required in combination with both of the justifications listed there (i.e., the new ruling and the undiscoverable factual predicate). See Note 7a, Supp. p. 219.

8th ed., p. 1667; add in lieu of Notes 3 and 4, pp. 1667–70:

SCHLUP v. DELO

513 U.S. 298, 115 S.Ct. 851, 130 L.Ed.2d 808 (1995).

Justice STEVENS delivered the opinion of the Court.

Petitioner Lloyd E. Schlup, Jr., a Missouri prisoner currently under a sentence of death, filed a second federal habeas corpus petition alleging that constitutional error deprived the jury of critical evidence that would have established his innocence. The District Court, without conducting an evidentiary hearing, declined to reach the merits of the petition, holding that petitioner could not satisfy the threshold showing of "actual innocence" required by *Sawyer v. Whitley,* 505 U.S. 333, 112 S.Ct. 2514, 120 L.Ed.2d 269 (1992). Under *Sawyer,* the petitioner must show "by clear and convincing evidence that but for a constitutional error, no reasonable juror would have found the petitioner" guilty. The Court of Appeals affirmed. We granted certiorari to consider whether the *Sawyer* standard provides adequate protection against the kind of miscarriage of justice that would result from the execution of a person who is actually innocent.

On February 3, 1984, on Walk 1 of the high security area of the Missouri State Penitentiary, a black inmate named Arthur Dade was stabbed to death. Three white inmates from Walk 2, including petitioner, were charged in connection with Dade's murder.

At petitioner's trial in December 1985, the State's evidence consisted principally of the testimony of two corrections officers who had witnessed the killing. On the day of the murder, Sergeant Roger Flowers was on duty on Walk 1 and Walk 2, the two walks on the lower floor of the prison's high security area. Flowers testified that he first released the inmates on Walk 2 for their noon meal and relocked their cells. After unlocking the cells to release the inmates on Walk 1, Flowers noticed an inmate named Rodnie Stewart moving against the flow of traffic carrying a container of steaming liquid. Flowers watched as Stewart threw the liquid in Dade's face. According to Flowers, Schlup then jumped on Dade's back, and Robert O'Neal joined in the attack. Flowers shouted for help, entered the walk, and grabbed Stewart as the two other assailants fled.

Officer John Maylee witnessed the attack from Walk 7, which is three levels and some 40–50 feet above Walks 1 and 2. Maylee first noticed Schlup, Stewart, and O'Neal as they were running from Walk 2 to Walk 1 against the flow of traffic. According to Maylee's testimony, Stewart threw a container of liquid at Dade's face, and then Schlup jumped on Dade's back. O'Neal then stabbed Dade several times in the chest, ran down the walk, and threw the weapon out a window. Maylee did not see what happened to Schlup or Stewart after the stabbing.

The State produced no physical evidence connecting Schlup to the killing, and no witness other than Flowers and Maylee testified to Schlup's involvement in the murder.

Schlup's defense was that the State had the wrong man. He relied heavily on a videotape from a camera in the prisoners' dining room. The tape showed that Schlup was the first inmate to walk into the dining room for the noon meal, and that he went through the line and got his food. Approximately 65 seconds after Schlup's entrance, several guards ran out of the dining room in apparent response to a distress call. Twenty-six seconds later, O'Neal ran into the dining room, dripping blood. Shortly thereafter, Schlup and O'Neal were taken into custody.

Schlup contended that the videotape, when considered in conjunction with testimony that he had walked at a normal pace from his cell to the dining room, demonstrated that he could not have participated in the assault. Because the videotape showed conclusively that Schlup was in the dining room 65 seconds before the guards responded to the distress call, a critical element of Schlup's defense was determining when the distress call went out. Had the distress call sounded shortly after the murder, Schlup would not have had time to get from the prison floor to the dining room, and thus he could not have participated in the murder. Conversely, had there been a delay of several minutes between the murder and the distress call, Schlup might have had sufficient time to participate in the murder and still get to the dining room over a minute before the distress call went out.[6]

The prosecutor adduced evidence tending to establish that such a delay had in fact occurred. First, Flowers testified that none of the officers on the prison floor had radios, thus implying that neither he nor any of the other officers on the floor was able to radio for help when the stabbing occurred. Second, Flowers testified that after he shouted for help, it took him "a couple [of] minutes" to subdue Stewart. Flowers

6. A necessary element of Schlup's defense was that Flowers and Maylee were mistaken in their identification of Schlup as one of the participants in the murder. Schlup suggested that Flowers had taken a visitor to Schlup's cell just 30 minutes before the murder. Schlup argued that Flowers therefore had Schlup "on the brain," Trial Tr. 493–494, thus explaining why, in the confusion surrounding the murder, Flowers might have mistakenly believed that he had seen Schlup. Schlup argued that Maylee's identification was suspect because Maylee was three floors away from the murder and did not have an unobstructed view of the murder scene. Schlup further suggested that Maylee's identification of Schlup had been influenced by a postincident conversation between Maylee and another officer who had talked to Flowers.
* * *

then brought Stewart downstairs, encountered Captain James Eberle, and told Eberle that there had been a "disturbance." Eberle testified that he went upstairs to the prison floor, and then radioed for assistance. Eberle estimated that the elapsed time from when he first saw Flowers until he radioed for help was "approximately a minute." The prosecution also offered testimony from a prison investigator who testified that he was able to run from the scene of the crime to the dining room in 33 seconds and to walk the distance at a normal pace in a minute and 37 seconds.

Neither the State nor Schlup was able to present evidence establishing the exact time of Schlup's release from his cell on Walk 2, the exact time of the assault on Walk 1, or the exact time of the radio distress call. Further, there was no evidence suggesting that Schlup had hurried to the dining room.

After deliberating overnight, the jury returned a verdict of guilty. Following the penalty phase, at which the victim of one of Schlup's prior offenses testified extensively about the sordid details of that offense, the jury sentenced Schlup to death. The Missouri Supreme Court affirmed Schlup's conviction and death sentence.

On January 5, 1989, after exhausting his state collateral remedies, Schlup filed a *pro se* petition for a federal writ of habeas corpus, asserting the claim, among others, that his trial counsel was ineffective for failing to interview and to call witnesses who could establish Schlup's innocence. The District Court concluded that Schlup's ineffectiveness claim was procedurally barred, and it denied relief on that claim without conducting an evidentiary hearing. The Court of Appeals affirmed, though it did not rely on the alleged procedural bar. Instead, based on its own examination of the record, the Court found that trial counsel's performance had not been constitutionally ineffective, both because counsel had reviewed statements that Schlup's potential witnesses had given to prison investigators, and because the testimony of those witnesses "would be repetitive of the testimony to be presented at trial."
* * *

On March 11, 1992, represented by new counsel, Schlup filed a second federal habeas corpus petition. That petition raised a number of claims, including that (1) Schlup was actually innocent of Dade's murder, and that his execution would therefore violate the Eighth and Fourteenth Amendments, cf. *Herrera v. Collins* [8th ed., pp. 1516, 1667]; (2) trial counsel was ineffective for failing to interview alibi witnesses; and (3) the State had failed to disclose critical exculpatory evidence. The petition was supported by numerous affidavits from inmates attesting to Schlup's innocence.

The State filed a response arguing that various procedural bars precluded the District Court from reaching the merits of Schlup's claims and that the claims were in any event meritless. Attached to the State's response were transcripts of inmate interviews conducted by prison investigators just five days after the murder. One of the transcripts contained an interview with John Green, an inmate who at the time was the clerk for the housing unit. In his interview, Green stated that he had been in his office at the end of the walks when the murder occurred. Green stated that Flowers had told him to call for help, and that Green had notified base of the disturbance shortly after it began.

Schlup immediately filed a traverse arguing that Green's affidavit provided conclusive proof of Schlup's innocence. Schlup contended that Green's statement demonstrated that a call for help had gone out shortly after the incident. Because the videotape showed that Schlup was in the dining room some 65 seconds before the guards received the distress call, Schlup argued that he could not have been involved in Dade's murder. Schlup emphasized that Green's statement was not likely to have been fabricated, because at the time of Green's interview, neither he nor anyone else would have realized the significance of Green's call to base. Schlup tried to buttress his claim of innocence with affidavits from inmates who stated that they had witnessed the event and that Schlup had not been present. Two of those affidavits suggested that Randy Jordan—who occupied the cell between O'Neal and Stewart in Walk 2, and who * * * is shown on the videotape arriving at lunch with O'Neal—was the third assailant.

On August 23, 1993, without holding a hearing, the District Court dismissed Schlup's second habeas petition and vacated the stay of execution that was then in effect. The District Court concluded that Schlup's various filings did not provide adequate cause for failing to raise his new claims more promptly. Moreover, the Court concluded that Schlup had failed to meet the *Sawyer v. Whitley* standard for showing that a refusal to entertain those claims would result in a fundamental miscarriage of justice. In its discussion of the evidence, the Court made no separate comment on the significance of Green's statement.

On September 7, 1993, petitioner filed a motion to set aside the order of dismissal, again calling the Court's attention to Green's statement. Two days later, Schlup filed a supplemental motion stating that his counsel had located John Green and had obtained an affidavit from him. That affidavit confirmed Green's postincident statement that he had called base shortly after the assault. Green's affidavit also identified Jordan rather than Schlup as the third assailant. The District Court denied the motion and the supplemental motion without opinion.

Petitioner then sought from the Court of Appeals a stay of execution pending the resolution of his appeal. Relying on Justice Powell's plurality opinion in *Kuhlmann v. Wilson* [8th ed., p. 1683, Note 6], Schlup argued that the District Court should have entertained his second habeas corpus petition, because he had supplemented his constitutional claim "with a colorable showing of factual innocence."

On October 15, 1993, the Court of Appeals denied the stay application. In an opinion that was subsequently vacated, the majority held that petitioner's claim of innocence was governed by the standard announced in *Sawyer v. Whitley,* and it concluded that under that standard, the evidence of Schlup's guilt that had been adduced at trial foreclosed consideration of petitioner's current constitutional claims. Judge Heaney dissented. Relying on Green's affidavit, the videotape, and the affidavits of four other eyewitnesses, Judge Heaney concluded that the petitioner had met both the *Kuhlmann* standard and a proper reading of the *Sawyer* standard. * * *

In the meantime, petitioner's counsel obtained an affidavit from Robert Faherty, the former lieutenant at the prison whom Schlup had passed on the way to lunch on the day of the murder and who had reprimanded Schlup for shouting out the window. Faherty's affidavit stated that Schlup had been in Faherty's presence for at least two and a half minutes; that Schlup was walking at a leisurely pace; and that Schlup "was not perspiring or breathing hard, and he was not nervous."

On November 15, 1993, the Court of Appeals vacated its earlier opinion and substituted a more comprehensive analysis of the law to support its decision to deny Schlup's request for a stay. The majority adhered to its earlier conclusion that *Sawyer* stated the appropriate standard for evaluating Schlup's claim of actual innocence. The opinion also contained an extended discussion of Schlup's new evidence. The Court noted in particular that Green's new affidavit was inconsistent in part with both his prison interview and his testimony at the Stewart trial. The Court viewed Faherty's affidavit as simply "an effort to embellish and expand upon his testimony" and concluded "that a habeas court should not permit retrial on such a basis." * * *

Judge Heaney again dissented, concluding that Schlup had "presented truly persuasive evidence that he is actually innocent," and that the District Court should therefore have addressed the merits of Schlup's constitutional claims. Judge Heaney also argued that Schlup's ineffectiveness claim was substantial. He noted that Schlup's trial counsel failed to conduct individual interviews with Griffin Bey, McCoy, or any of the other inmates who told investigators that they had seen the killing. Moreover, counsel failed to interview Green about his statement that he had called base. In fact, counsel apparently failed to conduct individual interviews with any of the potential witnesses to the crime. Judge Heaney adhered to his conclusion that Schlup's counsel was ineffective, even though counsel allegedly had reviewed 100 interviews conducted by prison investigators. Judge Heaney argued that counsel's review of the interview transcripts—rather than demonstrating counsel's effectiveness—made counsel's failure to conduct his own interviews with Green and the few inmates who admitted seeing the attack even more troubling. * * *

On November 17, 1993, the Court of Appeals denied a suggestion for rehearing en banc. Dissenting from that denial, three judges joined an opinion describing the question whether the majority should have applied the standard announced in *Sawyer v. Whitley, supra,* rather than the *Kuhlmann* standard as "a question of great importance in habeas

corpus jurisprudence.'' We granted certiorari to consider that question.
* * *

As a preliminary matter, it is important to explain the difference between Schlup's claim of actual innocence and the claim of actual innocence asserted in *Herrera v. Collins* [8th ed., p. 1667, fn. c]. In *Herrera,* the petitioner advanced his claim of innocence to support a novel substantive constitutional claim, namely that the execution of an innocent person would violate the Eighth Amendment. Under petitioner's theory in *Herrera,* even if the proceedings that had resulted in his conviction and sentence were entirely fair and error-free, his innocence would render his execution a "constitutionally intolerable event."

Schlup's claim of innocence, on the other hand, is procedural, rather than substantive. His constitutional claims are based not on his innocence, but rather on his contention that the ineffectiveness of his counsel, see *Strickland v. Washington,* and the withholding of evidence by the prosecution, see *Brady v. Maryland,* denied him the full panoply of protections afforded to criminal defendants by the Constitution. Schlup, however, faces procedural obstacles that he must overcome before a federal court may address the merits of those constitutional claims. Because Schlup has been unable to establish "cause and prejudice" sufficient to excuse his failure to present his evidence in support of his first federal petition, see *McCleskey v. Zant* [8th ed., p. 1660, Note 6], Schlup may obtain review of his constitutional claims only if he falls within the "narrow class of cases ... implicating a fundamental miscarriage of justice." *Id.* Schlup's claim of innocence is offered only to bring him within this "narrow class of cases."

Schlup's claim thus differs in at least two important ways from that presented in *Herrera.* First, Schlup's claim of innocence does not by itself provide a basis for relief. Instead, his claim for relief depends critically on the validity of his *Strickland* and *Brady* claims. Schlup's claim of innocence is thus "not itself a constitutional claim, but instead a gateway through which a habeas petitioner must pass to have his otherwise barred constitutional claim considered on the merits." *Herrera.*

More importantly, a court's assumptions about the validity of the proceedings that resulted in conviction are fundamentally different in Schlup's case than in Herrera's. In *Herrera,* petitioner's claim was evaluated on the assumption that the trial that resulted in his conviction had been error-free. In such a case, when a petitioner has been "tried before a jury of his peers, with the full panoply of protections that our Constitution affords criminal defendants," it is appropriate to apply an " 'extraordinarily high' " standard of review. Id. (O'Connor, J., concurring).

Schlup, in contrast, accompanies his claim of innocence with an assertion of constitutional error at trial. For that reason, Schlup's conviction may not be entitled to the same degree of respect as one, such as Herrera's, that is the product of an error-free trial. Without any new evidence of innocence, even the existence of a concededly meritorious constitutional violation is not in itself sufficient to establish a miscarriage of justice that would allow a habeas court to reach the merits of a barred claim. However, if a petitioner such as Schlup presents evidence of innocence so strong that a court cannot have confidence in the outcome of the trial unless the court is also satisfied that the trial was free of nonharmless constitutional error, the petitioner should be allowed to pass through the gateway and argue the merits of his underlying claims.

Consequently, Schlup's evidence of innocence need carry less of a burden. In *Herrera* (on the assumption that petitioner's claim was, in principle, legally well founded), the evidence of innocence would have had to be strong enough to make his execution "constitutionally intolerable" *even if* his conviction was the product of a fair trial. For Schlup, the evidence must establish sufficient doubt about his guilt to justify the conclusion that his execution would be a miscarriage of justice *unless* his conviction was the product of a fair trial.

Our rather full statement of the facts illustrates the foregoing distinction between a substantive *Herrera* claim and Schlup's procedural claim. Three items of evidence are particularly relevant: the affidavit of black inmates attesting to the innocence of a white defendant in a racially motivated killing; the affidavit of Green describing his prompt call for assistance; and the affidavit of Lieutenant Faherty describing Schlup's unhurried walk to the dining room. If there were no question about the fairness of the criminal trial, a *Herrera*–type claim would have to fail unless the federal habeas court is itself convinced that those new facts unquestionably establish Schlup's innocence. On the other hand, if the habeas court were merely convinced that those new facts raised sufficient doubt about Schlup's guilt to undermine confidence in the result of the trial without the assurance that that trial was untainted by constitutional error, Schlup's threshold showing of innocence would justify a review of the merits of the constitutional claims. * * *

* * * [The] Court [has] held that a habeas court may not ordinarily reach the merits of successive claims, *Kuhlmann v. Wilson,* or abusive claims, *McCleskey,* absent a showing of cause and prejudice, see *Wainwright v. Sykes.* The application of cause and prejudice to successive and abusive claims conformed to this Court's treatment of procedurally defaulted claims. * * * At the same time, the Court has adhered to the principle that habeas corpus is, at its core, an equitable remedy. * * * We firmly established the importance of the equitable inquiry required by the ends of justice in "a trio of 1986 decisions" handed down on the same day. *Sawyer* (referring to *Kuhlmann, Carrier* [8th ed., p. 1667], and *Smith v. Murray* [8th ed., p. 1667]). * * * Thus, while recognizing that successive petitions are generally precluded from review, Justice Powell's plurality opinion [in *Kuhlmann*] expressly noted that there are "limited circumstances under which the interests of the prisoner in relitigating constitutional claims held meritless on a prior petition may outweigh the countervailing interests served by according finality to the

prior judgment." Similarly, writing for the Court in *Carrier,* Justice O'Connor observed that the Court had adopted the cause and prejudice standard in part because of its confidence that that standard would provide adequate protection to " 'victims of a fundamental miscarriage of justice.' " For that reason, " '[i]n appropriate cases,' the principles of comity and finality that inform the concepts of cause and prejudice 'must yield to the imperative of correcting a fundamentally unjust incarceration.' " Id. In subsequent cases, we have consistently reaffirmed the existence and importance of the exception for fundamental miscarriages of justice. See, e.g., *Sawyer.*

To ensure that the fundamental miscarriage of justice exception would remain "rare" and would only be applied in the "extraordinary case," while at the same time ensuring that the exception would extend relief to those who were truly deserving, this Court explicitly tied the miscarriage of justice exception to the petitioner's innocence. In *Kuhlmann,* for example, Justice Powell concluded that a prisoner retains an overriding "interest in obtaining his release from custody if he is innocent of the charge for which he was incarcerated. That interest does not extend, however, to prisoners whose guilt is conceded or plain." Similarly, Justice O'Connor wrote in *Carrier* that "in an extraordinary case, where a constitutional violation has probably resulted in the conviction of one who is actually innocent, a federal habeas court may grant the writ even in the absence of a showing of cause for the procedural default."

The general rule announced in *Kuhlmann, Carrier,* and *Smith,* and confirmed in this Court's more recent decisions, rests in part on the fact that habeas corpus petitions that advance a substantial claim of actual innocence are extremely rare. Judge Friendly's observation a quarter of a century ago [Friendly, 8th ed., p. 1684] that "the one thing almost never suggested on collateral attack is that the prisoner was innocent of the crime" remains largely true today. Explicitly trying the miscarriage of justice exception to innocence thus accommodates both the systemic interests in finality, comity, and conservation of judicial resources, and the overriding individual interest in doing justice in the "extraordinary case," *Carrier.*

In addition to linking miscarriages of justice to innocence, *Carrier,* and *Kuhlmann* also expressed the standard of proof that should govern consideration of those claims. In *Carrier,* for example, the Court stated that the petitioner must show that the constitutional error "probably" resulted in the conviction of one who was actually innocent. The *Kuhlmann* plurality, though using the term "colorable claim of factual innocence," elaborated that the petitioner would be required to establish, by a " 'fair probability,' " that " 'the trier of the facts would have entertained a reasonable doubt of his guilt.' "

In the years following *Kuhlmann* and *Carrier,* we did not expound further on the actual innocence exception. In those few cases that mentioned the standard, the Court continued to rely on the formulations set forth in *Kuhlmann* and *Carrier.* * * * Then, in *Sawyer,* the Court examined the miscarriage of justice exception as applied to a petitioner who claimed he was "actually innocent of the death penalty." In that opinion, the Court struggled to define "actual innocence" in the context of a petitioner's claim that his death sentence was inappropriate. The Court concluded that such actual innocence "must focus on those elements which render a defendant eligible for the death penalty." However, in addition to defining what it means to be "innocent" of the death penalty, the Court departed from *Carrier's* use of "probably" and adopted a more exacting standard of proof to govern these claims: the Court held that a habeas petitioner "must show by *clear and convincing* evidence that but for a constitutional error, no reasonable juror would have found the petitioner eligible for the death penalty." (emphasis added). No attempt was made in *Sawyer* to reconcile this stricter standard with *Carrier's* use of "probably."

In evaluating Schlup's claim of innocence, the Court of Appeals applied Eighth Circuit precedent holding that *Sawyer,* rather than *Carrier,* supplied the proper legal standard. The Court then purported to apply the *Sawyer* standard. Schlup argues that *Sawyer* has no application to a petitioner who claims that he is actually innocent of the crime, and that the Court of Appeals misapplied *Sawyer* in any event. Respondent contends that the Court of Appeals was correct in both its selection and its application of the *Sawyer* standard. Though the Court of Appeals seems to have misapplied *Sawyer,* we do not rest our decision on that ground because we conclude that in a case such as this, the *Sawyer,* standard does not apply.

As we have stated, the fundamental miscarriage of justice exception seeks to balance the societal interests in finality, comity, and conservation of scarce judicial resources with the individual interest in justice that arises in the extraordinary case. We conclude that *Carrier,* rather than *Sawyer,* properly strikes that balance when the claimed injustice is that constitutional error has resulted in the conviction of one who is actually innocent of the crime.

Claims of actual innocence pose less of a threat to scarce judicial resources and to principles of finality and comity than do claims that focus solely on the erroneous imposition of the death penalty. Though challenges to the propriety of imposing a sentence of death are routinely asserted in capital cases, experience has taught us that a substantial claim that constitutional error has caused the conviction of an innocent person is extremely rare. To be credible, such a claim requires petitioner to support his allegations of constitutional error with new reliable evidence—whether it be exculpatory scientific evidence, trustworthy eyewitness accounts, or critical physical evidence—that was not presented at trial. Because such evidence is obviously unavailable in the vast majority of cases, claims of actual innocence are rarely successful. Even under the pre-*Sawyer* regime, "in virtually every case, the allegation of actual innocence has been summarily rejected." Steiker, Innocence and Federal Habeas, 41 UCLA L.Rev. 303 (1993). The threat to judicial resources, finality, and comity posed by claims of actual innocence is thus significantly less than that posed by claims relating only to sentencing.

Of greater importance, the individual interest in avoiding injustice is most compelling in the context of actual innocence. The quintessential miscarriage of justice is the execution of a person who is entirely innocent. Indeed, concern about the injustice that results from the conviction of an innocent person has long been at the core of our criminal justice system. That concern is reflected, for example, in the "fundamental value determination of our society that it is far worse to convict an innocent man than to let a guilty man go free." *In re Winship* [8th ed., p. 850]. * * * The overriding importance of this greater individual interest merits protection by imposing a somewhat less exacting standard of proof on a habeas petitioner alleging a fundamental miscarriage of justice than on one alleging that his sentence is too severe. * * * Though the *Sawyer* standard was fashioned to reflect the relative importance of a claim of an erroneous sentence, application of that standard to petitioners such as Schlup would give insufficient weight to the correspondingly greater injustice that is implicated by a claim of actual innocence. The paramount importance of avoiding the injustice of executing one who is actually innocent thus requires application of the *Carrier* standard.

We recognize, as the State has reminded us, that in *Sawyer* the Court applied its new standard not only to the penalty phase of the case but also to Sawyer's responsibility for arson, one of the elements of the offense of first-degree murder. This fact does not require application of the *Sawyer* standard to a case such as Schlup's. Though formulated as an element of the offense of first-degree murder, the arson functioned essentially as a sentence enhancer. That claim, therefore, is readily distinguishable from a claim, like the one raised by Schlup, that the petitioner is actually innocent.[a] Fealty to the doctrine of *stare decisis* does not, therefore, preclude application of the *Carrier* standard to the facts of this case. * * *

The *Carrier* standard requires the habeas petitioner to show that "a constitutional violation has probably resulted in the conviction of one

a. In Calderon v. Thompson, ___ U.S. ___, 118 S.Ct. 1489, 140 L.Ed.2d 728 (1998), also discussed in footnote a at Supp. p. 185, the Court held that Ninth Circuit's recall of its mandate constituted an abuse of discretion because not justified by the "miscarriage of justice exception." As to the branch of that exception applicable to the case before it, the Court noted:

"A claim like Thompson's could present some difficulty concerning whether to apply *Schlup* or *Sawyer*. Thompson makes no appreciable effort to assert his innocence of Fleischli's murder. Instead, he challenges, first, his rape conviction, and second, the jury's finding of the special circumstance [for capital sentencing] of rape. The former challenge is subject to the *Schlup* 'more likely than not' standard; the latter challenge is subject to the *Sawyer* 'clear and convincing' standard. In theory, then, it would be possible to vacate Thompson's stand-alone conviction of rape but to let stand his conviction of murder and sentence of death. This anomaly perhaps reflects some tension between *Sawyer* and the later-decided *Schlup*. The anomaly need not detain us, however, for Thompson's claims fail under either standard."

who is actually innocent." To establish the requisite probability, the petitioner must show that it is more likely than not that no reasonable juror would have convicted him in the light of the new evidence. The petitioner thus is required to make a stronger showing than that needed to establish prejudice. See *Strickland, Bagley*. At the same time, the showing of "more likely than not" imposes a lower burden of proof than the "clear and convincing" standard required under *Sawyer*. The *Carrier* standard thus ensures that petitioner's case is truly "extraordinary," *McCleskey*, while still providing petitioner a meaningful avenue by which to avoid a manifest injustice.

Carrier requires a petitioner to show that he is "actually innocent." As used in *Carrier*, actual innocence is closely related to the definition set forth by this Court in *Sawyer*. To satisfy the *Carrier* gateway standard, a petitioner must show that it is more likely than not that no reasonable juror would have found petitioner guilty beyond a reasonable doubt.

Several observations about this standard are in order. The *Carrier* standard is intended to focus the inquiry on actual innocence. In assessing the adequacy of petitioner's showing, therefore, the district court is not bound by the rules of admissibility that would govern at trial. Instead, the emphasis on "actual innocence" allows the reviewing tribunal also to consider the probative force of relevant evidence that was either excluded or unavailable at trial. Indeed, with respect to this aspect of the *Carrier* standard, we believe that Judge Friendly's description of the inquiry is appropriate: the habeas court must make its determination concerning the petitioner's innocence "in light of all the evidence, including that alleged to have been illegally admitted (but with due regard to any unreliability of it) and evidence tenably claimed to have been wrongly excluded or to have become available only after the trial."

The consideration in federal habeas proceedings of a broader array of evidence does not modify the essential meaning of "innocence." The *Carrier* standard reflects the proposition, firmly established in our legal system, that the line between innocence and guilt is drawn with reference to a reasonable doubt. See *In re Winship*. Indeed, even in *Sawyer*, with its emphasis on eligibility for the death penalty, the Court did not stray from the understanding that the eligibility determination must be made with reference to reasonable doubt. Thus, whether a court is assessing eligibility for the death penalty under *Sawyer*, or is deciding whether a petitioner has made the requisite showing of innocence under *Carrier*, the analysis must incorporate the understanding that proof beyond a reasonable doubt marks the legal boundary between guilt and innocence.

The meaning of actual innocence as formulated by *Sawyer*, and *Carrier* does not merely require a showing that a reasonable doubt exists in the light of the new evidence, but rather that no reasonable juror would have found the defendant guilty. It is not the district court's independent judgment as to whether reasonable doubt exists that the standard addresses; rather the standard requires the district court to make a probabilistic determination about what reasonable, properly instructed jurors would do.   Thus, a petitioner does not meet the threshold requirement unless he persuades the district court that, in light of the new evidence, no juror, acting reasonably, would have voted to find him guilty beyond a reasonable doubt.

We note finally that the *Carrier* standard requires a petitioner to show that it is more likely than not that "no reasonable juror" would have convicted him.   The word "reasonable" in that formulation is not without meaning.   It must be presumed that a reasonable juror would consider fairly all of the evidence presented.   It must also be presumed that such a juror would conscientiously obey the instructions of the trial court requiring proof beyond a reasonable doubt.[48]

Though the *Carrier* standard requires a substantial showing, it is by no means equivalent to the standard [of *Jackson v. Virginia,* 443 U.S. 307, 99 S.Ct. 2781, 61 L.Ed.2d 560 (1979)] that governs review of claims of insufficient evidence.   The *Jackson* standard, which focuses on whether any rational juror could have convicted, looks to whether there is sufficient evidence which, if credited, could support the conviction.   The *Jackson* standard thus differs in at least two important ways from the *Carrier* standard.   First, under *Jackson,* the assessment of the credibility of witnesses is generally beyond the scope of review.   In contrast, under the gateway standard we describe today, the newly presented evidence may indeed call into question the credibility of the witnesses presented at trial.   In such a case, the habeas court may have to make some credibility assessments.   Second, and more fundamentally, the focus of the inquiry is different under *Jackson* than under *Carrier.*   Under *Jackson,* the use of the word "could" focuses the inquiry on the power of the trier of the fact to reach its conclusion.   Under *Carrier,* the use of the word "would" focuses the inquiry on the likely behavior of the trier of fact.

Indeed, our adoption of the phrase "more likely than not" reflects this distinction.   Under *Jackson,* the question whether the trier of fact has power to make a finding of guilt requires a binary response: either the trier of fact has power as a matter of law or it does not.   Under *Carrier,* in contrast, the habeas court must consider what reasonable triers of fact are likely to do.   Under this probabilistic inquiry, it makes

---

48.   The Chief Justice suggests that the *Carrier* standard is "a classic mixing of apples and oranges."   That standard, however, is no more a mixing of apples and oranges than is the standard adopted by the Court in *Sawyer.*   Though it is true that " '[m]ore likely than not' " is a "quintessential charge to a finder of fact," that is equally true of the "clear and convincing evidence" component of the *Sawyer* formulation.   There is thus no reason to believe that the *Carrier* standard is any more likely

than the *Sawyer* standard to be "a source of confusion."

Nor do we accept The Chief Justice's description of the *Carrier* standard as a "hybrid."   Finders of fact are often called upon to make predictions about the likely actions of hypothetical "reasonable" actors.   Thus, the application of "more likely than not" to the habeas court's assessment of the actions of reasonable jurors is neither illogical nor unusual.

sense to have a probabilistic standard such as "more likely than not." Thus, though under *Jackson* the mere existence of sufficient evidence to convict would be determinative of petitioner's claim, that is not true under *Carrier*.

We believe that the Eighth Circuit's erroneous application of the *Sawyer* standard below illustrates this difference. In determining that Schlup had failed to satisfy the *Sawyer* standard, the majority noted that "two prison officials, who were eyewitnesses to the crime, positively identified Mr. Schlup as one of the three perpetrators of the murder. This evidence was clearly admissible and stands unrefuted except to the extent that Mr. Schlup now questions its credibility." The majority then continued:

> "[E]ven if we disregard the source of the new evidence, the eleventh-hour nature of the information, and a presentation coming almost six years after the trial; it is simply not possible to say that the appellant has shown by clear and convincing evidence that but for a constitutional error no reasonable jury would have found him guilty."

However, Schlup's evidence includes the sworn statements of several eyewitnesses that Schlup was not involved in the crime. Moreover, Schlup has presented statements from Green and Faherty that cast doubt on whether Schlup could have participated in the murder and still arrived at the dining room 65 seconds before the distress call was received. Those new statements may, of course, be unreliable. But if they are true—as the Court of Appeals assumed for the purpose of applying its understanding of the *Sawyer* standard—it surely cannot be said that a juror, conscientiously following the judge's instructions requiring proof beyond a reasonable doubt, would vote to convict. Under a proper application of either *Sawyer* or *Carrier*, petitioner's showing of innocence is not insufficient solely because the trial record contained sufficient evidence to support the jury's verdict.

In this case, the application of the *Carrier* standard arises in the context of a request for an evidentiary hearing. In applying the *Carrier* standard to such a request, the District Court must assess the probative force of the newly presented evidence in connection with the evidence of guilt adduced at trial. Obviously, the Court is not required to test the new evidence by a standard appropriate for deciding a motion for summary judgment. * * * Instead, the Court may consider how the timing of the submission and the likely credibility of the affiants bear on the probable reliability of that evidence.

Because both the Court of Appeals and the District Court evaluated the record under an improper standard, further proceedings are necessary. The fact-intensive nature of the inquiry, together with the District Court's ability to take testimony from the few key witnesses if it deems that course advisable, convinces us that the most expeditious procedure is to order that the decision of the Court of Appeals be vacated and that the case be remanded to the Court of Appeals with instructions to remand to the District Court for further proceedings consistent with this opinion.

Justice O'CONNOR, concurring.

I write to explain, in light of the dissenting opinions, what I understand the Court to decide and what it does not.

The Court holds that, in order to have an abusive or successive habeas claim heard on the merits, a petitioner who cannot demonstrate cause and prejudice "must show that it is more likely than not that no reasonable juror would have convicted him" in light of newly discovered evidence of innocence. This standard is higher than that required for prejudice, which requires only "a reasonable probability that, absent the errors, the factfinder would have had a reasonable doubt respecting guilt," *Strickland v. Washington.* Instead, a petitioner does not pass through the gateway erected by *Murray v. Carrier* if the district court believes it more likely than not that there is any juror who, acting reasonably, would have found the petitioner guilty beyond a reasonable doubt. And the Court's standard, which focuses the inquiry on the likely behavior of jurors, is substantively different from the rationality standard of *Jackson v. Virginia * * *. Jackson,* which emphasizes the authority of the factfinder to make conclusions from the evidence, establishes a standard of review for the sufficiency of record evidence—a standard that would be ill-suited as a burden of proof. * * * The Court today does not sow confusion in the law. Rather, it properly balances the dictates of justice with the need to ensure that the actual innocence exception remains only a " 'safety valve' for the 'extraordinary case.' "

Moreover, the Court does not, and need not, decide whether the fundamental miscarriage of justice exception is a discretionary remedy. It is a paradigmatic abuse of discretion for a court to base its judgment on an erroneous view of the law. Having decided that the district court committed legal error, and thus abused its discretion, by relying on *Sawyer v. Whitley,* instead of *Murray v. Carrier,* the Court need not decide the question—neither argued by the parties nor passed upon by the Court of Appeals—whether abuse of discretion is the proper standard of review. In reversing the judgment of the Court of Appeals, therefore, the Court does not disturb the traditional discretion of district courts in this area, nor does it speak to the standard of appellate review for such judgments. * * * With these observations, I join the Court's opinion.

Chief Justice REHNQUIST, with whom Justice KENNEDY and Justice THOMAS join, dissenting.

* * * In *Sawyer,* we described in some detail the showing of actual innocence required when a habeas petitioner brings an otherwise abusive, successive, or procedurally defaulted claim challenging the imposition of his death sentence, rather than his guilt of the crime. * * * We have never until today had to similarly flesh out the standard of "actual innocence" in the context of a habeas petitioner claiming innocence of the crime. Thus, I agree that the question of what threshold standard should govern is an open one. * * * I disagree with the Court's

conclusion that *Carrier,* and not *Sawyer,* provides the proper standard. But far more troubling than the choice of *Carrier* over *Sawyer* is the watered down and confusing version of *Carrier* which is served up by the Court.

* * * The Court informs us that a showing of "actual innocence" requires a habeas petitioner to "show that it is more likely than not that no reasonable juror would have convicted him in the light of the new evidence." But this is a classic mixing of apples and oranges. "More likely than not" is a quintessential charge to a finder of fact, while "no reasonable juror would have convicted him in the light of the new evidence" is an equally quintessential conclusion of law similar to the standard that courts constantly employ in deciding motions for judgment of acquittal in criminal cases. The hybrid which the Court serves up is bound to be a source of confusion. Because new evidence not presented at trial will almost always be involved in these claims of actual innocence, the legal standard for judgment of acquittal cannot be bodily transposed for the determination of "actual innocence," but the sensible course would be to modify that familiar standard, rather than to create a confusing hybrid.

In the course of elaborating the *Carrier* standard, the Court takes pains to point out that it differs from the standard enunciated in *Jackson v. Virginia,* for review of the sufficiency of the evidence to meet the constitutional standard of proof beyond a reasonable doubt. Under *Jackson,* "the relevant question is whether, after viewing the evidence in the light most favorable to the prosecution, *any* rational trier of fact could have found the essential elements of the crime beyond a reasonable doubt." This standard requires a solely retrospective analysis of the evidence considered by the jury and reflects a healthy respect for the trier of fact's "responsibility . . . to resolve conflicts in the testimony, to weigh the evidence, and to draw reasonable inferences from basic facts to the ultimate facts."

The Court fails to acknowledge expressly the similarities between the standard it has adopted and the *Jackson* standard. A habeas court reviewing a claim of actual innocence does not write on a clean slate. * * * Therefore, as the Court acknowledges, a petitioner making a claim of actual innocence under *Carrier* falls short of satisfying his burden if the reviewing court determines that *any* juror reasonably would have found petitioner guilty of the crime. * * * The situation presented by a claim of actual innocence in a federal habeas petition is obviously different from that presented in *Jackson* because the habeas court analyzing an "actual innocence" claim is faced with a body of evidence that has been supplemented since the original trial. The reviewing court must somehow predict the effect that this new evidence would have had on the deliberations of reasonable jurors. It must necessarily weigh this new evidence in some manner, and may need to make credibility determinations as to witnesses who did not appear before the original jury. This new evidence, however, is not a license for the reviewing court to disregard the presumptively proper determination by the original trier of fact.

I think the standard enunciated in *Jackson,* properly modified because of the different body of evidence which must be considered, faithfully reflects the language used in *Carrier.* The habeas judge should initially consider the motion on the basis of the written submissions made by the parties. As the Court suggests, habeas courts will be able to resolve the great majority of "actual innocence" claims routinely without any evidentiary hearing. This fact is important because, as we noted in *Sawyer:* "In the every day context of capital penalty proceedings, a federal district judge typically will be presented with a successive or abusive habeas petition a few days before, or even on the day of, a scheduled execution, and will have only a limited time to determine whether a petitioner has shown that his case falls within the 'actual innocence' exception if such a claim is made."

But in the highly unusual case where the district court believes on the basis of written submissions that the necessary showing of "actual innocence" may be made out, it should conduct a limited evidentiary hearing at which the affiants whose testimony the Court believes to be crucial to the showing of actual innocence are present and may be cross examined as to veracity, reliability, and all of the other elements which affect the weight to be given the testimony of a witness. After such a hearing, the district court would be in as good a position as possible to make the required determination as to the showing of actual innocence.

The present state of our habeas jurisprudence is less than ideal in its complexity, but today's decision needlessly adds to that complexity. I believe that by adopting the *Sawyer* standard both for attacks on the sentence and on the judgment of conviction, we would take a step in the direction of simplifying this jurisprudence. * * * The *Sawyer* standard strikes the proper balance among the State's interest in finality, *McCleskey,* the federal courts' respect for principles of federalism, see, e.g., *Teague v. Lane* [8th ed., p. 1670] and "the ultimate equity on the prisoner's side—a sufficient showing of actual innocence," *Withrow v. Williams* [8th ed., p. 1640] (O'Connor, J., concurring in part and dissenting in part). The Court of Appeals fully analyzed petitioner's new evidence and determined that that petitioner fell way short of " 'show[ing] by clear and convincing evidence [that] no reasonable juror would find him [guilty of murder].' " * * * I agree and therefore would affirm. * * * But if we are to adopt the *Carrier* standard, it should not be the confusing exegesis of that standard contained in the Court's opinion. It should be based on a modified version of *Jackson v. Virginia,* with a clearly defined area in which the district court may exercise its discretion to hold an evidentiary hearing.

Justice SCALIA, with whom Justice THOMAS joins, dissenting.

A federal statute entitled "Finality of Determination"—to be found at § 2244 of Title 28 of the United States Code—specifically addresses the problem of second and subsequent petitions for the writ of habeas corpus. The reader of today's opinion will be unencumbered with knowledge of this law, since it is not there discussed or quoted, and indeed is only cited *en passant*. Rather than asking what the statute says, or even what we have said the statute says, the Court asks only what is the fairest standard to apply, and answers that question by looking to the various semi-consistent standards articulated in our most recent decisions—minutely parsing phrases, and seeking shades of meaning in the interstices of sentences and words, as though a discursive judicial opinion were a statute. * * *

[Under § 2244(b)], a federal district court that receives a second or subsequent petition for the writ of habeas corpus, when a prior petition has been denied on the merits, "need not ... entertai[n]" (i.e. may dismiss) the petition unless it is neither (to use our shorthand terminology) successive nor abusive. * * * Today, however, the Court obliquely but unmistakably pronounces that a successive or abusive petition *must* be entertained and may *not* be dismissed so long as the petitioner makes a sufficiently persuasive showing that a "fundamental miscarriage of justice" has occurred. * * * ("if a petitioner such as Schlup presents [adequate] evidence of innocence ... the petitioner should be allowed to pass through the gateway and argue the merits"), *ante* at [Supp. p. 163, 1st ¶].[1] That conclusion flatly contradicts the statute, and is not required by our precedent.

* * * Three years after *Sanders* [8th ed., p. 1683, Note 6] * * *, Congress amended § 2244 to establish different finality rules for federal prisoner petitions (filed under § 2255) and state prisoner petitions (filed under § 2254). Section 2244(a), which addresses petitions by federal prisoners, retains the "ends of justice" proviso from the old statute; but § 2244(b) omits it, thus restricting the district courts' *obligation* to entertain petitions by state prisoners to cases where the petition is neither successive nor abusive. One might have expected that this not-so-subtle change in the statute would change our interpretation of it, and that we would modify *Sanders* by holding that a district court could exercise its discretion to give controlling weight to the prior denial * * *. Yet when the new version of § 2244(b) was first construed, in *Kuhlmann v. Wilson* [8th ed., p. 1683, Note 6], a plurality of the Court announced that it would "continue to rely on the reference in *Sanders* to the 'ends of justice,'" and concluded that "the 'ends of justice' require federal courts to entertain [successive] petitions only where the prisoner supplements his constitutional claim with a colorable showing of factual innocence." That conclusion contains two complementary propositions. The first is that a habeas court may *not* reach the merits of a barred claim *unless* actual innocence is shown; this was the actual judgment of the opinion (one cannot say the holding, since the opinion was a mere

---

1. The claim that "the Court does not, and need not, decide whether the fundamental miscarriage of justice exception is a discretionary remedy" (O'Connor, J., concurring), is not in my view an accurate description of what the Court's opinion says. Of course the concurrence's merely making the claim causes it to be an accurate description of what the Court today *holds*, since the narrower ground taken by one of the Justices comprising a five-Justice majority becomes the law.

plurality).   * * * The second is that a habeas court *must* hear a claim of actual innocence and reach the merits of the petition if the claim is sufficiently persuasive; this was the purest dictum.   It is the Court's prerogative to adopt that dictum today, but to adopt it without analysis, as though it were binding precedent, will not do.   The *Kuhlmann* plurality opinion lacks formal status as authority, and * * * no holding of this Court binds us to it.   A decision to follow it must be justified by reason, not simply asserted by will.   * * *

And if reasons are to be given, justification of the *Kuhlmann* opinion will be found difficult indeed.   The plurality's central theory is that ''the permissive language of § 2244(b) gives federal courts discretion to entertain successive petitions under some circumstances,'' so that ''[u]nless [the] 'rare instances' [in which successive petitions will be entertained] are to be identified by whim or caprice, district judges must be given guidance for determining when to exercise the limited discretion granted them by § 2244(b).''   What the plurality then proceeds to do, however, is not to ''guide'' the discretion, but to eliminate it entirely, dividing the entire universe of successive and abusive petitions into those that *must not* be entertained (where there is no showing of innocence) and those that *must* be entertained (where there is such a showing).   This converts a statute redolent of permissiveness (''*need not* entertain'') into a rigid command.

The *Kuhlmann* plurality's concern about caprice is met—as it is met for all decisions committed by law to the discretion of lower courts—by applying traditional ''abuse of discretion'' standards.   A judge who dismisses a successive petition because he misconceives some question of law, because he detests the petitioner's religion, or because he would rather play golf, may be reversed.   A judge who dismisses a successive petition because it is the petitioner's twenty-second, rather than his second, because its ''only purpose is to vex, harass, or delay,'' *Sanders,* or because the constitutional claims can be seen to be frivolous on the face of the papers—for any of the numerous considerations that have ''a *rational* bearing on the propriety of the discharge sought,'' *Salinger [v. Loisel,* 265 U.S. 224 (1924)] (emphasis added)—may not be commanded to reach the merits because ''the ends of justice'' require.   Here as elsewhere in the law, to say that a district judge may not abuse his discretion is merely to say that the action in question (dismissing a successive petition) may not be done without considering relevant factors and giving a ''justifying reason'' * * *.   It is a failure of logic, and an arrogation of authority, to ''guide'' that discretion by holding that what Congress authorized the district court to do may not be done at all.

The Court's assumption that the requirement imposed by the *Kuhlmann* plurality should be taken as law can find no support in our subsequent decisions.   * * * There is thus no route of escape from the Court's duty to confront the statute today.   I would say, as the statute does, that habeas courts need not entertain successive or abusive petitions.   The courts whose decisions we review declined to entertain the petition, and I find no abuse of discretion in the record.   (I agree with

The Chief Justice that they were correct to use *Sawyer v. Whitley,* supra, as the legal standard for determining claims of innocence.) Therefore, "we should sustain [their] action without saying more." *Salinger.*

Notes and Questions

1. On remand, the district court ordered a hearing on the merits of petitioner Schlup's constitutional claims after concluding, on the "basis of all the materials presented on the * * * actual innocence issue," that "it is more likely than not that no reasonable juror would have convicted petitioner in light of the new evidence." The court noted that the favorable testimony of inmates who stated that they had witnessed the murder was "credible and believable" even though most had denied witnessing the murder when originally interviewed in 1984, as those denials were explained by a "code of silence" that existed among the inmates at that time. See *Schlup v. Delo,* 912 F.Supp. 448 (E.D.Mo. 1995). On hearing the merits, the court concluded that the petitioner had established his ineffective assistance of counsel due to the trial attorney's failure to interview known, easily accessible eyewitness who said Schlup was not involved in the killing. See Marcia Coyle, *Law: Innocent Dead Men Walking,* 18 Nat'l L.J., n. 18, p. A1 (May 20, 1996).

2. What is left of *Schlup* and the fundamental miscarriage of justice doctrine in light of the 1996 Antiterrorism and Effective Death Penalty Act? Schlup involved a second habeas petition, which today would bring into play § 2244(b). Insofar as petitioner Schlup was presenting a claim not presented in a prior application, the failure to have included that claim in the prior petition would be excused under § 2244(b)(2)(B) only if (i) the factual predicate could not have been discovered previously through the exercise of due diligence and (ii) "the facts underlying the claim, if proven and viewed in light of the evidence as a whole, would be sufficient to establish by clear and convincing evidence that, but for constitutional error, no reasonable factfinder would have found the applicant guilty of the underlying offense." Is this second component essentially the showing that would have been required by the *Schlup* dissenters? Since the lower court in *Schlup* had held that petitioner could not meet the "cause" component of the cause and prejudice standard, does it follow that *Schlup* also could not have met the first component of the § 2244(b)(2)(B) standard?

In Calderon v. Thompson, ___ U.S. ___, 118 S.Ct. 1489, 140 L.Ed.2d 728 (1998), the Court characterized the *Schlup* and *Sawyer* standards as "somewhat more lenient than the standard in § 2244(b)(2)(B)," adding a "see e.g." citation to the § 2244(b)(2)(B) requirement that the factual predicate not have been previously discoverable with due diligence.

3. Assume that the claims presented in *Schlup* were today present- ed in an initial habeas petition, that those claims had been procedurally defaulted in the state proceedings, and that the state had a counsel- appointment procedure for its postconviction proceedings in capital cases

that satisfies the standards of chapter 154. Assume also that the habeas court finds that the factual predicate for the claim could have been discovered with due diligence at a point where that claim would have been cognizable before the state courts. Under § 2264, would the petitioner be precluded from presenting those claims—even if he could meet a "clear and convincing" standard as to the actual innocence issue? See Note 5b, Supp. p. 180.

4. Assume that the claims presented in *Schlup* were today presented in an initial habeas petition, that those claims had been procedurally defaulted in the state proceedings, and that the state does not have a counsel appointment procedure that meets the standards of chapter 154. Assume also that the habeas court concludes that the default in the state courts was not excused by "cause." Would the habeas court be free to rely upon *Schlup* and reach the merits of the constitutional claim if it found that it was "more likely than not" that no reasonable juror would have convicted the defendant in light of the evidence underlying those constitutional claims? Consider in this connection the possible bearing of § 2254(e)? See Note 7a, Supp. p. 219.

5. Do the various provisions of the Antiterrorism and Effective Death Penalty Act preclude litigating actual innocence on habeas as an independent constitutional claim (see the *Schlup* discussion of *Herrera v. Collins*) where that claim relies on evidence not presented at trial? See *Felker v. Turpin,* 83 F.3d 1303 (11th Cir.1996) (raising but finding no need to resolve that issue).

6. While the provisions of the 1996 amendments that refer to the actual innocence concept utilize the "clear and convincing evidence" standard of *Sawyer v. Whitley,* they require that showing as to habeas petitioner's guilt on the "underlying offense." See e.g., § 2254(e)(2)(B). Does this mean that in the context of successive petitions, or claims as to which the factual basis was not developed in state court proceedings, the petitioner may not raise a constitutional claim limited to the erroneous imposition of the death penalty—even where the factual predicate of that claim was not previously discoverable?

7. BOUSLEY v. UNITED STATES, __ U.S. __, 118 S.Ct. 1604, 140 L.Ed.2d 828 (1998), applied *Schlup* in the context of a guilty plea. In 1990, petitioner pleaded guilty to "using" a firearm in violation of § 924(c)(1). In 1995, *Bailey v. United States,* 516 U.S. 137, 116 S.Ct. 501, 133 L.Ed.2d 472 (1955) held that § 924(c)(1)'s "use" prong requires the prosecution to show "active employment of the firearm," such as "brandishing, displaying, bartering, striking with, * * * [or] firing"; "mere possession of the firearm" was not sufficient. Petitioner sought to take advantage of this ruling in his pending collateral attack under § 2255, claiming that his "guilty plea was not knowing and intelligent because he was misinformed by the District Court as to the nature of the charged crime." The Supreme Court majority (per REHNQUIST, C.J.) held that petitioner's claim had been procedurally defaulted, but peti-

tioner should be given the opportunity to establish his "actual innocence" in accordance with *Schlup*.

The Court initially noted that petitioner's involuntariness claim had been procedurally defaulted because it had not been raised on petitioner's direct appeal from his conviction (that appeal having challenged only the sentence imposed on the guilty plea). Where, as here, the voluntariness challenge does not depend on facts that must be developed apart from the record below, it "can be attacked on collateral review only if first challenged on direct review." The majority rejected the argument of Justice Stevens (dissenting on this point) that constitutional challenges to a guilty plea may be presented initially on collateral attack.[a] It noted that habeas review generally "will not be allowed to do service for an appeal," and the concern for finality underlying this limitation has "special force with respect to convictions based on guilty pleas."

The majority also concluded that the procedural default here was not excused by "cause" as that concept had been developed in *Wainwright v. Sykes* and its progeny. Although *Bailey* was decided long after petitioner's direct appeal, its reading of § 924(c)(1) was hardly so novel as not to have been reasonably available to counsel (see *Reed v. Ross*, 8th ed., p. 1662), and the petitioner's failure to present it on appeal was not excused by the fact that such a reading would not have been accepted by the appellate court (see *Engle v. Isaac*, 8th ed., p. 1661). With cause eliminated, the defaulted claim could be considered only if defendant met the "actual innocence" standard as developed in *Schlup*. As to this possibility, the Court noted:

"To establish actual innocence, petitioner must demonstrate that, 'in light of all the evidence,' 'it is more likely than not that no reasonable juror would have convicted him.' *Schlup v. Delo.* * * * It is important to note in this regard that 'actual innocence' means factual innocence, not mere legal insufficiency. See *Sawyer v. Whitley* * * *. In other words, the Government is not limited to the existing record to rebut any showing that petitioner might make. Rather, on remand, the Government should be permitted to present any admissible evidence of petitioner's guilt even if that evidence was not presented during petitioner's plea colloquy and would not normally have been offered before our decision in *Bailey*.[3] In

---

a. Justice Stevens argued that the *Timmreck* ruling [8th ed., p. 1376] cited by the majority dealt only with non-constitutional challenges to guilty pleas, and the Court had never previously held that "the constitutionality of a guilty plea cannot be attacked collaterally unless it is first challenged on direct review." "Moreover," he noted, "the facts of this case demonstrate, such a holding would be unwise and would defeat the very purpose of collateral review. A layman who justifiably relied on incorrect advice from the court and counsel in deciding to plead guilty to a crime that he did not commit will ordinarily continue to as-

sume that such advice was accurate during the time for taking an appeal. The injustice of his conviction is not mitigated by the passage of time. His plea should be treated as a nullity and the conviction based on such a plea should be voided."

3. Justice Scalia contends that this factual innocence inquiry will be unduly complicated by the absence of a trial transcript in the guilty plea context. We think his concerns are overstated. In the federal system, where this case arose, guilty pleas must be accompanied by proffers, recorded verbatim on the record, demonstrating a

cases where the Government has forgone more serious charges in the course of plea bargaining, petitioner's showing of actual innocence must also extend to those charges."

In dissent, SCALIA, J. (joined by Thomas, J.) argued that the "actual innocence" exception to the bar of a procedural default should not be available to the habeas petitioner challenging a guilty plea. He reasoned:

"No criminal-law system can function without rules of procedure conjoined with a rule of finality. Evidence not introduced, or objections not made, at the appropriate time cannot be brought forward to reopen the conviction after judgment has been rendered. In the United States, we have developed generous exceptions to the rule of finality, one of which permits reopening, via habeas corpus, when the petitioner shows 'cause' excusing the procedural default, and 'actual prejudice' resulting from the alleged error. * * * We have gone even beyond that generous exception in a certain class of cases: cases that have actually gone to trial. There we have held that, 'even in the absence of a showing of cause for the procedural default," habeas corpus will be granted 'where a constitutional violation has probably resulted in the conviction of one who is actually innocent.' *Schlup v. Delo*. In every one of our cases that has considered the possibility of applying this so-called actual-innocence exception, a defendant had asked a habeas court to adjudicate a successive or procedurally defaulted constitutional claim after his conviction by a jury. * * *

"There are good reasons for this limitation: First and foremost, it is feasible to make an accurate assessment of 'actual innocence' when a trial has been had. * * * As the Court's opinion today makes clear, the Government is permitted to supplement the trial record with any additional evidence of guilt, but the court begins with (and ordinarily ends with) a complete trial transcript to rely upon. But how is the court to determined 'actual innocence' upon our remand in the present case, where conviction was based upon an admission of guilt? Presumably the defendant will introduce evidence (perhaps nothing more than his own testimony) showing that he did not 'use' a firearm in committing the crime to which he pleaded guilty, and the Government, eight years after the fact, will have to find and produce witnesses saying that he did. This seems to me not to remedy a miscarriage of justice, but to produce one.*

"Secondly, the Court has given as one of its justifications for the super-generous miscarriage-of-justice exception to inexcusable default, 'the fact that habeas corpus petitions that advance a substantial claim of actual innocence are extremely rare.' *Schlup*. That may be true enough of petitions challenging jury convictions; it assuredly will not be true of

factual basis for the plea. See Fed. Rules Crim. Proc. 11(f), (g).

* The Court believes these concerns are overstated because, in the federal system, the court must be satisfied that there is a factual basis for the plea. See n.3. This displays a sad lack of solicitude for state courts, which handle the overwhelming majority of criminal cases. But even in the federal system, the "factual basis" requirement will typically be of no use. * * *

petitions challenging the 'voluntariness' of guilty pleas. I put 'voluntariness' in quotation marks, because we are not dealing here with only coerced confessions, which may indeed be rare enough. The present case is here because, in *Henderson v. Morgan* [8th ed., p. 1367], this Court held that where neither the indictment, defense counsel, nor the trial court explained to the defendant that intent to kill was an element of second-degree murder, his plea to that offense was 'involuntary.' * * * It is well established that 'when this Court construes a statute, it is explaining its understanding of what the statute has meant continuously since the date when it became law.' * * * Thus, every time this Court resolves a Circuit split regarding the elements of a crime defined in a federal statute, most if not all defendants who pleaded guilty in those Circuits on the losing end of the split will have confessed 'involuntarily,' having been advised by the Court, or by their counsel, that the law was what (as it turns out) it was not—or even (since this would suffice for application of *Henderson*) merely not having been advised that the law was what (as it turns out) it was. Indeed the latter basis for 'involuntariness' (mere lack of 'real notice of the charge against him,' *Henderson*), might be available even to those defendants pleading guilty in the Circuits on the winning side of the split. Thus, our decision in *Bailey v. United States,* has generated a flood of 28 U.S.C. § 2255 habeas petitions, each asserting actual innocence of 'using' a firearm in violation of 18 U.S.C. § 924(c). * * * To the undeniable fact that the claim of 'actual innocence' is much more likely to be available in guilty-plea cases than in jury-trial cases, there must be added the further undeniable fact that guilty-plea cases are very much more numerous than jury-trial cases. Last year, 51,647 of the 55,648 defendants convicted and sentenced in federal court (or nearly 93 percent) pleaded guilty. * * *

"When all these factors are taken into account, it could not be clearer that the premise for our adoption in *Schlup* of the supergenerous 'miscarriage of justice' exception to normal finality rules—viz., that the cases in which defendants seek to invoke the exception would be 'extremely rare'—is simply not true when the exception is extended to guilty pleas. To the contrary, the cases will be extremely frequent, placing upon the criminal-justice system a burden it will be unable to bear—especially in light of the fact, discussed earlier, that on remand the habeas trial court will not have any trial record on the basis of which to make the 'actual innocence' determination.

"Not only does the disposition agreed upon today overload the criminal-justice system; it makes relief available where equity demands that relief be denied. When a defendant pleads guilty, he waives his right to a have a jury make the requisite findings of guilt—typically in exchange for a lighter sentence of reduced charges. Thus, defendants plead guilty to charges that have not been proven—that perhaps could not be proven—in order to avoid conviction on charges of which they are 'actually guilty,' which carry a harsher penalty. Under today's holding, a defendant who is the 'wheel-man' in a bank robbery in which a person is shot and killed, and who pleads guilty in state court to the offense of voluntary manslaughter in order to avoid trial on felony-murder charges, is entitled to federal habeas review of his contention that his guilty plea was 'involuntary' because he was not advised that intent-to-kill was an element of the manslaughter offense, and that he was 'actually innocent' of manslaughter because he had no intent to kill. In such a case, it is excusing the petitioner from his procedural default, not holding him to it, that would be the miscarriage of justice.

"The Court evidently seeks to avoid this absurd consequence by prescribing that the defendant's 'showing of actual innocence must also extend' to any charge the Government has 'forgone.' This is not even a fully satisfactory solution in theory, since it assumes that the 'forgone' charge is identifiable. If, as is often the case, the bargaining occurred before the charge was filed ('charge-bargaining' instead of 'plea-bargaining'), it will almost surely not be identifiable. And of course in practical terms, the solution is no solution at all. To avoid the patent inequity, the Government will be called upon to refute, without any factual record to rely upon, not only the defendant's testimony of his innocence of the charge of conviction, but his testimony of innocence on the 'forgone' charge as well—and as to the second, even the finding of 'factual basis' required in federal courts, will not exist. But even if rebuttal evidence existed, it is a bizarre waste of judicial resources to require mini-trials on charges made in dusty indictments (or indeed, if they could be identified, on charges never made), just to determine whether the defendant can litigate a procedurally defaulted challenge to a guilty plea on a different offense. Rube Goldberg would envy the scheme the Court has created.

* * *

"It would be marvellously inspiring to be able to boast that we have a criminal-justice system in which a claim of 'actual innocence' will always be heard, no matter how late it is brought forward, and no matter how much the failure to bring it forward at the proper time is the defendant's own fault. But of course we do not have such a system, and no society unwilling to devote unlimited resources to repetitive criminal litigation ever could. The 'actual innocence' exception this Court has invoked to overcome inexcusable procedural default in cases decided by a jury 'seeks to balance the societal interests in finality, comity, and conservation of scarce judicial resources with the individual interest in justice that arises in the extraordinary case.' *Schlup*. Since the balance struck there simply does not obtain in the guilty-plea context, today's decision is not a logical extension of *Schlup*, and it is a grave mistake."

SECTION 4. THE GOVERNING LEGAL STANDARD

8th ed., p. 1683; after Note 5, add:

5a. *Retroactivity and the 1996 amendments.* The Antiterrorism and Effective Death Penalty Act in several provisions incorporates the "new rule" and retroactivity analysis of *Teague*. The failure to comply with various procedural prerequisites is excused where the claim is based on a subsequently established new rule held by the Supreme Court to be retroactively applicable in federal habeas proceedings. See Note 2a, Supp. p. 188. Does this standard implicitly incorporate the current Supreme Court jurisprudence as to what constitutes a new rule and what type of new rule will be applied retroactively, or does it leave the Court free to modify or expand upon those concepts (see e.g., Note 4, 8th ed., p. 1682)?

5b. *Standard of review and § 2254(d).* Although a plurality in *Wright v. West* (8th ed., p. 1692) insisted that *Teague* "did not establish a deferential standard of review of state court decisions on federal law," but simply a "principle of retroactivity" (see 8th ed., p. 1695, opinion of Justice O'Connor and 8th ed., p. 1697, opinion of Justice Kennedy), Congress looked to *Teague* to impose explicitly a deferential standard of review in the Antiterrorism and Effective Death Penalty Act. Newly adopted § 2254(d) provides:

> (d) An application for a writ of habeas corpus on behalf of a person in custody pursuant to the judgment of a State court shall not be granted with respect to any claim that was adjudicated on the merits in State court proceedings unless the adjudication of the claim—(1) resulted in a decision that was contrary to, or involved an unreasonable application of, clearly established Federal law, as determined by the Supreme Court of the United States; or (2) resulted in a decision that was based on an unreasonable determination of the facts in light of the evidence presented in the State court proceeding.

Does subsection (d)(1) simply restate the substance of the "new rule" principle developed in the Court's post-*Teague* rulings (see Notes 2 and 3, 8th ed., p. 1680)? Does it impose, as Justice Brennan suggested the Court had done in his *Butler* dissent (see 8th ed., p. 1681), a "clearly erroneous" standard of review in federal habeas cases?

Congress in § 2254(d) sought to ensure that the deferential standard of review suggested by *Teague* and its progeny would also be applied to mixed questions of law and fact (thereby rejecting the position of the plurality in *Wright v. West,* 8th ed., p. 1692). Does the combination of (d)(1) and (d)(2) now mandate that all State court determinations, whether described as purely legal, purely factual, or mixed, be judged under the same deferential standard of review? Does the language of § 2254(d)(1) instead suggest that a distinction is to be drawn between claims that the state court erred in the legal principle it derived from Supreme Court precedent (the "contrary to" standard) and claims that the state court erred in the application a correctly derived principle to facts of the case (the "unreasonable application" standard)? Consider also, in this connection, the bearing of subsection (e)(1) of § 2254, discussed in Note 7a, Supp. p. 219.

Subsection (d)(1) makes no reference to the possibility that a claim adjudicated on the merits in the state court may be the subject of a subsequently recognized new rule that has been held to have retroactive application. Are new rules held to be retroactive part of the "clearly established federal law" at it stood at the time of the adjudication in the state court proceedings? Is an exception for such new rules implicit in their recognition in other provisions adopted as part of Antiterrorism and Effective Death Penalty Act (see Note 5a, Supp. p. 215)? Consider, in this connection, the treatment of such new rules under § 2244(b)(1), discussed below.

8th ed., p. 1684; after Note 6, add:

6a. The Antiterrorism and Effective Death Penalty Act replaced the provision interpreted in *Kuhlmann* with a new § 2244(b)(1), which simply states:

> A claim presented in a second or successive habeas corpus application under section 2254 that was presented in a prior application shall be dismissed.

Does this provision render irrelevant the petitioner's current capacity to supplement his constitutional claim with a colorable showing of "actual innocence"?

Subsection (b)(2) of § 2244 prohibits consideration of claims not presented in a prior petition, but creates an exception where the applicant shows that claim relies on "a new rule of constitutional law, made retroactive to cases collateral review by the Supreme Court, that was previously unavailable." See Note 6a, Supp. p. 185. Where petitioner raised a particular constitutional objection in the state proceedings, that objection was presented in an initial habeas petition but was rejected because the state ruling reflected a reasonable reading of prevailing Supreme Court precedent, and a subsequent Supreme Court ruling then established a new rule that both enhanced the petitioner's claim and fell within one of the classes of new rulings held retroactive, does that ruling in effect create a "new claim" that was not presented in the original petition—therefore allowing the petitioner to utilize subsection (b)(2) and escaping the absolute language of (b)(1)? The 1996 amendments leave to the courts in this section and others the task of determining what constitutes a new "claim."

8th ed., p. 1687; at the end of the Note on Brecht, add:

In O'NEAL v. McANINCH, 513 U.S. 432, 115 S.Ct. 992, 130 L.Ed.2d 947 (1995), the Sixth Circuit, relying in part on *Brecht,* held that the habeas petitioner must bear the "burden of establishing" that the alleged constitutional error was prejudicial under the *Brecht–Kotteakos* harmless-error standard—i.e., the habeas petitioner had to establish by a preponderance of the evidence that the error had a " 'substantial and injurious effect or influence in determining the jury's verdict' " (quoting *Brecht,* in turn quoting *Kotteakos*). A divided Supreme Court (6–3), per BREYER, J., held that the Sixth Circuit had erred. The Court concluded: "As a practical matter, this statement [that the petitioner bears the burden of establishing prejudice] apparently means that, if a judge is in grave doubt about the effect on the jury of this kind of error, the petitioner must lose. Thus, O'Neal might have lost in the Court of Appeals, not because the judges concluded that the error *was* harmless, but because the record of the trial left them in grave doubt about the effect of the error. * * * [But] [w]hen a federal judge in a habeas proceeding is in grave doubt about whether a trial error of federal law had 'substantial and injurious effect or influence in determining the jury's verdict,' that error is not harmless. And, the petitioner must win."

In reaching this conclusion, the Court initially noted: "As an initial matter, * * * we deliberately phrase the issue in this case in terms of a judge's grave doubt, instead of in terms of 'burden of proof.' The case before us does not involve a judge who shifts a 'burden' to help control the presentation of evidence at a trial, but rather involves judges who apply a legal standard (harmlessness) to a record that the presentation of evidence is no longer likely to affect. In such a case, we think it conceptually clearer for the judge to ask directly, 'Do I, the judge, think that the error substantially influenced the jury's decision?' than for the judge to try to put the same question in terms of proof burdens (e.g., 'Do I believe the party has borne its burden of showing ...?'). As Chief Justice Traynor said:

> 'Whether or not counsel are helpful, it is still the responsibility of the ... court, once it concludes there was error, to determine whether the error affected the judgment. It must do so without benefit of such aids as presumptions or allocated burdens of proof that expedite fact-finding at the trial.' R. Traynor, The Riddle of Harmless Error 26 (1970).

The case may sometimes arise, however, where the record is so evenly balanced that a conscientious judge is in grave doubt as to the harmlessness of an error. This is the narrow circumstance we address here."

Justice Breyer then turned to "three considerations" that supported "our legal conclusion—that in cases of grave doubt as to harmlessness the petitioner must win." First, that conclusion was supported by precedent. Admittedly, *Brecht* spoke of habeas petitioners not being "entitled to habeas relief based on trial error unless they can establish that it resulted in 'actual prejudice'" (8th ed., p. 1686). But *Brecht* incorporated the *Kotteakos* standard, and the Court there had specifically noted that "*if one is left in grave doubt*, the conviction cannot stand" (emphasis added). So too, as the Court had noted in *Chapman*, " 'the original common-law harmless-error rule put the burden on the beneficiary of the error [here the State] to prove that there was no injury' " (8th ed., p. 1607).

Second, the Court's conclusion was "consistent with the basic purposes underlying the writ of habeas corpus": "[A] legal rule requiring issuance of the writ * * * [where a grave doubt exists] will, at least often avoid a grievous wrong—holding a person 'in custody in violation of the Constitution.' 28 U.S.C. § 2241(c)(3), § 2254(a). * * * [T]he *opposite* rule, denying the writ in cases of grave uncertainty, would virtually guarantee that many, *in fact,* will be held in unlawful custody."

Third, the Court's conclusion would have "certain administrative virtues": "It is consistent with the way that courts have long treated important trial errors.   * * * In a highly technical area such as this one, consistency brings with it simplicity, a body of existing case law available for consultation, see *Brecht,* and a consequently diminished risk of further, error-produced, proceedings.   Moreover, our rule avoids the need for judges to read lengthy records to determine prejudice in every habeas case.   These factors are not determinative, but offer a practical caution against a legal rule that, in respect to precedent and purpose, would run against the judicial grain."

Justice THOMAS' dissent argued that the Court was giving insufficient weight to "the state's interest in finality and the promotion of federal-state comity" in "balancing the costs and benefits associated with disturbing judgments when a court is in grave doubt as to harm." That those interests must be balanced against the potential for ensuring against unlawful imprisonment was acknowledged implicitly by the Court itself in "drawing the line at 'grave doubt' rather than 'significant doubt' or 'any doubt.' "   In the habeas context, the dissent argued, these additional interests should produce a harmless error inquiry that shifts to the petitioner a burden that is carried by the state on direct appeal (as in *Kotteakos* and *Chapman*).   While the majority viewed the language of the habeas statute as providing no direction as to how an appellate court should apply the harmless error standard, the dissent argued that statute clearly placed the burden of showing prejudice on the petitioner. Unless the petitioner can establish that the constitutional violation "had a 'substantial and injurious effect or influence in determining the jury's verdict,' " he cannot establish that he is being held in custody "in violation of the Constitution"—i.e., that there is a "causal link between the [constitutional] violation and the custody."   The dissent concluded by noting that it was "fortunate" that "the rule announced today will affect only a minuscule fraction of cases"—those "in which a judge, after a thorough review of the record remains in equipoise."

SECTION 5.   THE SPECIAL STATUS OF FACTFINDING

8th ed., p. 1692; after Note 7, add:

7a.   The 1996 amendments replaced former § 2254(d) with a much less complex subsection (e).[a]   That section provides initially in subdivi-

---

a. Subsection (d) provided:

"(d) In any proceeding instituted in a Federal court by an application for a writ of habeas corpus by a person in custody pursuant to the judgment of a State court, a determination after a hearing on the merits of a factual issue, made by a State court of

competent jurisdiction in a proceeding to which the applicant for the writ and the State or an officer or agent thereof were parties, evidenced by a written finding, written opinion, or other reliable and adequate written indicia, shall be presumed to be correct, unless the applicant shall estab-

sion (1) that "a determination of a factual issue by a State court shall be presumed to be correct," with the applicant having the "burden of rebutting the presumption of correctness by clear and convincing evidence." It then provides in subdivision (2) that the federal habeas court shall not hold an evidentiary hearing on a claim as to which there was "a failure to develop the factual basis" in state court proceedings unless that claim rests on either (i) an intervening new rule held to be retroactive (see Note 2a, Supp. p. 188) or (ii) a factual predicate not previously discoverable with due diligence (see Note 5b, Supp. p. 190), *and* the facts underlying the claim would be sufficient to "establish by clear and convincing evidence that but for the constitutional error, no reasonable factfinder would have found the applicant guilty of the underlying offense" (see Note 2, Supp. p. 210).

Under the former subsection (d), it was important to distinguish between a determination of historic fact and a "mixed determination of law and fact" because the presumption of correctness applied only to the former and *de novo* review governed as to the latter. See Notes 5–8, 8th ed., pp. 1688–92. Assuming that the presumption recognized in new subsection (e) also applies only to a determination of historic fact, is that distinction still of great significance in light of § 2254(d), discussed in Note 5b, Supp. p. 216?

How many of the 8 grounds listed in former subsection (d) (see fn. a supra) would today rebut the presumption of correctness? Where the "material facts were not adequately developed at the state court hearing" [ground (3) in the former subsection (d)], must the state court's finding nonetheless be accepted unless the petitioner meets the requirements for additional hearings under subsection (e)(ii)? Assuming that the facts were fully and fairly developed in the state courts, does the

lish or it shall otherwise appear, or the respondent shall admit—

(1) that the merits of the factual dispute were not resolved in the State court hearing; (2) that the factfinding procedure employed by the State court was not adequate to afford a full and fair hearing; (3) that the material facts were not adequately developed at the State court hearing; (4) that the State court lacked jurisdiction of the subject matter or over the person of the applicant in the State court proceeding; (5) that the applicant was an indigent and the State court, in deprivation of his constitutional right, failed to appoint counsel to represent him in the State court proceeding; (6) that the applicant did not receive a full, fair, and adequate hearing in the State court proceeding; or (7) that the applicant was otherwise denied due process of law in the State court proceeding; (8) or unless that part of the record of the State court proceeding in which the determination of such factual issue was made, pertinent to a determination of the sufficiency of the evidence to support such factual determination, is produced as provided for hereinafter, and the Federal court on a consideration of such part of the record as a whole concludes that such factual determination is not fairly supported by the record:

And in an evidentiary hearing in the proceeding in the Federal court, when due proof of such factual determination has been made, unless the existence of one or more of the circumstances respectively set forth in paragraphs numbered (1) to (7), inclusive, is shown by the applicant, otherwise appears, or is admitted by the respondent, or unless the court concludes pursuant to the provisions of paragraph numbered (8) that the record in the State court proceeding, considered as a whole, does not fairly support such factual determination, the burden shall rest upon the applicant to establish by convincing evidence that the factual determination by the State court was erroneous."

combination of § 2254(e)(2) and § 2254(d)(1) and (Note 5b, Supp. p. 216) leave the petitioner in approximately the same position as former subsection (d) in challenging a state court finding as against the weight of the evidence?

Does subsection (e) now fully supplant the *Townsend* standards as to when a habeas court must or may hold an evidentiary hearing? Does subsection (e)(ii), in particular, narrow the district court's authority, as recognized in *Keeney v. Tamayo–Reyes* (fn. a, 8th ed., p. 1688), to hold a hearing based on newly discovered evidence where the petitioner could meet the cause and prejudice standard of *Wainwright v. Sykes* or its "fundamental miscarriage of justice" exception? Consider Note 2a, Supp. p. 188; Note 5b, Supp. p. 190; Note 6a, Supp. p. 191; and Note 2, Supp. p. 210.

8th ed., p. 1698; after Wright v. West, add:

Notes and Questions

1. As for the impact of the Antiterrorism and Effective Death Penalty Act upon the issue presented in *West,* see Note 5b, Supp. p. 216, and Note 7a, Supp. p. 219.

Appendix A

SELECTED PROVISIONS OF THE UNITED STATES CONSTITUTION

Article I

Section 9.   * * *

[2] The privilege of the Writ of Habeas Corpus shall not be suspended, unless when in Cases of Rebellion or Invasion the public Safety may require it.

[3] No Bill of Attainder or ex post facto Law shall be passed.

Article III

Section 1.   The judicial Power of the United States, shall be vested in one supreme Court, and in such inferior Courts as the Congress may from time to time ordain and establish.   The Judges, both of the supreme and inferior Courts, shall hold their Offices during good Behaviour, and shall, at stated Times, receive for their Services a Compensation, which shall not be diminished during their Continuance in Office.

Section 2.   [1] The judicial Power shall extend to all Cases, in Law and Equity, arising under this Constitution, the Laws of the United States, and Treaties made, or which shall be made, under their Authority;—to all Cases affecting Ambassadors, other public Ministers and Consuls;—to all Cases of admiralty and maritime Jurisdiction;—to Controversies to which the United States shall be a Party;—to Controversies between two or more States;—between a State and Citizens of another State;—between Citizens of different States;—between Citizens of the same State claiming Lands under the Grants of different States, and between a State, or the Citizens thereof, and foreign States, Citizens or Subjects.

[3] The trial of all Crimes, except in Cases of Impeachment, shall be by Jury; and such Trial shall be held in the State where the said Crimes shall have been committed; but when not committed within any State, the Trial shall be at such Place or Places as the Congress may by Law have directed.

Section 3.   [1] Treason against the United States, shall consist only in levying War against them, or, in adhering to their Enemies, giving them Aid and Comfort.   No Person shall be convicted of Treason unless on the Testimony of two Witnesses to the same overt Act, or on Confession in open Court.

[2] The Congress shall have Power to declare the Punishment of Treason, but no Attainder of Treason shall work Corruption of Blood, or Forfeiture except during the Life of the Person attainted.

ARTICLE IV

Section 2.   [1] The Citizens of each State shall be entitled to all Privileges and Immunities of Citizens in the several States.

[2] A Person charged in any State with Treason, Felony, or other Crime, who shall flee from Justice, and be found in another State, shall on demand of the executive Authority of the State from which he fled, be delivered up, to be removed to the State having Jurisdiction of the Crime.

ARTICLE VI

[2] This Constitution, and the Laws of the United States which shall be made in Pursuance thereof; and all Treaties made, or which shall be made, under the Authority of the United States, shall be the supreme Law.

AMENDMENT I [1791]

Congress shall make no law respecting an establishment of religion, or prohibiting the free exercise thereof; or abridging the freedom of speech, or of the press; or the right of the people peaceably to assemble, and to petition the Government for a redress of grievances.

AMENDMENT II [1791]

A well regulated Militia, being necessary to the security of a free State, the right of the people to keep and bear Arms, shall not be infringed.

AMENDMENT III [1791]

No Soldier shall, in time of peace be quartered in any house, without the consent of the Owner, nor in time of war, but in a manner to be prescribed by law.

AMENDMENT IV [1791]

The right of the people to be secure in their persons, houses, papers, and effects, against unreasonable searches and seizures, shall not be violated, and no Warrants shall issue, but upon probable cause, supported by Oath or affirmation, and particularly describing the place to be searched, and the persons or things to be seized.

AMENDMENT V [1791]

No person shall be held to answer for a capital, or otherwise infamous crime, unless on a presentment or indictment of a Grand Jury, except in cases arising in the land or naval forces, or in the Militia, when in actual service in time of War or public danger; nor shall any person be subject for the same offence to be twice put in jeopardy of life or limb; nor shall be compelled in any criminal case to be a witness against himself, nor be deprived of life, liberty, or property, without due process of law; nor shall private property be taken for public use, without just compensation.

AMENDMENT VI [1791]

In all criminal prosecutions, the accused shall enjoy the right to a speedy and public trial, by an impartial jury of the State and district wherein the crime shall have been committed, which district shall have been previously ascertained by law, and to be informed of the nature and cause of the accusation; to be confronted with the witnesses against him; to have compulsory process for obtaining witnesses in his favor, and to have the Assistance of Counsel for his defence.

AMENDMENT VII [1791]

In Suits at common law, where the value in controversy shall exceed twenty dollars, the right of trial by jury shall be preserved, and no fact tried by jury, shall be otherwise re-examined in any Court of the United States, than according to the rules of the common law.

AMENDMENT VIII [1791]

Excessive bail shall not be required, nor excessive fines imposed, nor cruel and unusual punishments inflicted.

AMENDMENT IX [1791]

The enumeration in the Constitution, of certain rights, shall not be construed to deny or disparage others retained by the people.

AMENDMENT X [1791]

The powers not delegated to the United States by the Constitution, nor prohibited by it to the States, are reserved to the States respectively, or to the people.

AMENDMENT XIII [1865]

Section 1. Neither slavery nor involuntary servitude, except as a punishment for crime whereof the party shall have been duly convicted, shall exist within the United States, or any place subject to their jurisdiction.

Section 2. Congress shall have power to enforce this article by appropriate legislation.

AMENDMENT XIV [1868]

Section 1. All persons born or naturalized in the United States, and subject to the jurisdiction thereof, are citizens of the United States and of the State wherein they reside. No State shall make or enforce any law which shall abridge the privileges or immunities of citizens of the United States; nor shall any State deprive any person of life, liberty, or property, without due process of law; nor deny to any person within its jurisdiction the equal protection of the laws.

Section 5. The Congress shall have power to enforce, by appropriate legislation, the provisions of the article.

AMENDMENT XV [1870]

Section 1. The right of citizens of the United States to vote shall not be denied or abridged by the United States or by any State on account of race, color, or previous condition of servitude.

Section 2. The Congress shall have power to enforce this article by appropriate legislation.

Appendix B

SELECTED FEDERAL STATUTORY PROVISIONS

Analysis

WIRE AND ELECTRONIC COMMUNICATIONS INTERCEPTION AND INTERCEPTION OF ORAL COMMUNICATIONS

(18 U.S.C. §§ 2510–2511, 2515–2518, 2520–2521).

§ 2510. Definitions

As used in this chapter—

(1) "wire communication" means any aural transfer made in whole or in part through the use of facilities for the transmission of communications by the aid of wire, cable, or other like connection between the point of origin and the point of reception (including the use of such connection in a switching station) furnished or operated by any person engaged in providing or operating such facilities for the transmission of interstate or foreign communications or communications affecting interstate or foreign commerce and such term includes any electronic storage of such communication;

(2) "oral communication" means any oral communication uttered by a person exhibiting an expectation that such communication is not subject to interception under circumstances justifying such expectation, but such term does not include any electronic communication;

(3) "State" means any State of the United States, the District of Columbia, the Commonwealth of Puerto Rico, and any territory or possession of the United States;

(4) "intercept" means the aural or other acquisition of the contents of any wire, electronic, or oral communication through the use of any electronic, mechanical, or other device;

(5) "electronic, mechanical, or other device" means any device or apparatus which can be used to intercept a wire, oral, or electronic communication other than—

(a) any telephone or telegraph instrument, equipment or facility, or any component thereof, (i) furnished to the subscriber or user by a provider of wire or electronic communication service in the ordinary course of its business and being used by the subscriber or user in the ordinary course of its business or furnished by such subscriber or user for connection to the facilities of such service and used in the ordinary course of its business; or (ii) being used by a provider of wire or electronic communication service in the ordinary course of its business, or by an investigative or law enforcement officer in the ordinary course of his duties;

(b) a hearing aid or similar device being used to correct subnormal hearing to not better than normal;

(6) "person" means any employee, or agent of the United States or any State or political subdivision thereof, and any individual, partnership, association, joint stock company, trust, or corporation;

(7) "Investigative or law enforcement officer" means any officer of the United States or of a State or political subdivision thereof, who is empowered by law to conduct investigations of or to make arrests for offenses enumerated in this chapter, and any attorney authorized by law to prosecute or participate in the prosecution of such offenses;

(8) "contents", when used with respect to any wire, oral, or electronic communication, includes any information concerning the substance, purport, or meaning of that communication;

(9) "Judge of competent jurisdiction" means—

(a) a judge of a United States district court or a United States court of appeals; and

(b) a judge of any court of general criminal jurisdiction of a State who is authorized by a statute of that State to enter orders authorizing interceptions of wire, oral, or electronic communications;

(10) "communication common carrier" shall have the same meaning which is given the term "common carrier" by section 153(h) of title 47 of the United States Code;

(11) "aggrieved person" means a person who was a party to any intercepted wire, oral, or electronic communication or a person against whom the interception was directed;

(12) "electronic communication" means any transfer of signs, signals, writing, images, sounds, data, or intelligence of any nature transmitted in whole or in part by a wire, radio, electromagnetic, photoelectronic or photooptical system that affects interstate or foreign commerce, but does not include—

(A) any wire or oral communication;

(B) any communication made through a tone-only paging device;

(C) any communication from a tracking device (as defined in section 3117 of this title); or

(D) electronic funds transfer information stored by a financial institution in a communications system used for the electronic storage and transfer of funds;

(13) "user" means any person or entity who—

(A) uses an electronic communication service; and

(B) is duly authorized by the provider of such service to engage in such use;

(14) "electronic communications system" means any wire, radio, electromagnetic, photooptical or photoelectronic facilities for the transmission of electronic communications, and any computer facilities or related electronic equipment for the electronic storage of such communications;

(15) "electronic communication service" means any service which provides to users thereof the ability to send or receive wire or electronic communications;

(16) "readily accessible to the general public" means, with respect to a radio communication, that such communication is not—

(A) scrambled or encrypted;

(B) transmitted using modulation techniques whose essential parameters have been withheld from the public with the intention of preserving the privacy of such communication;

(C) carried on a subcarrier or other signal subsidiary to a radio transmission;

(D) transmitted over a communication system provided by a common carrier, unless the communication is a tone only paging system communication; or

(E) transmitted on frequencies allocated under part 25, subpart D, E, or F of part 74, or part 94 of the Rules of the Federal Communications Commission, unless, in the case of a communication transmitted on a frequency allocated under part 74 that is not exclusively allocated to broadcast auxiliary services, the communication is a two-way voice communication by radio;

(17) "electronic storage" means—

(A) any temporary, intermediate storage of a wire or electronic communication incidental to the electronic transmission thereof; and

(B) any storage of such communication by an electronic communication service for purposes of backup protection of such communication; and

(18) "aural transfer" means a transfer containing the human voice at any point between and including the point of origin and the point of reception.

§ 2511. Interception and disclosure of wire, oral, or electronic communications prohibited

(1) Except as otherwise specifically provided in this chapter any person who—

(a) intentionally intercepts, endeavors to intercept, or procures any other person to intercept or endeavor to intercept, any wire, oral, or electronic communication;

(b) intentionally uses, endeavors to use, or procures any other person to use or endeavor to use any electronic, mechanical, or other device to intercept any oral communication when—

(i) such device is affixed to, or otherwise transmits a signal through, a wire, cable, or other like connection used in wire communication; or

(ii) such device transmits communications by radio, or interferes with the transmission of such communication; or

(iii) such person knows, or has reason to know, that such device or any component thereof has been sent through the mail or transported in interstate or foreign commerce; or

(iv) such use or endeavor to use (A) takes place on the premises of any business or other commercial establishment the operations of which affect interstate or foreign commerce; or (B) obtains or is for the purpose of obtaining information relating to the operations of any business or other commercial establishment the operations of which affect interstate or foreign commerce; or

(v) such person acts in the District of Columbia, the Commonwealth of Puerto Rico, or any territory or possession of the United States;

(c) intentionally discloses, or endeavors to disclose, to any other person the contents of any wire, oral, or electronic communication, knowing or having reason to know that the information was obtained through the interception of a wire, oral, or electronic communication in violation of this subsection;

(d) intentionally uses, or endeavors to use, the contents of any wire, oral, or electronic communication, knowing or having reason to know that the information was obtained through the interception of a wire, oral, or electronic communication in violation of this subsection; or

(e)(i) intentionally discloses, or endeavors to disclose, to any other person the contents of any wire, oral, or electronic communication, intercepted by means authorized by sections 2511(2)(A)(ii), 2511(b)–(c), 2511(e), 2516, and 2518 of this subchapter, (ii) knowing or having reason to know that the information was obtained through the interception of such a communication in connection with a criminal investigation, (iii) having obtained or received the information in connection with a criminal investigation, and (iv) with intent to improperly obstruct, impede, or interfere with a duly authorized criminal investigation, shall be punished as provided in subsection (4) or shall be subject to suit as provided in subsection (5).

(2)(a)(i) It shall not be unlawful under this chapter for an operator of a switchboard, or an officer, employee, or agent of a provider of wire or electronic communication service, whose facilities are used in the transmission of a wire or electronic communication, to intercept, disclose, or use that communication in the normal course of his employment while engaged in any activity which is a necessary incident to the rendition of his service or to the protection of the rights or property of the provider of that service, except that a provider of wire communication service to the public shall not utilize service observing or random monitoring except for mechanical or service quality control checks.

(ii) Notwithstanding any other law, providers of wire or electronic communication service, their officers, employees, and agents, landlords, custodians, or other persons, are authorized to provide information, facilities, or technical assistance to persons authorized by law to intercept wire, oral, or electronic communications or to conduct electronic surveillance, as defined in section 101 of the Foreign Intelligence Surveillance Act of 1978, if such provider, its officers, employees, or agents, landlord, custodian, or other specified person, has been provided with—

(A) a court order directing such assistance signed by the authorizing judge, or

(B) a certification in writing by a person specified in section 2518(7) of this title or the Attorney General of·the United States that no warrant or court order is required by law, that all statutory requirements have been met, and that the specified assistance is required,

setting forth the period of time during which the provision of the information, facilities, or technical assistance is authorized and specifying the information, facilities, or technical assistance required. No provider of wire or electronic communication service, officer, employee, or agent thereof, or landlord, custodian, or other specified person shall disclose the existence of any interception or surveillance or the device used to accomplish the interception or surveillance with respect to which the person has been furnished a court order or certification under this chapter except as may otherwise be required by legal process and then only after prior notification to the Attorney General or to the principal prosecuting attorney of a State or any political subdivision of a State, as may be appropriate. Any such disclosure, shall render such person liable for the civil damages provided for in section 2520. No cause of action shall lie in any court against any provider of wire or electronic communication service, its officers, employees, or agents, landlord, custodian, or other specified person for providing information, facilities, or assistance in accordance with the terms of an order or certification under this subpar.

(b) It shall not be unlawful under this chapter for an officer, employee, or agent of the Federal Communications Commission, in the normal course of his employment and in discharge of the monitoring responsibilities exercised by the Commission in the enforcement of chapter 5 of title 47 of the United States Code, to intercept a wire or electronic communication, or oral communication transmitted by radio, or to disclose or use the information thereby obtained.

(c) It shall not be unlawful under this chapter for a person acting under color of law to intercept a wire, oral, or electronic communication, where such person is a party to the communication or one of the parties to the communication has given prior consent to such interception.

(d) It shall not be unlawful under this chapter for a person not acting under color of law to intercept a wire, oral, or electronic communication where such person is a party to the communication or where one of the parties to the communication has given prior consent to such interception unless such communication is intercepted for the purpose of committing any criminal or tortious act in violation of the Constitution or laws of the United States or of any State.

(e) Notwithstanding any other provision of this title or section 705 or 706 of the Communications Act of 1934, it shall not be unlawful for an officer, employee, or agent of the United States in the normal course of his official duty to conduct electronic surveillance, as defined in section 101 of the Foreign Intelligence Surveillance Act of 1978, as authorized by that Act.

(f) Nothing contained in this chapter or chapter 121, or section 705 of the Communications Act of 1934, shall be deemed to affect the acquisition by the United States Government of foreign intelligence information from international or foreign communications, or foreign intelligence activities conducted in accordance with otherwise applicable Federal law involving a foreign electronic communications system, utilizing a means other than electronic surveillance as defined in section 101 of the Foreign Intelligence Surveillance Act of 1978, and procedures in this chapter and the Foreign Intelligence Surveillance Act of 1978 shall be the exclusive means by which electronic surveillance, as defined in section 101 of such Act, and the interception of domestic wire and oral communications may be conducted.

(g) It shall not be unlawful under this chapter or chapter 121 of this title for any person—

(i) to intercept or access an electronic communication made through an electronic communication system that is configured so that such electronic communication is readily accessible to the general public;

(ii) to intercept any radio communication which is transmitted—

(I) by any station for the use of the general public, or that relates to ships, aircraft, vehicles, or persons in distress;

(II) by any governmental, law enforcement, civil defense, private land mobile, or public safety communications system, including police and fire, readily accessible to the general public;

(III) by a station operating on an authorized frequency within the bands allocated to the amateur, citizens band, or general mobile radio services; or

(IV) by any marine or aeronautical communications system;

(iii) to engage in any conduct which—

(I) is prohibited by section 633 of the Communications Act of 1934; or

(II) is excepted from the application of section 705(a) of the Communications Act of 1934 by section 705(b) of that Act;

(iv) to intercept any wire or electronic communication the transmission of which is causing harmful interference to any lawfully operating station or consumer electronic equipment, to the extent necessary to identify the source of such interference; or

(v) for other users of the same frequency to intercept any radio communication made through a system that utilizes frequencies monitored by individuals engaged in the provision or the use of such system, if such communication is not scrambled or encrypted.

(h) It shall not be unlawful under this chapter—

(i) to use a pen register or a trap and trace device (as those terms are defined for the purposes of chapter 206 (relating to pen registers and trap and trace devices) of this title); or

(ii) for a provider of electronic communication service to record the fact that a wire or electronic communication was initiated or completed in order to protect such provider, another provider furnishing service toward the completion of the wire or electronic communication, or a user of that service, from fraudulent, unlawful or abusive use of such service.

(3)(a) Except as provided in paragraph (b) of this subsection, a person or entity providing an electronic communication service to the public shall not intentionally divulge the contents of any communication (other than one to such person or entity, or an agent thereof) while in transmission on that service to any person or entity other than an addressee or intended recipient of such communication or an agent of such addressee or intended recipient.

(b) A person or entity providing electronic communication service to the public may divulge the contents of any such communication—

(i) as otherwise authorized in section 2511(2)(a) or 2517 of this title;

(ii) with the lawful consent of the originator or any addressee or intended recipient of such communication;

(iii) to a person employed or authorized, or whose facilities are used, to forward such communication to its destination; or

(iv) which were inadvertently obtained by the service provider and which appear to pertain to the commission of a crime, if such divulgence is made to a law enforcement agency.

(4)(a) Except as provided in paragraph (b) of this subsection or in subsection (5), whoever violates subsection (1) of this section shall be fined under this title or imprisoned not more than five years, or both.

(b) If the offense is a first offense under paragraph (a) of this subsection and is not for a tortious or illegal purpose or for purposes of direct or indirect commercial advantage or private commercial gain, and the wire or electronic communication with respect to which the offense under paragraph

(a) is a radio communication that is not scrambled or encrypted, or transmitted using modulation techniques the essential parameters of which have been withheld from the public with the intention of preserving the privacy of such communication, then—

(i) if the communication is not the radio portion of a cellular telephone communication, a cordless telephone communication that is transmitted between the cordless telephone handset and the base unit, a public land mobile radio service communication or a paging service communication, and the conduct is not that described in subsection (5), the offender shall be fined under this title or imprisoned not more than one year or both; and

(ii) if the communication is the radio portion of a cellular telephone communication, a cordless telephone communication that is transmitted between the cordless telephone handset and the base unit, a public land mobile radio service communication or a paging service communication, the offender shall be fined not more than $500.

(c) Conduct otherwise an offense under this subsection that consists of or relates to the interception of a satellite transmission that is not encrypted or scrambled and that is transmitted—

(i) to a broadcasting station for purposes of retransmission to the general public; or

(ii) as an audio subcarrier intended for redistribution to facilities open to the public, but not including data transmissions or telephone calls,

is not an offense under this subsection unless the conduct is for the purposes of direct or indirect commercial advantage or private financial gain.

(5)(a)(i) If the communication is—

(A) a private satellite video communication that is not scrambled or encrypted and the conduct in violation of this chapter is the private viewing of that communication and is not for a tortious or illegal purpose or for purposes of direct or indirect commercial advantage or private commercial gain; or

(B) a radio communication that is transmitted on frequencies allocated under subpart D of part 74 of the rules of the Federal Communications Commission that is not scrambled or encrypted and the conduct in violation of this chapter is not for a tortious or illegal purpose or for purposes of direct or indirect commercial advantage or private commercial gain,

then the person who engages in such conduct shall be subject to suit by the Federal Government in a court of competent jurisdiction.

(ii) In an action under this subsection—

(A) if the violation of this chapter is a first offense for the person under paragraph (a) of subsection (4) and such person has not been found liable in a civil action under section 2520 of this title, the Federal Government shall be entitled to appropriate injunctive relief; and

(B) if the violation of this chapter is a second or subsequent offense under paragraph (a) of subsection (4) or such person has been found liable in any prior civil action under section 2520, the person shall be subject to a mandatory $500 civil fine.

(b) The court may use any means within its authority to enforce an injunction issued under paragraph (ii)(A), and shall impose a civil fine of not less than $500 for each violation of such an injunction.

§ 2515. Prohibition of use as evidence of intercepted wire or oral communications

Whenever any wire or oral communication has been intercepted, no part of the contents of such communication and no evidence derived therefrom may be received in evidence in any trial, hearing, or other proceeding in or before any court, grand jury, department, officer, agency, regulatory body, legislative committee, or other authority of the United States, a State, or a political subdivision thereof if the disclosure of that information would be in violation of this chapter.

§ 2516. Authorization for interception of wire, oral, or electronic communications

(1) The Attorney General, Deputy Attorney General, Associate Attorney General, any Assistant Attorney General, any acting Assistant Attorney General, or any Deputy Assistant Attorney General or acting Deputy Assistant Attorney General in the Criminal Division specially designated by the Attorney General, may authorize an application to a Federal judge of competent jurisdiction for, and such judge may grant in conformity with section 2518 of this chapter an order authorizing or approving the interception of wire or oral communications by the Federal Bureau of Investigation, or a Federal agency having responsibility for the investigation of the offense as to which the application is made, when such interception may provide or has provided evidence of—

(a) any offense punishable by death or by imprisonment for more than one year under sections 2274 through 2277 of title 42 of the United States Code (relating to the enforcement of the Atomic Energy Act of 1954), section 2284 of title 42 of the United States Code (relating to sabotage of nuclear facilities or fuel), or under the following chapters of this title: chapter 37 (relating to espionage), chapter 105 (relating to sabotage), chapter 115 (relating to treason), chapter 102 (relating to riots); chapter 65 (relating to malicious mischief), chapter 111 (relating to destruction of vessels), or chapter 81 (relating to piracy);

(b) a violation of section 186 or section 501(c) of title 29, United States Code (dealing with restrictions on payments and loans to labor organizations), or any offense which involves murder, kidnapping, robbery, or extortion, and which is punishable under this title;

(c) any offense which is punishable under the following sections of this title: section 201 (bribery of public officials and witnesses), section 224 (bribery in sporting contests), subsection (d), (e), (f), (g), (h), or (i) of section 844 (unlawful use of explosives), section 1084 (transmission of wagering information), section 751 (relating to escape), sections 1503,

1512, and 1513 (influencing or injuring an officer, juror, or witness generally), section 1510 (obstruction of criminal investigations), section 1511 (obstruction of State or local law enforcement), section 1751 (Presidential and Presidential staff assassination, kidnapping, and assault), section 1951 (interference with commerce by threats or violence), section 1952 (interstate and foreign travel or transportation in aid of racketeering enterprises), section 1952A (relating to use of interstate commerce facilities in the commission of murder for hire), section 1952B (relating to violent crimes in aid of racketeering activity), section 1954 (offer, acceptance, or solicitation to influence operations of employee benefit plan), section 1955 (prohibition of business enterprises of gambling), section 1956 (laundering of monetary instruments), section 1957 (relating to engaging in monetary transactions in property derived from specified unlawful activity), section 659 (theft from interstate shipment), section 664 (embezzlement from pension and welfare funds), section 1343 (fraud by wire, radio, or television), sections 2251 and 2252 (sexual exploitation of children), sections 2312, 2313, 2314, and 2315 (interstate transportation of stolen property), the second section 2320 (relating to trafficking in certain motor vehicles or motor vehicle parts), section 1203 (relating to hostage taking), section 1029 (relating to fraud and related activity in connection with access devices), section 3146 (relating to penalty for failure to appear), section 3521(b)(3)(relating to witness relocation and assistance), section 32 (relating to destruction of aircraft or aircraft facilities), section 1963 (violations with respect to racketeer influenced and corrupt organizations), section 115 (relating to threatening or retaliating against a Federal official), the section in chapter 65 (relating to destruction of an energy facility), and section 1341 (relating to mail fraud), section 351 (violations with respect to congressional, Cabinet, or Supreme Court assassinations, kidnapping, and assault), section 831 (relating to prohibited transactions involving nuclear materials), section 33 (relating to destruction of motor vehicles or motor vehicle facilities), section 175 (relating to biological weapons), or section 1992 (relating to wrecking trains);

(d) any offense involving counterfeiting punishable under section 471, 472, or 473 of this title;

(e) any offense involving fraud connected with a case under title 11 or the manufacture, importation, receiving, concealment, buying, selling, or otherwise dealing in narcotic drugs, marihuana, or other dangerous drugs, punishable under any law of the United States;

(f) any offense including extortionate credit transactions under sections 892, 893, or 894 of this title;

(g) a violation of section 5322 of title 31, United States Code (dealing with the reporting of currency transactions);

(h) any felony violation of sections 2511 and 2512 (relating to interception and disclosure of certain communications and to certain intercepting devices) of this title;

(i) any felony violation of chapter 71 (relating to obscenity) of this title;

(j) any violation of section 60123(b)(relating to destruction of a natural gas pipeline) or 46502 (relating to aircraft piracy) of title 49;

(k) any criminal violation of section 2778 of title 22 (relating to the Arms Export Control Act);

(*l*) the location of any fugitive from justice from an offense described in this section;

(m) any conspiracy to commit any of the foregoing offenses;

(n) any felony violation of sections 922 and 924 of title 18, United States Code (relating to firearms);

(o) a felony violation of section 1028 (relating to production of false identification documents), section 1542 (relating to false statements in passport applications), section 1546 (relating to fraud and misuse of visas, permits, and other documents) of this title or a violation of section 274, 277, or 278 of the Immigration and Nationality Act (relating to the smuggling of aliens); or

(p) any violation of section 5861 of the Internal Revenue Code of 1986 (relating to firearms).

(2) The principal prosecuting attorney of any State, or the principal prosecuting attorney of any political subdivision thereof, if such attorney is authorized by a statute of that State to make application to a State court judge of competent jurisdiction for an order authorizing or approving the interception of wire, oral, or electronic communications, may apply to such judge for, and such judge may grant in conformity with section 2518 of this chapter and with the applicable State statute an order authorizing, or approving the interception of wire, oral, or electronic communications by investigative or law enforcement officers having responsibility for the investigation of the offense as to which the application is made, when such interception may provide or has provided evidence of the commission of the offense of murder, kidnapping, gambling, robbery, bribery, extortion, or dealing in narcotic drugs, marihuana or other dangerous drugs, or other crime dangerous to life, limb, or property, and punishable by imprisonment for more than one year, designated in any applicable State statute authorizing such interception, or any conspiracy to commit any of the foregoing offenses.

(3) Any attorney for the Government (as such term is defined for the purposes of the Federal Rules of Criminal Procedure) may authorize an application to a Federal judge of competent jurisdiction for, and such judge may grant, in conformity with section 2518 of this title, an order authorizing or approving the interception of electronic communications by an investigative or law enforcement officer having responsibility for the investigation of the offense as to which the application is made, when such interception may provide or has provided evidence of any Federal felony.

§ 2517. Authorization for disclosure and use of intercepted wire, oral, or electronic communications

(1) Any investigative or law enforcement officer who, by any means authorized by this chapter, has obtained knowledge of the contents of any wire, oral, or electronic communication, or evidence derived therefrom, may

disclose such contents to another investigative or law enforcement officer to the extent that such disclosure is appropriate to the proper performance of the official duties of the officer making or receiving the disclosure.

(2) Any investigative or law enforcement officer who, by any means authorized by this chapter, has obtained knowledge of the contents of any wire, oral, or electronic communication or evidence derived therefrom may use such contents to the extent such use is appropriate to the proper performance of his official duties.

(3) Any person who has received, by any means authorized by this chapter, any information concerning a wire, oral, or electronic communication, or evidence derived therefrom intercepted in accordance with the provisions of this chapter may disclose the contents of that communication or such derivative evidence while giving testimony under oath or affirmation in any proceeding held under the authority of the United States or of any State or political subdivision thereof.

(4) No otherwise privileged wire, oral, or electronic communication intercepted in accordance with, or in violation of, the provisions of this chapter shall lose its privileged character.

(5) When an investigative or law enforcement officer, while engaged in intercepting wire, oral, or electronic communications in the manner authorized herein, intercepts wire, oral, or electronic communications relating to offenses other than those specified in the order of authorization or approval, the contents thereof, and evidence derived therefrom, may be disclosed or used as provided in subsections (1) and (2) of this section. Such contents and any evidence derived therefrom may be used under subsection (3) of this section when authorized or approved by a judge of competent jurisdiction where such judge finds on subsequent application that the contents were otherwise intercepted in accordance with the provisions of this chapter. Such application shall be made as soon as practicable.

§ 2518. Procedure for interception of wire, oral, or electronic communications

(1) Each application for an order authorizing or approving the interception of a wire, oral, or electronic communication under this chapter shall be made in writing upon oath or affirmation to a judge of competent jurisdiction and shall state the applicant's authority to make such application. Each application shall include the following information:

(a) the identity of the investigative or law enforcement officer making the application, and the officer authorizing the application;

(b) a full and complete statement of the facts and circumstances relied upon by the applicant, to justify his belief that an order should be issued, including (i) details as to the particular offense that has been, is being, is about to be committed, (ii) except as provided in subsection (11), a particular description of the nature and location of the facilities from which or the place where the communication is to be intercepted, (iii) a particular description of the type of communications sought to be intercepted, (iv) the identity of the person, if known, committing the offense and whose communications are to be intercepted;

(c) a full and complete statement as to whether or not other investigative procedures have been tried and failed or why they reasonably appear to be unlikely to succeed if tried or to be too dangerous;

(d) a statement of the period of time for which the interception is required to be maintained. If the nature of the investigation is such that the authorization for interception should not automatically terminate when the described type of communication has been first obtained, a particular description of facts establishing probable cause to believe that additional communications of the same type will occur thereafter;

(e) a full and complete statement of the facts concerning all previous applications known to the individual authorizing and making the application, made to any judge for authorization to intercept, or for approval of interceptions of, wire, oral, or electronic communications involving any of the same persons, facilities or places specified in the application, and the action taken by the judge on each such application; and

(f) where the application is for the extension of an order, a statement setting forth the results thus far obtained from the interception, or a reasonable explanation of the failure to obtain such results.

(2) The judge may require the applicant to furnish additional testimony or documentary evidence in support of the application.

(3) Upon such application the judge may enter an ex parte order, as requested or as modified, authorizing or approving interception of wire, oral, or electronic communications within the territorial jurisdiction of the court in which the judge is sitting (and outside that jurisdiction but within the United States in the case of a mobile interception device authorized by a Federal court within such jurisdiction), if the judge determines on the basis of the facts submitted by the applicant that—

(a) there is probable cause for belief that an individual is committing, has committed, or is about to commit a particular offense enumerated in section 2516 of this chapter;

(b) there is probable cause for belief that particular communications concerning that offense will be obtained through such interception;

(c) normal investigative procedures have been tried and have failed or reasonably appear to be unlikely to succeed if tried or to be too dangerous;

(d) except as provided in subsection (11), there is probable cause for belief that the facilities from which, or the place where, the wire, oral, or electronic communications are to be intercepted are being used, or are about to be used, in connection with the commission of such offense, or are leased to, listed in the name of, or commonly used by such person.

(4) Each order authorizing or approving the interception of any wire, oral, or electronic communication under this chapter shall specify—

(a) the identity of the person, if known, whose communications are to be intercepted;

(b) the nature and location of the communications facilities as to which, or the place where, authority to intercept is granted;

(c) a particular description of the type of communication sought to be intercepted, and a statement of the particular offense to which it relates;

(d) the identity of the agency authorized to intercept the communications, and of the person authorizing the application; and

(e) the period of time during which such interception is authorized, including a statement as to whether or not the interception shall automatically terminate when the described communication has been first obtained.

An order authorizing the interception of a wire, oral, or electronic communication under this chapter shall, upon request of the applicant, direct that a provider of wire or electronic communication service, landlord, custodian or other person shall furnish the applicant forthwith all information, facilities, and technical assistance necessary to accomplish the interception unobtrusively and with a minimum of interference with the services that such service provider, landlord, custodian, or person is according the person whose communications are to be intercepted. Any provider of wire or electronic communication service, landlord, custodian or other person furnishing such facilities or technical assistance shall be compensated therefor by the applicant for reasonable expenses incurred in providing such facilities or assistance. Pursuant to section 2522 of this chapter, an order may also be issued to enforce the assistance capability requirements under the Communication Assistance for Law Enforcement Act.

(5) No order entered under this section may authorize or approve the interception of any wire, oral, or electronic communication for any period longer than is necessary to achieve the objective of the authorization, nor in any event longer than thirty days. Such thirty-day period begins on the earlier of the day on which the investigative or law enforcement officer first begins to conduct an interception under the order or ten days after the order is entered. Extensions of an order may be granted, but only upon application for an extension made in accordance with subsection (1) of this section and the court making the findings required by subsection (3) of this section. The period of extension shall be no longer than the authorizing judge deems necessary to achieve the purposes for which it was granted and in no event for longer than thirty days. Every order and extension thereof shall contain a provision that the authorization to intercept shall be executed as soon as practicable, shall be conducted in such a way as to minimize the interception of communications not otherwise subject to interception under this chapter, and must terminate upon attainment of the authorized objective, or in any event in thirty days. In the event the intercepted communication is in a code or foreign language, and an expert in that foreign language or code is not reasonably available during the interception period, minimization may be accomplished as soon as practicable after such interception. An interception under this chapter may be conducted in whole or in part by Government personnel, or by an individual operating under a contract with the Government, acting under the supervision of an investigative or law enforcement officer authorized to conduct the interception.

(6) Whenever an order authorizing interception is entered pursuant to this chapter, the order may require reports to be made to the judge who

issued the order showing what progress has been made toward achievement of the authorized objective and the need for continued interception. Such reports shall be made at such intervals as the judge may require.

(7) Notwithstanding any other provision of this chapter, any investigative or law enforcement officer, specially designated by the Attorney General, the Deputy Attorney General, the Associate Attorney General or by the principal prosecuting attorney of any State or subdivision thereof acting pursuant to a statute of that State, who reasonably determines that—

    (a) an emergency situation exists that involves—

        (i) immediate danger of death or serious physical injury to any person,

        (ii) conspiratorial activities threatening the national security interest, or

        (iii) conspiratorial activities characteristic of organized crime,

that requires a wire, oral, or electronic communication to be intercepted before an order authorizing such interception can, with due diligence, be obtained, and

    (b) there are grounds upon which an order could be entered under this chapter to authorize such interception,

may intercept such wire, oral, or electronic communication if an application for an order approving the interception is made in accordance with this section within forty-eight hours after the interception has occurred, or begins to occur. In the absence of an order, such interception shall immediately terminate when the communication sought is obtained or when the application for the order is denied, whichever is earlier. In the event such application for approval is denied, or in any other case where the interception is terminated without an order having been issued, the contents of any wire, oral, or electronic communication intercepted shall be treated as having been obtained in violation of this chapter, and an inventory shall be served as provided for in subsection (d) of this section on the person named in the application.

(8)(a) The contents of any wire, oral, or electronic communication intercepted by any means authorized by this chapter shall, if possible, be recorded on tape or wire or other comparable device. The recording of the contents of any wire, oral or electronic communication under this subsection shall be done in such way as will protect the recording from editing or other alterations. Immediately upon the expiration of the period of the order, or extensions thereof, such recordings shall be made available to the judge issuing such order and sealed under his directions. Custody of the recordings shall be wherever the judge orders. They shall not be destroyed except upon an order of the issuing or denying judge and in any event shall be kept for ten years. Duplicate recordings may be made for use or disclosure pursuant to the provisions of subsections (1) and (2) of section 2517 of this chapter for investigations. The presence of the seal provided for by this subsection, or a satisfactory explanation for the absence thereof, shall be a prerequisite for the use or disclosure of the contents of any wire, oral, or electronic communication or evidence derived therefrom under subsection (3) of section 2517.

(b) Applications made and orders granted under this chapter shall be sealed by the judge. Custody of the applications and orders shall be wherever the judge directs. Such applications and orders shall be disclosed only upon a showing of good cause before a judge of competent jurisdiction and shall not be destroyed except on order of the issuing or denying judge, and in any event shall be kept for ten years.

(c) Any violation of the provisions of this subsection may be punished as contempt of the issuing or denying judge.

(d) Within a reasonable time but not later than ninety days after the filing of an application for an order of approval under section 2518(7)(b) which is denied or the termination of the period of an order or extensions thereof, the issuing or denying judge shall cause to be served, on the persons named in the order or the application, and such other parties to intercepted communications as the judge may determine in his discretion that is in the interest of justice, an inventory which shall include notice of—

(1) the fact of the entry of the order or the application;

(2) the date of the entry and the period of authorized, approved or disapproved interception, or the denial of the application; and

(3) the fact that during the period wire, oral or electronic communications were or were not intercepted.

The judge, upon the filing of a motion, may in his discretion make available to such person or his counsel for inspection such portions of the intercepted communications, applications and orders as the judge determines to be in the interest of justice. On an ex parte showing of good cause to a judge of competent jurisdiction the serving of the inventory required by this subsection may be postponed.

(9) The contents of any wire, oral, or electronic communication intercepted pursuant to this chapter or evidence derived therefrom shall not be received in evidence or otherwise disclosed in any trial, hearing, or other proceeding in a Federal or State court unless each party, not less than ten days before the trial, hearing, or proceeding, has been furnished with a copy of the court order, and accompanying application, under which the interception was authorized or approved. This ten-day period may be waived by the judge if he finds that it was not possible to furnish the party with the above information ten days before the trial, hearing, or proceeding and that the party will not be prejudiced by the delay in receiving such information.

(10)(a) Any aggrieved person in any trial, hearing, or proceeding in or before any court, department, officer, agency, regulatory body, or other authority of the United States, a State, or a political subdivision thereof, may move to suppress the contents of any wire or oral communication intercepted pursuant to this chapter, or evidence derived therefrom, on the grounds that—

(i) the communication was unlawfully intercepted;

(ii) the order of authorization or approval under which it was intercepted is insufficient on its face; or

(iii) the interception was not made in conformity with the order of authorization or approval.

Such motion shall be made before the trial, hearing, or proceeding unless there was no opportunity to make such motion or the person was not aware of the grounds of the motion. If the motion is granted, the contents of the intercepted wire or oral communication, or evidence derived therefrom, shall be treated as having been obtained in violation of this chapter. The judge, upon the filing of such motion by the aggrieved person, may in his discretion make available to the aggrieved person or his counsel for inspection such portions of the intercepted communication or evidence derived therefrom as the judge determines to be in the interests of justice.

(b) In addition to any other right to appeal, the United States shall have the right to appeal from an order granting a motion to suppress made under paragraph (a) of this subsection, or the denial of an application for an order of approval, if the United States attorney shall certify to the judge or other official granting such motion or denying such application that the appeal is not taken for purposes of delay. Such appeal shall be taken within thirty days after the date the order was entered and shall be diligently prosecuted.

(c) The remedies and sanctions described in this chapter with respect to the interception of electronic communications are the only judicial remedies and sanctions for nonconstitutional violations of this chapter involving such communications.

(11) The requirements of subsections (1)(b)(ii) and (3)(d) of this section relating to the specification of the facilities from which, or the place where, the communication is to be intercepted do not apply if—

(a) in the case of an application with respect to the interception of an oral communication—

(i) the application is by a Federal investigative or law enforcement officer and is approved by the Attorney General, the Deputy Attorney General, the Associate Attorney General, an Assistant Attorney General, or an acting Assistant Attorney General;

(ii) the application contains a full and complete statement as to why such specification is not practical and identifies the person committing the offense and whose communications are to be intercepted; and

(iii) the judge finds that such specification is not practical; and

(b) in the case of an application with respect to a wire or electronic communication—

(i) the application is by a Federal investigative or law enforcement officer and is approved by the Attorney General, the Deputy Attorney General, the Associate Attorney General, an Assistant Attorney General, or an acting Assistant Attorney General;

(ii) the application identifies the person believed to be committing the offense and whose communications are to be intercepted and the applicant makes a showing of a purpose, on the part of that person, to thwart interception by changing facilities; and

(iii) the judge finds that such purpose has been adequately shown.

(12) An interception of a communication under an order with respect to which the requirements of subsections (1)(b)(ii) and (3)(d) of this section do not apply by reason of subsection (11) shall not begin until the facilities from which, or the place where, the communication is to be intercepted is ascertained by the person implementing the interception order. A provider of wire or electronic communications service that has received an order as provided for in subsection (11)(b) may move the court to modify or quash the order on the ground that its assistance with respect to the interception cannot be performed in a timely or reasonable fashion. The court, upon notice to the government, shall decide such a motion expeditiously.

§ 2520. Recovery of civil damages authorized

(a) In general.—Except as provided in section 2511(2)(a)(ii), any person whose wire, oral, or electronic communication is intercepted, disclosed, or intentionally used in violation of this chapter may in a civil action recover from the person or entity which engaged in that violation such relief as may be appropriate.

(b) Relief.—In an action under this section, appropriate relief includes—

(1) such preliminary and other equitable or declaratory relief as may be appropriate;

(2) damages under subsection (c) and punitive damages in appropriate cases; and

(3) a reasonable attorney's fee and other litigation costs reasonably incurred.

(c) Computation of damages.—(1) In an action under this section, if the conduct in violation of this chapter is the private viewing of a private satellite video communication that is not scrambled or encrypted or if the communication is a radio communication that is transmitted on frequencies allocated under subpart D of part 74 of the rules of the Federal Communications Commission that is not scrambled or encrypted and the conduct is not for a tortious or illegal purpose or for purposes of direct or indirect commercial advantage or private commercial gain, then the court shall assess damages as follows:

(A) If the person who engaged in that conduct has not previously been enjoined under section 2511(5) and has not been found liable in a prior civil action under this section, the court shall assess the greater of the sum of actual damages suffered by the plaintiff, or statutory damages of not less than $50 and not more than $500.

(B) If, on one prior occasion, the person who engaged in that conduct has been enjoined under section 2511(5) or has been found liable in a civil action under this section, the court shall assess the greater of the sum of actual damages suffered by the plaintiff, or statutory damages of not less than $100 and not more than $1000.

(2) In any other action under this section, the court may assess as damages whichever is the greater of—

(A) the sum of the actual damages suffered by the plaintiff and any profits made by the violator as a result of the violation; or

(B) statutory damages of whichever is the greater of $100 a day for each day of violation or $10,000.

(d) Defense.—A good faith reliance on—

(1) a court warrant or order, a grand jury subpoena, a legislative authorization, or a statutory authorization;

(2) a request of an investigative or law enforcement officer under section 2518(7) of this title; or

(3) a good faith determination that section 2511(3) of this title permitted the conduct complained of;

is a complete defense against any civil or criminal action brought under this chapter or any other law.

(e) Limitation.—A civil action under this section may not be commenced later than two years after the date upon which the claimant first has a reasonable opportunity to discover the violation.

§ 2521. Injunction against illegal interception

Whenever it shall appear that any person is engaged or is about to engage in any act which constitutes or will constitute a felony violation of this chapter, the Attorney General may initiate a civil action in a district court of the United States to enjoin such violation. The court shall proceed as soon as practicable to the hearing and determination of such an action, and may, at any time before final determination, enter such a restraining order or prohibition, or take such other action, as is warranted to prevent a continuing and substantial injury to the United States or to any person or class of persons for whose protection the action is brought. A proceeding under this section is governed by the Federal Rules of Civil Procedure, except that, if an indictment has been returned against the respondent, discovery is governed by the Federal Rules of Criminal Procedure.

CRIMINAL JUSTICE ACT

(18 U.S.C. § 3006A).

§ 3006A. Adequate representation of defendants

(a) Choice of plan.—Each United States district court, with the approval of the judicial council of the circuit, shall place in operation throughout the district a plan for furnishing representation for any person financially unable to obtain adequate representation in accordance with this section. Representation under each plan shall include counsel and investigative, expert, and other services necessary for adequate representation. Each plan shall provide the following:

(1) Representation shall be provided for any financially eligible person who—

(A) is charged with a felony or a Class A misdemeanor;

(B) is a juvenile alleged to have committed an act of juvenile delinquency as defined in section 5031 of this title;

(C) is charged with a violation of probation;

(D) is under arrest, when such representation is required by law;

(E) is charged with a violation of supervised release or faces modification, reduction, or enlargement of a condition, or extension or revocation of a term of supervised release;

(F) is subject to a mental condition hearing under chapter 313 of this title;

(G) is in custody as a material witness;

(H) is entitled to appointment of counsel under the sixth amendment to the Constitution; or

(I) faces loss of liberty in a case, and Federal law requires the appointment of counsel; or

(J) is entitled to the appointment of counsel under section 4019 of this title.

(2) Whenever the United States magistrate or the court determines that the interests of justice so require, representation may be provided for any financially eligible person who—

(A) is charged with a Class B or C misdemeanor, or an infraction for which a sentence to confinement is authorized; or

(B) is seeking relief under section 2241, 2254, or 2255 of title 28.

(3) Private attorneys shall be appointed in a substantial proportion of the cases. Each plan may include, in addition to the provisions for private attorneys, either of the following or both:

(A) Attorneys furnished by a bar association or a legal aid agency.

(B) Attorneys furnished by a defender organization established in accordance with the provisions of subsection (g).

Prior to approving the plan for a district, the judicial council of the circuit shall supplement the plan with provisions for representation on appeal. The district court may modify the plan at any time with the approval of the judicial council of the circuit. It shall modify the plan when directed by the judicial council of the circuit. The district court shall notify the Administrative Office of the United States Courts of any modification of its plan.

(b) Appointment of counsel.—Counsel furnishing representation under the plan shall be selected from a panel of attorneys designated or approved by the court, or from a bar association, legal aid agency, or defender organization furnishing representation pursuant to the plan. In every case in which a person entitled to representation under a plan approved under subsection (a) appears without counsel, the United States magistrate or the court shall advise the person that he has the right to be represented by counsel and that counsel will be appointed to represent him if he is financially unable to obtain counsel. Unless the person waives representation by counsel, the United States magistrate or the court, if satisfied after appropriate inquiry that the person is financially unable to obtain counsel, shall appoint counsel to represent him. Such appointment may be made retroactive to include any representation furnished pursuant to the plan prior to appointment. The United States magistrate or the court shall appoint separate counsel for persons having interests that cannot properly be represented by the same counsel, or when other good cause is shown.

(c) Duration and substitution of appointments.—A person for whom counsel is appointed shall be represented at every stage of the proceedings from his initial appearance before the United States magistrate or the court through appeal, including ancillary matters appropriate to the proceedings. If at any time after the appointment of counsel the United States magistrate or the court finds that the person is financially able to obtain counsel or to make partial payment for the representation, it may terminate the appointment of counsel or authorize payment as provided in subsection (f), as the interests of justice may dictate. If at any stage of the proceedings, including an appeal, the United States magistrate or the court finds that the person is financially unable to pay counsel whom he had retained, it may appoint counsel as provided in subsection (b) and authorize payment as provided in subsection (d), as the interests of justice may dictate. The United States magistrate or the court may, in the interests of justice, substitute one appointed counsel for another at any stage of the proceedings.

(d) Payment for representation.—

(1) Hourly rate.—Any attorney appointed pursuant to this section or a bar association or legal aid agency or community defender organization which has provided the appointed attorney shall, at the conclusion of the representation or any segment thereof, be compensated at a rate not exceeding $60 per hour for time expended in court or before a United States magistrate and $40 per hour for time reasonably expended out of court, unless the Judicial Conference determines that a higher rate of not in excess of $75 per hour is justified for a circuit or for particular districts within a circuit, for time expended in court or before a United States magistrate and for time expended out of court. The Judicial Conference shall develop guidelines for determining the maximum hourly rates for each circuit in accordance with the preceding sentence, with variations by district, where appropriate, taking into account such factors as the minimum range of the prevailing hourly rates for qualified attorneys in the district in which the representation is provided and the recommendations of the judicial councils of the circuits. Not less than 3 years after the effective date of the Criminal Justice Act Revision of 1986, the Judicial Conference is authorized to raise the maximum hourly rates specified in this paragraph up to the aggregate of the overall average percentages of the adjustments in the rates of pay under the General Schedule made pursuant to section 5305 of title 5 on or after such effective date. After the rates are raised under the preceding sentence, such maximum hourly rates may be raised at intervals of not less than 1 year each, up to the aggregate of the overall average percentages of such adjustments made since the last raise was made under this paragraph. Attorneys shall be reimbursed for expenses reasonably incurred, including the costs of transcripts authorized by the United States magistrate or the court.

(2) **Maximum amounts.**—For representation of a defendant before the United States magistrate or the district court, or both, the compensation to be paid to an attorney or to a bar association or legal aid agency or community defender organization shall not exceed $3,500 for each attorney in a case in which one or more felonies are charged, and $1,000 for each attorney in a case in which only misdemeanors are charged. For representation of a defendant in an appellate court, the compensation to be paid to an attorney or to a bar association or legal aid agency or community defender organization shall not exceed $2,500 for each attorney in each court. For representation of an offender before the United States Parole Commission in a proceeding under section 4106A of this title, the compensation shall not exceed $750 for each attorney in each proceeding; for representation of an offender in an appeal from a determination of such Commission under such section, the compensation shall not exceed 2,500 for each attorney in each court. For any other representation required or authorized by this section, the compensation shall not exceed $750 for each attorney in each proceeding.

(3) **Waiving maximum amounts.**—Payment in excess of any maximum amount provided in paragraph (2) of this subsection may be made for extended or complex representation whenever the court in which the representation was rendered, or the United States magistrate if the representation was furnished exclusively before him, certifies that the amount of the excess payment is necessary to provide fair compensation and the payment is approved by the chief judge of the circuit. The chief judge of the circuit may delegate such approval authority to an active circuit judge.

(4) **Disclosure of Fees.**—The amounts paid under this subsection, for representation in any case, shall be made available to the public.

(5) **Filing claims.**—A separate claim for compensation and reimbursement shall be made to the district court for representation before the United States magistrate and the court, and to each appellate court before which the attorney provided representation to the person involved. Each claim shall be supported by a sworn written statement specifying the time expended, services rendered, and expenses incurred while the case was pending before the United States magistrate and the court, and the compensation and reimbursement applied for or received in the same case from any other source. The court shall fix the compensation and reimbursement to be paid to the attorney or to the bar association or legal aid agency or community defender organization which provided the appointed attorney. In cases where representation is furnished exclusively before a United States magistrate, the claim shall be submitted to him and he shall fix the compensation and reimbursement to be paid. In cases where representation is furnished other than before the United States magistrate, the district court, or an appellate court, claims shall be submitted to the district court which shall fix the compensation and reimbursement to be paid.

(6) **New trials.**—For purposes of compensation and other payments authorized by this section, an order by a court granting a new trial shall be deemed to initiate a new case.

(7) Proceedings before appellate courts.—If a person for whom counsel is appointed under this section appeals to an appellate court or petitions for a writ of certiorari, he may do so without prepayment of fees and costs or security therefor and without filing the affidavit required by section 1915(a) of title 28.

(e) Services other than counsel.—

(1) Upon request.—Counsel for a person who is financially unable to obtain investigative, expert, or other services necessary for an adequate representation may request them in an ex parte application. Upon finding, after appropriate inquiry in an ex parte proceeding, that the services are necessary and that the person is financially unable to obtain them, the court, or the United States magistrate if the services are required in connection with a matter over which he has jurisdiction, shall authorize counsel to obtain the services.

(2) Without prior request.—(A) Counsel appointed under this section may obtain, subject to later review, investigative, expert, and other services without prior authorization if necessary for adequate representation. Except as provided in subparagraph (B) of this paragraph, the total cost of services obtained without prior authorization may not exceed $300 and expenses reasonably incurred.

(B) The court, or the United States magistrate (if the services were rendered in a case disposed of entirely before the United States magistrate), may, in the interest of justice, and upon the finding that timely procurement of necessary services could not await prior authorization, approve payment for such services after they have been obtained, even if the cost of such services exceeds $300.

(3) Maximum amounts.—Compensation to be paid to a person for services rendered by him to a person under this subsection, or to be paid to an organization for services rendered by an employee thereof, shall not exceed $1,000, exclusive of reimbursement for expenses reasonably incurred, unless payment in excess of that limit is certified by the court, or by the United States magistrate if the services were rendered in connection with a case disposed of entirely before him, as necessary to provide fair compensation for services of an unusual character or duration, and the amount of the excess payment is approved by the chief judge of the circuit. The chief judge of the circuit may delegate such approval authority to an active circuit judge.

(4) Disclosure of fees.—The amounts paid under this subsection for services in any case shall be made available to the public.

(f) Receipt of other payments.—Whenever the United States magistrate or the court finds that funds are available for payment from or on behalf of a person furnished representation, it may authorize or direct that such funds be paid to the appointed attorney, to the bar association or legal aid agency or community defender organization which provided the appointed attorney, to any person or organization authorized pursuant to subsection (e) to render investigative, expert, or other services, or to the court for deposit in the Treasury as a reimbursement to the appropriation, current at the time of payment, to carry out the provisions of this section. Except as so authorized or directed, no such person or organization may request or accept any payment or promise of payment for representing a defendant.

(g) Defender organization.—

(1) Qualifications.—A district or a part of a district in which at least two hundred persons annually require the appointment of counsel may establish a defender organization as provided for either under subparagraphs (A) or (B) of paragraph (2) of this subsection or both. Two adjacent districts or parts of districts may aggregate the number of persons required to be represented to establish eligibility for a defender organization to serve both areas. In the event that adjacent districts or parts of districts are located in different circuits, the plan for furnishing representation shall be approved by the judicial council of each circuit.

(2) Types of defender organizations.—

(A) Federal Public Defender Organization.—A Federal Public Defender Organization shall consist of one or more full-time salaried attorneys. An organization for a district or part of a district or two adjacent districts or parts of districts shall be supervised by a Federal Public Defender appointed by the court of appeals of the circuit, without regard to the provisions of title 5 governing appointments in the competitive service, after considering recommendations from the district court or courts to be served. Nothing contained herein shall be deemed to authorize more than one Federal Public Defender within a single judicial district. The Federal Public Defender shall be appointed for a term of four years, unless sooner removed by the court of appeals of the circuit for incompetency, misconduct in office, or neglect of duty. Upon the expiration of his term, a Federal Public Defender may, by a majority vote of the judges of the court of appeals, continue to perform the duties of his office until his successor is appointed, or until one year after the expiration of such Defender's term, whichever is earlier. The compensation of the Federal Public Defender shall be fixed by the court of appeals of the circuit at a rate not to exceed the compensation received by the United States attorney for the district where representation is furnished or, if two districts or parts of districts are involved, the compensation of the higher paid United States attorney of the districts. The Federal Public Defender may appoint, without regard to the provisions of title 5 governing appointments in the competitive service, full-time attorneys in such number as may be approved by the court of appeals of the circuit and other personnel in such number as may be approved by the Director of the Administrative Office of the United States Courts. Compensation paid to such attorneys and other personnel of the organization shall be fixed by the Federal Public Defender at a rate not to exceed that paid to attorneys and other personnel of similar qualifications and experience in the Office of the United States attorney in the district where representation is furnished or, if two districts or parts of districts are involved, the higher compensation paid to persons of similar qualifications and experience in the districts. Neither the Federal Public Defender nor any attorney so appointed by him may engage in the private practice of law. Each organization shall submit to the Director of the Administrative Office of the United States Courts, at the time and in the form prescribed by him, reports of its activities and financial position and its proposed budget. The Director of the Administrative Office shall submit, in accordance with section 605 of title 28, a budget for each organization for each fiscal year and shall out of the appropriations therefor make payments to and on behalf of each organization. Payments under this subparagraph to an organization shall be in lieu of payments under subsection (d) or (e).

(B) Community Defender Organization.—A Community Defender Organization shall be a nonprofit defense counsel service established and administered by any group authorized by the plan to provide representation. The organization shall be eligible to furnish attorneys and receive payments under this section if its bylaws are set forth in the plan of the district or districts in which it will serve. Each organization shall submit to the Judicial Conference of the United States an annual report setting forth its activities and financial position and the anticipated caseload and expenses for the next fiscal year. Upon application an organization may, to the extent approved by the Judicial Conference of the United States:

    (i) receive an initial grant for expenses necessary to establish the organization; and

    (ii) in lieu of payments under subsection (d) or (e), receive periodic sustaining grants to provide representation and other expenses pursuant to this section. * * *

BAIL REFORM ACT OF 1984

(18 U.S.C. §§ 3141–3150).

§ 3141. Release and detention authority generally

(a) Pending Trial.—A judicial officer authorized to order the arrest of a person under section 3041 of this title before whom an arrested person is brought shall order that such person be released or detained, pending judicial proceedings, under this chapter.

(b) Pending sentence or appeal.—A judicial officer of a court of original jurisdiction over an offense, or a judicial officer of a Federal appellate court, shall order that, pending imposition or execution of sentence, or pending appeal of conviction or sentence, a person be released or detained under this chapter.

§ 3142. Release or detention of a defendant pending trial

(a) In general.—Upon the appearance before a judicial officer of a person charged with an offense, the judicial officer shall issue an order that, pending trial, the person be—

    (1) released on his personal recognizance or upon execution of an unsecured appearance bond, under subsection (b) of this section;

    (2) released on a condition or combination of conditions under subsection (c) of this section;

    (3) temporarily detained to permit revocation of conditional release, deportation, or exclusion under subsection (d) of this section; or

    (4) detained under subsection (e) of this section.

(b) Release on personal recognizance or unsecured appearance bond.—The judicial officer shall order the pretrial release of the person on personal recognizance, or upon execution of an unsecured appearance bond in an amount specified by the court, subject to the condition that the person not commit a Federal, State, or local crime during the period of release, unless the judicial officer determines that such release will not reasonably assure the appearance of the person as required or will endanger the safety of any other person or the community.

(c) Release on conditions.—(1) If the judicial officer determines that the release described in subsection (b) of this section will not reasonably assure the appearance of the person as required or will endanger the safety of any other person or the community, such judicial officer shall order the pretrial release of the person—

(A) subject to the condition that the person not commit a Federal, State, or local crime during the period of release; and

(B) subject to the least restrictive further condition, or combination of conditions, that such judicial officer determines will reasonably assure the appearance of the person as required and the safety of any other person and the community, which may include the condition that the person—

(i) remain in the custody of a designated person, who agrees to assume supervision and to report any violation of a release condition to the court, if the designated person is able reasonably to assure the judicial officer that the person will appear as required and will not pose a danger to the safety of any other person or the community;

(ii) maintain employment, or, if unemployed, actively seek employment;

(iii) maintain or commence an educational program;

(iv) abide by specified restrictions on personal associations, place of abode, or travel;

(v) avoid all contact with an alleged victim of the crime and with a potential witness who may testify concerning the offense;

(vi) report on a regular basis to a designated law enforcement agency, pretrial services agency, or other agency;

(vii) comply with a specified curfew;

(viii) refrain from possessing a firearm, destructive device, or other dangerous weapon;

(ix) refrain from excessive use of alcohol, or any use of a narcotic drug or other controlled substance, as defined in section 102 of the Controlled Substances Act (21 U.S.C. 802), without a prescription by a licensed medical practitioner;

(x) undergo available medical or psychiatric treatment, including treatment for drug or alcohol dependency, and remain in a specified institution if required for that purpose;

(xi) execute an agreement to forfeit upon failing to appear as required, such designated property, including money, as is reasonably necessary to assure the appearance of the person as required, and post with the court such indicia of ownership of the property or such percentage of the money as the judicial officer may specify;

(xii) execute a bail bond with solvent sureties in such amount as is reasonably necessary to assure the appearance of the person as required;

(xiii) return to custody for specified hours following release for employment, schooling, or other limited purposes; and

(xiv) satisfy any other condition that is reasonably necessary to assure the appearance of the person as required and to assure the safety of any other person and the community.

(2) The judicial officer may not impose a financial condition that results in the pretrial detention of the person.

(3) The judicial officer may at any time amend the order to impose additional or different conditions of release.

(d) Temporary detention to permit revocation of conditional release, deportation, or exclusion.—If the judicial officer determines that—

(1) the person—

(A) is, and was at the time the offense was committed, on—

(i) release pending trial for a felony under Federal, State, or local law;

(ii) release pending imposition or execution of sentence, appeal of sentence or conviction, or completion of sentence, for any offense under Federal, State, or local law; or

(iii) probation or parole for any offense under Federal, State, or local law; or

(B) is not a citizen of the United States or lawfully admitted for permanent residence, as defined in section 101(a)(20) of the Immigration and Nationality Act (8 U.S.C. 1101(a)(20)); and

(2) the person may flee or pose a danger to any other person or the community;

such judicial officer shall order the detention of the person, for a period of not more than ten days, excluding Saturdays, Sundays, and holidays, and direct the attorney for the Government to notify the appropriate court, probation or parole official, or State or local law enforcement official, or the appropriate official of the Immigration and Naturalization Service. If the official fails or declines to take the person into custody during that period, the person shall be treated in accordance with the other provisions of this section, notwithstanding the applicability of other provisions of law governing release pending trial or deportation or exclusion proceedings. If temporary detention is sought under paragraph (1)(B) of this subsection, the person has the burden of proving to the court such person's United States citizenship or lawful admission for permanent residence.

(e) Detention.—If, after a hearing pursuant to the provisions of subsection (f) of this section, the judicial officer finds that no condition or combination of conditions will reasonably assure the appearance of the person as required and the safety of any other person and the community, such judicial officer shall order the detention of the person before trial. In a case described in (f)(1) of this section, a rebuttable presumption arises that no condition or combination of conditions will reasonably assure the safety of any other person and the community if such judicial officer finds that—

(1) the person has been convicted of a Federal offense that is described in subsection (f)(1) of this section, or of a State or local offense that would have been an offense described in subsection (f)(1) of this section if a circumstance giving rise to Federal jurisdiction had existed;

(2) the offense described in paragraph (1) of this subsection was committed while the person was on release pending trial for a Federal, State, or local offense; and

(3) a period of not more than five years has elapsed since the date of conviction, or the release of the person from imprisonment, for the offense described in paragraph (1) of this subsection, whichever is later.

Subject to rebuttal by the person, it shall be presumed that no condition or combination of conditions will reasonably assure the appearance of the person as required and the safety of the community if the judicial officer finds that there is probable cause to believe that the person committed an offense for which a maximum term of imprisonment of ten years or more is prescribed in the Controlled Substances Act (21 U.S.C. 801 et seq.), the Controlled Substances Import and Export Act (21 U.S.C. 951 et seq.), section 1 of the Act of September 15, 1980 (21 U.S.C. 955a), or an offense under section 924(c), 956(a), or 2332(b) of title 18 of the United States Code.

(f) Detention hearing.—The judicial officer shall hold a hearing to determine whether any condition or combination of conditions set forth in subsection (c) of this section will reasonably assure the appearance of the person as required and the safety of any other person and the community in a case—

(1) upon motion of the attorney for the Government, that involves—

(A) a crime of violence;*

(B) an offense for which the maximum sentence is life imprisonment or death;

(C) an offense for which a maximum term of imprisonment of ten years or more is prescribed in the Controlled Substances Act (21 U.S.C. 801 et seq.), the Controlled Substances Import and Export Act (21 U.S.C. 951 et seq.), or section 1 of the Act of September 15, 1980 (21 U.S.C. 955a); or

* The phrase "crime of violence" is defined in 18 U.S.C. § 3156(a)(4) as meaning: "(A) an offense that has an element of the offense the use, attempted use, or threatened use of physical force against the person or property of another, or (B) any other offense that is a felony and that, by its nature, involves a substantial risk that physical force against the person or property of another may be used in the course of committing the offense."

(D) any felony if the person had been convicted of two or more prior offenses described in subparagraphs (A) through (C) of this paragraph, or two or more State or local offenses that would have been offenses described in subparagraphs (A) through (C) of this paragraph if a circumstance giving rise to Federal jurisdiction had existed or a combination of such offenses; or

(2) upon motion of the attorney for the Government or upon the judicial officer's own motion in a case, that involves—

(A) a serious risk that such person will flee;

(B) a serious risk that the person will obstruct or attempt to obstruct justice, or threaten, injure, or intimidate, or attempt to threaten, injure, or intimidate, a prospective witness or juror.

The hearing shall be held immediately upon the person's first appearance before the judicial officer unless that person, or the attorney for the Government, seeks a continuance. Except for good cause, a continuance on motion of the person may not exceed five days, and a continuance on motion of the attorney for the Government may not exceed three days. During a continuance, the person shall be detained, and the judicial officer, on motion of the attorney for the Government or sua sponte, may order that, while in custody, a person who appears to be a narcotics addict receive a medical examination to determine whether such person is an addict. At the hearing, the person has the right to be represented by counsel, and, if financially unable to obtain adequate representation, to have counsel appointed. The person shall be afforded an opportunity to testify, to present witnesses, to cross-examine witnesses who appear at the hearing, and to present information by proffer or otherwise. The rules concerning admissibility of evidence in criminal trials do not apply to the presentation and consideration of information at the hearing. The facts the judicial officer uses to support a finding pursuant to subsection (e) that no condition or combination of conditions will reasonably assure the safety of any other person and the community shall be supported by clear and convincing evidence. The person may be detained pending completion of the hearing. The hearing may be reopened before or after a determination by the judicial officer, at any time before trial if the judicial officer finds that information exists that was not known to the movant at the time of the hearing and that has a material bearing on the issue of whether there are conditions of release that will reasonably assure the appearance of the person as required and the safety of any other person and the community.

(g) Factors to be considered.—The judicial officer shall, in determining whether there are conditions of release that will reasonably assure the appearance of the person as required and the safety of any other person and the community, take into account the available information concerning—

(1) the nature and circumstances of the offense charged, including whether the offense is a crime of violence or involves a narcotic drug;

(2) the weight of the evidence against the person;

(3) the history and characteristics of the person, including—

(A) the person's character, physical and mental condition, family ties, employment, financial resources, length of residence in the community, community ties, past conduct, history relating to drug or alcohol abuse, criminal history, and record concerning appearance at court proceedings; and

(B) whether, at the time of the current offense or arrest, the person was on probation, on parole, or on other release pending trial, sentencing, appeal, or completion of sentence for an offense under Federal, State, or local law; and

(4) the nature and seriousness of the danger to any person or the community that would be posed by the person's release. In considering the conditions of release described in subsection (c)(2)(K) or (c)(2)(L) [eds. note: intended references are to what is now subsection (c)(1)(B)(xi) or (c)(1)(B)(xii)], the judicial officer may upon his own motion, or shall upon the motion of the Government, conduct an inquiry into the source of the property to be designated for potential forfeiture or offered as collateral to secure a bond, and shall decline to accept the designation, or the use as collateral, of property that, because of its source, will not reasonably assure the appearance of the person as required.

(h) Contents of release order.—In a release order issued under subsection (b) or (c) of this section, the judicial officer shall—

(1) include a written statement that sets forth all the conditions to which the release is subject, in a manner sufficiently clear and specific to serve as a guide for the person's conduct; and

(2) advise the person of—

(A) the penalties for violating a condition of release, including the penalties for committing an offense while on pretrial release;

(B) the consequences of violating a condition of release, including the immediate issuance of a warrant for the person's arrest; and

(C) the provisions of sections 1503 of this title (relating to intimidation of witnesses, jurors, and officers of the court), 1510 (relating to obstruction of criminal investigations), 1512 (tampering with a witness, victim, or an informant), and 1513 (retaliating against a witness, victim, or an informant).

(i) Contents of detention order.—In a detention order issued under subsection (e) of this section, the judicial officer shall—

(1) include written findings of fact and a written statement of the reasons for the detention;

(2) direct that the person be committed to the custody of the Attorney General for confinement in a corrections facility separate, to the extent practicable, from persons awaiting or serving sentences or being held in custody pending appeal;

(3) direct that the person be afforded reasonable opportunity for private consultation with counsel; and

(4) direct that, on order of a court of the United States or on request of an attorney for the Government, the person in charge of the

corrections facility in which the person is confined deliver the person to a United States marshal for the purpose of an appearance in connection with a court proceeding.

The judicial officer may, by subsequent order, permit the temporary release of the person, in the custody of a United States marshal or another appropriate person, to the extent that the judicial officer determines such release to be necessary for preparation of the person's defense or for another compelling reason.

(j) Presumption of innocence.—Nothing in this section shall be construed as modifying or limiting the presumption of innocence.

§ 3143. Release or detention of a defendant pending sentence or appeal

(a) Release or detention pending sentence.—(1) Except as provided in paragraph (2), the judicial officer shall order that a person who has been found guilty of an offense and who is awaiting imposition or execution of sentence, other than a person for whom the applicable guideline promulgated pursuant to 28 U.S.C. 994 does not recommend a term of imprisonment, be detained, unless the judicial officer finds by clear and convincing evidence that the person is not likely to flee or pose a danger to the safety of any other person or the community if released under section 3142(b) or (c). If the judicial officer makes such a finding, such judicial officer shall order the release of the person in accordance with section 3142(b) or (c).

(2) The judicial officer shall order that a person who has been found guilty of an offense in a case described in subparagraph (A), (B), or (C) of subsection (f)(1) of section 3142 and is awaiting imposition or execution of sentence be detained unless—

    (A)(i) the judicial officer finds there is a substantial likelihood that a motion for acquittal or new trial will be granted; or

    (ii) an attorney for the Government has recommended that no sentence of imprisonment be imposed on the person; and

    (B) the judicial officer finds by clear and convincing evidence that the person is not likely to flee or pose a danger to any other person or the community.

(b) Release or detention pending appeal by the defendant.—(1) Except as provided in subparagraph (B)(iv) of this paragraph, the judicial officer shall order that a person who has been found guilty of an offense and sentenced to a term of imprisonment, and who has filed an appeal or a petition for a writ of certiorari, be detained, unless the judicial officer finds—

    (A) by clear and convincing evidence that the person is not likely to flee or pose a danger to the safety of any other person or the community if released under section 3142(b) or (c) of this title; and

    (B) that the appeal is not for the purpose of delay and raises a substantial question of law or fact likely to result in—

        (i) reversal,

        (ii) an order for a new trial,

(iii) a sentence that does not include a term of imprisonment, or

(iv) a reduced sentence to a term of imprisonment less than the total of the time already served plus the expected duration of the appeal process.

If the judicial officer makes such findings, such judicial officer shall order the release of the person in accordance with section 3142(b) or (c) of this title, except that in the circumstance described in subparagraph (B)(iv) of this paragraph, the judicial officer shall order the detention terminated at the expiration of the likely reduced sentence.

(2) The judicial officer shall order that a person who has been found guilty of an offense in a case described in subparagraph (A), (B), or (C) of subsection (f)(1) of section 3142 and sentenced to a term of imprisonment, and who has filed an appeal or a petition for a writ of certiorari, be detained.

(c) Release or detention pending appeal by the government.— The judicial officer shall treat a defendant in a case in which an appeal has been taken by the United States under section 3731 of this title, in accordance with section 3142 of this title, unless the defendant is otherwise subject to a release or detention order.

Except as provided in subsection (b) of this section, the judicial officer, in a case in which an appeal has been taken by the United States under section 3742, shall—

(1) if the person has been sentenced to a term of imprisonment, order that person detained; and

(2) in any other circumstance, release or detain the person under section 3142.

§ 3144. Release or detention of a material witness

If it appears from an affidavit filed by a party that the testimony of a person is material in a criminal proceeding, and if it is shown that it may become impracticable to secure the presence of the person by subpena, a judicial officer may order the arrest of the person and treat the person in accordance with the provisions of section 3142 of this title. No material witness may be detained because of inability to comply with any condition of release if the testimony of such witness can adequately be secured by deposition, and if further detention is not necessary to prevent a failure of justice. Release of a material witness may be delayed for a reasonable period of time until the deposition of the witness can be taken pursuant to the Federal Rules of Criminal Procedure.

§ 3145. Review and appeal of a release or detention order

(a) Review of a release order.—If a person is ordered released by a magistrate, or by a person other than a judge of a court having original jurisdiction over the offense and other than a Federal appellate court—

(1) the attorney for the Government may file, with the court having original jurisdiction over the offense, a motion for revocation of the order or amendment of the conditions of release; and

(2) the person may file, with the court having original jurisdiction over the offense, a motion for amendment of the conditions of release.

The motion shall be determined promptly.

(b) Review of a detention order.—If a person is ordered detained by a magistrate, or by a person other than a judge of a court having original jurisdiction over the offense and other than a Federal appellate court, the person may file, with the court having original jurisdiction over the offense, a motion for revocation or amendment of the order. The motion shall be determined promptly.

(c) Appeal from a release or detention order.—An appeal from a release or detention order, or from a decision denying revocation or amendment of such an order, is governed by the provisions of section 1291 of title 28 and section 3731 of this title. The appeal shall be determined promptly. A person subject to detention pursuant to section 3143(a)(2) or (b)(2), and who meets the conditions of release set forth in section 3143(a)(1) or (b)(1), may be ordered released, under appropriate conditions, by the judicial officer, if it is clearly shown that there are exceptional reasons why such person's detention would not be appropriate.

§ 3146. Penalty for failure to appear

(a) Offense.—Whoever, having been released under this chapter knowingly—

(1) fails to appear before a court as required by the conditions of his release; or

(2) fails to surrender for service of sentence pursuant to a court order; shall be punished as provided in subsection (b) of this section.

(b) Punishment.—(1) The punishment for an offense under this section is—

(A) if the person was released in connection with a charge of, or while awaiting sentence, surrender for service of sentence, or appeal or certiorari after conviction, for—

(i) an offense punishable by death, life imprisonment, or imprisonment for a term of 15 years or more, a fine under this title or imprisonment for not more than ten years, or both;

(ii) an offense punishable by imprisonment for a term of five years or more, a fine under this title or imprisonment for not more than five years, or both;

(iii) any other felony, a fine under this title or imprisonment for not more than two years, or both; or

(iv) a misdemeanor, a fine under this title or imprisonment for not more than one year, or both; and

(B) if the person was released for appearance as a material witness, a fine under this chapter or imprisonment for not more than one year, or both.

(2) A term of imprisonment imposed under this section shall be consecutive to the sentence of imprisonment for any other offense.

(c) Affirmative defense.—It is an affirmative defense to a prosecution under this section that uncontrollable circumstances prevented the person from appearing or surrendering, and that the person did not contribute to the creation of such circumstances in reckless disregard of the requirement that he appear or surrender, and that the person appeared or surrendered as soon as such circumstances ceased to exist.

(d) Declaration of forfeiture.—If a person fails to appear before a court as required, and the person executed an appearance bond pursuant to section 3142(b) of this title or is subject to the release condition set forth in clause (xi) or (xii) of section 3142(c)(1)(B) of this title, the judicial officer may, regardless of whether the person has been charged with an offense under this section, declare any property designated pursuant to that section to be forfeited to the United States.

§ 3147. Penalty for an offense committed while on release

A person convicted of an offense committed while released under this chapter shall be sentenced, in addition to the sentence prescribed for the offense to—

> (1) a term of imprisonment of not less than two years and not more than ten years if the offense is a felony; or

> (2) a term of imprisonment of not less than ninety days and not more than one year if the offense is a misdemeanor.

A term of imprisonment imposed under this section shall be consecutive to any other sentence of imprisonment.

§ 3148. Sanctions for violation of a release condition

(a) Available sanctions.—A person who has been released under section 3142 of this title, and who has violated a condition of his release, is subject to a revocation of release, an order of detention, and a prosecution for contempt of court.

(b) Revocation of release.—The attorney for the Government may initiate a proceeding for revocation of an order of release by filing a motion with the district court. A judicial officer may issue a warrant for the arrest of a person charged with violating a condition of release, and the person shall be brought before a judicial officer in the district in which such person's arrest was ordered for a proceeding in accordance with this section. To the extent practicable, a person charged with violating the condition of release that such person not commit a Federal, State, or local crime during the period of release shall be brought before the judicial officer who ordered the release and whose order is alleged to have been violated. The judicial officer shall enter an order of revocation and detention if, after a hearing, the judicial officer—

> (1) finds that there is—

>> (A) probable cause to believe that the person has committed a Federal, State, or local crime while on release; or

>> (B) clear and convincing evidence that the person has violated any other condition of his release; and

(2) finds that—

(A) based on the factors set forth in section 3142(g) of this title, there is no condition or combination of conditions of release that will assure that the person will not flee or pose a danger to the safety of any other person or the community; or

(B) the person is unlikely to abide by any condition or combination of conditions of release.

If there is probable cause to believe that, while on release, the person committed a Federal, State, or local felony, a rebuttable presumption arises that no condition or combination of conditions will assure that the person will not pose a danger to the safety of any other person or the community. If the judicial officer finds that there are conditions of release that will assure that the person will not flee or pose a danger to the safety of any other person or the community, and that the person will abide by such conditions, the judicial officer shall treat the person in accordance with the provisions of section 3142 of this title and may amend the conditions of release accordingly.

(c) Prosecution for contempt.—The judge may commence a prosecution for contempt, pursuant to the provisions of section 401 of this title, if the person has violated a condition of release.

§ 3149. Surrender of an offender by a surety

A person charged with an offense, who is released upon the execution of an appearance bond with a surety, may be arrested by the surety, and if so arrested, shall be delivered promptly to a United States marshal and brought before a judicial officer. The judicial officer shall determine in accordance with the provisions of section 3148(b) whether to revoke the release of the person, and may absolve the surety of responsibility to pay all or part of the bond in accordance with the provisions of Rule 46 of the Federal Rules of Criminal Procedure. The person so committed shall be held in official detention until released pursuant to this chapter or another provision of law.

§ 3150. Applicability to a case removed from a State court

The provisions of this chapter apply to a criminal case removed to a Federal court from a State court.

SPEEDY TRIAL ACT OF 1974 (AS AMENDED)

(18 U.S.C. §§ 3161–3162, 3164).

§ 3161. Time limits and exclusions

(a) In any case involving a defendant charged with an offense, the appropriate judicial officer, at the earliest practicable time, shall, after consultation with the counsel for the defendant and the attorney for the Government, set the case for trial on a day certain, or list it for trial on a weekly or other short-term trial calendar at a place within the judicial district, so as to assure a speedy trial.

(b) Any information or indictment charging an individual with the commission of an offense shall be filed within thirty days from the date on which such individual was arrested or served with a summons in connection with such charges. If an individual has been charged with a felony in a district in which no grand jury has been in session during such thirty-day period, the period of time for filing of the indictment shall be extended an additional thirty days.

(c)(1) In any case in which a plea of not guilty is entered, the trial of a defendant charged in an information or indictment with the commission of an offense shall commence within seventy days from the filing date (and making public) of the information or indictment, or from the date the defendant has appeared before a judicial officer of the court in which such charge is pending, whichever date last occurs. If a defendant consents in writing to be tried before a magistrate on a complaint, the trial shall commence within seventy days from the date of such consent.

(2) Unless the defendant consents in writing to the contrary, the trial shall not commence less than thirty days from the date on which the defendant first appears through counsel or expressly waives counsel and elects to proceed pro se.

(d)(1) If any indictment or information is dismissed upon motion of the defendant, or any charge contained in a complaint filed against an individual is dismissed or otherwise dropped, and thereafter a complaint is filed against such defendant or individual charging him with the same offense or an offense based on the same conduct or arising from the same criminal episode, or an information or indictment is filed charging such defendant with the same offense or an offense based on the same conduct or arising from the same criminal episode, the provisions of subsections (b) and (c) of this section shall be applicable with respect to such subsequent complaint, indictment, or information, as the case may be.

(2) If the defendant is to be tried upon an indictment or information dismissed by a trial court and reinstated following an appeal, the trial shall commence within seventy days from the date the action occasioning the trial becomes final, except that the court retrying the case may extend the period for trial not to exceed one hundred and eighty days from the date the action occasioning the trial becomes final if the unavailability of witnesses or other factors resulting from the passage of time shall make trial within seventy days impractical. The periods of delay enumerated in section 3161(h) are excluded in computing the time limitations specified in this section. The sanctions of section 3162 apply to this subsection.

(e) If the defendant is to be tried again following a declaration by the trial judge of a mistrial or following an order of such judge for a new trial, the trial shall commence within seventy days from the date the action occasioning the retrial becomes final. If the defendant is to be tried again following an appeal or a collateral attack, the trial shall commence within seventy days from the date the action occasioning the retrial becomes final, except that the court retrying the case may extend the period for retrial not to exceed one hundred and eighty days from the date the action occasioning the retrial becomes final if unavailability of witnesses or other factors resulting from passage of time shall make trial within seventy days impractical. The periods of delay enumerated in section 3161(h) are excluded in computing the time limitations specified in this section. The sanctions of section 3162 apply to this subsection. * * *

(h) The following periods of delay shall be excluded in computing the time within which an information or an indictment must be filed, or in computing the time within which the trial of any such offense must commence:

(1) Any period of delay resulting from other proceedings concerning the defendant, including but not limited to—

(A) delay resulting from any proceeding, including any examinations, to determine the mental competency or physical capacity of the defendant;

(B) delay resulting from any proceeding, including any examination of the defendant, pursuant to section 2902 of title 28, United States Code;

(C) delay resulting from deferral of prosecution pursuant to section 2902 of title 28, United States Code;

(D) delay resulting from trial with respect to other charges against the defendant;

(E) delay resulting from any interlocutory appeal;

(F) delay resulting from any pretrial motion, from the filing of the motion through the conclusion of the hearing on, or other prompt disposition of, such motion;

(G) delay resulting from any proceeding relating to the transfer of a case or the removal of any defendant from another district under the Federal Rules of Criminal Procedure;

(H) delay resulting from transportation of any defendant from another district, or to and from places of examination or hospitalization, except that any time consumed in excess of ten days from the date an order of removal or an order directing such transportation, and the defendant's arrival at the destination shall be presumed to be unreasonable;

(I) delay resulting from consideration by the court of a proposed plea agreement to be entered into by the defendant and the attorney for the Government; and

(J) delay reasonably attributable to any period, not to exceed thirty days, during which any proceeding concerning the defendant is actually under advisement by the court.

(2) Any period of delay during which prosecution is deferred by the attorney for the Government pursuant to written agreement with the defendant, with the approval of the court, for the purpose of allowing the defendant to demonstrate his good conduct.

(3) (A) Any period of delay resulting from the absence or unavailability of the defendant or an essential witness.

(B) For purposes of subparagraph (A) of this paragraph, a defendant or an essential witness shall be considered absent when his whereabouts are unknown and, in addition, he is attempting to avoid apprehension or prosecution or his whereabouts cannot be determined by due diligence. For purposes of such subparagraph, a defendant or an essential witness shall be considered unavailable whenever his whereabouts are known but his presence for trial cannot be obtained by due diligence or he resists appearing at or being returned for trial.

(4) Any period of delay resulting from the fact that the defendant is mentally incompetent or physically unable to stand trial.

(5) Any period of delay resulting from the treatment of the defendant pursuant to section 2902 of title 28, United States Code.

(6) If the information or indictment is dismissed upon motion of the attorney for the Government and thereafter a charge is filed against the defendant for the same offense, or any offense required to be joined with that offense, any period of delay from the date the charge was dismissed to the date the time limitation would commence to run as to the subsequent charge had there been no previous charge.

(7) A reasonable period of delay when the defendant is joined for trial with a codefendant as to whom the time for trial has not run and no motion for severance has been granted.

(8) (A) Any period of delay resulting from a continuance granted by any judge on his own motion or at the request of the defendant or his counsel or at the request of the attorney for the Government, if the judge granted such continuance on the basis of his findings that the ends of justice served by taking such action outweigh the best interest of the public and the defendant in a speedy trial. No such period of delay resulting from a continuance granted by the court in accordance with this paragraph shall be excludable under this subsection unless the court sets forth, in the record of the case, either orally or in writing, its reasons for finding that the ends of justice served by the granting of such continuance outweigh the best interests of the public and the defendant in a speedy trial.

(B) The factors, among others, which a judge shall consider in determining whether to grant a continuance under subparagraph (A) of this paragraph in any case are as follows:

(i) Whether the failure to grant such a continuance in the proceeding would be likely to make a continuation of such proceeding impossible, or result in a miscarriage of justice.

(ii) Whether the case is so unusual or so complex, due to the number of defendants, the nature of the prosecution, or the existence of novel questions of fact or law, that it is unreasonable to expect adequate preparation for pretrial proceedings or for the trial itself within the time limits established by this section.

(iii) Whether, in a case in which arrest precedes indictment, delay in the filing of the indictment is caused because the arrest occurs at a time such that it is unreasonable to expect return and filing of the indictment within the period specified in section 3161(b), or because the facts upon which the grand jury must base its determination are unusual or complex.

(iv) Whether the failure to grant such a continuance in a case which, taken as a whole, is not so unusual or so complex as to fall within clause (ii), would deny the defendant reasonable time to obtain counsel, would unreasonably deny the defendant or the Government continuity of counsel, or would deny counsel for the defendant or the attorney for the Government the reasonable time necessary for effective preparation, taking into account the exercise of due diligence.

(C) No continuance under subparagraph (A) of this paragraph shall be granted because of general congestion of the court's calendar, or lack of diligent preparation or failure to obtain available witnesses on the part of the attorney for the Government.

(9) Any period of delay, not to exceed one year, ordered by a district court upon an application of a party and a finding by a preponderance of the evidence that an official request, as defined in section 3292 of this title, has been made for evidence of any such offense and that it reasonably appears, or reasonably appeared at the time the request was made, that such evidence is, or was, in such foreign country.

(i) If trial did not commence within the time limitation specified in section 3161 because the defendant had entered a plea of guilty or nolo contendere subsequently withdrawn to any or all charges in an indictment or information, the defendant shall be deemed indicted with respect to all charges therein contained within the meaning of section 3161, on the day the order permitting withdrawal of the plea becomes final.

(j) (1) If the attorney for the Government knows that a person charged with an offense is serving a term of imprisonment in any penal institution, he shall promptly—

(A) undertake to obtain the presence of the prisoner for trial; or

(B) cause a detainer to be filed with the person having custody of the prisoner and request him to so advise the prisoner and to advise the prisoner of his right to demand trial.

(2) If the person having custody of such prisoner receives a detainer, he shall promptly advise the prisoner of the charge and of the prisoner's right to demand trial. If at any time thereafter the prisoner informs the person having custody that he does demand trial, such person shall cause notice to that effect to be sent promptly to the attorney for the Government who caused the detainer to be filed.

(3) Upon receipt of such notice, the attorney for the Government shall promptly seek to obtain the presence of the prisoner for trial.

(4) When the person having custody of the prisoner receives from the attorney for the Government a properly supported request for temporary custody of such prisoner for trial, the prisoner shall be made available to that attorney for the Government (subject, in cases of interjurisdictional transfer, to any right of the prisoner to contest the legality of his delivery).

(k)(1) If the defendant is absent (as defined by subsection (h)(3)) on the day set for trial, and the defendant's subsequent appearance before the court on a bench warrant or other process or surrender to the court occurs more than 21 days after the day set for trial, the defendant shall be deemed to have first appeared before a judicial officer of the court in which the information or indictment is pending within the meaning of subsection (c) on the date of the defendant's subsequent appearance before the court.

(2) If the defendant is absent (as defined by subsection (h)(3)) on the day set for trial, and the defendant's subsequent appearance before the court on a bench warrant or other process or surrender to the court occurs not more than 21 days after the day set for trial, the time limit required by subsection (c), as extended by subsection (h), shall be further extended by 21 days.

§ 3162. Sanctions

(a) (1) If, in the case of any individual against whom a complaint is filed charging such individual with an offense, no indictment or information is filed within the time limit required by section 3161(b) as extended by section 3161(h) of this chapter, such charge against that individual contained in such complaint shall be dismissed or otherwise dropped. In determining whether to dismiss the case with or without prejudice, the court shall consider, among others, each of the following factors: the seriousness of the offense; the facts and circumstances of the case which led to the dismissal; and the impact of a reprosecution on the administration of this chapter and on the administration of justice.

(2) If a defendant is not brought to trial within the time limit required by section 3161(c) as extended by section 3161(h), the information or indictment shall be dismissed on motion of the defendant. The defendant shall have the burden of proof of supporting such motion but the Government shall have the burden of going forward with the evidence in connection with any exclusion of time under subparagraph 3161(h)(3). In determining whether to dismiss the case with or without prejudice, the court shall consider, among others, each of the following factors: the seriousness of the offense; the facts and circumstances of the case which led to the dismissal; and the impact of a reprosecution on the administration of this chapter and on the administration of justice. Failure of the defendant to move for dismissal prior to trial or entry of a plea of guilty or nolo contendere shall constitute a waiver of the right to dismissal under this section.

(b) In any case in which counsel for the defendant or the attorney for the Government (1) knowingly allows the case to be set for trial without disclosing the fact that a necessary witness would be unavailable for trial; (2) files a motion solely for the purpose of delay which he knows is totally frivolous and without merit; (3) makes a statement for the purpose of obtaining a continuance which he knows to be false and which is material to the granting of a continuance; or (4) otherwise willfully fails to proceed to trial without justification consistent with section 3161 of this chapter, the court may punish any such counsel or attorney, as follows:

(A) in the case of an appointed defense counsel, by reducing the amount of compensation that otherwise would have been paid to such counsel pursuant to section 3006A of this title in an amount not to exceed 25 per centum thereof;

(B) in the case of a counsel retained in connection with the defense of a defendant, by imposing on such counsel a fine of not to exceed 25 per centum of the compensation to which he is entitled in connection with his defense of such defendant;

(C) by imposing on any attorney for the Government a fine of not to exceed $250;

(D) by denying any such counsel or attorney for the Government the right to practice before the court considering such case for a period of not to exceed ninety days; or

(E) by filing a report with an appropriate disciplinary committee.

The authority to punish provided for by this subsection shall be in addition to any other authority or power available to such court.

(c) The court shall follow procedures established in the Federal Rules of Criminal Procedure in punishing any counsel or attorney for the Government pursuant to this section.

§ 3164. Persons detained or designated as being of high risk

(a) The trial or other disposition of cases involving—

(1) a detained person who is being held in detention solely because he is awaiting trial, and

(2) a released person who is awaiting trial and has been designated by the attorney for the Government as being of high risk,

shall be accorded priority.

(b) The trial of any person described in subsection (a)(1) or (a)(2) of this section shall commence not later than ninety days following the beginning of such continuous detention or designation of high risk by the attorney for the Government. The periods of delay enumerated in section 3161(h) are excluded in computing the time limitation specified in this section.

(c) Failure to commence trial of a detainee as specified in subsection (b), through no fault of the accused or his counsel, or failure to commence trial of a designated releasee as specified in subsection (b), through no fault of the attorney for the Government, shall result in the automatic review by the court of the conditions of release. No detainee, as defined in subsection (a), shall be held in custody pending trial after the expiration of such ninety-day period required for the commencement of his trial. A designated releasee, as defined in subsection (a), who is found by the court to have intentionally delayed the trial of his case shall be subject to an order of the court modifying his nonfinancial conditions of release under this title to insure that he shall appear at trial as required.

LITIGATION CONCERNING SOURCES OF EVIDENCE

(18 U.S.C. § 3504).

§ 3504. Litigation concerning sources of evidence

(a) In any trial, hearing, or other proceeding in or before any court, grand jury, department, officer, agency, regulatory body, or other authority of the United States—

(1) upon a claim by a party aggrieved that evidence is inadmissible because it is the primary product of an unlawful act or because it was obtained by the exploitation of an unlawful act, the opponent of the claim shall affirm or deny the occurrence of the alleged unlawful act;

(2) disclosure of information for a determination if evidence is inadmissible because it is the primary product of an unlawful act occurring prior to June 19, 1968, or because it was obtained by the exploitation of an unlawful act occurring prior to June 19, 1968, shall not be required unless such information may be relevant to a pending claim of such inadmissibility; and

(3) no claim shall be considered that evidence of an event is inadmissible on the ground that such evidence was obtained by the exploitation of an unlawful act occurring prior to June 19, 1968, if such event occurred more than five years after such allegedly unlawful act.

(b) As used in this section "unlawful act" means any act the use of any electronic, mechanical, or other device (as defined in section 2510(5) of this title) in violation of the Constitution or laws of the United States or any regulation or standard promulgated pursuant thereto.

CRIMINAL APPEALS ACT OF 1970
(AS AMENDED)

(18 U.S.C. § 3731).

§ 3731. Appeal by United States

In a criminal case an appeal by the United States shall lie to a court of appeals from a decision, judgment, or order of a district court dismissing an indictment or information or granting a new trial after verdict or judgment, as to any one or more counts, except that no appeal shall lie where the double jeopardy clause of the United States Constitution prohibits further prosecution.

An appeal by the United States shall lie to a court of appeals from a decision or order of a district court suppressing or excluding evidence or requiring the return of seized property in a criminal proceeding, not made after the defendant has been put in jeopardy and before the verdict or finding on an indictment or information, if the United States attorney certifies to the district court that the appeal is not taken for purpose of delay and that the evidence is a substantial proof of a fact material in the proceeding.

An appeal by the United States shall lie to a court of appeals from a decision or order, entered by a district court of the United States, granting the release of a person charged with or convicted of an offense, or denying a motion for revocation of, or modification of the conditions of, a decision or order granting release.

The appeal in all such cases shall be taken within thirty days after the decision, judgment or order has been rendered and shall be diligently prosecuted.

The provisions of this section shall be liberally construed to effectuate its purposes.

JURY SELECTION AND SERVICE ACT OF 1968 (AS AMENDED)

(28 U.S.C. §§ 1861–1863, 1865–1867).

§ 1861. Declaration of policy

It is the policy of the United States that all litigants in Federal courts entitled to trial by jury shall have the right to grand and petit juries selected at random from a fair cross section of the community in the district or division wherein the court convenes. It is further the policy of the United States that all citizens shall have the opportunity to be considered for service on grand and petit juries in the district courts of the United States, and shall have an obligation to serve as jurors when summoned for that purpose.

§ 1862. Discrimination prohibited

No citizen shall be excluded from service as a grand or petit juror in the district courts of the United States or in the Court of International Trade on account of race, color, religion, sex, national origin, or economic status.

§ 1863. Plan for random jury selection

(a) Each United States district court shall devise and place into operation a written plan for random selection of grand and petit jurors that shall be designed to achieve the objectives of sections 1861 and 1862 of this title, and that shall otherwise comply with the provisions of this title. The plan shall be placed into operation after approval by a reviewing panel consisting of the members of the judicial council of the circuit and either the chief judge of the district whose plan is being reviewed or such other active district judge of that district as the chief judge of the district may designate. The panel shall examine the plan to ascertain that it complies with the provisions of this title. * * * The district court may modify a plan at any time and it shall modify the plan when so directed by the reviewing panel. * * *

(b) Among other things, such plan shall—

(1) either establish a jury commission, or authorize the clerk of the court, to manage the jury selection process. If the plan establishes a jury commission, the district court shall appoint one citizen to serve with the clerk of the court as the jury commission. * * * The citizen jury commissioner shall not belong to the same political party as the clerk serving with him. The clerk or the jury commission, as the case may be, shall act under the supervision and control of the chief judge of the district court or such other judge of the district court as the plan may provide. * * *

(2) specify whether the names of prospective jurors shall be selected from the voter registration lists or the lists of actual voters of the political subdivisions within the district or division. The plan shall prescribe some other source or sources of names in addition to voter

lists where necessary to foster the policy and protect the rights secured by sections 1861 and 1862 of this title. * * *

(3) specify detailed procedures to be followed by the jury commission or clerk in selecting names from the sources specified in paragraph (2) of this subsection. These procedures shall be designed to ensure the random selection of a fair cross section of the persons residing in the community in the district or division wherein the court convenes. They shall ensure that names of persons residing in each of the counties, parishes, or similar political subdivisions within the judicial district or division are placed in a master jury wheel; and shall ensure that each county, parish, or similar political subdivision within the district or division is substantially proportionally represented in the master jury wheel for that judicial district, division, or combination of divisions. For the purposes of determining proportional representation in the master jury wheel, either the number of actual voters at the last general election in each county, parish, or similar political subdivision, or the number of registered voters if registration of voters is uniformly required throughout the district or division, may be used.

(4) provide for a master jury wheel (or a device similar in purpose and function) into which the names of those randomly selected shall be placed. The plan shall fix a minimum number of names to be placed initially in the master jury wheel, which shall be at least one-half of 1 per centum of the total number of persons on the lists used as a source of names for the district or division; but if this number of names is believed to be cumbersome and unnecessary, the plan may fix a smaller number of names to be placed in the master wheel, but in no event less than one thousand. The chief judge of the district court, or such other district court judge as the plan may provide, may order additional names to be placed in the master jury wheel from time to time as necessary. The plan shall provide for periodic emptying and refilling of the master jury wheel at specified times, the interval for which shall not exceed four years.

(5) (A) except as provided in subparagraph (B), specify those groups of persons or occupational classes whose members shall, on individual request therefor, be excused from jury service. Such groups or classes shall be excused only if the district court finds, and the plan states, that jury service by such class or group would entail undue hardship or extreme inconvenience to the members thereof, and excuse of members thereof would not be inconsistent with sections 1861 and 1862 of this title.

(B) specify that volunteer safety personnel, upon individual request, shall be excused from jury service. For purposes of this subparagraph, the term "volunteer safety personnel" means individuals serving a public agency (as defined in section 1203(6) of title I of the Omnibus Crime Control and Safe Streets Act of 1968) in an official capacity, without compensation, as firefighters or members of a rescue squad or ambulance crew.

(6) specify that the following persons are barred from jury service on the ground that they are exempt: (A) members in active service in

the Armed Forces of the United States; (B) members of the fire or police departments of any State, the District of Columbia, any territory or possession of the United States, or any subdivision of a State, the District of Columbia, or such territory or possession; (C) public officers in the executive, legislative, or judicial branches of the Government of the United States, or of any State, the District of Columbia, any territory or possession of the United States, or any subdivision of a State, the District of Columbia, or such territory or possession, who are actively engaged in the performance of official duties.

(7) fix the time when the names drawn from the qualified jury wheel shall be disclosed to parties and to the public. If the plan permits these names to be made public, it may nevertheless permit the chief judge of the district court, or such other district court judge as the plan may provide, to keep these names confidential in any case where the interests of justice so require.

(8) specify the procedures to be followed by the clerk or jury commission in assigning persons whose names have been drawn from the qualified jury wheel to grand and petit jury panels. * * *

§ 1865. Qualifications for jury service

(a) The chief judge of the district court, or such other district court judge as the plan may provide, on his initiative or upon recommendation of the clerk or jury commission, shall determine solely on the basis of information provided on the juror qualification form and other competent evidence whether a person is unqualified for, or exempt, or to be excused from jury service. The clerk shall enter such determination in the space provided on the juror qualification form and the alphabetical list of names drawn from the master jury wheel. If a person did not appear in response to a summons, such fact shall be noted on said list.

(b) In making such determination the chief judge of the district court, or such other district court judge as the plan may provide, shall deem any person qualified to serve on grand and petit juries in the district court unless he—

(1) is not a citizen of the United States eighteen years old who has resided for a period of one year within the judicial district;

(2) is unable to read, write, and understand the English language with a degree of proficiency sufficient to fill out satisfactorily the juror qualification form;

(3) is unable to speak the English language;

(4) is incapable, by reason of mental or physical infirmity, to render satisfactory jury service; or

(5) has a charge pending against him for the commission of, or has been convicted in a State or Federal court of record of, a crime punishable by imprisonment for more than one year and his civil rights have not been restored.

§ 1866. Selection and summoning of jury panels

* * *

(c) Except as provided in section 1865 of this title or in any jury selection plan provision adopted pursuant to paragraph (5) or (6) of section 1863(b) of this title, no person or class of persons shall be disqualified, excluded, excused, or exempt from service as jurors: *Provided*, That any person summoned for jury service may be (1) excused by the court, or by the clerk under supervision of the court if the court's jury selection plan so authorizes, upon a showing of undue hardship or extreme inconvenience, for such period as the court deems necessary, at the conclusion of which such person either shall be summoned again for jury service under subsections (b) and (c) of this section or, if the court's jury selection plan so provides, the name of such person shall be reinserted into the qualified jury wheel for selection pursuant to subsection (a) of this section, or (2) excluded by the court on the ground that such person may be unable to render impartial jury service or that his service as a juror would be likely to disrupt the proceedings, or (3) excluded upon peremptory challenge as provided by law, or (4) excluded pursuant to the procedure specified by law upon a challenge by any party for good cause shown, or (5) excluded upon determination by the court that his service as a juror would be likely to threaten the secrecy of the proceedings, or otherwise adversely affect the integrity of jury deliberations. No person shall be excluded under clause (5) of this subsection unless the judge, in open court, determines that such is warranted and that exclusion of the person will not be inconsistent with sections 1861 and 1862 of this title. The number of persons excluded under clause (5) of this subsection shall not exceed one per centum of the number of persons who return executed jury qualification forms during the period, specified in the plan, between two consecutive fillings of the master jury wheel. The names of persons excluded under clause (5) of this subsection, together with detailed explanations for the exclusions, shall be forwarded immediately to the judicial council of the circuit, which shall have the power to make any appropriate order, prospective or retroactive, to redress any misapplication of clause (5) of this subsection, but otherwise exclusions effectuated under such clause shall not be subject to challenge under the provisions of this title. Any person excluded from a particular jury under clause (2), (3), or (4) of this subsection shall be eligible to sit on another jury if the basis for his initial exclusion would not be relevant to his ability to serve on such other jury. * * *

§ 1867. Challenging compliance with selection procedures

(a) In criminal cases, before the voir dire examination begins, or within seven days after the defendant discovered or could have discovered, by the exercise of diligence, the grounds therefor, whichever is earlier, the defendant may move to dismiss the indictment or stay the proceedings against him on the ground of substantial failure to comply with the provisions of this title in selecting the grand or petit jury.

(b) In criminal cases, before the voir dire examination begins, or within seven days after the Attorney General of the United States discovered or could have discovered, by the exercise of diligence, the grounds therefor, whichever is earlier, the Attorney General may move to dismiss the indictment or stay the proceedings on the ground of substantial failure to comply with the provisions of this title in selecting the grand or petit jury. * * *

(d) Upon motion filed under subsection (a), (b), or (c) of this section, containing a sworn statement of facts which, if true, would constitute a substantial failure to comply with the provisions of this title, the moving party shall be entitled to present in support of such motion the testimony of the jury commission or clerk, if available, any relevant records and papers not public or otherwise available used by the jury commissioner or clerk, and any other relevant evidence. If the court determines that there has been a substantial failure to comply with the provisions of this title in selecting a grand jury, the court shall stay the proceedings pending the selection of a grand jury in conformity with this title or dismiss the indictment, whichever is appropriate. If the court determines that there has been a substantial failure to comply with the provisions of this title in selecting the petit jury, the court shall stay the proceedings pending the selection of a petit jury in conformity with this title.

(e) The procedures prescribed by this section shall be the exclusive means by which a person accused of a Federal crime, the Attorney General of the United States or a party in a civil case may challenge any jury on the ground that such jury was not selected in conformity with the provisions of this title. Nothing in this section shall preclude any person or the United States from pursuing any other remedy, civil or criminal, which may be available for the vindication or enforcement of any law prohibiting discrimination on account of race, color, religion, sex, national origin or economic status in the selection of persons for service on grand or petit juries. * * *

HABEAS CORPUS

(28 U.S.C. §§ 2241–2244, 2254–2255).

§ 2241. Power to grant writ

(a) Writs of habeas corpus may be granted by the Supreme Court, any justice thereof, the district courts and any circuit judge within their respective jurisdictions. The order of a circuit judge shall be entered in the records of the district court of the district wherein the restraint complained of is had.

(b) The Supreme Court, any justice thereof, and any circuit judge may decline to entertain an application for a writ of habeas corpus and may transfer the application for hearing and determination to the district court having jurisdiction to entertain it.

(c) The writ of habeas corpus shall not extend to a prisoner unless—

(1) He is in custody under or by color of the authority of the United States or is committed for trial before some court there of; or

(2) He is in custody for an act done or omitted in pursuance of an Act of Congress, or an order, process, judgment or decree of a court or judge of the United States; or

(3) He is in custody in violation of the Constitution or laws or treaties of the United States; or

(4) He, being a citizen of a foreign state and domiciled therein is in custody for an act done or omitted under any alleged right, title,

authority, privilege, protection, or exemption claimed under the commission, order or sanction of any foreign state, or under color thereof, the validity and effect of which depend upon the law of nations; or

(5) It is necessary to bring him into court to testify or for trial.

(d) Where an application for a writ of habeas corpus is made by a person in custody under the judgment and sentence of a State court of a State which contains two or more Federal judicial districts, the application may be filed in the district court for the district wherein such person is in custody or in the district court for the district within which the State court was held which convicted and sentenced him and each of such district courts shall have concurrent jurisdiction to entertain the application. The district court for the district wherein such an application is filed in the exercise of its discretion and in furtherance of justice may transfer the application to the other district court for hearing and determination.

§ 2242. Application

Application for a writ of habeas corpus shall be in writing signed and verified by the person for whose relief it is intended or by someone acting in his behalf.

It shall allege the facts concerning the applicant's commitment or detention, the name of the person who has custody over him and by virtue of what claim or authority, if known.

It may be amended or supplemented as provided in the rules of procedure applicable to civil actions.

If addressed to the Supreme Court, a justice thereof or a circuit judge it shall state the reasons for not making application to the district court of the district in which the applicant is held.

§ 2243. Issuance of writ; return; hearing; decision

A court, justice or judge entertaining an application for a writ of habeas corpus shall forthwith award the writ or issue an order directing the respondent to show cause why the writ should not be granted, unless it appears from the application that the applicant or person detained is not entitled thereto.

The writ, or order to show cause shall be directed to the person having custody of the person detained. It shall be returned within three days unless for good cause additional time, not exceeding twenty days, is allowed.

The person to whom the writ or order is directed shall make a return certifying the true cause of the detention.

When the writ or order is returned a day shall be set for hearing, not more than five days after the return unless for good cause additional time is allowed.

Unless the application for the writ and the return present only issues of law the person to whom the writ is directed shall be required to produce at the hearing the body of the person detained.

The applicant or the person detained may, under oath, deny any of the facts set forth in the return or allege any other material facts.

The return and all suggestions made against it may be amended, by leave of court, before or after being filed.

The court shall summarily hear and determine the facts, and dispose of the matter as law and justice require.

§ 2244. Finality of determination

(a) No circuit or district judge shall be required to entertain an application for a writ of habeas corpus to inquire into the detention of a person pursuant to a judgment of a court of the United States if it appears that the legality of such detention has been determined by a judge or court of the United States on a prior application for a writ of habeas corpus, except as provided in section 2255.

(b)(1) A claim presented in a second or successive habeas corpus application under section 2254 that was presented in a prior application shall be dismissed.

(2) A claim presented in a second or successive habeas corpus application under section 2254 that was not presented in a prior application shall be dismissed unless—

(A) the applicant shows that the claim relies on a new rule of constitutional law, made retroactive to cases on collateral review by the Supreme Court, that was previously unavailable; or

(B)(i) the factual predicate for the claim could not have been discovered previously through the exercise of due diligence; and

(ii) the facts underlying the claim, if proven and viewed in light of the evidence as a whole, would be sufficient to establish by clear and convincing evidence that, but for constitutional error, no reasonable factfinder would have found the applicant guilty of the underlying offense.

(3)(A) Before a second or successive application permitted by this section is filed in the district court, the applicant shall move in the appropriate court of appeals for an order authorizing the district court to consider the application.

(B) A motion in the court of appeals for an order authorizing the district court to consider a second or successive application shall be determined by a three-judge panel of the court of appeals.

(C) The court of appeals may authorize the filing of a second or successive application only if it determines that the application makes a prima facie showing that the application satisfies the requirements of this subsection.

(D) The court of appeals shall grant or deny the authorization to file a second or successive application not later than 30 days after the filing of the motion.

(E) The grant or denial of an authorization by a court of appeals to file a second or successive application shall not be appealable and shall not be the subject of a petition for rehearing or for a writ of certiorari.

(4) A district court shall dismiss any claim presented in a second or successive application that the court of appeals has authorized to be filed unless the applicant shows that the claim satisfies the requirements of this section.

(c) In a habeas corpus proceeding brought in behalf of a person in custody pursuant to the judgment of a State court, a prior judgment of the Supreme Court of the United States on an appeal or review by a writ of certiorari at the instance of the prisoner of the decision of such State court, shall be conclusive as to all issues of fact or law with respect to an asserted denial of a Federal right which constitutes ground for discharge in a habeas corpus proceeding, actually adjudicated by the Supreme Court therein, unless the applicant for the writ of habeas corpus shall plead and the court shall find the existence of a material and controlling fact which did not appear in the record of the proceeding in the Supreme Court and the court shall further find that the applicant for the writ of habeas corpus could not have caused such fact to appear in such record by the exercise of reasonable diligence.

(d)(1) A 1-year period of limitation shall apply to an application for a writ of habeas corpus by a person in custody pursuant to the judgment of a State court. The limitation period shall run from the latest of—

(A) the date on which the judgment became final by the conclusion of direct review or the expiration of the time for seeking such review;

(B) the date on which the impediment to filing an application created by State action in violation of the Constitution or laws of the United States is removed, if the applicant was prevented from filing by such State action;

(C) the date on which the constitutional right asserted was initially recognized by the Supreme Court, if the right has been newly recognized by the Supreme Court and made retroactively applicable to cases on collateral review; or

(D) the date on which the factual predicate of the claim or claims presented could have been discovered through the exercise of due diligence.

(2) The time during which a properly filed application for State post-conviction or other collateral review with respect to the pertinent judgment or claim is pending shall not be counted toward any period of limitation under this subsection.

§ 2253. Appeal

(a) In a habeas corpus proceeding or a proceeding under section 2255 before a district judge, the final order shall be subject to review, on appeal, by the court of appeals for the circuit in which the proceeding is held.

(b) There shall be no right of appeal from a final order in a proceeding to test the validity of a warrant to remove to another district or place for commitment or trial a person charged with a criminal offense against the United States, or to test the validity of such person's detention pending removal proceedings.

(c)(1) Unless a circuit justice or judge issues a certificate of appealability, an appeal may not be taken to the court of appeals from—

(A) the final order in a habeas corpus proceeding in which the detention complained of arises out of process issued by a State court; or

(B) the final order in a proceeding under section 2255.

(2) A certificate of appealability may issue under paragraph (1) only if the applicant has made a substantial showing of the denial of a constitutional right.

(3) The certificate of appealability under paragraph (1) shall indicate which specific issue or issues satisfy the showing required by paragraph (2).

§ 2254. State custody; remedies in State courts

(a) The Supreme Court, a Justice thereof, a circuit judge, or a district court shall entertain an application for a writ of habeas corpus in behalf of a person in custody pursuant to the judgment of a State court only on the ground that he is in custody in violation of the Constitution or laws or treaties of the United States.

(b)(1) An application for a writ of habeas corpus on behalf of a person in custody pursuant to the judgment of a State court shall not be granted unless it appears that—

(A) the applicant has exhausted the remedies available in the courts of the State; or

(B)(i) there is an absence of available State corrective process; or

(ii) circumstances exist that render such process ineffective to protect the rights of the applicant.

(2) An application for a writ of habeas corpus may be denied on the merits, notwithstanding the failure of the applicant to exhaust the remedies available in the courts of the State.

(3) A State shall not be deemed to have waived the exhaustion requirement or be estopped from reliance upon the requirement unless the State, through counsel, expressly waives the requirement.

(c) An applicant shall not be deemed to have exhausted the remedies available in the courts of the State, within the meaning of this section, if he has the right under the law of the State to raise, by any available procedure, the question presented.

(d) An application for a writ of habeas corpus on behalf of a person in custody pursuant to the judgment of a State court shall not be granted with respect to any claim that was adjudicated on the merits in State court proceedings unless the adjudication of the claim—

(1) resulted in a decision that was contrary to, or involved an unreasonable application of, clearly established Federal law, as determined by the Supreme Court of the United States; or

(2) resulted in a decision that was based on an unreasonable determination of the facts in light of the evidence presented in the State court proceeding.

(e)(1) In a proceeding instituted by an application for a writ of habeas corpus by a person in custody pursuant to the judgment of a State court, a determination of a factual issue made by a State court shall be presumed to be correct. The applicant shall have the burden of rebutting the presumption of correctness by clear and convincing evidence.

(2) If the applicant has failed to develop the factual basis of a claim in State court proceedings, the court shall not hold an evidentiary hearing on the claim unless the applicant shows that—

(A) the claim relies on—

(i) a new rule of constitutional law, made retroactive to cases on collateral review by the Supreme Court, that was previously unavailable; or

(ii) a factual predicate that could not have been previously discovered through the exercise of due diligence; and

(B) the facts underlying the claim would be sufficient to establish by clear and convincing evidence that but for constitutional error, no reasonable factfinder would have found the applicant guilty of the underlying offense.

(f) If the applicant challenges the sufficiency of the evidence adduced in such State court proceeding to support the State court's determination of a factual issue made therein, the applicant, if able, shall produce that part of the record pertinent to a determination of the sufficiency of the evidence to support such determination. If the applicant, because of indigency or other reason is unable to produce such part of the record, then the State shall produce such part of the record and the Federal court shall direct the State to do so by order directed to an appropriate State official. If the State cannot provide such pertinent part of the record, then the court shall determine under the existing facts and circumstances what weight shall be given to the State court's factual determination.

(g) A copy of the official records of the State court, duly certified by the clerk of such court to be a true and correct copy of a finding, judicial opinion, or other reliable written indicia showing such a factual determination by the State court shall be admissible in the Federal court proceeding.

(h) Except as provided in section 408 of the Controlled Substances Act, in all proceedings brought under this section, and any subsequent proceedings on review, the court may appoint counsel for an applicant who is or becomes financially unable to afford counsel, except as provided by a rule promulgated by the Supreme Court pursuant to statutory authority. Appointment of counsel under this section shall be governed by section 3006A of title 18.

(i) The ineffectiveness or incompetence of counsel during Federal or State collateral post-conviction proceedings shall not be a ground for relief in a proceeding arising under section 2254.

§ 2255. Federal custody; remedies on motion attacking sentence

A prisoner in custody under sentence of a court established by Act of Congress claiming the right to be released upon the ground that the sentence was imposed in violation of the Constitution or laws of the United States, or that the court was without jurisdiction to impose such sentence, or that the sentence was in excess of the maximum authorized by law, or is otherwise subject to collateral attack, may move the court which imposed the sentence to vacate, set aside or correct the sentence.

Unless the motion and the files and records of the case conclusively show that the prisoner is entitled to no relief, the court shall cause notice thereof to be served upon the United States attorney, grant a prompt hearing thereon, determine the issues and make findings of fact and conclusions of law with respect thereto. If the court finds that the judgment was rendered without jurisdiction, or that the sentence imposed was not authorized by law or otherwise open to collateral attack, or that there has been such a denial or infringement of the constitutional rights of the prisoner as to render the judgment vulnerable to collateral attack, the court shall vacate and set the judgment aside and shall discharge the prisoner or resentence him or grant a new trial or correct the sentence as may appear appropriate.

A court may entertain and determine such motion without requiring the production of the prisoner at the hearing.

A 1-year period of limitation shall apply to a motion under this section. The limitation period shall run from the latest of—

(1) the date on which the judgment of conviction becomes final;

(2) the date on which the impediment to making a motion created by governmental action in violation of the Constitution or laws of the United States is removed, if the movant was prevented from making a motion by such governmental action;

(3) the date on which the right asserted was initially recognized by the Supreme Court, if that right has been newly recognized by the Supreme Court and made retroactively applicable to cases on collateral review; or

(4) the date on which the facts supporting the claim or claims presented could have been discovered through the exercise of due diligence.

Except as provided in section 408 of the Controlled Substances Act, in all proceedings brought under this section, and any subsequent proceedings on review, the court may appoint counsel, except as provided by a rule promulgated by the Supreme Court pursuant to statutory authority. Appointment of counsel under this section shall be governed by section 3006A of title 18.

A second or successive motion must be certified as provided in section 2244 by a panel of the appropriate court of appeals to contain—

(1) newly discovered evidence that, if proven and viewed in light of the evidence as a whole, would be sufficient to establish by clear and convincing evidence that no reasonable factfinder would have found the movant guilty of the offense; or

(2) a new rule of constitutional law, made retroactive to cases on collateral review by the Supreme Court, that was previously unavailable.

An appeal may be taken to the court of appeals from the order entered on the motion as from a final judgment on application for a writ of habeas corpus.

An application for a writ of habeas corpus in behalf of a prisoner who is authorized to apply for relief by motion pursuant to this section, shall not be entertained if it appears that the applicant has failed to apply for relief, by motion, to the court which sentenced him, or that such court has denied him relief, unless it also appears that the remedy by motion is inadequate or ineffective to test the legality of his detention.

§ 2261. Prisoners in State custody subject to capital sentence; appointment of counsel; requirement of rule of court or statute; procedures for appointment

(a) This chapter shall apply to cases arising under section 2254 brought by prisoners in State custody who are subject to a capital sentence. It shall apply only if the provisions of subsections (b) and (c) are satisfied.

(b) This chapter is applicable if a State establishes by statute, rule of its court of last resort, or by another agency authorized by State law, a mechanism for the appointment, compensation, and payment of reasonable litigation expenses of competent counsel in State post-conviction proceedings brought by indigent prisoners whose capital convictions and sentences have been upheld on direct appeal to the court of last resort in the State or have otherwise become final for State law purposes. The rule of court or statute must provide standards of competency for the appointment of such counsel.

(c) Any mechanism for the appointment, compensation, and reimbursement of counsel as provided in subsection (b) must offer counsel to all State prisoners under capital sentence and must provide for the entry of an order by a court of record—

(1) appointing one or more counsels to represent the prisoner upon a finding that the prisoner is indigent and accepted the offer or is unable competently to decide whether to accept or reject the offer;

(2) finding, after a hearing if necessary, that the prisoner rejected the offer of counsel and made the decision with an understanding of its legal consequences; or

(3) denying the appointment of counsel upon a finding that the prisoner is not indigent.

(d) No counsel appointed pursuant to subsections (b) and (c) to represent a State prisoner under capital sentence shall have previously represented the prisoner at trial or on direct appeal in the case for which the appointment is made unless the prisoner and counsel expressly request continued representation.

(e) The ineffectiveness or incompetence of counsel during State or Federal post-conviction proceedings in a capital case shall not be a ground for relief in a proceeding arising under section 2254. This limitation shall not preclude the appointment of different counsel, on the court's own motion or at the request of the prisoner, at any phase of State or Federal post-conviction proceedings on the basis of the ineffectiveness or incompetence of counsel in such proceedings.

§ 2262. Mandatory stay of execution; duration; limits on stays of execution; successive petitions

(a) Upon the entry in the appropriate State court of record of an order under section 2261(c), a warrant or order setting an execution date for a

State prisoner shall be stayed upon application to any court that would have jurisdiction over any proceedings filed under section 2254. The application shall recite that the State has invoked the post-conviction review procedures of this chapter and that the scheduled execution is subject to stay.

(b) A stay of execution granted pursuant to subsection (a) shall expire if—

(1) a State prisoner fails to file a habeas corpus application under section 2254 within the time required in section 2263;

(2) before a court of competent jurisdiction, in the presence of counsel, unless the prisoner has competently and knowingly waived such counsel, and after having been advised of the consequences, a State prisoner under capital sentence waives the right to pursue habeas corpus review under section 2254; or

(3) a State prisoner files a habeas corpus petition under section 2254 within the time required by section 2263 and fails to make a substantial showing of the denial of a Federal right or is denied relief in the district court or at any subsequent stage of review.

(c) If one of the conditions in subsection (b) has occurred, no Federal court thereafter shall have the authority to enter a stay of execution in the case, unless the court of appeals approves the filing of a second or successive application under section 2244(b).

§ 2263. Filing of habeas corpus application; time requirements; tolling rules

(a) Any application under this chapter for habeas corpus relief under section 2254 must be filed in the appropriate district court not later than 180 days after final State court affirmance of the conviction and sentence on direct review or the expiration of the time for seeking such review.

(b) The time requirements established by subsection (a) shall be tolled—

(1) from the date that a petition for certiorari is filed in the Supreme Court until the date of final disposition of the petition if a State prisoner files the petition to secure review by the Supreme Court of the affirmance of a capital sentence on direct review by the court of last resort of the State or other final State court decision on direct review;

(2) from the date on which the first petition for post-conviction review or other collateral relief is filed until the final State court disposition of such petition; and

(3) during an additional period not to exceed 30 days, if—

(A) a motion for an extension of time is filed in the Federal district court that would have jurisdiction over the case upon the filing of a habeas corpus application under section 2254; and

(B) a showing of good cause is made for the failure to file the habeas corpus application within the time period established by this section.

§ 2264. Scope of Federal review; district court adjudications

(a) Whenever a State prisoner under capital sentence files a petition for habeas corpus relief to which this chapter applies, the district court shall only consider a claim or claims that have been raised and decided on the merits in the State courts, unless the failure to raise the claim properly is—

(1) the result of State action in violation of the Constitution or laws of the United States;

(2) the result of the Supreme Court's recognition of a new Federal right that is made retroactively applicable; or

(3) based on a factual predicate that could not have been discovered through the exercise of due diligence in time to present the claim for State or Federal post-conviction review.

(b) Following review subject to subsections (a), (d), and (e) of section 2254, the court shall rule on the claims properly before it.

§ 2265. Application to State unitary review procedure

(a) For purposes of this section, a 'unitary review' procedure means a State procedure that authorizes a person under sentence of death to raise, in the course of direct review of the judgment, such claims as could be raised on collateral attack. This chapter shall apply, as provided in this section, in relation to a State unitary review procedure if the State establishes by rule of its court of last resort or by statute a mechanism for the appointment, compensation, and payment of reasonable litigation expenses of competent counsel in the unitary review proceedings, including expenses relating to the litigation of collateral claims in the proceedings. The rule of court or statute must provide standards of competency for the appointment of such counsel.

(b) To qualify under this section, a unitary review procedure must include an offer of counsel following trial for the purpose of representation on unitary review, and entry of an order, as provided in section 2261(c), concerning appointment of counsel or waiver or denial of appointment of counsel for that purpose. No counsel appointed to represent the prisoner in the unitary review proceedings shall have previously represented the prisoner at trial in the case for which the appointment is made unless the prisoner and counsel expressly request continued representation.

(c) Sections 2262, 2263, 2264, and 2266 shall apply in relation to cases involving a sentence of death from any State having a unitary review procedure that qualifies under this section. References to State 'post-conviction review' and 'direct review' in such sections shall be understood as referring to unitary review under the State procedure. The reference in section 2262(a) to 'an order under section 2261(c)' shall be understood as referring to the post-trial order under subsection (b) concerning representation in the unitary review proceedings, but if a transcript of the trial proceedings is unavailable at the time of the filing of such an order in the appropriate State court, then the start of the 180–day limitation period under section 2263 shall be deferred until a transcript is made available to the prisoner or counsel of the prisoner.

§ 2266. Limitation periods for determining applications and motions

(a) The adjudication of any application under section 2254 that is subject to this chapter, and the adjudication of any motion under section 2255 by a person under sentence of death, shall be given priority by the district court and by the court of appeals over all noncapital matters.

(b)(1)(A) A district court shall render a final determination and enter a final judgment on any application for a writ of habeas corpus brought under this chapter in a capital case not later than 180 days after the date on which the application is filed.

(B) A district court shall afford the parties at least 120 days in which to complete all actions, including the preparation of all pleadings and briefs, and if necessary, a hearing, prior to the submission of the case for decision.

(C)(i) A district court may delay for not more than one additional 30–day period beyond the period specified in subparagraph (A), the rendering of a determination of an application for a writ of habeas corpus if the court issues a written order making a finding, and stating the reasons for the finding, that the ends of justice that would be served by allowing the delay outweigh the best interests of the public and the applicant in a speedy disposition of the application.

(ii) The factors, among others, that a court shall consider in determining whether a delay in the disposition of an application is warranted are as follows:

(I) Whether the failure to allow the delay would be likely to result in a miscarriage of justice.

(II) Whether the case is so unusual or so complex, due to the number of defendants, the nature of the prosecution, or the existence of novel questions of fact or law, that it is unreasonable to expect adequate briefing within the time limitations established by subparagraph (A).

(III) Whether the failure to allow a delay in a case that, taken as a whole, is not so unusual or so complex as described in subclause (H), but would otherwise deny the applicant reasonable time to obtain counsel, would unreasonably deny the applicant or the government continuity of counsel, or would deny counsel for the applicant or the government the reasonable time necessary for effective preparation, taking into account the exercise of due diligence.

(iii) No delay in disposition shall be permissible because of general congestion of the court's calendar.

(iv) The court shall transmit a copy of any order issued under clause (i) to the Director of the Administrative Office of the United States Courts for inclusion in the report under paragraph (5).

(2) The time limitations under paragraph (1) shall apply to—

(A) an initial application for a writ of habeas corpus;

(B) any second or successive application for a writ of habeas corpus; and

(C) any redetermination of an application for a writ of habeas corpus following a remand by the court of appeals or the Supreme Court for further proceedings, in which case the limitation period shall run from the date the remand is ordered.

(3)(A) The time limitations under this section shall not be construed to entitle an applicant to a stay of execution, to which the applicant would otherwise not be entitled, for the purpose of litigating any application or appeal.

(B) No amendment to an application for a writ of habeas corpus under this chapter shall be permitted after the filing of the answer to the application, except on the grounds specified in section 2244(b).

(4)(A) The failure of a court to meet or comply with a time limitation under this section shall not be a ground for granting relief from a judgment of conviction or sentence.

(B) The State may enforce a time limitation under this section by petitioning for a writ of mandamus to the court of appeals. The court of appeals shall act on the petition for a writ of mandamus not later than 30 days after the filing of the petition.

(5)(A) The Administrative Office of the United States Courts shall submit to Congress an annual report on the compliance by the district courts with the time limitations under this section.

(B) The report described in subparagraph (A) shall include copies of the orders submitted by the district courts under paragraph (1)(B)(iv).

(c)(1)(A) A court of appeals shall hear and render a final determination of any appeal of an order granting or denying, in whole or in part, an application brought under this chapter in a capital case not later than 120 days after the date on which the reply brief is filed, or if no reply brief is filed, not later than 120 days after the date on which the answering brief is filed.

(B)(i) A court of appeals shall decide whether to grant a petition for rehearing or other request for rehearing en banc not later than 30 days after the date on which the petition for rehearing is filed unless a responsive pleading is required, in which case the court shall decide whether to grant the petition not later than 30 days after the date on which the responsive pleading is filed.

(ii) If a petition for rehearing or rehearing en banc is granted, the court of appeals shall hear and render a final determination of the appeal not later than 120 days after the date on which the order granting rehearing or rehearing en banc is entered.

(2) The time limitations under paragraph (1) shall apply to—

(A) an initial application for a writ of habeas corpus;

(B) any second or successive application for a writ of habeas corpus; and

(C) any redetermination of an application for a writ of habeas corpus or related appeal following a remand by the court of appeals en banc or the Supreme Court for further proceedings, in which case the limitation period shall run from the date the remand is ordered.

(3) The time limitations under this section shall not be construed to entitle an applicant to a stay of execution, to which the applicant would otherwise not be entitled, for the purpose of litigating any application or appeal.

(4)(A) The failure of a court to meet or comply with a time limitation under this section shall not be a ground for granting relief from a judgment of conviction or sentence.

(B) The State may enforce a time limitation under this section by applying for a writ of mandamus to the Supreme Court.

(5) The Administrative Office of the United States Courts shall submit to Congress an annual report on the compliance by the courts of appeals with the time limitations under this section.[a]

PRIVACY PROTECTION ACT OF 1980

(42 U.S.C. §§ 2000aa–2000aa–12).

§ 2000aa. Searches and seizures by government officers and employees in connection with investigation or prosecution of criminal offenses

(a) Notwithstanding any other law, it shall be unlawful for a government officer or employee, in connection with the investigation or prosecution of a criminal offense, to search for or seize any work product materials possessed by a person reasonably believed to have a purpose to disseminate to the public a newspaper, book, broadcast, or other similar form of public communication, in or affecting interstate or foreign commerce; but this provision shall not impair or affect the ability of any government officer or employee, pursuant to otherwise applicable law, to search for or seize such materials, if—

(1) there is probable cause to believe that the person possessing such materials has committed or is committing the criminal offense to which the materials relate: *Provided, however,* That a government officer or employee may not search for or seize such materials under the provisions of this paragraph if the offense to which the materials relate consists of the receipt, possession, communication, or withholding of such materials or the information contained therein (but such a search or seizure may be conducted under the provisions of this paragraph if the offense consists of the receipt, possession, or communication of information relating to the national defense, classified information, or restricted data under the provisions of section 793, 794, 797, or 798 of Title 18, or section 2274, 2275 or 2277 of this title, or section 783 of Title 50, or if the offense involves the production, possession, receipt,

a. The enacting legislation states that new sections 2261–2266 "shall apply to cases pending on or after the date of enactment of this Act."

mailing, sale, distribution, shipment, or transportation of child pornography, the sexual exploitation of children, or the sale or purchase of children under section 2251, 2251A, 2252, or 2252A of Title 18); or

(2) there is reason to believe that the immediate seizure of such materials is necessary to prevent the death of, or serious bodily injury to, a human being.

(b) Notwithstanding any other law, it shall be unlawful for a government officer or employee, in connection with the investigation or prosecution of a criminal offense, to search for or seize documentary materials, other than work product materials, possessed by a person in connection with a purpose to disseminate to the public a newspaper, book, broadcast, or other similar form of public communication, in or affecting interstate or foreign commerce; but this provision shall not impair or affect the ability of any government officer or employee, pursuant to otherwise applicable law, to search for or seize such materials, if—

(1) there is probable cause to believe that the person possessing such materials has committed or is committing the criminal offense to which the materials relate: *Provided, however,* That a government officer or employee may not search for or seize such materials under the provisions of this paragraph if the offense to which the materials relate consists of the receipt, possession, communication, or withholding of such materials or the information contained therein (but such a search or seizure may be conducted under the provisions of this paragraph if the offense consists of the receipt, possession, or communication of information relating to the national defense, classified information, or restricted data under the provisions of section 793, 794, 797, or 798 of Title 18, or section 2274, 2275 or 2277 of this title, or section 783 of Title 50, or if the offense involves the production, possession, receipt, mailing, sale, distribution, shipment, or transportation of child pornography, the sexual exploitation of children, or the sale or purchase of children under section 2251, 2251A, 2252, or 2252A of Title 18);

(2) there is reason to believe that the immediate seizure of such materials is necessary to prevent the death of, or serious bodily injury to, a human being;

(3) there is reason to believe that the giving of notice pursuant to a subpena duces tecum would result in the destruction, alteration, or concealment of such materials; or

(4) such materials have not been produced in response to a court order directing compliance with a subpena duces tecum, and—

(A) all appellate remedies have been exhausted; or

(B) there is reason to believe that the delay in an investigation or trial occasioned by further proceedings relating to the subpena would threaten the interests of justice.

(c) In the event a search warrant is sought pursuant to paragraph (4)(B) of subsection (b) of this section, the person possessing the materials shall be afforded adequate opportunity to submit an affidavit setting forth the basis for any contention that the materials sought are not subject to seizure.

§ 2000aa–5. Border and customs searches

This chapter shall not impair or affect the ability of a government officer or employee, pursuant to otherwise applicable law, to conduct searches and seizures at the borders of, or at international points of, entry into the United States in order to enforce the customs laws of the United States.

§ 2000aa–6. Civil actions by aggrieved persons

(a) A person aggrieved by a search for or seizure of materials in violation of this chapter shall have a civil cause of action for damages for such search or seizure—

(1) against the United States, against a State which has waived its sovereign immunity under the Constitution to a claim for damages resulting from a violation of this chapter, or against any other governmental unit, all of which shall be liable for violations of this chapter by their officers or employees while acting within the scope or under color of their office or employment; and

(2) against an officer or employee of a State who has violated this chapter while acting within the scope or under color of his office or employment, if such State has not waived its sovereign immunity as provided in paragraph (1).

(b) It shall be a complete defense to a civil action brought under paragraph (2) of subsection (a) of this section that the officer or employee had a reasonable good faith belief in the lawfulness of his conduct.

(c) The United States, a State, or any other governmental unit liable for violations of this chapter under subsection (a)(1) of this section, may not assert as a defense to a claim arising under this chapter the immunity of the officer or employee whose violation is complained of or his reasonable good faith belief in the lawfulness of his conduct, except that such a defense may be asserted if the violation complained of is that of a judicial officer.

(d) The remedy provided by subsection (a)(1) of this section against the United States, a State, or any other governmental unit is exclusive of any other civil action or proceeding for conduct constituting a violation of this chapter, against the officer or employee whose violation gave rise to the claim, or against the estate of such officer or employee.

(e) Evidence otherwise admissible in a proceeding shall not be excluded on the basis of a violation of this chapter.

(f) A person having a cause of action under this section shall be entitled to recover actual damages but not less than liquidated damages of $1,000, and such reasonable attorneys' fees and other litigation costs reasonably incurred as the court, in its discretion, may award: *Provided, however*, That the United States, a State, or any other governmental unit shall not be liable for interest prior to judgment.

(g) The Attorney General may settle a claim for damages brought against the United States under this section, and shall promulgate regulations to provide for the commencement of an administrative inquiry following a determination of a violation of this chapter by an officer or employee of the United States and for the imposition of administrative sanctions against such officer or employee, if warranted.

(h) The district courts shall have original jurisdiction of all civil actions arising under this section.

§ 2000aa–7. Definitions

(a) "Documentary materials", as used in this chapter, means materials upon which information is recorded, and includes, but is not limited to, written or printed materials, photographs, motion picture films, negatives, video tapes, audio tapes, and other mechanically, magnetically or electronically recorded cards, tapes, or discs, but does not include contraband or the fruits of a crime or things otherwise criminally possessed, or property designed or intended for use, or which is or has been used as, the means of committing a criminal offense.

(b) "Work product materials", as used in this chapter, means materials, other than contraband or the fruits of a crime or things otherwise criminally possessed, or property designed or intended for use, or which is or has been used, as the means of committing a criminal offense, and—

(1) in anticipation of communicating such materials to the public, are prepared, produced, authored, or created, whether by the person in possession of the materials or by any other person;

(2) are possessed for the purposes of communicating such materials to the public; and

(3) include mental impressions, conclusions, opinions, or theories of the person who prepared, produced, authored, or created such material.

(c) "Any other governmental unit", as used in this chapter, includes the District of Columbia, the Commonwealth of Puerto Rico, any territory or possession of the United States, and any local government, unit of local government, or any unit of State government.

§ 2000aa–11. Guidelines for federal officers and employees

(a) The Attorney General shall * * * issue guidelines for the procedures to be employed by any Federal officer or employee, in connection with the investigation or prosecution of an offense, to obtain documentary materials in the private possession of a person when the person is not reasonably believed to be a suspect in such offense or related by blood or marriage to such a suspect, and when the materials sought are not contraband or the fruits or instrumentalities of an offense. * * *

§ 2000aa–12. Binding nature of guidelines; disciplinary actions for violations; legal proceedings for non-compliance prohibited

Guidelines issued by the Attorney General under this subchapter shall have the full force and effect of Department of Justice regulations and any violation of these guidelines shall make the employee or officer involved subject to appropriate administrative disciplinary action. However, an issue relating to the compliance, or the failure to comply, with guidelines issued pursuant to this subchapter may not be litigated, and a court may not entertain such an issue as the basis for the suppression or exclusion of evidence.

[EDITOR'S NOTE: These guidelines appear in 28 C.F.R. Pt. 59. The procedural provisions are set out below.]

§ 59.4 Procedures

(a) *Provisions governing the use of search warrants generally.*

(1) A search warrant should not be used to obtain documentary materials believed to be in the private possession of a disinterested third party unless it appears that the use of a subpoena, summons, request, or other less intrusive alternative means of obtaining the materials would substantially jeopardize the availability or usefulness of the materials sought, and the application for the warrant has been authorized as provided in paragraph (a)(2) of this section.

(2) No federal officer or employee shall apply for a warrant to search for and seize documentary materials believed to be in the private possession of a disinterested third party unless the application for the warrant has been authorized by an attorney for the government. Provided, however, that in an emergency situation in which the immediacy of the need to seize the materials does not permit an opportunity to secure the authorization of an attorney for the government, the application may be authorized by a supervisory law enforcement officer in the applicant's department or agency, if the appropriate United States Attorney (or where the case is not being handled by a United States Attorney's Office, the appropriate supervisory official of the Department of Justice) is notified of the authorization and the basis for justifying such authorization under this part within 24 hours of the authorization.

(b) *Provisions governing the use of search warrants which may intrude upon professional, confidential relationships.*

(1) A search warrant should not be used to obtain documentary materials believed to be in the private possession of a disinterested third party physician, lawyer, or clergyman, under circumstances in which the materials sought, or other materials likely to be reviewed during the execution of the warrant, contain confidential information on patients, clients, or parishioners which was furnished or developed for the purposes of professional counseling or treatment, unless—

(i) It appears that the use of a subpoena, summons, request or other less intrusive alternative means of obtaining the materials would substantially jeopardize the availability or usefulness of the materials sought;

(ii) Access to the documentary materials appears to be of substantial importance to the investigation or prosecution for which they are sought; and

(iii) The application for the warrant has been approved as provided in paragraph (b)(2) of this section.

(2) No federal officer or employee shall apply for a warrant to search for and seize documentary materials believed to be in the private possession of a

disinterested third party physician, lawyer, or clergyman under the circumstances described in paragraph (b)(1) of this section, unless, upon the recommendation of the United States Attorney (or where a case is not being handled by a United States Attorney's Office, upon the recommendation of the appropriate supervisory official of the Department of Justice), an appropriate Deputy Assistant Attorney General has authorized the application for the warrant. Provided, however, that in an emergency situation in which the immediacy of the need to seize the materials does not permit an opportunity to secure the authorization of a Deputy Assistant Attorney General, the application may be authorized by the United States Attorney (or where the case is not being handled by a United States Attorney's Office, by the appropriate supervisory official of the Department of Justice) if an appropriate Deputy Assistant Attorney General is notified of the authorization and the basis for justifying such authorization under this part within 72 hours of the authorization.

(3) Whenever possible, a request for authorization by an appropriate Deputy Assistant Attorney General of a search warrant application pursuant to paragraph (b)(2) of this section shall be made in writing and shall include:

(i) The application for the warrant; and

(ii) A brief description of the facts and circumstances advanced as the basis for recommending authorization of the application under this part.

If a request for authorization of the application is made orally or if, in an emergency situation, the application is authorized by the United States Attorney or a supervisory official of the Department of Justice as provided in paragraph (b)(2) of this section, a written record of the request including the materials specified in paragraphs (b)(3)(i) and (ii) of this section shall be transmitted to an appropriate Deputy Assistant Attorney General within 7 days. The Deputy Assistant Attorneys General shall keep a record of the disposition of all requests for authorizations of search warrant applications made under paragraph (b) of this section.

(4) A search warrant authorized under paragraph (b)(2) of this section shall be executed in such a manner as to minimize, to the greatest extent practicable, scrutiny of confidential materials.

(5) Although it is impossible to define the full range of additional doctor-like therapeutic relationships which involve the furnishing or development of private information, the United States Attorney (or where a case is not being handled by a United States Attorney's Office, the appropriate supervisory official of the Department of Justice) should determine whether a search for documentary materials held by other disinterested third party professionals involved in such relationships (e.g. psychologists or psychiatric social workers or nurses) would implicate the special privacy concerns which are addressed in paragraph (b) of this section. If the United States Attorney (or other supervisory official of the Department of Justice) determines that such a search would require review of extremely confidential information furnished or developed for the purposes of professional counseling or treatment, the provisions of this subsection should be applied. Otherwise, at a minimum, the requirements of paragraph (a) of this section must be met.

(c) *Considerations bearing on choice of methods.*

In determining whether, as an alternative to the use of a search warrant, the use of a subpoena or other less intrusive means of obtaining documentary materials would substantially jeopardize the availability or usefulness of the materials sought, the following factors, among others, should be considered:

(1) Whether it appears that the use of a subpoena or other alternative which gives advance notice of the government's interest in obtaining the materials would be likely to result in the destruction, alteration, concealment, or transfer of the materials sought; considerations, among others, bearing on this issue may include:

(i) Whether a suspect has access to the materials sought;

(ii) Whether there is a close relationship of friendship, loyalty, or sympathy between the possessor of the materials and a suspect;

(iii) Whether the possessor of the materials is under the domination or control of a suspect;

(iv) Whether the possessor of the materials has an interest in preventing the disclosure of the materials to the government;

(v) Whether the possessor's willingness to comply with a subpoena or request by the government would be likely to subject him to intimidation or threats of reprisal;

(vi) Whether the possessor of the materials has previously acted to obstruct a criminal investigation or judicial proceeding or refused to comply with or acted in defiance of court orders; or

(vii) Whether the possessor has expressed an intent to destroy, conceal, alter, or transfer the materials;

(2) The immediacy of the government's need to obtain the materials; considerations, among others, bearing on this issue may include:

(i) Whether the immediate seizure of the materials is necessary to prevent injury to persons or property;

(ii) Whether the prompt seizure of the materials is necessary to preserve their evidentiary value;

(iii) Whether delay in obtaining the materials would significantly jeopardize an ongoing investigation or prosecution; or

(iv) Whether a legally enforceable form of process, other than a search warrant, is reasonably available as a means of obtaining the materials.

The fact that the disinterested third party possessing the materials may have grounds to challenge a subpoena or other legal process is not in itself a legitimate basis for the use of a search warrant.

Appendix C

FEDERAL RULES OF CRIMINAL PROCEDURE FOR THE UNITED STATES DISTRICT COURTS

I. SCOPE, PURPOSE, AND CONSTRUCTION

Rule 1. Scope

These rules govern the procedure in all criminal proceedings in the courts of the United States, as provided in Rule 54(a); and, whenever specifically provided in one of the rules, to preliminary, supplementary, and special proceedings before United States magistrate judges and at proceedings before state and local judicial officers.

Rule 2. Purpose and Construction

These rules are intended to provide for the just determination of every criminal proceeding. They shall be construed to secure simplicity in procedure, fairness in administration and the elimination of unjustifiable expense and delay.

II. PRELIMINARY PROCEEDINGS

Rule 3. The Complaint

The complaint is a written statement of the essential facts constituting the offense charged. It shall be made upon oath before a magistrate judge.

Rule 4. Arrest Warrant or Summons upon Complaint

(a) Issuance. If it appears from the complaint, or from an affidavit or affidavits filed with the complaint, that there is probable cause to believe that an offense has been committed and that the defendant has committed it, a warrant for the arrest of the defendant shall issue to any officer authorized by law to execute it. Upon the request of the attorney for the government a summons instead of a warrant shall issue. More than one warrant or summons may issue on the same complaint. If a defendant fails to appear in response to the summons, a warrant shall issue.

(b) Probable Cause. The finding of probable cause may be based upon hearsay evidence in whole or in part.

(c) Form.

(1) Warrant. The warrant shall be signed by the magistrate judge and shall contain the name of the defendant or, if the defendant's name is unknown, any name or description by which the defendant can be identified with reasonable certainty. It shall describe the offense charged in the complaint. It shall command that the defendant be arrested and brought before the nearest available magistrate judge.

(2) Summons. The summons shall be in the same form as the warrant except that it shall summon the defendant to appear before a magistrate at a stated time and place.

(d) Execution or Service; and Return.

(1) By Whom. The warrant shall be executed by a marshal or by some other officer authorized by law. The summons may be served by any person authorized to serve a summons in a civil action.

(2) Territorial Limits. The warrant may be executed or the summons may be served at any place within the jurisdiction of the United States.

(3) Manner. The warrant shall be executed by the arrest of the defendant. The officer need not have the warrant at the time of the arrest but upon request shall show the warrant to the defendant as soon as possible. If the officer does not have the warrant at the time of the arrest, the officer shall then inform the defendant of the offense charged and of the fact that a warrant has been issued. The summons shall be served upon a defendant by delivering a copy to the defendant personally, or by leaving it at the defendant's dwelling house or usual place of abode with some person of suitable age and discretion then residing therein and by mailing a copy of the summons to the defendant's last known address.

(4) Return. The officer executing a warrant shall make return thereof to the magistrate judge or other officer before whom the defendant is brought pursuant to Rule 5. At the request of the attorney for the government any unexecuted warrant shall be returned to and canceled by the magistrate judge by whom it was issued. On or before the return day the person to whom a summons was delivered for service shall make return thereof to the magistrate judge before whom the summons is returnable. At the request of the attorney for the government made at any time while the complaint is pending, a warrant returned unexecuted and not canceled or a summons returned unserved or a duplicate thereof may be delivered by the magistrate judge to the marshal or other authorized person for execution or service.

Rule 5. Initial Appearance Before the Magistrate Judge

(a) In General. Except as otherwise provided in this rule, an officer making an arrest under a warrant issued upon a complaint or any person making an arrest without a warrant shall take the arrested person without unnecessary delay before the nearest available federal magistrate judge or, if a federal magistrate judge is not reasonably available, before a state or local judicial officer authorized by 18 U.S.C. § 3041. If a person arrested without a warrant is brought before a magistrate judge, a complaint, satisfying the probable cause requirements of Rule 4(a), shall be promptly filed. When a person, arrested with or without a warrant or given a summons, appears initially before the magistrate judge, the magistrate judge shall proceed in accordance with the applicable subdivisions of this rule. An officer making an arrest under a warrant issued upon a complaint charging solely a violation of 18 U.S.C. § 1073 need not comply with this rule if the person arrested is transferred without unnecessary delay to the custody of appropriate state or local authorities in the district of arrest and an attorney for the government moves promptly, in the district in which the warrant was issued, to dismiss the complaint.

(b) Misdemeanors and Other Petty Offenses. If the charge against the defendant is a misdemeanor or other petty offense triable by a United States magistrate judge under 18 U.S.C. § 3401, the United States magistrate judge shall proceed in accordance with Rule 58.

(c) Offenses Not Triable by the United States Magistrate Judge. If the charge against the defendant is not triable by the United States magistrate judge, the defendant shall not be called upon to plead. The magistrate judge shall inform the defendant of the complaint against the defendant and of any affidavit filed therewith, of the defendant's right to retain counsel or to request the assignment of counsel if the defendant is unable to obtain counsel, and of the general circumstances under which the defendant may secure pretrial release. The magistrate judge shall inform the defendant that the defendant is not required to make a statement and that any statement made by the defendant may be used against the defendant. The magistrate judge shall also inform the defendant of the right to a preliminary examination. The magistrate judge shall allow the defendant reasonable time and opportunity to consult counsel and shall detain or conditionally release the defendant as provided by statute or in these rules.

A defendant is entitled to a preliminary examination, unless waived, when charged with any offense, other than a petty offense, which is to be tried by a judge of the district court. If the defendant waives preliminary examination, the magistrate judge shall forthwith hold the defendant to answer in the district court. If the defendant does not waive the preliminary examination, the magistrate judge shall schedule a preliminary examination. Such examination shall be held within a reasonable time but in any event not later than 10 days following the initial appearance if the defendant is in custody and no later than 20 days if the defendant is not in custody, provided, however, that the preliminary examination shall not be held if the defendant is indicted or if an information against the defendant is filed in district court before the date set for the preliminary examination. With the consent of the defendant and upon a showing of good cause, taking into account the public interest in the prompt disposition of criminal cases, time limits specified in this subdivision may be extended one or more times by a federal magistrate judge. In the absence of such consent by the defendant, time limits may be extended by a judge of the United States only upon a showing that extraordinary circumstances exist and that delay is indispensable to the interests of justice.

Rule 5.1. Preliminary Examination

(a) Probable Cause Finding. If from the evidence it appears that there is probable cause to believe that an offense has been committed and that the defendant committed it, the federal magistrate judge shall forthwith hold the defendant to answer in district court. The finding of probable cause may be based upon hearsay evidence in whole or in part. The defendant may cross-examine adverse witnesses and may introduce evidence. Objections to evidence on the ground that it was acquired by unlawful means are not properly made at the preliminary examination. Motions to suppress must be made to the trial court as provided in Rule 12.

(b) Discharge of Defendant. If from the evidence it appears that there is no probable cause to believe that an offense has been committed or that the defendant committed it, the federal magistrate judge shall dismiss the complaint and discharge the defendant. The discharge of the defendant shall not preclude the government from instituting a subsequent prosecution for the same offense.

(c) Records. After concluding the proceeding the federal magistrate judge shall transmit forthwith to the clerk of the district court all papers in the proceeding. The magistrate judge shall promptly make or cause to be made a record or summary of such proceeding.

(1) On timely application to a federal magistrate judge, the attorney for a defendant in a criminal case may be given the opportunity to have the recording of the hearing on preliminary examination made available to that attorney in connection with any further hearing or preparation for trial. The court may, by local rule, appoint the place for and define the conditions under which such opportunity may be afforded counsel.

(2) On application of a defendant addressed to the court or any judge thereof, an order may issue that the federal magistrate judge make available a copy of the transcript, or of a portion thereof, to defense counsel. Such order shall provide for prepayment of costs of such transcript by the defendant unless the defendant makes a sufficient affidavit that the defendant is unable to pay or to give security therefor, in which case the expense shall be paid by the Director of the Administrative Office of the United States Courts from available appropriated funds. Counsel for the government may move also that a copy of the transcript, in whole or in part, be made available to it, for good cause shown, and an order may be entered granting such motion in whole or in part, on appropriate terms, except that the government need not prepay costs nor furnish security therefor.

III. INDICTMENT AND INFORMATION
Rule 6. The Grand Jury

(a) Summoning Grand Juries.

(1) Generally. The court shall order one or more grand juries to be summoned at such time as the public interest requires. The grand jury shall consist of not less than 16 nor more than 23 members. The court shall direct that a sufficient number of legally qualified persons be summoned to meet this requirement.

(2) Alternate Jurors. The court may direct that alternate jurors may be designated at the time a grand jury is selected. Alternate jurors in the order in which they were designated may thereafter be impanelled as provided in subdivision (g) of this rule. Alternate jurors shall be drawn in the same manner and shall have the same qualifications as the regular jurors, and if impanelled shall be subject to the same challenges, shall take the same oath and shall have the same functions, powers, facilities and privileges as the regular jurors.

(b) Objections to Grand Jury and to Grand Jurors.

(1) Challenges. The attorney for the government or a defendant who has been held to answer in the district court may challenge the array of jurors on the ground that the grand jury was not selected, drawn or summoned in accordance with law, and may challenge an individual juror on the ground that the juror is not legally qualified. Challenges shall be made before the administration of the oath to the jurors and shall be tried by the court.

(2) Motion to Dismiss. A motion to dismiss the indictment may be based on objections to the array or on the lack of legal qualification of an individual juror, if not previously determined upon challenge. It shall be made in the manner prescribed in 28 U.S.C. § 1867(e) and shall be granted under the conditions prescribed in that statute. An indictment shall not be dismissed on the ground that one or more members of the grand jury were not legally qualified if it appears from the record kept pursuant to subdivision (c) of this rule that 12 or more jurors, after deducting the number not legally qualified, concurred in finding the indictment.

(c) Foreperson and Deputy Foreperson. The court shall appoint one of the jurors to be foreperson and another to be deputy foreperson. The foreperson shall have power to administer oaths and affirmations and shall sign all indictments. The foreperson or another juror designated by the foreperson shall keep record of the number of jurors concurring in the finding of every indictment and shall file the record with the clerk of the court, but the record shall not be made public except on order of the court. During the absence of the foreperson, the deputy foreperson shall act as foreperson.

(d) Who May Be Present. Attorneys for the government, the witness under examination, interpreters when needed and, for the purpose of taking the evidence, a stenographer or operator of a recording device may be present while the grand jury is in session, but no person other than the jurors may be present while the grand jury is deliberating or voting.

(e) Recording and Disclosure of Proceedings.

(1) Recording of Proceedings. All proceedings, except when the grand jury is deliberating or voting, shall be recorded stenographically or by an electronic recording device. An unintentional failure of any recording to reproduce all or any portion of a proceeding shall not affect the validity of the prosecution. The recording or reporter's notes or any transcript prepared therefrom shall remain in the custody or control of the attorney for the government unless otherwise ordered by the court in a particular case.

(2) General Rule of Secrecy. A grand juror, an interpreter, a stenographer, an operator of a recording device, a typist who transcribes recorded testimony, an attorney for the government, or any person to whom disclosure is made under paragraph (3)(A)(ii) of this subdivision shall not disclose matters occurring before the grand jury, except as otherwise provided for in these rules. No obligation of secrecy may be imposed on any person except in accordance with this rule. A knowing violation of Rule 6 may be punished as a contempt of court.

(3) Exceptions.

(A) Disclosure otherwise prohibited by this rule of matters occurring before the grand jury, other than its deliberations and the vote of any grand juror, may be made to—

> (i) an attorney for the government for use in the performance of such attorney's duty; and

> (ii) such government personnel (including personnel of a state or subdivision of a state) as are deemed necessary by an attorney for the government to assist an attorney for the government in the performance of such attorney's duty to enforce federal criminal law.

(B) Any person to whom matters are disclosed under subparagraph (A)(ii) of this paragraph shall not utilize that grand jury material for any purpose other than assisting the attorney for the government in the performance of such attorney's duty to enforce federal criminal law. An attorney for the government shall promptly provide the district court, before which was impaneled the grand jury whose material has been so disclosed, with the names of the persons to whom such disclosure has been made, and shall certify that the attorney has advised such persons of their obligation of secrecy under this rule.

(C) Disclosure otherwise prohibited by this rule of matters occurring before the grand jury may also be made—

> (i) when so directed by a court preliminarily to or in connection with a judicial proceeding;

> (ii) when permitted by a court at the request of the defendant, upon a showing that grounds may exist for a motion to dismiss the indictment because of matters occurring before the grand jury;

> (iii) when the disclosure is made by an attorney for the government to another federal grand jury; or

> (iv) when permitted by a court at the request of an attorney for the government, upon a showing that such matters may disclose a violation of state criminal law, to an appropriate official of a state or subdivision of a state for the purpose of enforcing such law.

If the court orders disclosure of matters occurring before the grand jury, the disclosure shall be made in such manner, at such time, and under such conditions as the court may direct.

(D) A petition for disclosure pursuant to subdivision (e)(3)(C)(i) shall be filed in the district where the grand jury convened. Unless the hearing is ex parte, which it may be when the petitioner is the government, the petitioner shall serve written notice of the petition upon (i) the attorney for the government, (ii) the parties to the judicial proceeding if disclosure is sought in connection with such a proceeding, and (iii) such other persons as the court may direct. The court shall afford those persons a reasonable opportunity to appear and be heard.

(E) If the judicial proceeding giving rise to the petition is in a federal district court in another district, the court shall transfer the matter to that court unless it can reasonably obtain sufficient knowledge of the proceeding to determine whether disclosure is proper. The court shall order transmitted to the court to which the matter is transferred the material sought to be disclosed, if feasible, and a written evaluation of the need for continued grand jury secrecy. The court to which the matter is transferred shall afford the aforementioned persons a reasonable opportunity to appear and be heard.

(4) Sealed Indictments. The federal magistrate judge to whom an indictment is returned may direct that the indictment be kept secret until the defendant is in custody or has been released pending trial. Thereupon the clerk shall seal the indictment and no person shall disclose the return of the indictment except when necessary for the issuance and execution of a warrant or summons.

(5) Closed Hearing. Subject to any right to an open hearing in contempt proceedings, the court shall order a hearing on matters affecting a grand jury proceeding to be closed to the extent necessary to prevent disclosure of matters occurring before a grand jury.

(6) Sealed Records. Records, orders and subpoenas relating to grand jury proceedings shall be kept under seal to the extent and for such time as is necessary to prevent disclosure of matters occurring before a grand jury.

(f) Finding and Return of Indictment. An indictment may be found only upon the concurrence of 12 or more jurors. The indictment shall be returned by the grand jury to a federal magistrate judge in open court. If a complaint or information is pending against the defendant and 12 jurors do not concur in finding an indictment, the foreperson shall so report to a federal magistrate judge in writing forthwith.

(g) Discharge and Excuse. A grand jury shall serve until discharged by the court, but no grand jury may serve more than 18 months unless the court extends the service of the grand jury for a period of six months or less upon a determination that such extension is in the public interest. At any time for cause shown the court may excuse a juror either temporarily or permanently, and in the latter event the court may impanel another person in place of the juror excused.

Rule 7. The Indictment and the Information

(a) Use of Indictment or Information. An offense which may be punished by death shall be prosecuted by indictment. An offense which may be punished by imprisonment for a term exceeding one year or at hard labor shall be prosecuted by indictment or, if indictment is waived, it may be prosecuted by information. Any other offense may be prosecuted by indictment or by information. An information may be filed without leave of court.

(b) Waiver of Indictment. An offense which may be punished by imprisonment for a term exceeding one year or at hard labor may be prosecuted by information if the defendant, after having been advised of the nature of the charge and of the rights of the defendant, waives in open court prosecution by indictment.

(c) Nature and Contents.

(1) In General. The indictment or the information shall be a plain, concise and definite written statement of the essential facts constituting the offense charged. It shall be signed by the attorney for the government. It need not contain a formal commencement, a formal conclusion or any other matter not necessary to such statement. Allegations made in one count may be incorporated by reference in another count. It may be alleged in a single count that the means by which the defendant committed the offense are unknown or that the defendant committed it by one or more specified means. The indictment or information shall state for each count the official or customary citation of the statute, rule, regulation or other provision of law which the defendant is alleged therein to have violated.

(2) Criminal Forfeiture. No judgment of forfeiture may be entered in a criminal proceeding unless the indictment or the information shall allege the extent of the interest or property subject to forfeiture.

(3) Harmless Error. Error in the citation or its omission shall not be ground for dismissal of the indictment or information or for reversal of a conviction if the error or omission did not mislead the defendant to the defendant's prejudice.

(d) Surplusage. The court on motion of the defendant may strike surplusage from the indictment or information.

(e) Amendment of Information. The court may permit an information to be amended at any time before verdict or finding if no additional or different offense is charged and if substantial rights of the defendant are not prejudiced.

(f) Bill of Particulars. The court may direct the filing of a bill of particulars. A motion for a bill of particulars may be made before arraignment or within ten days after arraignment or at such later time as the court may permit. A bill of particulars may be amended at any time subject to such conditions as justice requires.

Rule 8.   Joinder of Offenses and of Defendants

(a) Joinder of Offenses. Two or more offenses may be charged in the same indictment or information in a separate count for each offense if the offenses charged, whether felonies or misdemeanors or both, are of the same or similar character or are based on the same act or transaction or on two or more acts or transactions connected together or constituting parts of a common scheme or plan.

(b) Joinder of Defendants. Two or more defendants may be charged in the same indictment or information if they are alleged to have participated in the same act or transaction or in the same series of acts or transactions constituting an offense or offenses. Such defendants may be charged in one or more counts together or separately and all of the defendants need not be charged in each count.

Rule 9. Warrant or Summons Upon Indictment or Information

(a) Issuance. Upon the request of the attorney for the government the court shall issue a warrant for each defendant named in an information supported by a showing of probable cause under oath as is required by Rule 4(a), or in an indictment. Upon the request of the attorney for the government a summons instead of a warrant shall issue. If no request is made, the court may issue either a warrant or a summons in its discretion. More than one warrant or summons may issue for the same defendant. The clerk shall deliver the warrant or summons to the marshal or other person authorized by law to execute or serve it. If a defendant fails to appear in response to the summons, a warrant shall issue. When a defendant arrested with a warrant or given a summons appears initially before a magistrate judge, the magistrate judge shall proceed in accordance with the applicable subdivisions of Rule 5.

(b) Form.

(1) Warrant. The form of the warrant shall be as provided in Rule 4(c)(1) except that it shall be signed by the clerk, it shall describe the offense charged in the indictment or information and it shall command that the defendant be arrested and brought before the nearest available magistrate judge. The amount of bail may be fixed by the court and endorsed on the warrant.

(2) Summons. The summons shall be in the same form as the warrant except that it shall summon the defendant to appear before a magistrate judge at a stated time and place.

(c) Execution or Service; and Return.

(1) Execution or Service. The warrant shall be executed or the summons served as provided in Rule 4(d)(1), (2) and (3). A summons to a corporation shall be served by delivering a copy to an officer or to a managing or general agent or to any other agent authorized by appointment or by law to receive service of process and, if the agent is one authorized by statute to receive service and the statute so requires, by also mailing a copy to the corporation's last known address within the district or at its principal place of business elsewhere in the United States. The officer executing the warrant shall bring the arrested person without unnecessary delay before the nearest available federal magistrate judge or, in the event that a federal magistrate judge is not reasonably available, before a state or local judicial officer authorized by 18 U.S.C. § 3041.

(2) Return. The officer executing a warrant shall make return thereof to the magistrate judge or other officer before whom the defendant is brought. At the request of the attorney for the government any unexecuted warrant shall be returned and cancelled. On or before the return day the person to whom a summons was delivered for service shall make return thereof. At the request of the attorney for the government made at any time while the indictment or information is pending, a warrant returned unexecuted and not cancelled or a summons returned unserved or a duplicate thereof may be delivered by the clerk to the marshal or other authorized person for execution or service.

[(d) Remand to United States Magistrate for Trial of Minor Offenses] (Abrogated Apr. 28, 1982, eff. Aug. 1, 1982).

IV. ARRAIGNMENT AND PREPARATION FOR TRIAL

Rule 10. Arraignment

Arraignment shall be conducted in open court and shall consist of reading the indictment or information to the defendant or stating to the defendant the substance of the charge and calling on the defendant to plead thereto. The defendant shall be given a copy of the indictment or information before being called upon to plead.

Rule 11. Pleas

(a) Alternatives.

(1) In General. A defendant may plead not guilty, guilty, or nolo contendere. If a defendant refuses to plead or if a defendant corporation fails to appear, the court shall enter a plea of not guilty.

(2) Conditional Pleas. With the approval of the court and the consent of the government, a defendant may enter a conditional plea of guilty or nolo contendere, reserving in writing the right, on appeal from the judgment, to review of the adverse determination of any specified pretrial motion. A defendant who prevails on appeal shall be allowed to withdraw the plea.

(b) Nolo Contendere. A defendant may plead nolo contendere only with the consent of the court. Such a plea shall be accepted by the court only after due consideration of the views of the parties and the interest of the public in the effective administration of justice.

(c) Advice to Defendant. Before accepting a plea of guilty or nolo contendere, the court must address the defendant personally in open court and inform the defendant of, and determine that the defendant understands, the following:

(1) the nature of the charge to which the plea is offered, the mandatory minimum penalty provided by law, if any, and the maximum possible penalty provided by law, including the effect of any special parole or supervised release term, the fact that the court is required to consider any applicable sentencing guidelines but many depart from those guidelines under some circumstances, and, when applicable, that the court may also order the defendant to make restitution to any victim of the offense; and

(2) if the defendant is not represented by an attorney, that the defendant has the right to be represented by an attorney at every stage of the proceeding and, if necessary, one will be appointed to represent the defendant; and

(3) that the defendant has the right to plead not guilty or to persist in that plea if it has already been made, the right to be tried by a jury and at that trial the right to the assistance of counsel, the right to confront and cross-examine adverse witnesses, and the right against compelled self-incrimination; and

(4) that if a plea of guilty or nolo contendere is accepted by the court there will not be a further trial of any kind, so that by pleading guilty or nolo contendere the defendant waives the right to a trial; and

(5) if the court intends to question the defendant under oath, on the record, and in the presence of counsel about the offense to which the defendant has pleaded, that the defendant's answers may later be used against the defendant in a prosecution for perjury or false statement.

(d) Insuring That the Plea is Voluntary. The court shall not accept a plea of guilty or nolo contendere without first, by addressing the defendant personally in open court, determining that the plea is voluntary and not the result of force or threats or of promises apart from a plea agreement. The court shall also inquire as to whether the defendant's willingness to plead guilty or nolo contendere results from prior discussions between the attorney for the government and the defendant or the defendant's attorney.

(e) Plea Agreement Procedure.

(1) In General. The attorney for the government and the attorney for the defendant or the defendant when acting pro se may engage in discussions with a view toward reaching an agreement that, upon the entering of a plea of guilty or nolo contendere to a charged offense or to a lesser or related offense, the attorney for the government will do any of the following:

(A) move for dismissal of other charges; or

(B) make a recommendation, or agree not to oppose the defendant's request, for a particular sentence, with the understanding that such recommendation or request shall not be binding upon the court; or

(C) agree that a specific sentence is the appropriate disposition of the case.

The court shall not participate in any such discussions.

(2) Notice of Such Agreement. If a plea agreement has been reached by the parties, the court shall, on the record, require the disclosure of the agreement in open court or, on a showing of good cause, in camera, at the time the plea is offered. If the agreement is of the type specified in subdivision (e)(1)(A) or (C), the court may accept or reject the agreement, or may defer its decision as to the acceptance or rejection until there has been an opportunity to consider the presentence report. If the agreement is of the type specified in subdivision (e)(1)(B), the court shall advise the defendant that if the court does not accept the recommendation or request the defendant nevertheless has no right to withdraw the plea.

(3) Acceptance of a Plea Agreement. If the court accepts the plea agreement, the court shall inform the defendant that it will embody in the judgment and sentence the disposition provided for in the plea agreement.

(4) Rejection of a Plea Agreement. If the court rejects the plea agreement, the court shall, on the record, inform the parties of this fact, advise the defendant personally in open court or, on a showing of good cause, in camera, that the court is not bound by the plea agreement, afford the defendant the opportunity to then withdraw the plea, and advise the defendant that if the defendant persists in a guilty plea or plea of nolo contendere the disposition of the case may be less favorable to the defendant than that contemplated by the plea agreement.

(5) Time of Plea Agreement Procedure. Except for good cause shown, notification to the court of the existence of a plea agreement shall be given at the arraignment or at such other time, prior to trial, as may be fixed by the court.

(6) Inadmissibility of Pleas, Plea Discussions, and Related Statements. Except as otherwise provided in this paragraph, evidence of the following is not, in any civil or criminal proceeding, admissible against the defendant who made the plea or was a participant in the plea discussions:

(A) a plea of guilty which was later withdrawn;

(B) a plea of nolo contendere;

(C) any statement made in the course of any proceedings under this rule regarding either of the foregoing pleas; or

(D) any statement made in the course of plea discussions with an attorney for the government which do not result in a plea of guilty or which result in a plea of guilty later withdrawn.

However, such a statement is admissible (i) in any proceeding wherein another statement made in the course of the same plea or plea discussions has been introduced and the statement ought in fairness be considered contemporaneously with it, or (ii) in a criminal proceeding for perjury or false statement if the statement was made by the defendant under oath, on the record, and in the presence of counsel.

(f) Determining Accuracy of Plea. Notwithstanding the acceptance of a plea of guilty, the court should not enter a judgment upon such plea without making such inquiry as shall satisfy it that there is a factual basis for the plea.

(1) By Whom. The warrant shall be executed by a marshal or by some other officer authorized by law. The summons may be served by any person authorized to serve a summons in a civil action.

(g) Record of Proceedings. A verbatim record of the proceedings at which the defendant enters a plea shall be made and, if there is a plea of guilty or nolo contendere, the record shall include, without limitation, the court's advice to the defendant, the inquiry into the voluntariness of the plea including any plea agreement, and the inquiry into the accuracy of a guilty plea.

(h) Harmless Error. Any variance from the procedures required by this rule which does not affect substantial rights shall be disregarded.

Rule 12. Pleadings and Motions Before Trial; Defenses and Objections

(a) Pleadings and Motions. Pleadings in criminal proceedings shall be the indictment and the information, and the pleas of not guilty, guilty and nolo contendere.   All other pleas, and demurrers and motions to quash are abolished, and defenses and objections raised before trial which heretofore could have been raised by one or more of them shall be raised only by motion to dismiss or to grant appropriate relief, as provided in these rules.

(b) Pretrial Motions.   Any defense, objection, or request which is capable of determination without the trial of the general issue may be raised before trial by motion.   Motions may be written or oral at the discretion of the judge.   The following must be raised prior to trial:

(1) Defenses and objections based on defects in the institution of the prosecution; or

(2) Defenses and objections based on defects in the indictment or information (other than that it fails to show jurisdiction in the court or to charge an offense which objections shall be noticed by the court at any time during the pendency of the proceedings); or

(3) Motions to suppress evidence; or

(4) Requests for discovery under Rule 16; or

(5) Requests for a severance of charges or defendants under Rule 14.

(c) Motion Date.   Unless otherwise provided by local rule, the court may, at the time of the arraignment or as soon thereafter as practicable, set a time for the making of pretrial motions or requests and, if required, a later date of hearing.

(d) Notice by the Government of the Intention to Use Evidence.

(1) At the Discretion of the Government.   At the arraignment or as soon thereafter as is practicable, the government may give notice to the defendant of its intention to use specified evidence at trial in order to afford the defendant an opportunity to raise objections to such evidence prior to trial under subdivision (b)(3) of this rule.

(2) At the Request of the Defendant.   At the arraignment or as soon thereafter as is practicable the defendant may, in order to afford an opportunity to move to suppress evidence under subdivision (b)(3) of this rule, request notice of the government's intention to use (in its evidence in chief at trial) any evidence which the defendant may be entitled to discover under Rule 16 subject to any relevant limitations prescribed in Rule 16.

(e) Ruling on Motion.   A motion made before trial shall be determined before trial unless the court, for good cause, orders that it be deferred for determination at the trial of the general issue or until after verdict, but no such determination shall be deferred if a party's right to appeal is adversely affected.   Where factual issues are involved in determining a motion, the court shall state its essential findings on the record.

(f) Effect of Failure To Raise Defenses or Objections.   Failure by a party to raise defenses or objections or to make requests which must be made prior to trial, at the time set by the court pursuant to subdivision (c), or prior to any extension thereof made by the court, shall constitute waiver thereof, but the court for cause shown may grant relief from the waiver.

(g) Records. A verbatim record shall be made of all proceedings at the hearing, including such findings of fact and conclusions of law as are made orally.

(h) Effect of Determination. If the court grants a motion based on a defect in the institution of the prosecution or in the indictment or information, it may also order that the defendant be continued in custody or that bail be continued for a specified time pending the filing of a new indictment or information. Nothing in this rule shall be deemed to affect the provisions of any Act of Congress relating to periods of limitations.

(i) Production of Statements at Suppression Hearing. Rule 26.2 applies at a hearing on a motion to suppress evidence under subdivision (b)(3) of this rule. For purposes of this subdivision, a law enforcement officer is deemed a government witness.

Rule 12.1. Notice of Alibi

(a) Notice by Defendant. Upon written demand of the attorney for the government stating the time, date, and place at which the alleged offense was committed, the defendant shall serve within ten days, or at such different time as the court may direct, upon the attorney for the government a written notice of the defendant's intention to offer a defense of alibi. Such notice by the defendant shall state the specific place or places at which the defendant claims to have been at the time of the alleged offense and the names and addresses of the witnesses upon whom the defendant intends to rely to establish such alibi.

(b) Disclosure of Information and Witness. Within ten days thereafter, but in no event less than ten days before trial, unless the court otherwise directs, the attorney for the government shall serve upon the defendant or the defendant's attorney a written notice stating the names and addresses of the witnesses upon whom the government intends to rely to establish the defendant's presence at the scene of the alleged offense and any other witnesses to be relied on to rebut testimony of any of the defendant's alibi witnesses.

(c) Continuing Duty to Disclose. If prior to or during trial, a party learns of an additional witness whose identity, if known, should have been included in the information furnished under subdivision (a) or (b), the party shall promptly notify the other party or the other party's attorney of the existence and identity of such additional witness.

(d) Failure to Comply. Upon the failure of either party to comply with the requirements of this rule, the court may exclude the testimony of any undisclosed witness offered by such party as to the defendant's absence from or presence at, the scene of the alleged offense. This rule shall not limit the right of the defendant to testify.

(e) Exceptions. For good cause shown, the court may grant an exception to any of the requirements of subdivisions (a) through (d) of this rule.

(f) Inadmissibility of Withdrawn Alibi. Evidence of an intention to rely upon an alibi defense, later withdrawn, or of statements made in connection with such intention, is not, in any civil or criminal proceeding, admissible against the person who gave notice of the intention.

Rule 12.2. Notice of Insanity Defense or Expert Testimony of Defendant's Mental Condition

(a) Defense of Insanity. If a defendant intends to rely upon the defense of insanity at the time of the alleged offense, the defendant shall, within the time provided for the filing of pretrial motions or at such later time as the court may direct, notify the attorney for the government in writing of such intention and file a copy of such notice with the clerk. If there is a failure to comply with the requirements of this subdivision, insanity may not be raised as a defense. The court may for cause shown allow late filing of the notice or grant additional time to the parties to prepare for trial or make such other order as may be appropriate.

(b) Expert Testimony of Defendant's Mental Condition. If a defendant intends to introduce expert testimony relating to a mental disease or defect or any other mental condition of the defendant bearing upon the issue of guilt, the defendant shall, within the time provided for the filing of pretrial motions or at such later time as the court may direct, notify the attorney for the government in writing of such intention and file a copy of such notice with the clerk. The court may for cause shown allow late filing of the notice or grant additional time to the parties to prepare for trial or make such other order as may be appropriate.

(c) Mental Examination of Defendant. In an appropriate case the court may, upon motion of the attorney for the government, order the defendant to submit to an examination pursuant to 18 U.S.C. 4241 or 4242. No statement made by the defendant in the course of any examination provided for by this rule, whether the examination be with or without the consent of the defendant, no testimony by the expert based upon such statement, and no other fruits of the statement shall be admitted in evidence against the defendant in any criminal proceeding except on an issue respecting mental condition on which the defendant has introduced testimony.

(d) Failure To Comply. If there is a failure to give notice when required by subdivision (b) of this rule or to submit to an examination when ordered under subdivision (c) of this rule, the court may exclude the testimony of any expert witness offered by the defendant on the issue of the defendant's guilt.

(e) Inadmissibility of Withdrawn Intention. Evidence of an intention as to which notice was given under subdivision (a) or (b), later withdrawn, is not, in any civil or criminal proceeding, admissible against the person who gave notice of the intention.

Rule 12.3. Notice of Defense Based Upon Public Authority

(a) Notice by Defendant; Government Response; Disclosure of Witnesses.

    (1) Defendant's Notice and Government's Response. A defendant intending to claim a defense of actual or believed exercise of public authority on behalf of a law enforcement or Federal intelligence agency at the time of the alleged offense shall, within the time provided for the filing of pretrial motions or at such later time as the court may direct, serve upon the attorney for the Government a written notice of such intention and file a copy of such notice with the clerk. Such notice shall identify the law enforcement or Federal intelligence agency and any member of such agency on behalf of which and the period of time in which the defendant claims the actual or believed exercise of public authority occurred. If the notice identifies a Federal intelligence agency, the copy filed with the clerk shall be under seal. Within ten days after receiving the defendant's notice, but in no event less than twenty days before the trial, the attorney for the Government shall serve upon the defendant or the defendant's attorney a written response which shall admit or deny that the defendant exercised the public authority identified in the defendant's notice.

(2) **Disclosure of Witnesses.** At the time that the Government serves its response to the notice or thereafter, but in no event less than twenty days before the trial, the attorney for the Government may serve upon the defendant or the defendant's attorney a written demand for the names and addresses of the witnesses, if any, upon whom the defendant intends to rely in establishing the defense identified in the notice. Within seven days after receiving the Government's demand, the defendant shall serve upon the attorney for the Government a written statement of the names and addresses of any such witnesses. Within seven days after receiving the defendant's written statement, the attorney for the Government shall serve upon the defendant or the defendant's attorney a written statement of the names and addresses of the witnesses, if any, upon whom the Government intends to rely in opposing the defense identified in the notice.

(3) **Additional Time.** If good cause is shown, the court may allow a party additional time to comply with any obligation imposed by this rule.

(b) **Continuing Duty to Disclose.** If, prior to or during trial, a party learns of any additional witness whose identity, if known, should have been included in the written statement furnished under subdivision (a)(2) of this rule, that party shall promptly notify in writing the other party or the other party's attorney of the name and address of any such witness.

(c) **Failure to Comply.** If a party fails to comply with the requirements of this rule, the court may exclude the testimony of any undisclosed witness offered in support of or in opposition to the defense, or enter such other order as it deems just under the circumstances. This rule shall not limit the right of the defendant to testify.

(d) **Protective Procedures Unaffected.** This rule shall be in addition to and shall not supersede the authority of the court to issue appropriate protective orders, or the authority of the court to order that any pleading be filed under seal.

(e) **Inadmissibility of Withdrawn Defense Based Upon Public Authority.** Evidence of an intention as to which notice was given under subdivision (a), later withdrawn, is not, in any civil or criminal proceeding, admissible against the person who gave notice of the intention.

Rule 13. Trial Together of Indictments or Informations

The court may order two or more indictments or informations or both to be tried together if the offenses, and the defendants if there is more than one, could have been joined in a single indictment or information. The procedure shall be the same as if the prosecution were under such single indictment or information.

Rule 14. Relief from Prejudicial Joinder

If it appears that a defendant or the government is prejudiced by a joinder of offenses or of defendants in an indictment or information or by such joinder for trial together, the court may order an election or separate trials of counts, grant a severance of defendants or provide whatever other relief justice requires. In ruling on a motion by a defendant for severance the court may order the attorney for the government to deliver to the court for inspection *in camera* any statements or confessions made by the defendants which the government intends to introduce in evidence at the trial.

Rule 15. Depositions

(a) When Taken. Whenever due to exceptional circumstances of the case it is in the interest of justice that the testimony of a prospective witness of a party be taken and preserved for use at trial, the court may upon motion of such party and notice to the parties order that testimony of such witness be taken by deposition and that any designated book, paper, document, record, recording, or other material not privileged, be produced at the same time and place. If a witness is detained pursuant to section 3144 of title 18, United States Code, the court on written motion of the witness and upon notice to the parties may direct that the witness' deposition be taken. After the deposition has been subscribed the court may discharge the witness.

(b) Notice of Taking. The party at whose instance a deposition is to be taken shall give to every party reasonable written notice of the time and place for taking the deposition. The notice shall state the name and address of each person to be examined. On motion of a party upon whom the notice is served, the court for cause shown may extend or shorten the time or change the place for taking the deposition. The officer having custody of a defendant shall be notified of the time and place set for the examination and shall, unless the defendant waives in writing the right to be present, produce the defendant at the examination and keep the defendant in the presence of the witness during the examination, unless, after being warned by the court that disruptive conduct will cause the defendant's removal from the place of the taking of the deposition, the defendant persists in conduct which is such as to justify exclusion from that place. A defendant not in custody shall have the right to be present at the examination upon request subject to such terms as may be fixed by the court, but a failure, absent good cause shown, to appear after notice and tender of expenses in accordance with subdivision (c) of this rule shall constitute a waiver of that right and of any objection to the taking and use of the deposition based upon that right.

(c) Payment of Expenses. Whenever a deposition is taken at the instance of the government, or whenever a deposition is taken at the instance of a defendant who is unable to bear the expenses of the taking of the deposition, the court may direct that the expense of travel and subsistence of the defendant and the defendant's attorney for attendance at the examination and the cost of the transcript of the deposition shall be paid by the government.

(d) How Taken. Subject to such additional conditions as the court shall provide, a deposition shall be taken and filed in the manner provided in civil actions except as otherwise provided in these rules, provided that (1) in no event shall a deposition be taken of a party defendant without that defendant's consent, and (2) the scope and manner of examination and cross-examination shall be such as would be allowed in the trial itself. The government shall make available to the defendant or the defendant's counsel for examination and use at the taking of the deposition any statement of the witness being deposed which is in the possession of the government and to which the defendant would be entitled at the trial.

(e) Use. At the trial or upon any hearing, a part or all of a deposition, so far as otherwise admissible under the rules of evidence, may be used as substantive evidence if the witness is unavailable, as unavailability is defined in Rule 804(a) of the Federal Rules of Evidence, or the witness gives testimony at the trial or hearing inconsistent with that witness' deposition. Any deposition may also be used by any party for the purpose of contradicting or impeaching the testimony of the deponent as a witness. If only a part of a deposition is offered in evidence by a party, an adverse party may require the offering of all of it which is relevant to the part offered and any party may offer other parts.

(f) Objections to Deposition Testimony. Objections to deposition testimony or evidence or parts thereof and the grounds for the objection shall be stated at the time of the taking of the deposition.

(g) Deposition by Agreement Not Precluded. Nothing in this rule shall preclude the taking of a deposition, orally or upon written questions, or the use of a deposition, by agreement of the parties with the consent of the court.

Rule 16. Discovery and Inspection

(a) Governmental Disclosure of Evidence.

(1) Information Subject to Disclosure.

(A) Statement of Defendant. Upon request of a defendant the government must disclose to the defendant and make available for inspection, copying, or photographing: any relevant written or recorded statements made by the defendant, or copies thereof, within the possession, custody, or control of the government, the existence of which is known, or by the exercise of due diligence may become known, to the attorney for the government; that portion of any written record containing the substance of any relevant oral statement made by the defendant whether before or after arrest in response to interrogation by any person then known to the defendant to be a government agent; and recorded testimony of the defendant before a grand jury which relates to the offense charged. The government must also disclose to the defendant the substance of any other relevant oral statement made by the defendant whether before or after arrest in response to interrogation by any person then known by the defendant to be a government agent if the government intends to use that statement at trial. Upon request of a defendant which is an organization such as a corporation, partnership, association or labor union, the government must disclose to the defendant any of the foregoing statements made by a person who the government contends (1) was, at the time of making the statement, so situated as a director, officer, employee, or agent as to have been able legally to bind the defendant in respect to the subject of the statement, or (2) was, at the time of the offense, personally involved in the alleged conduct constituting the offense and so situated as a director, officer, employee, or agent as to have been able legally to bind the defendant in respect to that alleged conduct in which the person was involved.

(B) Defendant's Prior Record. Upon request of the defendant, the government shall furnish to the defendant such copy of the defendant's prior criminal record, if any, as is within the possession, custody, or control of the government, the existence of which is known, or by the exercise of due diligence may become known, to the attorney for the government.

(C) Documents and Tangible Objects. Upon request of the defendant the government shall permit the defendant to inspect and copy or photograph books, papers, documents, photographs, tangible objects, buildings or places, or copies or portions thereof, which are within the possession, custody or control of the government, and which are material to the preparation of the defendant's defense or are intended for use by the government as evidence in chief at the trial, or were obtained from or belong to the defendant.

(D) Reports of Examinations and Tests. Upon request of a defendant the government shall permit the defendant to inspect and copy or photograph any results or reports of physical or mental examinations, and of scientific tests or experiments, or copies thereof, which are within the possession, custody, or control of the government, the existence of which is known, or by the exercise of due diligence may become known, to the attorney for the government, and which are material to the preparation of the defense or are intended for use by the government as evidence in chief at the trial.

(E) Expert Witnesses. At the defendant's request, the government shall disclose to the defendant a written summary of testimony that the government intends to use under Rules 702, 703, or 705 of the Federal Rules of Evidence during its case-in-chief at trial. If the government requests discovery under subdivision (b)(1)(C)(ii) of this rule and the defendant complies, the government shall, at the defendant's request, disclose to the defendant a written summary of testimony the government intends to use under Rules 702, 703, or 705 as evidence at trial on the issue of the defendant's mental condition. The summary provided under this subdivision shall describe the witnesses' opinions, the bases and the reasons for those opinions, and the witnesses' qualifications.

(2) Information Not Subject to Disclosure. Except as provided in paragraphs (A), (B), (D), and (E) of subdivision (a)(1), this rule does not authorize the discovery or inspection of reports, memoranda, or other internal government documents made by the attorney for the government or any other government agent investigating or prosecuting the case. Nor does the rule authorize the discovery or inspection of statements made by government witnesses or prospective government witnesses except as provided in 18 U.S.C. § 3500.

(3) Grand Jury Transcripts. Except as provided in Rules 6, 12(i) and 26.2, and subdivision (a)(1)(A) of this rule, these rules do not relate to discovery or inspection of recorded proceedings of a grand jury.

[(4) Failure to Call Witness.] (Deleted Dec. 12, 1975)

(b) The Defendant's Disclosure of Evidence.

(1) Information Subject to Disclosure.

(A) Documents and Tangible Objects. If the defendant requests disclosure under subdivision (a)(1)(C) or (D) of this rule, upon compliance with such request by the government, the defendant, on request of the government, shall permit the government to inspect and copy or photograph books, papers, documents, photographs, tangible objects, or copies or portions thereof, which are within the possession, custody, or control of the defendant and which the defendant intends to introduce as evidence in chief at the trial.

(B) Reports of Examinations and Tests. If the defendant requests disclosure under subdivision (a)(1)(C) or (D) of this rule, upon compliance with such request by the government, the defendant, on request of the government, shall permit the government to inspect and copy or photograph any results or reports of physical or mental examinations and of scientific tests or experiments made in connection with the particular case, or copies thereof, within the possession or control of the defendant, which the defendant intends to introduce as evidence in chief at the trial or which were prepared by a witness whom the defendant intends to call at the trial when the results or reports relate to that witness' testimony.

(C) Expert Witnesses. Under the following circumstances, the defendant shall, at the government's request, disclose to the government a written summary of testimony that the defendant intends to use under Rules 702, 703, or 705 of the Federal Rules of Evidence as evidence at trial: (i) if the defendant requests disclosure under subdivision (a)(1)(E) of this rule and the government complies, or (ii) if the defendant has given notice under Rule 12.2(b) of an intent to present expert testimony on the defendant's mental condition. This summary shall describe the witnesses' opinions, the bases and reasons for those opinions, and the witnesses' qualifications.

(2) Information Not Subject To Disclosure. Except as to scientific or medical reports, this subdivision does not authorize the discovery or inspection of reports, memoranda, or other internal defense documents made by the defendant, or the defendant's attorneys or agents in connection with the investigation or defense of the case, or of statements made by the defendant, or by government or defense witnesses, or by prospective government or defense witnesses, to the defendant, the defendant's agents or attorneys.

[**(3) Failure to Call Witness.**]   (Deleted Dec. 12, 1975)

(c) Continuing Duty to Disclose. If, prior to or during trial, a party discovers additional evidence or material previously requested or ordered, which is subject to discovery or inspection under this rule, such party shall promptly notify the other party or that other party's attorney or the court of the existence of the additional evidence or material.

(d) Regulation of Discovery.

(1) Protective and Modifying Orders. Upon a sufficient showing the court may at any time order that the discovery or inspection be denied, restricted, or deferred, or make such other order as is appropriate. Upon motion by a party, the court may permit the party to make such showing, in whole or in part, in the form of a written statement to be inspected by the judge alone. If the court enters an order granting relief following such an ex parte showing, the entire text of the party's statement shall be sealed and preserved in the records of the court to be made available to the appellate court in the event of an appeal.

(2) Failure To Comply With a Request. If at any time during the course of the proceedings it is brought to the attention of the court that a party has failed to comply with this rule, the court may order such party to permit the discovery or inspection, grant a continuance, or prohibit the party from introducing evidence not disclosed, or it may enter such other order as it deems just under the circumstances. The court may specify the time, place and manner of making the discovery and inspection and may prescribe such terms and conditions as are just.

(e) Alibi Witnesses. Discovery of alibi witnesses is governed by Rule 12.1.

Rule 17. Subpoena

(a) For Attendance of Witnesses; Form; Issuance. A subpoena shall be issued by the clerk under the seal of the court. It shall state the name of the court and the title, if any, of the proceeding, and shall command each person to whom it is directed to attend and give testimony at the time and place specified therein. The clerk shall issue a subpoena, signed and sealed but otherwise in blank to a party requesting it, who shall fill in the blanks before it is served. A subpoena shall be issued by a United States magistrate judge in a proceeding before that magistrate judge, but it need not be under the seal of the court.

(b) Defendants Unable to Pay. The court shall order at any time that a subpoena be issued for service on a named witness upon an *ex parte* application of a defendant upon a satisfactory showing that the defendant is financially unable to pay the fees of the witness and that the presence of the witness is necessary to an adequate defense. If the court orders the subpoena to be issued the costs incurred by the process and the fees of the witness so subpoenaed shall be paid in the same manner in which similar costs and fees are paid in case of a witness subpoenaed in behalf of the government.

(c) For Production of Documentary Evidence and of Objects. A subpoena may also command the person to whom it is directed to produce the books, papers, documents or other objects designated therein. The court on motion made promptly may quash or modify the subpoena if compliance would be unreasonable or oppressive. The court may direct that books, papers, documents or objects designated in the subpoena be produced before the court at a time prior to the trial or prior to the time when they are to be offered in evidence and may upon their production permit the books, papers, documents or objects or portions thereof to be inspected by the parties and their attorneys.

(d) Service. A subpoena may be served by the marshal, by a deputy marshal or by any other person who is not a party and who is not less than 18 years of age. Service of a subpoena shall be made by delivering a copy thereof to the person named and by tendering to that person the fee for 1 day's attendance and the mileage allowed by law. Fees and mileage need not be tendered to the witness upon service of a subpoena issued in behalf of the United States or an officer or agency thereof.

(e) Place of Service.

(1) In United States. A subpoena requiring the attendance of a witness at a hearing or trial may be served at any place within the United States.

(2) Abroad. A subpoena directed to a witness in a foreign country shall issue under the circumstances and in the manner and be served as provided in Title 28, U.S.C., § 1783.

(f) For Taking Deposition; Place of Examination.

(1) Issuance. An order to take a deposition authorizes the issuance by the clerk of the court for the district in which the deposition is to be taken of subpoenas for the persons named or described therein.

(2) Place. The witness whose deposition is to be taken may be required by subpoena to attend at any place designated by the trial court, taking into account the convenience of the witness and the parties.

(g) Contempt. Failure by any person without adequate excuse to obey a subpoena served upon that person may be deemed a contempt of the court from which the subpoena issued or of the court for the district in which it issued if it was issued by a United States magistrate judge.

(h) Information Not Subject to Subpoena. Statements made by witnesses or prospective witnesses may not be subpoenaed from the government or the defendant under this rule, but shall be subject to production only in accordance with the provisions of Rule 26.2.

Rule 17.1. Pretrial Conference

At any time after the filing of the indictment or information the court upon motion of any party or upon its own motion may order one or more conferences to consider such matters as will promote a fair and expeditious trial. At the conclusion of a conference the court shall prepare and file a memorandum of the matters agreed upon. No admissions made by the defendant or the defendant's attorney at the conference shall be used against the defendant unless the admissions are reduced to writing and signed by the defendant and the defendant's attorney. This rule shall not be invoked in the case of a defendant who is not represented by counsel.

V. VENUE

Rule 18. Place of Prosecution and Trial

Except as otherwise permitted by statute or by these rules, the prosecution shall be had in a district in which the offense was committed. The court shall fix the place of trial within the district with due regard to the convenience of the defendant and the witnesses and the prompt administration of justice.

Rule 19. Rescinded Feb. 28, 1966, eff. July 1, 1966

Rule 20. Transfer From the District for Plea and Sentence

(a) Indictment or Information Pending. A defendant arrested, held, or present in a district other than that in which an indictment or information is pending against that defendant may state in writing a wish to plead guilty or nolo contendere, to waive trial in the district in which the indictment or information is pending, and to consent to disposition of the case in the district in which that defendant was arrested, held, or present, subject to the approval of the United States attorney for each district. Upon receipt of the defendant's statement and of the written approval of the United States attorneys, the clerk of the court in which the indictment or information is pending shall transmit the papers in the proceeding or certified copies thereof to the clerk of the court for the district in which the defendant is arrested, held, or present, and the prosecution shall continue in that district.

(b) Indictment or Information Not Pending. A defendant arrested, held, or present, in a district other than the district in which a complaint is pending against that defendant may state in writing a wish to plead guilty or nolo contendere, to waive venue and trial in the district in which the warrant was issued, and to consent to disposition of the case in the district in which that defendant was arrested, held, or present, subject to the approval of the United States attorney for each district. Upon filing the written waiver of venue in the district in which the defendant is present, the prosecution may proceed as if venue were in such district.

(c) Effect of Not Guilty Plea. If after the proceeding has been transferred pursuant to subdivision (a) or (b) of this rule the defendant pleads not guilty, the clerk shall return the papers to the court in which the prosecution was commenced, and the proceeding shall be restored to the docket of that court. The defendant's statement that the defendant wishes to plead guilty or nolo contendere shall not be used against that defendant.

(d) Juveniles. A juvenile (as defined in 18 U.S.C. § 5031) who is arrested, held, or present in a district other than that in which the juvenile is alleged to have committed an act in violation of a law of the United States not punishable by death or life imprisonment may, after having been advised by counsel and with the approval of the court and the United States attorney for each district, consent to be proceeded against as a juvenile delinquent in the district in which the juvenile is arrested, held, or present. The consent shall be given in writing before the court but only after the court has apprised the juvenile of the juvenile's rights, including the right to be returned to the district in which the juvenile is alleged to have committed the act, and of the consequences of such consent.

Rule 21. Transfer From the District for Trial

(a) For Prejudice in the District. The court upon motion of the defendant shall transfer the proceeding as to that defendant to another district whether or not such district is specified in the defendant's motion if the court is satisfied that there exists in the district where the prosecution is pending so great a prejudice against the defendant that the defendant cannot obtain a fair and impartial trial at any place fixed by law for holding court in that district.

(b) Transfer in Other Cases. For the convenience of parties and witnesses, and in the interest of justice, the court upon motion of the defendant may transfer the proceeding as to that defendant or any one or more of the counts thereof to another district.

(c) Proceedings on Transfer. When a transfer is ordered the clerk shall transmit to the clerk of the court to which the proceeding is transferred all papers in the proceeding or duplicates thereof and any bail taken, and the prosecution shall continue in that district.

Rule 22. Time of Motion to Transfer

A motion to transfer under these rules may be made at or before arraignment or at such other time as the court or these rules may prescribe.

VI. TRIAL

Rule 23. Trial by Jury or by the Court

(a) Trial by Jury. Cases required to be tried by jury shall be so tried unless the defendant waives a jury trial in writing with the approval of the court and the consent of the government.

(b) Jury of Less Than Twelve. Juries shall be of 12 but at any time before verdict the parties may stipulate in writing with the approval of the court that the jury shall consist of any number less than 12 or that a valid verdict may be returned by a jury of less than 12 should the court find it necessary to excuse one or more jurors for any just cause after trial commences. Even absent such stipulation, if the court finds it necessary to excuse a juror for just cause after the jury has retired to consider its verdict, in the discretion of the court a valid verdict may be returned by the remaining 11 jurors.

(c) Trial Without a Jury. In a case tried without a jury the court shall make a general finding and shall in addition, on request made before the general finding, find the facts specially. Such findings may be oral. If an opinion or memorandum of decision is filed, it will be sufficient if the findings of fact appear therein.

Rule 24. Trial Jurors

(a) Examination. The court may permit the defendant or the defendant's attorney and the attorney for the government to conduct the examination of prospective jurors or may itself conduct the examination. In the latter event the court shall permit the defendant or the defendant's attorney and the attorney for the government to supplement the examination by such further inquiry as it deems proper or shall itself submit to the prospective jurors such additional questions by the parties or their attorneys as it deems proper.

(b) Peremptory Challenges. If the offense charged is punishable by death, each side is entitled to 20 peremptory challenges. If the offense charged is punishable by imprisonment for more than one year, the government is entitled to 6 peremptory challenges and the defendant or defendants jointly to 10 peremptory challenges. If the offense charged is punishable by imprisonment for not more than one year or by fine or both, each side is entitled to 3 peremptory challenges. If there is more than one defendant, the court may allow the defendants additional peremptory challenges and permit them to be exercised separately or jointly.

(c) Alternate Jurors. The court may direct that not more than 6 jurors in addition to the regular jury be called and impanelled to sit as alternate jurors. Alternate jurors in the order in which they are called shall replace jurors who, prior to the time the jury retires to consider its verdict, become or are found to be unable or disqualified to perform their duties. Alternate jurors shall be drawn in the same manner, shall have the same qualifications, shall be subject to the same examination and challenges, shall take the same oath and shall have the same functions, powers, facilities and privileges as the regular jurors. An alternate juror who does not replace a regular juror shall be discharged after the jury retires to consider its verdict. Each side is entitled to 1 peremptory challenge in addition to those otherwise allowed by law if 1 or 2 alternate jurors are to be impanelled, 2 peremptory challenges if 3 or 4 alternate jurors are to be impanelled, and 3 peremptory challenges if 5 or 6 alternate jurors are to be impanelled. The additional peremptory challenges may be used against an alternate juror only, and the other peremptory challenges allowed by these rules may not be used against an alternate juror.

Rule 25. Judge; Disability

(a) During Trial. If by reason of death, sickness or other disability the judge before whom a jury trial has commenced is unable to proceed with the trial, any other judge regularly sitting in or assigned to the court, upon certifying familiarity with the record of the trial, may proceed with and finish the trial.

(b) After Verdict or Finding of Guilt. If by reason of absence, death, sickness or other disability the judge before whom the defendant has been tried is unable to perform the duties to be performed by the court after a verdict or finding of guilt, any other judge regularly sitting in or assigned to the court may perform those duties; but if that judge is satisfied that a judge who did not preside at the trial cannot perform those duties or that it is appropriate for any other reason, that judge may grant a new trial.

Rule 26. Taking of Testimony

In all trials the testimony of witnesses shall be taken orally in open court, unless otherwise provided by an Act of Congress or by these rules, the Federal Rules of Evidence, or other rules adopted by the Supreme Court.

Rule 26.1. Determination of Foreign Law

A party who intends to raise an issue concerning the law of a foreign country shall give reasonable written notice. The court, in determining foreign law, may consider any relevant material or source, including testimony, whether or not submitted by a party or admissible under the Federal Rules of Evidence. The court's determination shall be treated as a ruling on a question of law.

Rule 26.2. Production of Witness Statements

(a) Motion for Production. After a witness other than the defendant has testified on direct examination, the court, on motion of a party who did not call the witness, shall order the attorney for the government or the defendant and the defendant's attorney, as the case may be, to produce, for the examination and use of the moving party, any statement of the witness that is in their possession and that relates to the subject matter concerning which the witness has testified.

(b) Production of Entire Statement. If the entire contents of the statement relate to the subject matter concerning which the witness has testified, the court shall order that the statement be delivered to the moving party.

(c) Production of Excised Statement. If the other party claims that the statement contains privileged information or matter that does not relate to the subject matter concerning which the witness has testified, the court shall order that it be delivered to the court in camera. Upon inspection, the court shall excise the portions of the statement that are privileged or that do not relate to the subject matter concerning which the witness has testified, and shall order that the statement, with such material excised, be delivered to the moving party. Any portion of the statement that is withheld from the defendant over the defendant's objection must be preserved by the attorney for the government, and, if the defendant appeals a conviction, shall be made available to the appellate court for the purpose of determining the correctness of the decision to excise the portion of the statement.

(d) Recess for Examination of Statement. Upon delivery of the statement to the moving party, the court, upon application of that party, may recess the proceedings so that counsel may examine the statement and prepare to use it in the proceedings.

(e) Sanction for Failure to Produce Statement. If the other party elects not to comply with an order to deliver a statement to the moving party, the court shall order that the testimony of the witness be stricken from the record and that the trial proceed, or, if it is the attorney for the government who elects not to comply, shall declare a mistrial if required by the interest of justice.

(f) Definition. As used in this rule, a "statement" of a witness means:

(1) a written statement made by the witness that is signed or otherwise adopted or approved by the witness;

(2) a substantially verbatim recital of an oral statement made by the witness that is recorded contemporaneously with the making of the oral statement and that is contained in a stenographic, mechanical, electrical, or other recording or a transcription thereof; or

(3) a statement, however taken or recorded, or a transcription thereof, made by the witness to a grand jury.

(g) Scope of Rule. This rule applies at a suppression hearing conducted under Rule 12, at trial under this rule, and to the extent specified:

(1) in Rule 32(f) at sentencing;

(2) in Rule 32.1(c) at a hearing to revoke or modify probation or supervised release;

(3) in Rule 46(i) at a detention hearing; and

(4) in Rule 8 of the Rules Governing Proceedings under 28 U.S.C. § 2255.

Rule 26.3. Mistrial

Before ordering a mistrial, the court shall provide an opportunity for the government and for each defendant to comment on the propriety of the order, including whether each party consents or objects to a mistrial, and to suggest any alternatives.

Rule 27. Proof of Official Record

An official record or an entry therein or the lack of such a record or entry may be proved in the same manner as in civil actions.

Rule 28. Interpreters

The court may appoint an interpreter of its own selection and may fix the reasonable compensation of such interpreter. Such compensation shall be paid out of funds provided by law or by the government, as the court may direct.

Rule 29. Motion for Judgment of Acquittal

(a) Motion Before Submission to Jury. Motions for directed verdict are abolished and motions for judgment of acquittal shall be used in their place. The court on motion of a defendant or of its own motion shall order the entry of judgment of acquittal of one or more offenses charged in the indictment or information after the evidence on either side is closed if the evidence is insufficient to sustain a conviction of such offense or offenses. If a defendant's motion for judgment of acquittal at the close of the evidence offered by the government is not granted, the defendant may offer evidence without having reserved the right.

(b) Reservation of Decision on Motion. The court may reserve decision on a motion for judgment of acquittal, proceed with the trial (where the motion is made before the close of all the evidence), submit the case to the jury and decide the motion either before the jury returns a verdict or after it returns a verdict of guilty or is discharged without having returned a verdict. If the court reserves decision, it must decide the motion on the basis of the evidence at the time the ruling was reserved.

(c) Motion After Discharge of Jury. If the jury returns a verdict of guilty or is discharged without having returned a verdict, a motion for judgment of acquittal may be made or renewed within 7 days after the jury is discharged or within such further time as the court may fix during the 7-day period. If a verdict of guilty is returned the court may on such motion set aside the verdict and enter judgment of acquittal. If no verdict is returned the court may enter judgment of acquittal. It shall not be necessary to the making of such a motion that a similar motion has been made prior to the submission of the case to the jury.

(d) Same: Conditional Ruling on Grant of Motion. If a motion for judgment of acquittal after verdict of guilty under this Rule is granted, the court shall also determine whether any motion for a new trial should be granted if the judgment of acquittal is thereafter vacated or reversed, specifying the grounds for such determination. If the motion for a new trial is granted conditionally, the order thereon does not affect the finality of the judgment. If the motion for a new trial has been granted conditionally and the judgment is reversed on appeal, the new trial shall proceed unless the appellate court has otherwise ordered. If such motion has been denied conditionally, the appellee on appeal may assert error in that denial, and if the judgment is reversed on appeal, subsequent proceedings shall be in accordance with the order of the appellate court.

Rule 29.1. Closing Argument

After the closing of evidence the prosecution shall open the argument. The defense shall be permitted to reply. The prosecution shall then be permitted to reply in rebuttal.

Rule 30. Instructions

At the close of the evidence or at such earlier time during the trial as the court reasonably directs, any party may file written requests that the court instruct the jury on the law as set forth in the requests. At the same time copies of such requests shall be furnished to all parties. The court shall inform counsel of its proposed action upon the requests prior to their arguments to the jury. The court may instruct the jury before or after the arguments are completed or at both times. No party may assign as error any portion of the charge or omission therefrom unless that party objects thereto before the jury retires to consider its verdict, stating distinctly the matter to which that party objects and the grounds of the objection. Opportunity shall be given to make the objection out of the hearing of the jury and, on request of any party, out of the presence of the jury.

Rule 31. Verdict

(a) Return. The verdict shall be unanimous. It shall be returned by the jury to the judge in open court.

(b) Several Defendants. If there are two or more defendants, the jury at any time during its deliberations may return a verdict or verdicts with respect to a defendant or defendants as to whom it has agreed; if the jury cannot agree with respect to all, the defendant or defendants as to whom it does not agree may be tried again.

(c) Conviction of Less Offense. The defendant may be found guilty of an offense necessarily included in the offense charged or of an attempt to commit either the offense charged or an offense necessarily included therein if the attempt is an offense.

(d) Poll of Jury. When a verdict is returned and before it is recorded the jury shall be polled at the request of any party or upon the court's own motion. If upon the poll there is not unanimous concurrence, the jury may be directed to retire for further deliberations or may be discharged.

(e) Criminal Forfeiture. If the indictment or the information alleges that an interest or property is subject to criminal forfeiture, a special verdict shall be returned as to the extent of the interest or property subject to forfeiture, if any.

VII.   JUDGMENT
Rule 32.   Sentence and Judgment

(a) In General; Time for Sentencing. When a presentence investigation and report are made under subdivision (b)(1), sentence should be imposed without unnecessary delay following completion of the process prescribed by subdivision (b)(6). The time limits prescribed in subdivision (b)(6) may be either shortened or lengthened for good cause.

(b) Presentence Investigation and Report.

(1) When Made. The probation officer must make a presentence investigation and submit a report to the court before the sentence is imposed, unless:

> (A) the court finds that the information in the record enables it to exercise its sentencing authority meaningfully under 18 U.S.C. § 3553; and

> (B) the court explains this finding on the record.

Notwithstanding the preceding sentence, a presentence investigation and report, or other report containing information sufficient for the court to enter an order of restitution, as the court may direct, shall be required in any case in which restitution is required to be ordered.

(2) Presence of Counsel. On request, the defendant's counsel is entitled to notice and a reasonable opportunity to attend any interview of the defendant by a probation officer in the course of a presentence investigation.

(3) Nondisclosure. The report must not be submitted to the court or its contents disclosed to anyone unless the defendant has consented in writing, has pleaded guilty or nolo contendere, or has been found guilty.

(4) Contents of the Presentence Report. The presentence report must contain—

(A) information about the defendant's history and characteristics, including any prior criminal record, financial condition, and any circumstances that, because they affect the defendant's behavior, may be helpful in imposing sentence or in correctional treatment;

(B) the classification of the offense and of the defendant under the categories established by the Sentencing Commission under 28 U.S.C. § 994(a), as the probation officer believes to be applicable to the defendant's case; the kinds of sentence and the sentencing range suggested for such a category of offense committed by such a category of defendant as set forth in the guidelines issued by the Sentencing Commission under 28 U.S.C. § 994(a)(1); and the probation officer's explanation of any factors that may suggest a different sentence—within or without the applicable guideline—that would be more appropriate, given all the circumstances;

(C) a reference to any pertinent policy statement issued by the Sentencing Commission under 28 U.S.C. § 994(a)(2);

(D) verified information, stated in a nonargumentative style, containing an assessment of the financial, social, psychological, and medical impact on any individual against whom the offense has been committed;

(E) in appropriate cases, information about the nature and extent of nonprison programs and resources available for the defendant;

(F) in appropriate cases, information sufficient for the court to enter an order of restitution;

(G) any report and recommendation resulting from a study ordered by the court under 18 U.S.C. § 3552(b); and

(H) any other information required by the court.

(5) Exclusions. The presentence report must exclude:

(A) any diagnostic opinions that, if disclosed, might seriously disrupt a program of rehabilitation;

(B) sources of information obtained upon a promise of confidentiality; or

(C) any other information that, if disclosed, might result in harm, physical or otherwise, to the defendant or other persons.

(6) Disclosure and Objections.

(A) Not less than 35 days before the sentencing hearing—unless the defendant waives this minimum period—the probation officer must furnish the presentence report to the defendant, the defendant's counsel, and the attorney for the Government. The court may, by local rule or in individual cases, direct that the probation officer not disclose the probation officer's recommendation, if any, on the sentence.

(B) Within 14 days after receiving the presentence report, the parties shall communicate in writing to the probation officer, and to each other, any objections to any material information, sentencing classifications, sentencing guideline ranges, and policy statements contained in or omitted from the presentence report. After receiving objections, the probation officer may meet with the defendant, the defendant's counsel, and the attorney for the Government to discuss those objections. The probation officer may also conduct a further investigation and revise the presentence report as appropriate.

(C) Not later than 7 days before the sentencing hearing, the probation officer must submit the presentence report to the court, together with an addendum setting forth any unresolved objections, the grounds for those objections, and the probation officer's comments on the objections. At the same time, the probation officer must furnish the revisions of the presentence report and the addendum to the defendant, the defendant's counsel, and the attorney for the Government.

(D) Except for any unresolved objection under subdivision (b)(6)(B), the court may, at the hearing, accept the presentence report as its findings of fact. For good cause shown, the court may allow a new objection to be raised at any time before imposing sentence.

(c) Sentence.

(1) Sentencing Hearing. At the sentencing hearing, the court must afford counsel for the defendant and for the Government an opportunity to comment on the probation officer's determinations and on other matters relating to the appropriate sentence, and must rule on any unresolved objections to the presentence report. The court may, in its discretion, permit the parties to introduce testimony or other evidence on the objections. For each matter controverted, the court must make either a finding on the allegation or a determination that no finding is necessary because the controverted matter will not be taken into account in, or will not affect, sentencing. A written record of these findings and determinations must be appended to any copy of the presentence report made available to the Bureau of Prisons.

(2) Production of Statements at Sentencing Hearing. Rule 26.2(a)–(d) and (f) applies at a sentencing hearing under this rule. If a party elects not to comply with an order under Rule 26.2(a) to deliver a statement to the movant, the court may not consider the affidavit or testimony of the witness whose statement is withheld.

(3) Imposition of Sentence. Before imposing sentence, the court must:

(A) verify that the defendant and defendant's counsel have read and discussed the presentence report made available under subdivision (b)(6)(A). If the court has received information excluded from the presentence report under subdivision (b)(5) the court—in lieu of making that information available—must summarize it in writing, if the information will be relied on in determining sentence. The court must also give the defendant and the defendant's counsel a reasonable opportunity to comment on that information;

(B) afford defendant's counsel an opportunity to speak on behalf of the defendant;

(C) address the defendant personally and determine whether the defendant wishes to make a statement and to present any information in mitigation of the sentence;

(D) afford the attorney for the Government an opportunity equivalent to that of the defendant's counsel to speak to the court; and

(E) if sentence is to be imposed for a crime of violence or sexual abuse, address the victim personally if the victim is present at the sentencing hearing and determine if the victim wishes to make a statement or present any information in relation to the sentence.

(4) In Camera Proceedings. The court's summary of information under subdivision (c)(3)(A) may be in camera. Upon joint motion by the defendant and by the attorney for the Government, the court may hear in camera the statements—made under subdivision (c)(3)(B), (C), (D), and (E)—by the defendant, the defendant's counsel, the victim, or the attorney for the Government.

(5) Notification of Right to Appeal. After imposing sentence in a case which has gone to trial on a plea of not guilty, the court must advise the defendant of the right to appeal. After imposing sentence in any case, the court must advise the defendant of any right to appeal the sentence, and of the right of a person who is unable to pay the cost of an appeal to apply for leave to appeal in forma pauperis. If the defendant so requests, the clerk of the court must immediately prepare and file a notice of appeal on behalf of the defendant.

(d) Judgment.

(1) In General. A judgment of conviction must set forth the plea, the verdict or findings, the adjudication, and the sentence. If the defendant is found not guilty or for any other reason is entitled to be discharged, judgment must be entered accordingly. The judgment must be signed by the judge and entered by the clerk.

(2) Criminal Forfeiture. If a verdict contains a finding that property is subject to a criminal forfeiture, or if a defendant enters a guilty plea subjecting property to such forfeiture, the court may enter a preliminary order of forfeiture after providing notice to the defendant and a reasonable opportunity to be heard on the timing and form of the order. The order of forfeiture shall authorize the Attorney General to seize the property subject to forfeiture, to conduct any discovery that the court considers proper to help identify, locate, or dispose of the property, and to begin proceedings consistent with any statutory requirements pertaining to ancillary hearings and the rights of third parties. At sentencing, a final order of forfeiture shall be made part of the sentence and included in the judgment. The court may include in the final order such conditions as may be reasonably necessary to preserve the value of the property pending any appeal.

(e) Plea Withdrawal. If a motion to withdraw a plea of guilty or nolo contendere is made before sentence is imposed, the court may permit the plea to be withdrawn if the defendant shows any fair and just reason. At any later time, a plea may be set aside only on direct appeal or by motion under 28 U.S.C. § 2255.

(f) Definitions. For purposes of this rule—

(1) "victim" means any individual against whom an offense has been committed for which a sentence is to be imposed, but the right of allocution under subdivision (c)(3)(E) may be exercised instead by—

(A) a parent or legal guardian if the victim is below the age of eighteen years or incompetent; or

(B) one or more family members or relatives designated by the court if the victim is deceased or incapacitated;

if such person or persons are present at the sentencing hearing, regardless of whether the victim is present; and

(2) "crime of violence or sexual abuse" means a crime that involved the use or attempted or threatened use of physical force against the person or property of another, or a crime under chapter 109A of title 18, United States Code.

Rule 32.1.   Revocation or Modification of Probation or Supervised Release

(a) Revocation of Probation or Supervised Release.

(1) Preliminary Hearing. Whenever a person is held in custody on the ground that the person has violated a condition of probation or supervised release, the person shall be afforded a prompt hearing before any judge, or a United States magistrate who has been given authority pursuant to 28 U.S.C. § 636 to conduct such hearings, in order to determine whether there is probable cause to hold the person for a revocation hearing. The person shall be given

(A) notice of the preliminary hearing and its purpose and of the alleged violation;

(B) an opportunity to appear at the hearing and present evidence in the person's own behalf;

(C) upon request, the opportunity to question witnesses against the person unless, for good cause, the federal magistrate decides that justice does not require the appearance of the witness; and

(D) notice of the person's right to be represented by counsel.

The proceedings shall be recorded stenographically or by an electronic recording device. If probable cause is found to exist, the person shall be held for a revocation hearing. The person may be released pursuant to Rule 46(c) pending the revocation hearing. If probable cause is not found to exist, the proceeding shall be dismissed.

(2) Revocation Hearing. The revocation hearing, unless waived by the person, shall be held within a reasonable time in the district of jurisdiction. The person shall be given

(A) written notice of the alleged violation;

(B) disclosure of the evidence against the person;

(C) an opportunity to appear and to present evidence in the person's own behalf;

(D) the opportunity to question adverse witnesses; and

(E) notice of the person's right to be represented by counsel.

(b) Modification of Probation or Supervised Release. A hearing and assistance of counsel are required before the terms or conditions of probation or supervised release can be modified, unless the relief to be granted to the person on probation or supervised release upon the person's request or the court's own motion is favorable to the person, and the attorney for the government, after having been given notice of the proposed relief and a reasonable opportunity to object, has not objected. An extension of the term of probation or supervised release is not favorable to the person for the purposes of this rule.

(c) Production of Statements.

(1) In General. Rule 26.2(a)–(d) and (f) applies at any hearing under this rule.

(2) Sanctions for Failure to Produce Statement. If a party elects not to comply with an order under Rule 26.2(a) to deliver a statement to the moving party, the court may not consider the testimony of a witness whose statement is withheld.

Rule 33. New Trial

The court on motion of a defendant may grant a new trial to that defendant if required in the interest of justice. If trial was by the court without a jury the court on motion of a defendant for a new trial may vacate the judgment if entered, take additional testimony and direct the entry of a new judgment. A motion for a new trial based on the ground of newly discovered evidence may be made only before or within two years after final judgment, but if an appeal is pending the court may grant the motion only on remand of the case. A motion for a new trial based on any other grounds shall be made within 7 days after verdict or finding of guilty or within such further time as the court may fix during the 7-day period.

Rule 34. Arrest of Judgment

The court on motion of a defendant shall arrest judgment if the indictment or information does not charge an offense or if the court was without jurisdiction of the offense charged. The motion in arrest of judgment shall be made within 7 days after verdict or finding of guilty, or after plea of guilty or *nolo contendere,* or within such further time as the court may fix during the 7–day period.

Rule 35. Correction of Sentence

(a) Correction of a Sentence on Remand. The court shall correct a sentence that is determined on appeal under 18 U.S.C. 3742 to have been imposed in violation of law, to have been imposed as a result of an incorrect application of the sentencing guidelines, or to be unreasonable, upon remand of the case to the court—

> (1) for imposition of a sentence in accord with the findings of the court of appeals; or

> (2) for further sentencing proceedings if, after such proceedings, the court determines that the original sentence was incorrect.

(b) Reduction of Sentence for Changed Circumstances. The court, on motion of the Government made within one year after the imposition of the sentence, may reduce a sentence to reflect a defendant's subsequent, substantial assistance in the investigation or prosecution of another person who has committed an offense, in accordance with the guidelines and policy statements issued by the Sentencing Commission pursuant to section 994 of title 28, United States Code. The court may consider a government motion to reduce a sentence made one year or more after imposition of the sentence where the defendant's substantial assistance involves information or evidence not known by the defendant until one year or more after imposition of sentence. The court's authority to reduce a sentence under this subsection includes the authority to reduce such sentence to a level below that established by statute as a minimum sentence.

(c) Correction of Sentence by Sentencing Court. The Court, acting within 7 days after the imposition of sentence, may correct a sentence that was imposed as a result of arithmetical, technical, or other clear error.

Rule 36. Clerical Mistakes

Clerical mistakes in judgments, orders or other parts of the record and errors in the record arising from oversight or omission may be corrected by the court at any time and after such notice, if any, as the court orders.

[VIII. APPEAL] (Abrogated Dec. 4, 1967, eff. July 1, 1968)

[Rule 37. Taking Appeal; and Petition for Writ of Certiorari.] (Abrogated Dec. 4, 1967, Eff. July 1, 1968)

Rule 38. Stay of Execution

(a) Death. A sentence of death shall be stayed if an appeal is taken from the conviction or sentence.

(b) Imprisonment. A sentence of imprisonment shall be stayed if an appeal is taken from the conviction or sentence and the defendant is released pending disposition of appeal pursuant to Rule 9(b) of the Federal Rules of Appellate Procedure. If not stayed, the court may recommend to the Attorney General that the defendant be retained at, or transferred to, a place of confinement near the place of trial or the place where an appeal is to be heard, for a period reasonably necessary to permit the defendant to assist in the preparation of an appeal to the court of appeals.

(c) Fine. A sentence to pay a fine or a fine and costs, if an appeal is taken, may be stayed by the district court or by the court of appeals upon such terms as the court deems proper. The court may require the defendant pending appeal to deposit the whole or any part of the fine and costs in the registry of the district court, or to give bond for the payment thereof, or to submit to an examination of assets, and it may make any appropriate order to restrain the defendant from dissipating such defendant's assets.

(d) Probation. A sentence of probation may be stayed if an appeal from the conviction or sentence is taken. If the sentence is stayed, the court shall fix the terms of the stay.

(e) Criminal Forfeiture, Notice to Victims, and Restitution. A sanction imposed as part of the sentence pursuant to 18 U.S.C. 3554, 3555, or 3556 may, if an appeal of the conviction or sentence is taken, be stayed by the district court or by the court of appeals upon such terms as the court finds appropriate. The court may issue such orders as may be reasonably necessary to ensure compliance with the sanction upon disposition of the appeal, including the entering of a restraining order or an injunction or requiring a deposit in whole or in part of the monetary amount involved into the registry of the district court or execution of a performance bond.

(f) Disabilities. A civil or employment disability arising under a Federal statute by reason of the defendant's conviction or sentence, may, if an appeal is taken, be stayed by the district court or by the court of appeals upon such terms as the court finds appropriate. The court may enter a restraining order or an injunction, or take any other action that may be reasonably necessary to protect the interest represented by the disability pending disposition of the appeal.

[Rule 39.   Supervision of Appeal.]   (Abrogated Dec. 4, 1967, Eff. July 1, 1968)

IX.   SUPPLEMENTARY AND SPECIAL PROCEEDINGS

Rule 40.   Commitment to Another District

(a) Appearance Before Federal Magistrate Judge. If a person is arrested in a district other than that in which the offense is alleged to have been committed, that person shall be taken without unnecessary delay before the nearest available federal magistrate judge, in accordance with the provisions of Rule 5. Preliminary proceedings concerning the defendant shall be conducted in accordance with Rules 5 and 5.1, except that if no preliminary examination is held because an indictment has been returned or an information filed or because the defendant elects to have the preliminary examination conducted in the district in which the prosecution is pending, the person shall be held to answer upon a finding that such person is the person named in the indictment, information or warrant. If held to answer, the defendant shall be held to answer in the district court in which the prosecution is pending—provided that a warrant is issued in that district if the arrest was made without a warrant—upon production of the warrant or a certified copy thereof. The warrant or certified copy may be produced by facsimile transmission.

(b) Statement by Federal Magistrate Judge. In addition to the statements required by Rule 5, the federal magistrate judge shall inform the defendant of the provisions of Rule 20.

(c) Papers. If a defendant is held or discharged, the papers in the proceeding and any bail taken shall be transmitted to the clerk of the district court in which the prosecution is pending.

(d) Arrest of Probationer or Supervised Releasee. If a person is arrested for a violation of probation or supervised release in a district other than the district having jurisdiction, such person must be taken without unnecessary delay before the nearest available federal magistrate judge. The person may be released under Rule 46(c). The federal magistrate judge shall:

(1) Proceed under Rule 32.1 if jurisdiction over the person is transferred to that district;

(2) Hold a prompt preliminary hearing if the alleged violation occurred in that district, and either (i) hold the person to answer in the district court of the district having jurisdiction or (ii) dismiss the proceedings and so notify that court; or

(3) Otherwise order the person held to answer in the district court of the district having jurisdiction upon production of certified copies of the judgment, the warrant, and the application for the warrant, and upon a finding that the person before the magistrate judge is the person named in the warrant.

(e) Arrest for Failure to Appear. If a person is arrested on a warrant in a district other than that in which the warrant was issued, and the warrant was issued because of the failure of the person named therein to appear as required pursuant to a subpoena or the terms of that person's release, the person arrested must be taken without unnecessary delay before the nearest available federal magistrate judge. Upon production of the warrant or a certified copy thereof and upon a finding that the person before the magistrate judge is the person named in the warrant, the federal magistrate judge shall hold the person to answer in the district in which the warrant was issued.

(f) Release or Detention. If a person was previously detained or conditionally released, pursuant to chapter 207 of title 18, United States Code, in another district where a warrant, information, or indictment issued, the federal magistrate judge shall take into account the decision previously made and the reasons set forth therefor, if any, but will not be bound by that decision. If the federal magistrate judge amends the release or detention decision or alters the conditions of release, the magistrate judge shall set forth the reasons therefore [1] in writing.

Rule 41.   Search and Seizure

(a) Authority to Issue Warrant.   Upon the request of a federal law enforcement officer or an attorney for the government, a search warrant authorized by this rule may be issued (1) by a federal magistrate judge, or a state court of record within the federal district, for a search of property or for a person within the district, (2) by a federal magistrate judge for a search of property or for a person either within or outside the district if the property or person is within the district when the warrant is sought but might move outside the district before the warrant is executed.

(b) Property or Persons Which May Be Seized With a Warrant. A warrant may be issued under this rule to search for and seize any (1) property that constitutes evidence of the commission of a criminal offense; or (2) contraband, the fruits of crime, or things otherwise criminally possessed; or (3) property designed or intended for use or which is or has been used as the means of committing a criminal offense; or (4) person for whose arrest there is probable cause, or who is unlawfully restrained.

(c) Issuance and Contents.

(1) Warrant Upon Affidavit.   A warrant other than a warrant upon oral testimony under paragraph (2) of this subdivision shall issue only on an affidavit or affidavits sworn to before the federal magistrate judge or state judge and establishing the grounds for issuing the warrant.   If the federal magistrate judge or state judge is satisfied that grounds for the application exist or that there is probable cause to believe that they exist, that magistrate judge or state judge shall issue a warrant identifying the property or person to be seized and naming or describing the person or place to be searched.   The finding of probable cause may be based upon hearsay evidence in whole or in part.   Before ruling on a request for a warrant the federal magistrate judge or state judge may require the affiant to appear personally and may examine under oath the affiant and any witnesses the affiant may produce, provided that such proceeding shall be taken down by a court reporter or recording equipment and made part of the affidavit.   The warrant shall be directed to a civil officer of the United States authorized to enforce or assist in enforcing any law thereof or to a person so authorized by the President of the United States.   It shall command the officer to search, within a specified period of time not to exceed 10 days, the person or place named for the property or person specified.   The warrant shall be served in the daytime, unless the issuing authority, by appropriate provision in the warrant, and for reasonable cause shown, authorizes its execution at times other than daytime.   It shall designate a federal magistrate judge to whom it shall be returned.

(2) Warrant Upon Oral Testimony.

(A) General Rule.   If the circumstances make it reasonable to dispense, in whole or in part, with a written affidavit, a Federal magistrate judge may issue a warrant based upon sworn testimony

[1] So in original.

communicated by telephone or other appropriate means, including facsimile transmission.

(B) Application. The person who is requesting the warrant shall prepare a document to be known as a duplicate original warrant and shall read such duplicate original warrant, verbatim, to the Federal magistrate judge. The Federal magistrate judge shall enter, verbatim, what is so read to such magistrate judge on a document to be known as the original warrant. The Federal magistrate judge may direct that the warrant be modified.

(C) Issuance. If the Federal magistrate judge is satisfied that the circumstances are such as to make it reasonable to dispense with a written affidavit and that grounds for the application exist or that there is probable cause to believe that they exist, the Federal magistrate judge shall order the issuance of a warrant by directing the person requesting the warrant to sign the Federal magistrate judge's name on the duplicate original warrant. The Federal magistrate judge shall immediately sign the original warrant and enter on the face of the original warrant the exact time when the warrant was ordered to be issued. The finding of probable cause for a warrant upon oral testimony may be based on the same kind of evidence as is sufficient for a warrant upon affidavit.

(D) Recording and Certification of Testimony. When a caller informs the Federal magistrate judge that the purpose of the call is to request a warrant, the Federal magistrate judge shall immediately place under oath each person whose testimony forms a basis of the application and each person applying for that warrant. If a voice recording device is available, the Federal magistrate judge shall record by means of such device all of the call after the caller informs the Federal magistrate judge that the purpose of the call is to request a warrant. Otherwise a stenographic or longhand verbatim record shall be made. If a voice recording device is used or a stenographic record made, the Federal magistrate judge shall have the record transcribed, shall certify the accuracy of the transcription, and shall file a copy of the original record and the transcription with the court. If a longhand verbatim record is made, the Federal magistrate judge shall file a signed copy with the court.

(E) Contents. The contents of a warrant upon oral testimony shall be the same as the contents of a warrant upon affidavit.

(F) Additional Rule for Execution. The person who executes the warrant shall enter the exact time of execution on the face of the duplicate original warrant.

(G) Motion to Suppress Precluded. Absent a finding of bad faith, evidence obtained pursuant to a warrant issued under this paragraph is not subject to a motion to suppress on the ground that the circumstances were not such as to make it reasonable to dispense with a written affidavit.

(d) Execution and Return with Inventory. The officer taking property under the warrant shall give to the person from whom or from whose premises the property was taken a copy of the warrant and a receipt for the property taken or shall leave the copy and receipt at the place from which the property was taken. The return shall be made promptly and shall be accompanied by a written inventory of any property taken. The inventory shall be made in the presence of the applicant for the warrant and the person from whose possession or premises the property was taken, if they are present, or in the presence of at least one credible person other than the applicant for the warrant or the person from whose possession or premises the property was taken, and shall be verified by the officer. The federal magistrate judge shall upon request deliver a copy of the inventory to the person from whom or from whose premises the property was taken and to the applicant for the warrant.

(e) Motion for Return of Property. A person aggrieved by an unlawful search and seizure or by the deprivation of property may move the district court for the district in which the property was seized for the return of the property on the ground that such person is entitled to lawful possession of the property. The court shall receive evidence on any issue of fact necessary to the decision of the motion. If the motion is granted, the property shall be returned to the movant, although reasonable conditions may be imposed to protect access and use of the property in subsequent proceedings. If a motion for return of property is made or comes on for hearing in the district of trial after an indictment or information is filed, it shall be treated also as a motion to suppress under Rule 12.

(f) Motion to Suppress. A motion to suppress evidence may be made in the court of the district of trial as provided in Rule 12.

(g) Return of Papers to Clerk. The federal magistrate judge before whom the warrant is returned shall attach to the warrant a copy of the return, inventory and all other papers in connection therewith and shall file them with the clerk of the district court for the district in which the property was seized.

(h) Scope and Definition. This rule does not modify any act, inconsistent with it, regulating search, seizure and the issuance and execution of search warrants in circumstances for which special provision is made. The term "property" is used in this rule to include documents, books, papers and any other tangible objects. The term "daytime" is used in this rule to mean the hours from 6:00 a.m. to 10:00 p.m. according to local time. The phrase "federal law enforcement officer" is used in this rule to mean any government agent, other than an attorney for the government as defined in Rule 54(c), who is engaged in the enforcement of the criminal laws and is within any category of officers authorized by the Attorney General to request the issuance of a search warrant.

Rule 42. Criminal Contempt

(a) Summary Disposition. A criminal contempt may be punished summarily if the judge certifies that the judge saw or heard the conduct constituting the contempt and that it was committed in the actual presence of the court. The order of contempt shall recite the facts and shall be signed by the judge and entered of record.

(b) Disposition Upon Notice and Hearing. A criminal contempt except as provided in subdivision (a) of this rule shall be prosecuted on notice. The notice shall state the time and place of hearing, allowing a reasonable time for the preparation of the defense, and shall state the essential facts constituting the criminal contempt charged and describe it as such. The notice shall be given orally by the judge in open court in the presence of the defendant or, on application of the United States attorney or of an attorney appointed by the court for that purpose, by an order to show cause or an order of arrest. The defendant is entitled to a trial by jury in any case in which an act of Congress so provides. The defendant is entitled to admission to bail as provided in these rules. If the contempt charged involves disrespect to or criticism of a judge, that judge is disqualified from presiding at the trial or hearing except with the defendant's consent. Upon a verdict or finding of guilt the court shall enter an order fixing the punishment.

X. GENERAL PROVISIONS
Rule 43. Presence of the Defendant

(a) Presence Required. The defendant shall be present at the arraignment, at the time of the plea, at every stage of the trial including the impaneling of the jury and the return of the verdict, and at the imposition of sentence, except as otherwise provided by this rule.

(b) Continued Presence Not Required. The further progress of the trial to and including the return of the verdict, and the imposition of sentence, will not be prevented and the defendant will be considered to have waived the right to be present whenever a defendant, initially present at trial, or having pleaded guilty or nolo contendere,

(1) is voluntarily absent after the trial has commenced (whether or not the defendant has been informed by the court of the obligation to remain during the trial),

(2) in a noncapital case, is voluntarily absent at the imposition of sentence, or

(3) after being warned by the court that disruptive conduct will cause the removal of the defendant from the courtroom, persists in conduct which is such as to justify exclusion from the courtroom.

(c) Presence Not Required. A defendant need not be present:

(1) when represented by counsel and the defendant is an organization, as defined in 18 U.S.C. s 18;

(2) when the offense is punishable by fine or by imprisonment for not more than one year or both, and the court, with the written consent of the defendant, permits arraignment, plea, trial, and imposition of sentence in the defendant's absence;

(3) when the proceeding involves only a conference or hearing upon a question of law; or

(4) when the proceeding involves a correction of sentence under Rule 35.

Rule 44. Right to and Assignment of Counsel

(a) Right to Assigned Counsel. Every defendant who is unable to obtain counsel shall be entitled to have counsel assigned to represent that defendant at every stage of the proceedings from initial appearance before the federal magistrate judge or the court through appeal, unless that defendant waives such appointment.

(b) Assignment Procedure. The procedures for implementing the right set out in subdivision (a) shall be those provided by law and by local rules of court established pursuant thereto.

(c) Joint Representation. Whenever two or more defendants have been jointly charged pursuant to Rule 8(b) or have been joined for trial pursuant to Rule 13, and are represented by the same retained or assigned counsel or by retained or assigned counsel who are associated in the practice of law, the court shall promptly inquire with respect to such joint representation and shall personally advise each defendant of the right to the effective assistance of counsel, including separate representation. Unless it appears that there is good cause to believe no conflict of interest is likely to arise, the court shall take such measures as may be appropriate to protect each defendant's right to counsel.

Rule 45. Time

(a) Computation. In computing any period of time the day of the act or event from which the designated period of time begins to run shall not be included. The last day of the period so computed shall be included, unless it is a Saturday, a Sunday, or a legal holiday, or, when the act to be done is the filing of some paper in court, a day on which weather or other conditions have made the office of the clerk of the district court inaccessible, in which event the period runs until the end of the next day which is not one of the aforementioned days. When a period of time prescribed or allowed is less than 11 days, intermediate Saturdays, Sundays and legal holidays shall be excluded in the computation. As used in these rules, "legal holiday" includes New Year's Day, Birthday of Martin Luther King, Jr., Washington's Birthday, Memorial Day, Independence Day, Labor Day, Columbus Day, Veterans Day, Thanksgiving Day, Christmas Day, and any other day appointed as a holiday by the President or the Congress of the United States, or by the state in which the district court is held.

(b) Enlargement. When an act is required or allowed to be done at or within a specified time, the court for cause shown may at any time in its discretion (1) with or without motion or notice, order the period enlarged if request therefor is made before the expiration of the period originally prescribed or as extended by a previous order or (2) upon motion made after the expiration of the specified period permit the act to be done if the failure to act was the result of excusable neglect; but the court may not extend the time for taking any action under Rules 29, 33, 34 and 35, except to the extent and under the conditions stated in them.

[(c) Unaffected by Expiration of Term.] (Rescinded Feb. 28, 1966, eff. July 1, 1966.)

(d) For Motions; Affidavits. A written motion, other than one which may be heard *ex parte,* and notice of the hearing thereof shall be served not later than 5 days before the time specified for the hearing unless a different period is fixed by rule or order of the court. For cause shown such an order may be made on *ex parte* application. When a motion is supported by affidavit, the affidavit shall be served with the motion; and opposing affidavits may be served not less than 1 day before the hearing unless the court permits them to be served at a later time.

(e) Additional Time After Service by Mail. Whenever a party has the right or is required to do an act within a prescribed period after the service of a notice or other paper upon that party and the notice or other paper is served by mail, 3 days shall be added to the prescribed period.

Rule 46.   Release From Custody

(a) Release Prior to Trial. Eligibility for release prior to trial shall be in accordance with 18 U.S.C. §§ 3142 and 3144.

(b) Release During Trial. A person released before trial shall continue on release during trial under the same terms and conditions as were previously imposed unless the court determines that other terms and conditions or termination of release are necessary to assure such person's presence during the trial or to assure that such person's conduct will not obstruct the orderly and expeditious progress of the trial.

(c) Pending Sentence and Notice of Appeal. Eligibility for release pending sentence or pending notice of appeal or expiration of the time allowed for filing notice of appeal, shall be in accordance with 18 U.S.C. § 3143. The burden of establishing that the defendant will not flee or pose a danger to any other person or to the community rests with the defendant.

(d) Justification of Sureties. Every surety, except a corporate surety which is approved as provided by law, shall justify by affidavit and may be required to describe in the affidavit the property by which the surety proposes to justify and the encumbrances thereon, the number and amount of other bonds and undertakings for bail entered into by the surety and remaining undischarged and all the other liabilities of the surety. No bond shall be approved unless the surety thereon appears to be qualified.

(e) Forfeiture.

(1) Declaration. If there is a breach of condition of a bond, the district court shall declare a forfeiture of the bail.

(2) Setting Aside. The court may direct that a forfeiture be set aside in whole or in part, upon such conditions as the court may impose, if a person released upon execution of an appearance bond with a surety is subsequently surrendered by the surety into custody or if it otherwise appears that justice does not require the forfeiture.

(3) Enforcement. When a forfeiture has not been set aside, the court shall on motion enter a judgment of default and execution may issue thereon. By entering into a bond the obligors submit to the jurisdiction of the district court and irrevocably appoint the clerk of the court as their agent upon whom any papers affecting their liability may be served. Their liability may be enforced on motion without the necessity of an independent action. The motion and such notice of the motion as the court prescribes may be served on the clerk of the court, who shall forthwith mail copies to the obligors to their last known addresses.

(4) Remission. After entry of such judgment, the court may remit it in whole or in part under the conditions applying to the setting aside of forfeiture in paragraph (2) of this subdivision.

(f) Exoneration. When the condition of the bond has been satisfied or the forfeiture thereof has been set aside or remitted, the court shall exonerate the obligors and release any bail. A surety may be exonerated by a deposit of cash in the amount of the bond or by a timely surrender of the defendant into custody.

(g) Supervision of Detention Pending Trial. The court shall exercise supervision over the detention of defendants and witnesses within the district pending trial for the purpose of eliminating all unnecessary detention. The attorney for the government shall make a biweekly report to the court listing each defendant and witness who has been held in custody pending indictment, arraignment or trial for a period in excess of ten days. As to each witness so listed the attorney for the government shall make a statement of the reasons why such witness should not be released with or without the taking of a deposition pursuant to Rule 15(a). As to each defendant so listed the attorney for the government shall make a statement of the reasons why the defendant is still held in custody.

(h) Forfeiture of Property. Nothing in this rule or in chapter 207 of title 18, United States Code, shall prevent the court from disposing of any charge by entering an order directing forfeiture of property pursuant to 18 U.S.C. 3142(c)(1)(B)(xi) if the value of the property is an amount that would be an appropriate sentence after conviction of the offense charged and if such forfeiture is authorized by statute or regulation.

(i) Production of Statements.

(1) In General. Rule 26.2(a)–(d) and (f) applies at a detention hearing held under 18 U.S.C. § 3144, unless the court, for good cause shown, rules otherwise in a particular case.

(2) Sanctions for Failure to Produce Statement. If a party elects not to comply with an order under Rule 26.2(a) to deliver a statement to the moving party, at the detention hearing the court may not consider the testimony of a witness whose statement is withheld.

Rule 47.   Motions

An application to the court for an order shall be by motion. A motion other than one made during a trial or hearing shall be in writing unless the court permits it to be made orally. It shall state the grounds upon which it is made and shall set forth the relief or order sought. It may be supported by affidavit.

Rule 48.   Dismissal

(a) By Attorney for Government. The Attorney General or the United States attorney may by leave of court file a dismissal of an indictment, information or complaint and the prosecution shall thereupon terminate. Such a dismissal may not be filed during the trial without the consent of the defendant.

(b) By Court. If there is unnecessary delay in presenting the charge to a grand jury or in filing an information against a defendant who has been held to answer to the district court, or if there is unnecessary delay in bringing a defendant to trial, the court may dismiss the indictment, information or complaint.

Rule 49.   Service and Filing of Papers

(a) Service: When Required. Written motions other than those which are heard ex parte, written notices, designations of record on appeal and similar papers shall be served upon each of the parties.

(b) Service: How Made. Whenever under these rules or by an order of the court service is required or permitted to be made upon a party represented by an attorney, the service shall be made upon the attorney unless service upon the party personally is ordered by the court. Service upon the attorney or upon a party shall be made in the manner provided in civil actions.

(c) Notice of Orders. Immediately upon the entry of an order made on a written motion subsequent to arraignment the clerk shall mail to each party a notice thereof and shall make a note in the docket of the mailing. Lack of notice of the entry by the clerk does not affect the time to appeal or relieve or authorize the court to relieve a party for failure to appeal within the time allowed, except as permitted by Rule 4(b) of the Federal Rules of Appellate Procedure.

(d) Filing. Papers required to be served shall be filed with the court. Papers shall be filed in the manner provided in civil actions.

Rule 50.   Calendars; Plan for Prompt Disposition

(a) Calendars. The district courts may provide for placing criminal proceedings upon appropriate calendars. Preference shall be given to criminal proceedings as far as practicable.

(b) Plans for Achieving Prompt Disposition of Criminal Cases. To minimize undue delay and to further the prompt disposition of criminal cases, each district court shall conduct a continuing study of the administration of criminal justice in the district court and before United States magistrate judges of the district and shall prepare plans for the prompt disposition of criminal cases in accordance with the provisions of Chapter 208 of Title 18, United States Code.

Rule 51.   Exceptions Unnecessary

Exceptions to rulings or orders of the court are unnecessary and for all purposes for which an exception has heretofore been necessary it is sufficient that a party, at the time the ruling or order of the court is made or sought, makes known to the court the action which that party desires the court to take or that party's objection to the action of the court and the grounds therefor; but if a party has no opportunity to object to a ruling or order, the absence of an objection does not thereafter prejudice that party.

Rule 52. Harmless Error and Plain Error

(a) Harmless Error. Any error, defect, irregularity or variance which does not affect substantial rights shall be disregarded.

(b) Plain Error. Plain errors or defects affecting substantial rights may be noticed although they were not brought to the attention of the court.

Rule 53. Regulation of Conduct in the Court Room

The taking of photographs in the court room during the progress of judicial proceedings or radio broadcasting of judicial proceedings from the court room shall not be permitted by the court.

Rule 54. Application and Exception

(a) Courts. These rules apply to all criminal proceedings in the United States District Courts; in the District Court of Guam; in the District Court for the Northern Mariana Islands, except as otherwise provided in articles IV and V of the covenant provided by the Act of March 24, 1976 (90 Stat. 263); in the District Court of the Virgin Islands; and (except as otherwise provided in the Canal Zone Code) in the United States District Court for the District of the Canal Zone; in the United States Courts of Appeals; and in the Supreme Court of the United States; except that the prosecution of offenses in the District Court of the Virgin Islands shall be by indictment or information as otherwise provided by law.

(b) Proceedings.

(1) Removed Proceedings. These rules apply to criminal prosecutions removed to the United States district courts from state courts and govern all procedure after removal, except that dismissal by the attorney for the prosecution shall be governed by state law.

(2) Offenses Outside a District or State. These rules apply to proceedings for offenses committed upon the high seas or elsewhere out of the jurisdiction of any particular state or district, except that such proceedings may be had in any district authorized by 18 U.S.C. § 3238.

(3) Peace Bonds. These rules do not alter the power of judges of the United States or of United States magistrate judges to hold to security of the peace and for good behavior under Revised Statutes, § 4069, 50 U.S.C. § 23, but in such cases the procedure shall conform to these rules so far as they are applicable.

(4) Proceedings Before United States Magistrate Judges. Proceedings involving misdemeanors and other petty offenses are governed by Rule 58.

(5) Other Proceedings. These rules are not applicable to extradition and rendition of fugitives; civil forfeiture of property for violation of a statute of the United States; or the collection of fines and penalties. Except as provided in Rule 20(d) they do not apply to proceedings under 18 U.S.C., Chapter 403—Juvenile Delinquency—so far as they are inconsistent with that chapter. They do not apply to summary trials for offenses against the navigation laws under Revised Statutes §§ 4300–4305, 33 U.S.C. §§ 391–396, or to proceedings involving disputes between seamen under Revised Statutes, §§ 4079–4081, as amended, 22 U.S.C. §§ 256–258, or to proceedings for fishery offenses under the Act of June 28, 1937, c. 392, 50 Stat. 325–327, 16 U.S.C. §§ 772–772i, or to proceedings against a witness in a foreign country under 28 U.S.C. § 1784.

(c) Application of Terms. As used in these rules the following terms have the designated meanings.

"Act of Congress" includes any act of Congress locally applicable to and in force in the District of Columbia, in Puerto Rico, in a territory or in an insular possession.

"Attorney for the government" means the Attorney General, an authorized assistant of the Attorney General, a United States Attorney, an authorized assistant of a United States Attorney, when applicable to cases arising under the laws of Guam the Attorney General of Guam or such other person or persons as may be authorized by the laws of Guam to act therein, and when applicable to cases arising under the laws of the Northern Mariana Islands the Attorney General of the Northern Mariana Islands or any other person or persons as may be authorized by the laws of the Northern Marianas to act therein.

"Civil action" refers to a civil action in a district court.

The words "demurrer," "motion to quash," "plea in abatement," "plea in bar" and "special plea in bar," or words to the same effect, in any act of Congress shall be construed to mean the motion raising a defense or objection provided in Rule 12.

"District court" includes all district courts named in subdivision (a) of this rule.

"Federal magistrate judge" means a United States magistrate judge as defined in 28 U.S.C. §§ 631–639, a judge of the United States or another judge or judicial officer specifically empowered by statute in force in any territory or possession, the Commonwealth of Puerto Rico, or the District of Columbia, to perform a function to which a particular rule relates.

"Judge of the United States" includes a judge of a district court, court of appeals, or the Supreme Court.

"Law" includes statutes and judicial decisions.

"Magistrate judge" includes a United States magistrate as defined in 28 U.S.C. §§ 631–639, a judge of the United States, another judge or judicial officer specifically empowered by statute in force in any territory or possession, the Commonwealth of Puerto Rico, or the District of Columbia, to perform a function to which a particular rule relates, and a state or local judicial officer, authorized by 18 U.S.C. § 3041 to perform the functions prescribed in Rules 3, 4, and 5.

"Oath" includes affirmations.

"Petty offense" is defined in 18 U.S.C. § 19.

"State" includes District of Columbia, Puerto Rico, territory and insular possession.

"United States magistrate judge" means the officer authorized by 28 U.S.C. §§ 631–639.

Rule 55. Records

The clerk of the district court and each United States magistrate judge shall keep records in criminal proceedings in such form as the Director of the Administrative Office of the United States Courts may prescribe. The clerk shall enter in the records each order or judgment of the court and the date such entry is made.

Rule 56. Courts and Clerks

The district court shall be deemed always open for the purpose of filing any proper paper, of issuing and returning process and of making motions and orders. The clerk's office with the clerk or a deputy in attendance shall be open during business hours on all days except Saturdays, Sundays, and legal holidays, but a court may provide by local rule or order that its clerk's office shall be open for specified hours on Saturdays or particular legal holidays other than New Year's Day, Birthday of Martin Luther King, Jr., Washington's Birthday, Memorial Day, Independence Day, Labor Day, Columbus Day, Veterans Day, Thanksgiving Day, and Christmas Day.

Rule 57. Rules by District Courts

(a) In General

(1) Each district court acting by a majority of its district judges may, after giving appropriate public notice and an opportunity to comment, make and amend rules governing its practice. A local rule shall be consistent with—but not duplicative of—Acts of Congress and rules adopted under 28 U.S.C. s 2072 and shall conform to any uniform numbering system prescribed by the Judicial Conference of the United States.

(2) A local rule imposing a requirement of form shall not be enforced in a manner that causes a party to lose rights because of a nonwillful failure to comply with the requirement.

(b) Procedure When There Is No Controlling Law. A judge may regulate practice in any manner consistent with federal law, these rules, and local rules of the district. No sanction or other disadvantage may be imposed for noncompliance with any requirement not in federal law, federal rules, or the local district rules unless the alleged violator has been furnished in the particular case with actual notice of the requirement.

(c) Effective Date And Notice. A local rule so adopted shall take effect upon the date specified by the district court and shall remain in effect unless amended by the district court or abrogated by the judicial council of the circuit in which the district is located. Copies of the rules and amendments so made by any district court shall upon their promulgation be furnished to the judicial council and the Administrative Office of the United States Courts and shall be made available to the public.

Rule 58. Procedure for Misdemeanors and Other Petty Offenses

(a) Scope.

(1) In General. This rule governs the procedure and practice for the conduct of proceedings involving misdemeanors and other petty offenses, and for appeals to district judges in such cases tried by United States magistrate judges.

(2) Applicability of Other Federal Rules of Criminal Procedure. In proceedings concerning petty offenses for which no sentence of imprisonment will be imposed the court may follow such provisions of these rules as it deems appropriate, to the extent not inconsistent with this rule. In all other proceedings the other rules govern except as specifically provided in this rule.

(3) Definition. The term "petty offenses for which no sentence of imprisonment will be imposed" as used in this rule, means any petty offenses as defined in 18 U.S.C. § 19 as to which the court determines, that, in the event of conviction, no sentence of imprisonment will actually be imposed.

(b) Pretrial Procedures.

(1) Trial Document. The trial of a misdemeanor may proceed on an indictment, information, or complaint or, in the case of a petty offense, on a citation or violation notice.

(2) Initial Appearance. At the defendant's initial appearance on a misdemeanor or other petty offense charge, the court shall inform the defendant of:

(A) the charge, and the maximum possible penalties provided by law, including payment of a special assessment under 18 U.S.C. § 3013, and restitution under 18 U.S.C. § 3663;

(B) the right to retain counsel;

(C) the right to request the appointment of counsel if the defendant is unable to obtain counsel, unless the charge is a petty offense for which an appointment of counsel is not required;

(D) the right to remain silent and that any statement made by the defendant may be used against the defendant;

(E) the right to trial, judgment, and sentencing before a district judge, unless:

(i) the charge is a Class B misdemeanor motor-vehicle offense, a Class C misdemeanor, or an infraction; or

(ii) the defendant consents to trial, judgment, and sentencing before a magistrate judge;

(F) the right to trial by jury before either a United States magistrate judge or a district judge, unless the charge is a petty offense; and

(G) the right to a preliminary examination in accordance with 18 U.S.C. § 3060, and the general circumstances under which the defendant may secure pretrial release, if the defendant is held in custody and charged with a misdemeanor other than a petty offense.

(3) Consent and Arraignment.

(a) Plea Before a United States Magistrate Judge. A magistrate judge shall take the defendant's plea in a Class B misdemeanor charging a motor-vehicle offense, a Class C misdemeanor, or an infraction. In every other misdemeanor case, a magistrate judge may take the plea only if the defendant consents either in writing or orally on the record to be tried before the magistrate judge and specifically waives trial before a district judge. The defendant may plead not guilty, guilty, or with the consent of the magistrate judge, nolo contendere.

(b) Failure to Consent. In a misdemeanor case—other than a Class B misdemeanor charging a motor—vehicle offense, a Class C misdemeanor, or an infraction—magistrate judge shall order the defendant to appear before a district judge for further proceedings on notice, unless the defendant consents to trial before the magistrate judge.

(c) Additional Procedures Applicable Only to Petty Offenses for Which No Sentence of Imprisonment Will be Imposed. With respect to petty offenses for which no sentence of imprisonment will be imposed, the following additional procedures are applicable:

(1) Plea of Guilty or Nolo Contendere. No plea of guilty or nolo contendere shall be accepted unless the court is satisfied that the defendant understands the nature of the charge and the maximum possible penalties provided by law.

(2) Waiver of Venue for Plea and Sentence. A defendant who is arrested, held, or present in a district other than that in which the indictment, information, complaint, citation or violation notice is pending against that defendant may state in writing a wish to plead guilty or nolo contendere, to waive venue and trial in the district in which the proceeding is pending, and to consent to disposition of the case in the district in which that defendant was arrested, is held, or is present. Unless the defendant thereafter pleads not guilty, the prosecution shall be had as if venue were in such district, and notice of the same shall be given to the magistrate judge in the district where the proceeding was originally commenced. The defendant's statement of a desire to plead guilty or nolo contendere is not admissible against the defendant.

(3) Sentence. The court shall afford the defendant an opportunity to be heard in mitigation. The court shall then immediately proceed to sentence the defendant, except that in the discretion of the court, sentencing may be continued to allow an investigation by the probation service or submission of additional information by either party.

(4) Notification of Right to Appeal After imposing sentence in a case which has gone to trial on a plea of not guilty, the court shall advise the defendant of the defendant's right to appeal including any right to appeal the sentence. There shall be no duty on the court to advise the defendant of any right of appeal after sentence is imposed following a plea of guilty or nolo contendere, except that the court shall advise the defendant of any right to appeal the sentence.

(d) Securing the Defendant's Appearance; Payment in Lieu of Appearance.

(1) Forfeiture of Collateral. When authorized by local rules of the district court, payment of a fixed sum may be accepted in suitable cases in lieu of appearance and as authorizing the termination of the proceedings. Local rules may make provision for increases in fixed sums not to exceed the maximum fine which could be imposed.

(2) Notice to Appear. If a defendant fails to pay a fixed sum, request a hearing, or appear in response to a citation or violation notice, the clerk or a magistrate judge may issue a notice for the defendant to appear before the court on a date certain. The notice may also afford the defendant an additional opportunity to pay a fixed sum in lieu of appearance, and shall be served upon the defendant by mailing a copy to the defendant's last known address.

(3) Summons or Warrant. Upon an indictment or a showing by one of the other documents specified in subdivision (b)(1) of probable cause to believe that an offense has been committed and that the defendant has committed it, the court may issue an arrest warrant or, if no warrant is requested by the attorney for the prosecution, a summons. The showing of probable cause shall be made in writing upon oath or under penalty for perjury, but the affiant need not appear before the court. If the defendant fails to appear before the court in response to a summons, the court may summarily issue a warrant for the defendant's immediate arrest and appearance before the court.

(e) Record. Proceedings under this rule shall be taken down by a reporter or recorded by suitable sound equipment.

(f) New Trial. The provisions of Rule 33 shall apply.

(g) Appeal.

(1) Decision, Order, Judgment or Sentence by a District Judge. An appeal from a decision, order, judgment or conviction or sentence by a district judge shall be taken in accordance with the Federal Rules of Appellate Procedure.

(2) Decision, Order, Judgment or Sentence by a United States Magistrate Judge.

(a) Interlocutory Appeal. A decision or order by a magistrate judge which, if made by a district judge, could be appealed by the government or defendant under any provision of law, shall be subject to an appeal to a district judge provided such appeal is taken within 10 days of the entry of the decision or order. An appeal shall be taken by filing with the clerk of court a statement specifying the decision or order from which an appeal is taken and by serving a copy of the statement upon the adverse party, personally or by mail, and by filing a copy with the magistrate judge.

(b) Appeal From Conviction or Sentence. An appeal from a judgment of conviction or sentence by a magistrate judge to a district judge shall be taken within 10 days after entry of the judgment. An appeal shall be taken by filing with the clerk of court a statement specifying the judgment from which an appeal is taken, and by serving a copy of the statement upon the United States Attorney, personally or by mail, and by filing a copy with the magistrate judge.

(c) Record. The record shall consist of the original papers and exhibits in the case together with any transcript, tape, or other recording of the proceedings and a certified copy of the docket entries which shall be transmitted promptly to the clerk of court. For purposes of the appeal, a copy of the record of such proceedings shall be made available at the expense of the United States to a person who establishes by affidavit the inability to pay or give security therefor, and the expense of such copy shall be paid by the Director of the Administrative Office of the United States Courts.

(d) Scope of Appeal. The defendant shall not be entitled to a trial de novo by a district judge. The scope of appeal shall be the same as an appeal from a judgment of a district court to a court of appeals.

(3) Stay of Execution; Release Pending Appeal. The provisions of Rule 38 relating to stay of execution shall be applicable to a judgment of conviction or sentence. The defendant may be released pending appeal in accordance with the provisions of law relating to release pending appeal from a judgment of a district court to a court of appeals.

Rule 59.   Effective Date

These rules take effect on the day which is 3 months subsequent to the adjournment of the first regular session of the 79th Congress, but if that day is prior to September 1, 1945, then they take effect on September 1, 1945. They govern all criminal proceedings thereafter commenced and so far as just and practicable all proceedings then pending.

Rule 60.   Title

These rules may be known and cited as the Federal Rules of Criminal Procedure.

Appendix D

PROPOSED AMENDMENTS TO FEDERAL RULES OF CRIMINAL PROCEDURE

[These amendments to the Rules were approved by the Supreme Court and submitted to Congress on April 24, 1998, and will take effect on December 1, 1998, unless Congress takes contrary action.]

Rule 5.1. Preliminary Examination

* * *

(d) PRODUCTION OF STATEMENTS.

(1) *In General*. Rule 26.2(a)–(d) and (f) applies at any hearing under this rule, unless the court, for good cause shown, rules otherwise in a particular case.

(2) *Sanctions for Failure to Produce Statement*. If a party elects not to comply with an order under Rule 26.2(a) to deliver a statement to the moving party, the court may not consider the testimony of a witness whose statement is withheld.

* * *

Rule 26.2. Production of Witness Statements

* * *

(g) SCOPE OF RULE. This rule applies at a suppression hearing conducted under Rule 12, at trial under this rule, and to the extent specified:

(1) in Rule ~~32(e)~~ 32(c)(2) at sentencing;

(2) in Rule 32.1(c) at a hearing to revoke or modify probation or supervised release;

(3) in Rule 46(i) at a detention hearing; ~~and~~

(4) in Rule 8 of the Rules Governing Proceedings under 28 U.S.C. § 2255~~.~~; and

(5) in Rule 5.1 at a preliminary examination.

Rule 31. Verdict

* * *

(d) POLL OF JURY. ~~When~~ After a verdict is returned ~~and~~ but before ~~it is recorded~~ the jury is discharged, the court shall, on a party's request, or

342

may on its own motion, poll the jurors individually, ~~jury shall be polled at the request of any party or upon the court's own motion~~. If ~~upon~~ the poll reveals a lack of unanimity ~~there is not unanimous concurrence~~, the court may direct the jury ~~may be directed~~ to deliberate ~~retire for~~ further ~~deliberations~~ or may declare a mistrial ~~be discharged~~ and discharged the jury.

* * *

Rule 33. New Trial

On a defendant's motion, the court ~~The court on motion of a defendant~~ may grant a new trial to that defendant if ~~required in the interest of justice,~~ the interests of justice so require. If trial was by the court without a jury, the court may—on defendant's motion for new trial—~~motion of a defendant for a new trial may~~ vacate the judgement~~, if entered~~, take additional testimony, and direct the entry of a new judgment. A motion for new trial based on ~~the ground of~~ newly discovered evidence may be made only ~~before or~~ within three ~~two~~ years after ~~final judgment,~~ the verdict or finding of guilty, ~~but~~ But if an appeal is pending, the court may grant the motion only on remand of the case. A motion for a new trial based on any other grounds ~~shall~~ may be made only within 7 days after the verdict or finding of guilty or within such further time as the court may fix during the 7–day period.

Rule 35. Correction or Reduction of Sentence

* * *

(b) REDUCTION OF SENTENCE FOR SUBSTANTIAL ASSISTANCE ~~CHANGED CIRCUMSTANCES. The court, on motion of~~ If the Government so moves ~~made~~ within one year after ~~the imposition of~~ the sentence, is imposed, the court may reduce a sentence to reflect a defendant's subsequent substantial assistance in ~~the investigation of prosecution of~~ investigating or prosecuting another person, ~~who has committed an offense,~~ in accordance with the ~~to section 994 of title 28, United States Code.~~ The court may consider a government motion to reduce a sentence made one year or more after ~~imposition of~~ the sentence is imposed if ~~where~~ the defendant's substantial assistance involves information or evidence not known by the defendant until one year or more after ~~imposition of~~ sentence is imposed. In evaluating whether substantial assistance has been rendered, the court may consider the defendant's pre-sentence assistance. ~~The court's authority to reduce a sentence under this subsection includes the authority to~~ In applying this subdivision, the court may reduce ~~such~~ the sentence to a level below that established by statute as a minimum sentence.

* * *

Rule 43. Presence of the Defendant

* * *

(c) **PRESENCE NOT REQUIRED.** A defendant need not be present:

(1) when represented by counsel and the defendant is an organization, as defined in 18 U.S.C. § 18;

(2) when the offense is punishable by fine or by imprisonment for not more than one year or both, and the court, with the written consent of the defendant, permits arraignment, plea, trial, and imposition of sentence in the defendants absence;

(3) when the proceeding involves only a conference or hearing upon a question of law; or

(4) when the proceeding involves a reduction or correction of sentence under Rule 35 35(b) or (c) or 18 U.S.C. § 3582(c).

Special Appendix
UNITED STATES v. SINGLETON

Chapter 5
ARREST, SEARCH AND SEIZURE

SECTION 1. THE EXCLUSIONARY RULE

8th ed., p. 157; after Note 6, add

7. *Suppression of the testimony of a government witness as a remedy for the government's use of testimony by promising the witness leniency in violation of § 201 (c) (2).* In UNITED STATES v. SINGLETON (discussed below at considerable length), the Tenth Circuit held that suppression of testimony for the prosecution is "the appropriate remedy" for the use of testimony obtained by the government in violation of 18 U.S.C. § 201 (c) (2) (which, according to the Tenth Circuit, prohibits the government from promising leniency to a witness in return for his or her testimony). In reaching this conclusion, the Tenth Circuit, per KELLY, J., relied heavily on the search and seizure exclusionary rule cases:

> "Although [the] application [of the exclusionary rule] to statutory violations is not automatic, we believe the policies of the rule require its use in this context. Suppression is a judicially fashioned rule whose primary purpose is to deter official misconduct, [citing, inter alia, *United States* v. *Calandra*]. We must balance the good of preventing future unlawful conduct with the evil of disallowing relevant evidence in an individual case.

> "We believe exclusion will effectively deter the unlawful conduct before us. Agreements to seek leniency [in] return for testimony are entered into with the intention of presenting to a court the testimony so acquired. Excluding that tainted testimony removes the sole purpose of the unlawful conduct and leaves no incentive to violate § 201 (c) (2). Courts declining to apply the exclusionary rule for violation of statutes have done so on the ground that it is 'inappropriate until such time as "widespread and repeated violations"' of the statute exist , and they have specifically held the remedy available for that situation. This approach is appropriate because deterrence is a preventive function

345

which cannot be served unless there is a significant likelihood of future violations to be deterred. See *Calandra*. [The] ingrained practice of buying testimony indicates that suppression is necessary to compel respect for the statutory protections Congress has placed around testimony in federal courts. Exclusion is also necessary to remove the incentive to disregard the statute. See *Calandra* [quoting *Elkins* v. *United States*, 8th ed., p. 133]. The benefits of deterrence outweigh the evil of excluding relevant evidence, and the balance falls heavily in favor of suppression.

"A second policy protected by the exclusionary rule is 'the imperative of judicial integrity.' *Elkins*. Courts will not be made party to lawlessness by permitting unhindered use of the fruits of illegality. Although this basis for the exclusionary rule exerts limited force, see *Stone* v. *Powell* [8th ed., p. 136], * * * we find it relevant because of the substance of the policy codified in § 201 (c) (2).

" * * * Congress evidenced an intent in § 201 (c) (2) to remove the temptation inherent in a witness's accepting value from a party for his testimony. That temptation, even if unconscious, is to color or falsify one's testimony in favor of the donor. [When] testimony [tainted by unlawful gratuities or inducements] is presented to the courts of the United States, judicial integrity is directly impugned in a way it is not by tangible evidence whose reliability is unaffected by an underlying illegality. And when the statutory policy of Congress is to protect courts and parties from that taint, suppression is particularly appropriate because it effectuates that purpose.

"For this reason we are unpersuaded by cases holding suppression inappropriate for statutory violations on the ground that where Congress has established other penalties the courts should not create a judicial remedy. Unlike all of these cases, the violation of § 201 (c) (2) at issue in our case directly tainted the reliability of the evidence."

Chapter 22

COERCED, INDUCED AND NEGOTIATED GUILTY PLEAS; PROFESSIONAL RESPONSIBILITY

SECTION 1. SOME VIEWS OF GUILTY PLEAS

8th ed., p. 1313; end of section; add new segment

F. Promising Leniency in Return for a Government Witness's Testimony

Section 201 (c) (2) of Title 18 of the U.S. Code provides that "whoever * * * gives, offers or promises anything of value" to a witness for or because of his or her testimony is guilty of a felony. In a ruling that startled law enforcement officials, see Joan Biskupic, *Govt. to Appeal Ban on Witness Leniency*, Washington Post, July 10, 1998, p. A03; Stuart Taylor, *Prosecutors Take Note: A Promise of Leniency Can Be a Bribe*, National Journal, July 11, 1998, p. 1606, UNITED STATES v. SINGLETON, 1998 WL 350507 (10th Cir.) held, per KELLY, J., that § 201 (c) (2) prohibits the government from promising leniency to witnesses in return for their testimony against criminal defendants.

The case arose as follows: Defendant was charged with multiple counts of money laundering and conspiracy to distribute cocaine. She moved to suppress the testimony of Mr. Douglas, a coconspirator who had entered into a plea agreement with the government, contending that the government had violated § 201 (c) (2) by promising Douglas something of value—leniency—in return for his testimony. The district court denied the motion, maintaining that § 201 (c) (2) did not apply to the government. The Tenth Circuit disagreed. In ruling that § 201 (c) (2) applied to the government as well as private persons—"the class of persons who can violate the statute is not limited"—the Tenth Circuit observed:

"The anti-gratuity provision of § 201 (c) (2) indicates Congress's belief that justice is undermined by giving, offering, or promising anything of value for testimony. If justice is perverted when a criminal defendant seeks to buy testimony from a witness, it is no less perverted when the government does so. Because § 201 (c) (2) addresses what Congress perceived to be a wrong, and operates to prevent fraud upon the federal courts in the form of inherently unreliable testimony, the proscription of § 201 (c) (2) must apply to the government. * * *

"The judicial process is tainted and justice cheapened when factual testimony is purchased, whether with leniency or money. Because prosecutors bear a weighty responsibility to do justice and observe the law in the course of a prosecution, it is particularly appropriate to apply the strictures of § 201 (c) (2) to their activities."

The court rejected the argument that "anything of value" should be restricted to things of monetary, commercial or tangible value. "The obvious purpose of the government's promised actions," noted the court, "was to reduce [Douglas's] jail term, and it is difficult to imagine anything more valuable than personal freedom."

The court also concluded that § 201 (c) (2) could be harmonized with the statute authorizing federal prosecutors to give immunity for testimony: "Both statutes can operate fully and independently; together they manifest a congressional intent to allow testimony obtained by the court's grant of immunity, but to criminalize the gift, offer or promise of any other thing of value for or because of testimony."

The court was not impressed by the government's argument that some overriding policy should prevent application of § 201 (c) (2) to "reasonable enforcement actions" by officers of the law: "The chasm between the government's present conduct and reasonable law enforcement actions can be illustrated by analogy to the FBI's Abscam operation, under which operatives and undercover agents offered bribes to public officials and arrested those who accepted the bribes. Although Abscam created controversy and dissent in the courts, it was held a legitimate means of detecting public corruption. The government's present inducement for testimony goes much further. Reasonable law enforcement actions stop with detecting crime and observing enough to prove it. The government's statutory violation unreasonably exceeds this purpose, and is the more egregious because the intended product of the violation is testimony presented in court."

As for the federal sentencing statute, which authorizes the court, upon the government's motion, to impose a sentence below the statutory minimum so as to reflect a defendant's "substantial assistance" in the investigation or prosecution of another defendant, neither this provision nor any other "authorizes the government to make a deal for testimony before it is given, as the government did with Mr. Douglas." Did the court's reading of § 201 (c) (2) significantly impair the "substantial assistance" provisions? The court thought not; "a defendant can substantially assist an investigation or prosecution in myriad ways other than by testifying."

The court recognized that the Eleventh Circuit had taken the position that § 201 (c) (2) is violated only when the resultant testimony is false, but disagreed: Under § 201 (c) (2), "the promise need not be intended to affect, and need not actually affect, the testimony in any way. Promising something of value to secure truthful testimony is as much prohibited as buying perjured testimony."

Relying heavily on search and seizure exclusionary rule cases (see first paragraph of Special Appendix), the Tenth Circuit then concluded that, considering the circumstances of this case, the appropriate remedy for the governments use of testimony obtained in violation of § 201 (c) (2) was suppression of its use. The court "emphasize[d] that the rule we apply today rests in no way on the Constitution; it is a creature solely of statute."

†